TO HAVE
AND
TO HOLD

A Daily Marriage Devotional

TO HAVE AND TO HOLD

A *Daily Marriage Devotional*

Barbara Canale

Liguori
LIGUORI, MISSOURI

Imprimi Potest:
Harry Grile, CSsR, Provincial
Denver Province, The Redemptorists

Published by Liguori Publications
Liguori, Missouri 63057

To order, call 800-325-9521 or visit Liguori.org

Library of Congress Cataloging-in-Publication Data
Canale, Barbara S.
   To have and to hold : a daily marriage devotional / Barbara Canale. — First
Edition.
      pages cm
1. Married people—Prayers and devotions. 2. Devotional calendars. I. Title.
   BV4596.M3C375 2014
   242'.644--dc23

                              2014005650

p ISBN 978-0-7648-2295-7
e ISBN 978-0-7648-6914-3

Liguori Publications, a nonprofit corporation, is an apostolate of
the Redemptorists. To learn more about the Redemptorists, visit
Redemptorists.com.

Printed in the United States of America
18 17 16 15 14 / 5 4 3 2 1
First Edition

Contents

This book is dedicated to Patrick Canale,
my soul mate, lifelong partner, and best friend.
Thank you for journeying through life with me.
I truly appreciate your brilliant ideas and heartfelt
stories to share with other married couples
who read this book. Your unwavering love and
devotion moved me through many roadblocks.
Without you, this book would not exist.

Acknowledgments

I thank my selfless parents, Joseph and Barbara Casper, who gave me my faith and fostered it throughout my life with an infinite stream of love and encouragement. In their sixty-plus years of marriage, I learned through their example the importance of living together in Christ's love.

I extend my gratitude to Patricia Ennis, creator of The Third Option. Her commitment to improving the lives of all married couples is commendable. I am indebted to her knowledge, friendship, and compassion; they provided numerous tools that enable my marriage to blossom.

This book wouldn't be complete without my friend and pastor, Reverend Monsignor J. Robert Yeazel, for his friendship, his spiritual guidance, and immeasurable words of inspiration.

I am sincerely grateful to Julia DiSalvo, who worked diligently on this book and saw it through to completion. Thanks to you and the Liguori staff for making it possible to enrich the lives of all married couples around the world.

To my loving Lord, who gives me everything and keeps my marriage on track: I thank you for it all.

Introduction

After twenty years of marriage, my relationship with Pat was in a lull. I thought attending a Marriage Encounter weekend at church might provide the kind of revitalization we needed, but we never followed through. Pat found The Third Option program, sponsored by the diocese of Syracuse, and presented it to me as a birthday gift. It turned out to be the best gift he ever gave me, because it transformed our marriage from one with an unknown future to a hopeful, meaningful, and spiritual one.

The change was a long process that we prayed our way through, trusting in God and his remarkable ways. Initially, we prayed individually and searched the Bible for answers. Sometimes we didn't completely understand the passages or couldn't find verses that matched our experiences at that point in our lives. While there are devotionals on the market for married couples, there isn't anything for couples who struggle to overcome issues or obstacles in their marriage. I believe all couples struggle in their relationship at one time or another.

Throughout this process I kept a journal of Scripture verses that brought me comfort, understanding, and resolve as it pertained to a difficulty we were trying to overcome in our marriage. Once Pat and I mastered The Third Option skills, we volunteered to become a mentor couple to others who wanted more from their marriages. Prayer cemented the bond between us.

After spending ten years working in this field, I put my notes to good use. I matched actual case examples with methods for overcoming quandaries to a pertinent Scripture and prayer. This book is the resulting amalgamation. Whether you are married, newly married, or getting married, this devotional is perfect for you.

"God is in Every Tomorrow"

God is in every tomorrow,
Therefore I live for today,
Certain of finding at sunrise,
Guidance and strength for the way;
Power for each moment of weakness,
Hope for each moment of pain,
Comfort for every sorrow,
Sunshine and joy after rain.

—Laura A. Barter Snow
"With Tongue and Pen"

January 1

He has endowed them with skill to execute all types of work: engraving, embroidering, the making of variegated cloth of violet, purple, and scarlet yarn and fine linen thread, weaving, and all other arts and crafts.

EXODUS 35:35

The first time I taught my daughter to knit, there were numerous mistakes. She pulled out more stitches than she stitched. When it was completed, the slipups were barely noticeable. Only she knew how much went into making it and repairing it.

The frustrations surrounding the time and energy to repair marriage blunders are worth the extra effort. You might make mistakes along the way, use improper approaches, inappropriate language, or even feel like giving up. Your marriage is a valuable gift that God intended for you to have: sharing your lives with each other forever. Ask God to cast off the unsuitable practices that wear your bonds down and allow you to evoke the best ways to tackle your quandaries. God has blessed you with many coping skills and strategies to resolve difficulties in your marriage.

You know the problems you need to face and the best methods to resolve them. If you are unsure of what the problem actually is, ask your spouse in a loving manner. Spouses usually can identify problematic areas. When tackling it, establish ground rules to guide you through it: stick to one topic at a time and don't move on to another matter until the first one is solved to both of your satisfactions. It is essential not to dredge up past mistakes, hurts, or problems. If the past continually resurfaces, it's an indication that those issues were never completely resolved and at some point you will have to revisit them to bring them closure.

After repeatedly practicing healthy conflict-resolution skills, perhaps through the art of compromise, they will become second nature, and you will be glad you invested the time and energy to enhance your marriage and brighten your future together. It is not enough to toil over problems; you must also pray on them. When you find yourself in the midst of conflict, how will you stop a quarrel and pray for God to enlighten you with the skills to resolve it amicably?

Dear Lord, help me to knit my marriage back together, one careful stitch at a time. Keep me focused on you so that I do what is right and just. Don't let me be offensive and hurtful to the mate you brought into my life. Fill me with grace, so that I convey my thoughts, feelings, and ideas tactfully and lovingly. I ask this in your sweet and holy name. Amen.

January 2

But the one who perseveres to the end will be saved.

MARK 13:13

Ice skate a few times each winter. I might enjoy it more if I didn't fall so much. No one likes bruises and tired, achy muscles, not to mention cold feet. If I practiced more, I might not fall and actually enjoy myself more.

When times are difficult in a marriage, it's exhausting to keep falling and getting back up only to fall again. If there are verbal attacks, bruises can result, taking even longer to recover. It's critical to remember that humans make mistakes. The key is to get back up and keep trying. God would not want you to give up. He brought you both together and equipped you with the skills and knowledge to continue on your journey through life. Do it prayerfully and peacefully in God's love.

Whatever you are struggling with, give it to God and ask for his guidance. God will never abandon you in your struggles and with his almighty power you will be able to overcome anything, no matter how big it is or how frightening it might seem. If you have cold feet in this matter, don't lose your nerve talking to God for help. God is only a breath away from you at all times. He will fill you with inspiration. If you have cold hands, God will take them and warm them and lead you safely to the place he wants you to be. If you have a cold heart, cry out to the Lord and let him build a fire of his blazing love in it. With God's love in your heart, you will succeed at everything you do, no matter how slippery the surface is that you are skating on.

Perhaps you frequently use "you" statements, making your spouse defensive, feeling as if he is being attacked or accused of something. Try replacing each "you" with an "I" statement: I feel, I wish, I love you. It is not easy changing the way you speak, but it will make a world of difference in your relationship. Can you spend the rest of week using "I" statements with your spouse?

Dear Lord, I feel fatigued from failing to make my marriage sound. I wish I could say the right words to my partner because I care so much about our future together. I desperately want to make my marriage work. I will keep trying, no matter how difficult it is. Stay close to me Lord, and help me back up on my feet each time I stumble and fall. You are my salvation. With you I have no fear. Amen.

January 3

I went down to the potter's house and there he was, working at the wheel.
Whenever the vessel of clay he was making turned out badly in his hand,
he tried again, making another vessel of whatever sort he pleased.

JEREMIAH 18:3–4

Watching a potter throw clay on a wheel is amusing because he can transform a glob of mud into an art form or a useful earthenware object. Centering the clay is critical because if it is not done accurately, it will be off balance, and the potter will struggle with it the entire time. Some potters smack the clay down with a bat, knowing that the success of the pot depends on the centering.

Every marriage is centered differently. Some are centered on sex or seeking pleasure solely through entertainment and vacations. Some are centered on their careers, while others are centered on hobbies or sports. Some are centered on rearing children. Contemplate what the center of your relationship is and what activity do you put the most time into. Whatever it is, consider molding it from that worldly function into a more spiritual one focused on God. When you put God first in your life, everything else will fall into perfect place.

Make it a goal to create an intimate relationship with God. Find a way each day to spend quality time with your partner in prayer. Connecting with God and your spouse on a deep spiritual level will strengthen your commitment to each other and reinforce your relationship. Allow him into all of the areas of your life. Upon waking each day, you could spend a few minutes in prayerful reflection and offer your prayers, works, and joys to him. Before each project you tackle, perhaps you could spend a few moments in heartfelt prayer, seeking God's guidance and direction. Praying before meals is another way to bring God into your world.

Your life is like a ball of clay that can be molded into something extraordinary if it is centered correctly and completely on the Lord. How will you and your spouse incorporate more prayer time together?

Dear Lord, allow me to keep working at my marriage, to enable it to withstand any distractions that could wear it down or possibly destroy it. Enable me to avert diversions, to push aside commotions, focus on what is really important: you. Don't let me squander my valuable time on petty nuances that consume my neighbors and friends. Instead, let me dwell in your infinite love and mercy that you so willingly provide. Help me to center my marriage around you so that together we can do all that is good, right, and just in this world and the next. Amen.

January 4

The just shall flourish like the palm tree, shall grow like a cedar of Lebanon.
Planted in the house of the Lord, they shall flourish in the courts of our God.

PSALM 92:13–14

When Ephesus Technologies, inventors and producers of LED lights, installed their fixtures in a dairy-cattle barn, the cows exposed to the new lights produced an additional five gallons of milk each day. It was concluded that happier cows produce more milk. It would be fantastic for couples to turn on a light in their marriages to make it better and brighter.

A happy marriage produces more love. Reflect on what is working in your relationship and focus on making that area better. After you feel satisfied with that success, you can contemplate other areas of your marriage that could use more enhancing. No one has a perfect marriage: everyone's relationship could use a little polishing and a little brightening. Perhaps you speak condescendingly to your partner and want to correct that behavior. Imagine your spouse is Christ; that might prompt you to treat him or her with more dignity. Let God influence your decisions to be more kind and compassionate to your spouse.

Consider what else you could do to make your marriage more productive and dynamic. Often, making simple modifications or adjustments is all that is necessary. Maybe you need more physical contact with your spouse; hug more often or acknowledge the good they do each day. Thank your spouse when he or she does something nice. Those simple gestures tell your spouse you care. Don't take your spouse for granted. Ponder if you give minimally to your partner or keep score who does the most to build up the relationship. Consider what changes you might make. Perhaps setting aside time to reconnect in prayer by bringing God into your relationship could be the brightness your marriage needs. Contemplate the many ways God can illuminate your union.

God is the light of the world and whoever walks with him will never be in darkness. How will you let God's love shine on your marriage this week?

Dear Lord, I don't want to live in the shadows of those around me or those who suppress me. Let me break out of the darkness. Shine forth your love and bless my marriage to make it more productive by teaching me to reach for a deeper level of trust and loyalty. Remind me to be more thoughtful, speak kinder, and act more compassionately to my partner. When I please my spouse, I am also pleasing you. You are the light of the world and I want my relationship to flourish in the brilliance of your unconditional love. Amen.

January 5

After a time, his master's wife looked at him with
longing and said, "Lie with me."

GENESIS 39:7

A whimsical mobile dangled lazily over my daughter's crib at the perfect distance, enabling her to admire it with curiosity. The temptation for her to grasp it was enticing. Through creative measures, she yanked off a trinket, forcing the mobile to be lopsided.

There will be myriad temptations that can derail a marriage if one person succumbs to it. If you feel temptation stirring within you, call out to Jesus, and he will strengthen you. He will give you the courage to boldly walk away. If you are addicted to food, alcohol, drugs, gambling, the Internet, or shopping, cry out to God to resist the lure. God is stronger than any enticement and he can help you avert any trap. The worldly pleasures that are addicting can create havoc in your marriage. It's not worth it to risk succumbing to a temptation if it will cause injury to your marriage. When you leave this world for the next, you will leave all earthly pleasures behind. If you cannot take it with you, leave it now. Instead, feed the hungry, talk to the lonely, share what you have with those who have nothing.

Implore the Holy Spirit to keep you focused on keeping your marriage the sacred union God intended it to be. Remember the marriage vows you made to your spouse, and honor them. If there are infidelities keeping your marriage askew, stop them immediately and seek advice from your parish priest or go to a marriage counselor. If there are impure thoughts, flush them out with prayer and fill your mind with loving thoughts of your Lord and savior. Pray for guidance. God will illuminate your path and show you the way out of your disparity. If there are betrayals, apologize for them, and make a plan to avoid that reckless behavior in the future. Seeking forgiveness is imperative. Start by going to confession and seeking the sacrament of reconciliation. You will experience peace and spiritual consolation after going to confession. Your encounter with a loving, merciful God will enable you to renew your strength to thwart temptations, turn away from sin, and walk together with God. What are healthy ways to you can work through your temptations so that your marriage doesn't become lopsided?

Dear Lord, exude your tender mercies on me. Keep me strong and holy as I journey onward with my spouse and strive for reconciliation in my marriage. Keep me on the right path, avoiding inducements in every alluring form. Enable me to see the good in my partner. Allow me to remember that you created [name] for me to share my life with. I trust in your plan even though I do not understand it. Amen.

January 6

Does the snow of Lebanon desert the rocky heights?

JEREMIAH 18:14

Each tiny snowflake is a beautiful ice crystal that forms in a wide variety of intricate shapes, making each one unique. When snowflakes stick together, whatever they attach to appears clean, bright, and magical. A snow-covered landscape is a remarkable sight.

Because people are different, when they stick together in marriage, they emanate the same mystique and radiance as the first snowfall. Think about the personality traits that you have in common with each other. Maybe you are both outgoing and enjoy socializing or perhaps you are both night owls. Other commonalities might be that you are both from the same town, the same nationality, or have the same religion. Perhaps you have similar traditions that you brought with you into your marriage. Contemplate what initially drew you and your spouse together. What was so appealing about those character traits; were they similar to yours or different? For today, dwell on those charming qualities and remind your partner about them.

Ask your spouse what unique traits he or she finds endearing about you. There are undoubtedly personality traits you have that are different from your spouse. Consider stretching to meet them and become a student of them, trying to be appreciative and learn as much as you can to be better-rounded. Opposites attract; perhaps that is your situation. If so, you can balance out each other's differences. If your spouse is a socialite and you are a recluse, you can learn from your mate how to step outside your comfort zone to be more social. And occasionally your spouse could enjoy quiet time at home with you. God made all of us different and he wants us to embrace those differences. This is one way we can honor God, by appreciating, tolerating, and caring about each other's variances. Our differences are what God loves about us the most. Therefore, it behooves us to accept and celebrate our spouse's uniqueness.

What activities do you especially enjoy sharing and participating with your spouse? Do you appreciate taking long walks together? What new endeavors might you do with your spouse? Perhaps you could teach a religion class together. As God for direction; he will guide your journey.

Dear Lord, thank you for bringing [*name*] into my life and for filling my days with abundant joy and love. Thank you for the ability to overcome the sorrows and disappointments I have experienced by not appreciating my spouse's differences. Teach me how to embrace them and to move beyond any idiosyncrasies that once held me back. I love you, Lord, for choosing such a wonderful life partner for me. Amen.

January 7

For this momentary light affliction is producing for us an eternal weight
of glory beyond all comparison, as we look not to what is seen but to what
is unseen; for what is seen is transitory, but what is unseen is eternal.

2 Corinthians 4:17–18

When the snow falls, it's understandable how some people are bothered by it. The leading complaints by northerners are being too cold and having to work to shovel it. Some southerners long for it. They think about building snow forts, snowmen, and having snowball fights. Many people fly to mountain resorts to ski or snowboard. Do you abhor the snow, or do you adore it?

There are positive and negative aspects of most everything, including marriages. Contemplate the favorable characteristics of your relationship. Perhaps you enjoy the companionship aspect, because you are never really alone and your partner is a great listener or conversationalist. Your mate shares a living space with you, and you might find sharing chores and responsibilities comforting. Marriage gives you the ability to pool your assets and to cohabitate more affordably. If one of you is down, the other one can lift you up and act as a sounding board to help you through your personal difficulties. God planned many benefits for you to enjoy as a couple. You might not actually see the benefits, but they are there.

When two people share a living space, there is room for conflict. Perhaps you might get annoyed with the way the laundry is done and your spouse might not like the way you shovel the driveway. However, find contentment in the fact that your partner makes attempts to share in the responsibilities, even if the job is not done to your satisfaction. Again, you might not actually see the intention, but it is there.

Tap into your creativity to generate better opportunities for a loving environment in your home. Maybe your spouse needs to hear you say, "Thank you" for doing the dishes, or "I love you." Perhaps your partner is struggling with health issues. Think of ways you can nurture your spouse while bringing happiness and love back into your union on a deeper level. One of the best ways to strengthen your marriage is to pray together and offer prayers for one another. Your holy union has been bound together in God's love. How can you promote an insightful commitment to your spouse while you weather the mechanics of living together in harmony?

Dear Lord, reaffirm the many respectable qualities in my relationship and help me be resilient to the struggles we face. Please, Lord, don't let me become ensnared in nitpicking and being overly critical. Open my eyes to the goodness of my partner that I sometimes overlook. Let me embrace the wonderful qualities and mature in your love. Amen.

January 8

These are the contributions you shall accept from them:
gold, silver and bronze; violet, purple, and scarlet yarn.

EXODUS 25:3–4

When artists paint pictures, they normally mix several different colors to create a totally unique shade. It often takes a few attempts to make the perfect color they are imagining. It rarely happens on the first try. But over time and with practice, it is easier to achieve the perfect color.

When two people marry, they are blending the colors of their past to form another hue that is exclusive to their union. Everyone brings their own individual emotional baggage with them into their marriage, including past hurts and emotional scars, childhood issues, medical problems, family traditions and beliefs, unrealistic expectations, and the tactics their parents used to settle disagreements. Contemplate what emotional baggage you dragged into your marriage and ask yourself if any of those issues have surfaced in marital spats. Ponder the significance of them and consider which ones you could cut loose and which ones need attention in order to put them into proper perspective, deal with them, and move on. Don't allow issues from your past to cloud your future.

God has blessed you with a partner who may not be aware of your baggage. You have the ability to shape your new life together in a new way, uncluttered from past events that may weigh too heavily on you. Your spouse has issues from his or her past as well. Together you can both discuss the events that are ingrained in you and the ones to let go of. It usually takes couples a while to get their relationship to be what they were envisioning.

Contemplate what childhood baggage or past issues you contributed and how well it works in your current relationship. Pray about whether or not it's worth keeping. What worked in the past may not work for your future with your spouse. Today, when you are upset by something, question if it is unfinished business from your youth; if it is, how will you handle it?

Dear Lord, help me to release the past struggles and pain that I brought into my marriage. Heal my brokenness and teach me to forge onward with the caring companion you brought into my life. Allow our hearts to soar in your endless stream of love. You have been so kind and merciful to me. Thank you for giving me the freedom to decide what I should keep from my past and what I should get rid of. I love you, Lord. Amen.

January 9

I have brushed away your offenses like a cloud, your sins like a mist; return to me, for I have redeemed you.

ISAIAH 44:22

Every January thaw brings rising temperatures that melt the snow in the northeast, leaving a bleak brown scene behind that is often a muddy mess. Within a few days the sky opens up and covers the landscape again with a merciful blanket of white, making everything appear clean and fresh; a somber reminder that winter is not over.

In a marriage, temperatures rise periodically as situations heat up and wipe away all that was good. It doesn't take much for tempers to flare: maybe work was grueling, you didn't get much sleep, the phone never stopped ringing, and demands for your time finally set you off. The pressures of life can unravel the best-made rug, but instead of pulling apart all of the good you have done, reinforce it with love in the form of prayer. Talk to God and then be still. Listen for his voice.

Perhaps it was your spouse who had the bad day; maybe the rug was pulled out from under him or her, and you need to take into consideration the good, kind, and honorable partner he or she is buried underneath the cumbersome stress of the day. Regardless of the pressure cooker you both were in, step away from it and talk to God. Let the Lord's tranquility wash over you, cleanse you, and fill you with the peace you need to move forward to either seek forgiveness or offer it.

The need to forgive and move on arises every day. If you can't be open to it, you will find yourself living in the muddy mess under the receding snow. When you find yourself at the crossroads in life, always choose compassion. Mercy is the antidote to bitterness. As your father in heaven forgives you for past transgressions, he provides you the power to pardon others. What has happened that caused you to consider forgiveness this week?

Dear Lord, pardon my sinfulness; fill me with your tender mercies and limitless, unconditional love. Cleanse me, Lord, and make my soul white as snow. With your graciousness, I can offer forgiveness to [name] and wrap our marriage up in a sweet blanket of warmth. Let my kindness trickle down from heaven like the delightful snowflakes that protect the earth with pureness. You are my kind and loving Lord. Thank you for raising me up and allowing me to raise others in your name holy name. Amen.

January 10

In peace I will lie down and fall asleep, for you alone, Lord, make me secure.

PSALM 4:9

Retired Cornell Professor Dr. James Maas says most adults are sleep deprived. Sleep deprivation increases moodiness, stress, accidents, and illness. Restful sleep allows you to concentrate, make critical and creative decisions, communicate credibly, and increases overall productivity.

Could you or your spouse be sleep deprived, causing difficulties in your relationship? It isn't easy sharing a bed with another person. Perhaps children or a cat or dog share a bed with you. As enjoyable as it may be to share your special space with other family members, resist the temptation and opt to keep your bed a private sanctuary for you and your spouse to enjoy as a couple.

Perhaps your marriage is sleep deprived. A marriage needs certain elements to work effectively: trustworthiness, loyalty, compassion, dependability, love. Therefore, it is essential to keep the fundamentals of your marriage sacred. If one area is lacking, they could all suffer, causing a rippling effect onto other components form a stable marriage. For example, communication problems could develop if there is a breakdown in loyalty. And the domino effect keeps going, interfering with jobs, raising children, and conducting a social life.

Perhaps your married life is not well balanced between work and obligations, and fun and recreation. Work is essential, but only in the correct proportions: too much or too little is not healthy for anyone and not good for your marriage. Family recreation is necessary to balance out the work component, but "alone time" as a couple is also vital. Where does prayer fit into your life? How can you make God the cement to hold together all aspects of your life?

If you question areas that are lacking in your relationship, ask God to intervene. Draw the Lord into your life and ask God to show you the way. He will never abandon you. In the quiet of your heart, God will tell you what to do.

Dear Lord, allow my marriage to operate like an efficient, well-oiled machine, and not be lethargic from depravation. Teach me what to do and how to do it, Lord. Bring the perfect people into my life that can help to make my marriage better. Open my eyes to see what needs to be done. Give me the tools and the means to carry it through. Let me hear you, Lord. I am here, waiting, longing, and listening. Amen.

January 11

When a thirsty man dreams he is drinking and awakens faint,
his throat parched, so shall the horde of all the nations be.

Isaiah 29:8

Two simple ingredients make a delicious drink: water and coffee beans. A cup of coffee is the most desired morning beverage because it tastes good, is satisfying, and the caffeine jumpstarts the day. Brewing coffee requires heat. It's a simple concept for a humble pick-me-up.

What gentle words can you offer your spouse to begin his or her day? Sometimes a tender compliment will boost his or her day more than a cup of coffee. Words are simple letters put together and the way they are arranged and presented can be a gift or a putdown. Words have enormous power. Accolades for your partner seem like a simple thing to do, but it is an extraordinary gesture that will pick up your spouse to new heights, knowing that love is behind your intention. It costs nothing, but is worth so much to your partner.

Instead of using harsh words to get a point across, try changing the words to have a more pleasant sound and message. Maybe you could sing the message. That would certainly put a smile on your spouse's face. Perhaps you could deliver the message your spouse needs to know, but finish with a compliment so feelings don't get hurt. It might not be what you have to say, but more about how you say it. Think of congenial ways you can communicate amicably to your partner.

Like a good cup of coffee needs heat to brew, your marriage needs warmth and affection too. Ponder the fondness you feel and ways to convey it to your partner. Perhaps you could caress your spouse when you have conversations. A back rub would ease tensions and set the mood for openness to discussions. Maybe your spouse thirsts to hear endearing words from you. Invoke the Holy Spirit to fill your heart with the right words. How will you converse with your partner in a more endearing way?

Dear Lord, transform me into the compassionate spouse you always wanted for me to be. Fill my heart with kind and remarkable words. Let them brew inside of me until they are just right. Teach me how to use genuine and sincere words to let my partner feel the love that grows in my heart. Let me put [*name*]'s feelings and desires above my own so that I am able to convey my message in a most loving way. Keep my marriage safe and holy for as long as we both shall live. Amen.

January 12

He touched her hand, the fever left her, and she rose and waited on him.

MATTHEW 8:15

When you have a bad cold, why does chicken soup make you feel better? It's warm and comforting and makes you feel cozy when you eat it. There is no medicine in it, but somehow it does help. It's not expensive, and it's readily available. Nasty colds can make you feel tired and worn down, and sometimes the only other thing that can help is a hug.

Sometimes you need a warm hug even if you're not sick. Hugs, like soup, can make you feel better. There is something healing in touch. A growing body of research on how emotions affect health has helped medical professionals recognize its value, and some hospitals incorporate supportive touch because it tempers stress and blood pressure.

Whether you crave physical touch or your spouse yearns for it, it is as rewarding to give a hug as it is to get one. Consider when the last time was that you hugged your mate. Hugs can give reassurance, sympathy, empathy, encouragement, or congratulatory support. Regardless of the reason, hugging your spouse conveys your love without saying a word, and you both reap the benefits of it.

Is there sufficient touch in your relationship? If you need more physical contact from your spouse, speak up and say something in a nonthreatening way. For example, "I could really use a hug right now," is perfectly acceptable. It is kind, direct, and leaves no room for guesswork. It might seem awkward at first to ask for what you want, but it is better than expecting your spouse to be a mind reader. It might be possible that you have to initiate hugs and physical touch if you feel it is lacking in your relationship. The key is knowing what you want and then having the courage to ask for it in a kindhearted way.

Contemplate how you can add more compassionate touching in your relationship. You might want to establish more eye contact and offer friendlier smiles, which can lay the foundation for it. Touch is a powerful means to convey marital love. When Jesus touched people, they were changed forever by it. How can you transform your spouse's heart through your gentle caress?

Dear Lord, let my loving touch heal my spouse's wounds, the ones I know about and the ones I am not aware of. Make my words be as soothing as my warm caress. Let my demeanor feel like the hug my spouse longs for. Teach me, loving and merciful Lord, to be a supportive partner and to be respectful of the times when my spouse needs aloneness. Amen.

January 13

Jehoshaphat therefore had wealth and glory in abundance;
but he became related to Ahab by marriage.
2 CHRONICLES 18:1

Ancient marriage was not a personal matter. The motives were to protect property, expand the wealth of the clan, and provide a secure environment for the next generation. The institution of marriage revolved around economic, political ,and cultural influences. Consider how that differs from your marriage.

Did you marry for love or for other reasons such as economic motives? Perhaps you knew your partner for a long time before your wedding, and it made sense that you both would eventually end up together. Did your extended families approve of your union? Perhaps you can stand back and see God's hand guiding you toward one another. Not fully understanding God's plan is normal, but acting in good faith on what you believe to be his divine plan is called trust.

Was your courtship long enough to get to know your partner's imaginings and inspirations? Did you marry too young or too old? Perhaps your lives together revolve around careers. Ascertain how your lives will encompass God, because journeying with Christ will give your lives a purpose and a richness you won't be able to find anywhere else. Ponder the significance of children in your marriage. Will you include them biologically or through adoption? Perhaps God has blessed you with biological children, but consider if there is room in your lives to adopt a needy orphan. The Lord God Almighty has molded a child's heart with pure heavenly faith, and it is a gift to experience it while you raise children.

Contemplate whether or not you had any expectation of marriage. Perhaps you were surprised to have complications with in-laws or money. The sacred union of marriage provides couples with countless delicate blessings that can become problematic if not handled carefully. Joining together two completely different families can present couples with a realm of complex dynamics: decisions over which families to celebrate holidays with, caring for elderly parents, or saving money for your own retirement. When storybooks relay messages of "living happily ever after," did it occur to you how different your married life would actually be? Out of the millions of people on earth, your path crossed with your partner's. Was it destiny, or did God select you both for a reason you haven't yet discovered? Trust in God's plan as you reflect today on what that plan might be for you.

Dear Lord, reveal your plan to me, Lord, or give me the patience to endure a while longer. I trust in your glorious ways. Amen.

January 14

Do you see those skilled at their work? They will stand in the presence of kings, but not in the presence of the obscure.

PROVERBS 22:29

As a child, I built forts out of sofa cushions and blankets; I played with boxes and turned pots and pans into musical instruments. Sometimes it's important to use ordinary items and tap into your creativity to turn a plain relationship into something quite remarkable. Reflect on past times with your partner where you turned a regular day into an extraordinary occasion. Perhaps the last time that happened revolved around your marriage proposal. Consider how Jesus turned an average day meandering through town into a miraculous event: curing the lame allowing them to walk and permitted the blind to see.

Perhaps you could transform a regular meal into an event by using a tablecloth, special dishes, and candlelight. You could play soft music while you prepare dinner. Or maybe you could spread a blanket on the living room floor and serve a picnic-style dinner on paper plates in the middle of winter. If you normally go out to dinner, switch it up by having breakfast at a local diner. Whatever creative measures you take, your partner will appreciate the kind gesture to make the day special.

You might want to draft a "bucket list" of fun things you can do together; it's something to aim for. Perhaps you could make a list of interesting spots to visit in your area and then expand it to a 100-mile radius of your town. Possibly you could visit every church in your town, admiring the stained glass windows and statuary inside. Day trips can certainly convert a typical day into something exceptional. Maybe you could plan your summer vacation today. Half of the fun is deciding where to go and planning where to stay and what you will do. Whatever creative measure you take, include God in it. You will go farther than you could imagine with the Lord in your life. How will you make this day an extra special one for you and your partner?

Dear Lord, remove the boredom from my life and fill my head with wondrous ideas, allowing my imagination to go wild. Let me hear my spouse laugh and get lost in the love we have for each other. Let me take what you have provided and build it up into something exquisite. You are my rock and my salvation. I love you, Lord, for all you have given to me and for all you will bless me with. Amen.

January 15

How beautiful is your love, my sister, my bride, how much better is your love than wine, and the fragrance of your perfumes than any spice!
SONG OF SONGS 4:10

The same perfume sprayed on different people has a different scent that is distinctive to the person wearing it because each person has a unique body chemistry that reacts with the fragrance. Many things affect how perfumes respond to the body: hormones, medications, stress, and the complexities of skin with compounds including fat, salt, sugar, proteins, and fibers.

There are also many complexities of the love in your marriage. Perhaps you feel the excitement you once had in your relationship wane and you are unsure how to recapture it. Many outside factors may contribute to that happening. There are extraneous distractions vying for your attention, such as computer games, social networking sites, online shopping, and watching TV. One thing you can do is avoid them and spend more time with your spouse. Ask your partner what one thing you can do to be a better mate. Then do that thing for the rest of the week.

Because God made each person different, it's important to adapt to those variances. Some things your spouse likes you might find revolting and vice versa. It's essential to convey those thoughts and feelings to each other to avoid the possibility of a miscommunication. One element that lends itself to communication conundrums is misinterpreting body language. When your partner speaks to you, give your undivided attention. Look up from the newspaper; don't keep watering the plants or insist on multitasking; stop, look, and listen to what your mate has to say.

Paying attention to your spouse makes him or her feel loved and respected, and that their message is important. If your spouse fidgets, reach out to caress his or her hand; this simple gesture reassures your partner that you care. Listen first with your heart, ingesting the message internally before offering a reply. While it is tempting to half-listen to devise a rebuttal, resist the temptation. It's equally important not to scramble the message with blaming, rationalizing, or denials. Think of how lovingly Jesus listened to people and how he listens to your prayers each day. Knowing how different you are from your spouse, what one thing will you do differently this week to demonstrate that you care about what he or she has to say?

Dear Lord, open my heart to hear your words and teach me to listen more closely to my spouse. When [name] listens to me, it feels like sweet perfume is poured over me. Teach me to listen with my eyes, my ears, and my heart. Expose my soul to your messages, Lord. Let me listen to my spouse the way you listen to me. Amen.

January 16

You shall not wear cloth made from wool and linen woven together.

DEUTERONOMY 22:11

Toile is a fabric with a repeated pattern depicting a multifaceted scene of a pastoral theme such as a couple picnicking by a lake. It's a classic design in one color on a white background, which is fascinating because every pattern tells a story. Some configurations show people hunting, working, fishing, drinking, and dancing. What story does your marriage tell?

Perhaps your marriage depicts a true love romance, a saga of heartache or adventure, or perhaps a combination. Reflect on past happenings, both good and bad, that describe your history as a couple. Maybe you took an extravagant honeymoon, traveling to a foreign place or fun destination. Reliving happier times is a good way to reconnect and begin dreaming of future adventures together.

Perhaps your toile pattern would depict a charitable couple who volunteer in a variety of worthy organizations in your community. God calls each of us to share our talents with the less fortunate. You could possibly sing in your church choir or teach religious education in your local parish. Volunteering could be the perfect venue for you to live your lives more purposefully as a couple the way Christ desires.

Who is in control of your life? Are you in control, or does money, your job, or your children define you? With so many obligations pulling at you, it's understandable how some people get derailed and out of control. If you sense it is happening to you, welcome the Lord into your life by devoting extra time each day meditating on your purpose and seeking God's wisdom in his time and place.

Are you attempting to control your spouse or your relationship? The Lord brought you and your partner together to work and live peaceably in unison as equal companions. Make Jesus a part of your marriage, and he will walk with you through each chapter of your life story. Reflect on the earlier years of your marriage and compare it to the way you and your spouse are now. If you were to draw that story, what would it look like?

Dear Lord, empower me to be in control of my life and to assert myself prayerfully in my marriage. Help me make poignant decisions to define my life with my spouse so that we can do your work peacefully here on earth to will prepare us for our lives with you in heaven. Amen.

January 17

*I praise you because you remember me in everything and hold
fast to the traditions, just as I handed them on to you. But I
want you to know that Christ is the head of every man, and a
husband the head of his wife, and God the head of Christ.*

1 CORINTHIANS 11:2–3

Anyone who flies in or out of the northeast in the winter will be familiar with waiting for a plane to be deiced. Chemicals are sprayed on the aircraft to prevent ice formation. What do you do to prevent ice from forming on your relationship?

While you cannot spray chemicals on it, there are other, more suitable, options. You could shower your spouse with gifts. They don't have to be expensive, just something meaningful from the heart. You might want to present your partner with a single red rose; it's small but packs a powerful punch. Maybe your spouse would appreciate a card with a heartfelt message inscribed in it. It's possible that your partner would enjoy an afternoon with his or her friends, away from the hectic home filled with responsibilities, chores, and obligations.

There are many different ways you can cultivate a loving relationship without spending any money at all. It can be done through the use of words. Just think of all of the wonderful things you could say to your spouse; there is no limit. Perhaps you could give your spouse a gift of compliments all week. After spending a considerable amount of time preparing dinner, it's nice to hear an earnest compliment, something more than "good dinner." Making the effort to build up your partner's self-esteem with a stream of accolades could have a compassionate effect on your marriage and the gesture might be reciprocated.

When you see your spouse, God is in him or her. What you say to your mate you also say to God. That could make your praises sweeter, kinder, and more loving. How do you keep the fire alive in your marriage?

Dear Lord, thank you for the ability to convey gentle and loving thoughts to my lifelong partner and friend. You made this special person exactly the way I need him or her to be. I promise to honor [*name*] with a stream of praises even when there is no reason for it. You have blessed me with the power to lift my partner's feelings with a few pleasant words. Thank you, sweet and generous Lord, for all you have given me and continue to give. You are my saving God. I love you, Lord. Amen.

January 18

Oh, would that my words were written down!

JOB 19:23

Handwriting analysis identifies and assesses personality traits through the patterns revealed in cursive script. The way you cross your t's and dot your i's speaks volumes about how you think and behave.

Instead of analyzing your cursive style, examine what makes you a kind and compassionate mate. Contemplate your actions last week and scrutinize what behaviors led you to act the way you did. Perhaps you struggled to keep your temper under control or had misdirected anger toward your mate.

Are your actions programmed by your brain or by your heart? Perhaps you could begin your work each day by first quieting yourself and saying a prayer before you do anything else. Ask God to formulate your thoughts and actions, keeping them pure, good, and just. When your thoughts are converted into words intellectually, allow them to pass through a filter in your heart before they are spoken to ensure the message is entwined with God's intentions.

Persistent prayer will ensure that God motivates your thoughts and actions toward your spouse. If you are bewildered with the words you want to say to your partner, ask God in the silence of your heart if it is the right message. He will direct your speech.

Contemplate what type of life partner you are and whether or not you need to make improvements on your behaviors. Often it's easier to say one thing but do another, because it's difficult to put your words into action. Have you ever told your spouse you would do the dishes, but the moment the meal was over you found something else more "important" to do? Reflect on times in the past when you may have said you would do something, but then failed to act. Your actions speak volumes, so be mindful of all you say and do.

It's possible that your actions are directly proportional to your personality traits. Perhaps your words, tone, body language, and actions are a result of how you were raised. It may appear to be intertwined; tease it all apart to understand each component individually. How will you bring God into everything you say, think, and do?

Dear Lord, thank you for making me in your image and blessing me with specific personality traits. Help me find the good in each mannerism, appreciate them, and make them work kindheartedly to serve you. Help me to include you in every utterance I make. Let each word I say pass through my heart before it rolls off my tongue. I want my thoughts to be conveyed lovingly and intelligently to my spouse, preventing heartache and disagreements. Amen.

January 19

Therefore, I will always remind you of these things, even though you already know them and are established in the truth you have.

2 PETER 1:12

I shoveled a narrow path down the driveway so my daughters wouldn't get covered in snow on their way to the bus stop. While one girl followed closely behind, the other plodded her own course through the snow that was knee-deep. Even though I raised my daughters in the same exact manner, they both developed specific personality differences and grew up to be unique individuals. It's not surprising that you have noticed many differences between you and your spouse.

Your lifelong marriage partner will not always follow everything you say and do, because you are both different; everyone is. Reflect on noticeable differences you observed this week that caused your relationship to be strained. For example, if your spouse spends excessive amounts of time mulling over decisions before making them, you might appreciate that each choice has been thought out extremely well. If this difference is bothersome to you, try learning from your partner how to give yourself more time prior to making important assessments. Instead of making a snap decision, give yourself an extra day to decide. Ask God to bless you with patience while you observe, learn, and practice spending more time controlling decisiveness.

Subtle personality differences also exist between you and your mate. Consider the ones that were the most bothersome last week and search earnestly for the goodness in them and see what you can learn from it. Remember that there are no "bad" personality traits.

Contemplate what personality differences you were attracted to when you first began dating. Perhaps your spouse is talkative and outgoing, and you are shy. Consider the benefits of this: when you're together at a social gathering, you have someone who will enjoy talking if you don't want to. Contemplate finding the silver lining in each personality difference between you. If you are unorganized, perhaps you could learn your partner's organizational capabilities. You can become a student of his or her select personality differences.

God gave you the opportunity to learn optimal skills from one another. What will you learn from your partner today?

Dear Lord, enable me to appreciate the difference in my spouse's character. Help me to understand, embrace it, and learn from it, so that I can improve and be a better version of myself. Teach me not to have unrealistic expectations of [*name*] or hold his or her characteristics against him or her; they are gifts from you and I adore all that is from you. Bless me with patience as I grow in your love. Amen.

January 20

"You shall not commit adultery."

EXODUS 20:14

Have you ever driven through a winter storm? It's critical to acquire special driving techniques and practices for the winter months. Some people insist on using snow tires or four-wheel-drive vehicles. They carry blankets, emergency flares, and keep shovels in their trunks in the event of an accident. Consider what emergency items are kept in the trunk of your car. Maybe you live in a warm climate, but it would behoove you to carry such emergency tools as jumper cables or a membership with a roadside-assistance club.

What special precautionary measures do you take to ensure your marriage stays on course? Most marriages have been tested, and one way to ensure your marriage doesn't succumb to such temptations is to keep a tight alliance to God. This can be achieved by reading holy Scriptures with your partner. The answer to every question can be found in the Bible.

If you sense an attraction to someone of the opposite sex or flirtatious behavior, don't meander a path that could lead to adultery. Don't be alone with this person, even if you think you can withstand the lure or set aside the desirability; always include your spouse. Evaluate your feelings honestly: is that friend more than a friend? If so, walk away. If you are tempted by a coworker, ask for a transfer. If you are tempted by a boss, quit that job. If you are tempted by a neighbor, move to another house. Nothing good can come from it; however, much evil can result from it. Resist the inducement by putting out the fire, not fanning it. Lustful thoughts and desires can be more powerful than the will to resist. Acknowledge your weakness and relish fulfillment with the Holy Spirit who is stronger than your nature to sin. Ask God to empower you with the ability to do what is right.

Remember to keep your marriage vows sacred and honor the commandments God established for you to live by. Take whatever measures are necessary to stay true to your vows to your spouse and to God. You will be richly blessed for it. How do you stay true to your commitment to your partner?

Dear Lord, keep my eyes on you as I walk the path of righteousness. Empower me to walk away from illicit affairs of the mind, heart, body, and soul. Let me overcome the stumbling blocks that clutter my path and live in your love forever and ever. Amen.

January 21

He disperses hail like crumbs. Who can withstand his cold?
PSALM 147:17

It's wise to wear a hat in the winter, but you won't lose more body heat through your head; heat dissipates from any part of your body that is exposed to the cold weather. Core body temperature is a measurement of how your body is doing. What do you use to measure the core emotions of your marriage?

How do you prevent your marriage from being exposed to unemotional or unkind behaviors? One way you can achieve this is not to contribute to negativity in your relationship. In its place, seek whatever is good, kind, and tranquil. If there is emotional detachment in your home, your relationship could be on a collision course with an unpredictable outcome. Instead, be involved in your spouse's interests, dreams, and passions by showing concern for his or her well-being. If you suspect you are drifting off course, call upon the Lord to guide you back on track. Ask yourself, "What would Jesus do in this situation?" and then do that.

An affective events theory suggests that emotions are swayed, initiated by happenings that influence attitudes and behaviors. For example, if you feel neutral walking into your home after work and your spouse has a wonderful dinner prepared; the table is set beautifully with china, crystal, and candlelight—that will influence how you feel and behave. If you walk into the house feeling neutral and are greeted with crying children who misbehaved all day, toys are strewn across the floor, you smell dinner burning on the stove—that will influence how you feel and behave. Reflect on past times where certain events influenced your attitude and behaviors.

Emotions such as anger, disgust, fear, happiness, sadness, and surprise connect thoughts, feelings, and dispositions. They can also be influenced by hormones and chemicals (such as dopamine, serotonin, and cortisol) that transport messages between nerve cells. When you walk into a messy kitchen to find a sink full of dirty dishes, much is happening internally to trigger your mood. God created your body to act that way. You have the ability to let the messy kitchen put you in a foul mood, or you can sympathize, knowing that your spouse was up all night working on a project for you, so you do the dishes quietly and lovingly. It's a choice you can make. You have the power to turn it into a fight or a rich, loving gift.

How do you meet your emotional need for love? You feel secure in your relationship when your mate accepts, loves, and is committed to your well-being. How can you ensure that your emotions are not "left out in the cold?"

Dear Lord, teach me to meet [*name*]'s emotional need to feel loved. Allow me to find the love that is needed. Amen.

January 22

Try to get here before winter....The Lord be with
your spirit. Grace be with all of you.

2 Timothy 4:21–22

A woman's hands and feet tend to be chilly before men's. The external temperature where a male and female's bodies conserve varies by three degrees. Your body conserves heat by reducing blood flow to the hands and feet, making them feel chilled. Many say, "Cold hands, warm heart." How warm is your heart toward your spouse?

One way to warm his or her heart is to be complimentary by using words that build up your partner. It could be as simple as saying, "You look nice today." If you really want to warm up your spouse's heart, try gazing into his or her eyes and say, "You have lovely eyes; they are as beautiful today as the day I married you." And then reflect on the intimate feelings you experienced on your wedding day. Maybe you could reminisce about the happenings of your wedding, which could stir up a cauldron of joyful feelings.

It is important for you to affirm and support your spouse in a positive light. Recall the favorable attributes that you find endearing and build off them. For example, if your spouse is a good father, explain why you reached that conclusion. Hearing positive feedback will boost your partner's self-esteem. Encouraging words add fuel to the fire of love that burns within his or her heart. If you don't do anything to feed that fire, eventually it will go out.

Kind words, and the manner in which you use them, can set the mood for the entire day. Compliments are powerful communicators of love and can add the warmth that your relationship longs for during the winter months. If you want a fire of love to burn passionately in your marriage, use kind words as kindling.

If you have ever tried to build a fire, you know you need to do more than toss a few logs in a pile and ignite it. Kindling is essential, but fanning it is what really gets it going. You can fan the fire of love in your spouse's heart by acknowledging every good thing that he or she does. For example, "Thank you for taking the trash out," or "Thank you for bringing in the mail." Each time you feel love, express it; don't hold back. It won't be long before you will be warm from head to toe. How will you fan the embers of love in your mate?

Dear Lord, fill my heart with loving compliments that my spouse yearns to hear. Erase all negativity from my vocabulary and let my language be encouraging, compassionate, generous, and agreeable. Show me your image in my mate. Amen.

January 23

*She is not concerned for her household when it snows—all her charges
are doubly clothed....She is clothed with strength and dignity,
and laughs at the days to come. She opens her mouth in wisdom;
kindly instruction is on her tongue. She watches over the affairs of
her household, and does not eat the bread of idleness. Her children
rise up and call her blessed; her husband, too, praises her: "Many
are the women of proven worth, but you have excelled them all."*
PROVERBS 31:21, 25–29

Cotton may be the "fabric of our lives," but it can be dangerous outside in the cold. If cotton gets wet from perspiration or rain, it saps body heat rapidly. Polypropylene is a synthetic substance that wicks moisture away from the skin to keep you warm and dry.

Making good clothing choices parallels the difference between your marriage making it or not. It is therefore imperative to make wise choices in your marriage. If you question a decision, pray on it before making it. Ask God to help you through it. He will never lead you astray. Sit patiently and quietly and wait for God to speak to you in the silence of your heart.

If you make a poor choice, admit your mistake, take responsibility for your actions, state corrective actions to fix it, and uphold it. When your spouse sees you acting conscientiously and maturely, he will gain better appreciation and respect for you. We are all human, subjected to making mistakes. Let go of it and move on. Learn from your mistakes so you don't repeat them.

You live by the decisions you make; therefore, choose honorably. Instead of making rash decisions, take time to ponder the pros and cons. Perhaps you could make a list and pray on it before acting on it. You might solicit input from your priest. When God is woven into the fabric of your life, the wear-ability and durability can powerhouse you through anything.

When you bring a decision to your spouse, be flexible with it. You can request input from your partner before acting on it also. You might include him or her in the decision making process; that would make your spouse feel important and show you care significantly about his or her feelings. What decision will you pray about this week?

Dear Lord, help me to make sound choices in my marriage. When I am wrong, give me the courage to admit my mistakes, give me the wisdom to amend my blunders, and the strength to move forward in love. Let me wipe the slate clean and start over in your mercy. Amen.

January 24

Wine is arrogant, strong drink is riotous;
none who are intoxicated by them are wise.

PROVERBS 20:1

During the chilly winter months, drinking alcohol makes you feel warm because it causes blood to rush to the surface of your skin. In actuality, blood vessels dilate, causing you to lose heat more rapidly. Additionally, drinking alcohol in the cold impairs both shivering and judgment. The mental and physical well-being of the drinker is at risk, but your relationship can be affected too.

If a spouse is an alcoholic, the effects can be life-shattering to both of you. Usually the alcoholic will deny that there is a problem and the partner won't know how to help. If the drinking continues, marriage problems can ensue and destroy their relationship. Alcoholism can cause males to experience impotence and low libido because excessive drinking decreases testosterone production. The sober person has little desire to engage in sexual activity with their drinking companion. Do you drink to escape problems, feel good, or drink compulsively?

There are psychological and other health-related ramifications that can be traumatic and long-lasting if you or your partner has a drinking problem. Often the hardest part to solving a problem is admitting that there is one. Reach out to someone: Alcoholics Anonymous, a priest or doctor, and God. With God you can get through anything.

If you drink alcoholic beverages with your spouse, friends, and coworkers, you may enjoy the social camaraderie while partaking to achieve intoxication. The irony of enjoying alcohol is that it presents both benefits and risks to your health and other significant realms of your life, including your work and marriage. Moderation is the key to safe alcohol consumption. Reflect on the amount of alcohol you have consumed thus far with your spouse and decide if it is within acceptable limits or if there is a problem. If you have concerns about it, what are you going to do?

Dear Lord, bring the right people into my life to open my eyes to see if there is a drinking problem in my family. Don't let me abuse alcohol or any other kind of drug or stimulant. Give me the strength I need to do something proactive to safeguard myself and my family. Cradle me in your loving embrace, Lord. Shine your all-encompassing love around me. I adore you, Lord, and desperately need your help. I call out to you in my darkest hour to hear and answer me. Amen.

January 25

*The workmen labored, and the task of restoration progressed
under their hands. They restored the house of God
according to its original form, and reinforced it.*

2 CHRONICLES 24:13

A piano requires maintenance and tuning to produce its best sound. When it is properly tuned, the music is intoxicating. The longer a piano is left out of tune, the more time and effort it takes to restore it to correct pitch.

Your marriage is akin to a piano, needing conservation and fine-tuning. Contemplate when the last time was that your marriage had upkeep, alterations, or tweaking. For a relationship to work properly, it needs work daily, maybe even hourly. Consider what you have done to fine-tune your marriage. One of the best things you can do as a couple is pray together. Try setting aside just five minutes each morning to connect with your spouse on a spiritual level.

Would it be possible to send your children to a family room to play quietly after dinner to allow you and your spouse extra time to talk without interruptions and enjoy a hot beverage? Or perhaps could you and your spouse take a brisk walk outside after dinner to catch up on family events and reconnect with each other? Maybe you could nix a TV program in favor of going to bed early to talk and read holy Scriptures before going to sleep. Whatever scenario works is what you should do. What type of marriage restoration is necessary to keep your relationship in perfect pitch?

Because the circumstances of your lives are in a constant state of flux with job changes, health, children, and friends, conflict is inevitable. It's important to maintain good communication to prevent any misunderstandings. It isn't easy to convert the life challenges into growth opportunities for your marriage, but with flexibility and consideration, seek ways to make the most of your circumstances. For example, if your spouse must travel for business, can you accompany him or her to make it a mini get-away? The key to making the struggle productive is to do it together as a team with open and honest communication.

During trying moments, commit to openly expressing your appreciation and affection for one another. It sets a loving tone for a more relaxing environment to sort out issues that constantly creep into a marriage. How will you plan to do that throughout the week?

Dear Lord, thank you for giving me a level-headed spouse to help me through our life struggles as one problem morphs into another. Your presence in my life enables me the endurance to get through them. I honor and praise you today and every day for as long as I shall live. I love you, Lord. Amen.

January 26

*I said in my heart, "Come, now, let me try you with
pleasure and the enjoyment of good things."*
ECCLESIASTES 2:1

Modern sledding began in St. Moritz during the early 1870s when visitors experimented with delivery sleds. Alpine events began among the privileged leisure set, but now it's available to everyone on any snow-covered slope. Creative imaginings inspired an enjoyable winter pastime.

Contemplate what ordinary experimentations could be transformed into a pleasurable creation with your spouse. Maybe you could go sledding with your spouse at night. Nighttime sledding or skiing is a totally different experience with shadows and slivers of light reflections from snowy surfaces. You might try cross-country skiing under a moonlit sky. Maybe this would be a good time to take a horse-drawn sleigh ride. It's not only beautiful, but it's romantic and exciting too.

Perhaps you could create a magical dining experience with candlelight and soft music, or eat on TV trays while watching a favorite movie. Maybe you could make a favorite meal together, a pot of soup, stew, or chili. You could enjoy a winter picnic or take a thermos of hot cocoa to go sledding. It takes a little creativity to turn something common into something exceptional to let your partner know you care about his or her happiness.

God wants you to have pleasurable experiences. Your life cannot be full of work and responsibilities or else you will burn out. It's essential to have balance between all you are accountable for and enjoyment. If you have been overworked for so long that you forgot how to have fun, go for a walk, listen to the songbirds, and be amazed with the wind blowing through the evergreen trees dusted with snow. For God is there. Look up at the powder-blue sky dotted with billowy clouds; God is there too. Everywhere you look, you will find the Lord and he will never abandon you. Call out to him to let your spirit soar.

Dear Lord, teach me how to close my books, turn off my computer, and leave work early to enjoy the beauty of the life you gave me. Let me celebrate the simple pleasures of life, my partner's smile, or a warm embrace on a chilly day. You tantalize me with the workings of the world and I thank you dearly for that. Thank you for the countless blessing you have given to lighten my heart and each footstep I take. Thank you for being such a kind and generous God. I love you, Lord. Amen.

January 27

*"Come, let us go down and there confuse their language,
so that no one will understand the speech of another."*
GENESIS 11:7

Downhill skiing is a popular winter activity. Avid skiers buy top-notch clothing to stay warm and safe. Skiing is a complicated process with many techniques to master before someone can actually enjoy it.

Like skiing, there are many intricate elements to accomplishing effective communication. You can say whatever pops into your head, but that could be disastrous if you say the wrong thing. Before you hit the slopes with Alpine skis, you get prepared. Do the same thing when speaking. Get ready by asking the Holy Spirit in the silence of your heart to fill your head with the right words and give you the ability to convey the true message laced with tranquility and love.

There are many things you can do to ensure your marriage vocabulary stays on track. It's important to be honest, not brutally honest, but sincere honesty. Brutal honesty is hurtful and offensive. Work to avoid anything that can be interpreted as cutting; strive for tactfulness. Omission is a form of dishonesty. To remain silent purposefully is hurtful by not sharing key information or knowledge that might enable your conversation to be successful. Take responsibility for your half of the dialog. Attempt to make it insightful and diplomatic.

Don't put more effort into sports instead of listening to your spouse with undivided attention. If your partner has something to say, stop what you are doing and listen with undivided attention: turn off the TV, unplug the mp3 player, and close the newspaper. What your body language says conveys how important you are to your spouse. Some couples touch each other's hands to ensure honest and open communication between them. Give this practice a try and see if it helps strengthen your conversations. If you can enhance your communication skills, making them a priority, you might see improvements in your marriage by the way you speak, listen, and understand.

When your spouse speaks to you, invoke the Holy Spirit to enable you to listen more intently. By conversing with God in your heart before you give a response, your words will be blessed with your good intentions. Before you engage your spouse in a conversation this week, can you pray for enlightenment from God first?

Dear Lord, let me see you in my spouse. Let me hear your voice. I want you to be intertwined with every loving word we use. Bless my marriage and the way we work to keep it together. Amen.

January 28

He said to her, "Please give me a little water to drink. I am thirsty."
So she opened a skin of milk, gave him a drink, and then covered him.

JUDGES 4:19

If we were all the same, life would certainly be boring, especially if our world was filled only with whistlers! Life is richer because there are wide vocal ranges: soprano, mezzo-soprano, contralto, tenor, baritone, and bass. We look differently, act differently, and sound differently. Sometimes we are attracted to opposites. And that is a good thing because when you blend the melody from a soprano and a baritone, it sounds beautiful. Each are good individually, too.

We all have fundamental rights. In marriage, you have the right to be different and celebrate your uniqueness. It's possible that your spouse found your personality uniqueness endearing. Reflect on some of your partner's characteristics that you are fond of. Maybe your spouse is a whistler, while you like to hum. Whatever your differences are, cherish that distinctiveness as a gift that God selected especially for him or her to be shared with you. The next time you hear your mate whistle, know that the song is a gift from God.

Do you appreciate your individuality? Your spouse also has the right to his or her distinctive personality. If you enjoy eating healthy foods and exercising, but your spouse eats different foods and likes to rest, perhaps you could take turns preparing meals for each other and try each other's individualized exercises and rest periods. In moderation both are good and you could learn something from each other. Are you respectful of your personal differences or do you seek to change him or her?

When your spouse's eccentricities become bothersome to you, pray to Jesus. Ask the Lord to show you how to embrace or overlook the oddities and appreciate them. Ponder ways you can demonstrate courteousness and acceptance of the variances. Jesus was different. Think of Jesus when your spouse's idiosyncrasies annoy you. If Jesus was different and admired and loved by so many, can you offer the same courtesy to your spouse? What do you thirst for in your marriage?

Dear Lord, mold me into your image and teach me how to be more loving and accepting of my spouse's peculiarities. Allow me to acquiesce to the personality differences between us and not let it be a source of contention in our marriage. Thank you for my spouse. Amen.

January 29

The start of strife is like the opening of a dam;
check a quarrel before it bursts forth!

PROVERBS 17:14

When the sun shines on freshly fallen snow, it glitters like a field of diamonds. While some might view winter as a frigid, barren landscape, others adore the thick gobs of snow stuck like marshmallow fluff to tree branches, creating a winter wonderland.

You and your partner don't have to agree on every issue; in fact, you have the right to disagree with your partner in your marriage. It's perfectly acceptable to have your own rights, opinions, and viewpoints about things such as politics. Reflect on a few differences of opinions you experienced with your spouse last week. Because you and your spouse are two totally different people, with dissimilar upbringings and viewpoints, acknowledge and appreciate that you will not always agree on everything.

If you don't see eye-to-eye on a subject, it isn't cause for an argument but a topic of a lighthearted discussion in which you can educate each other about your actual feelings. That could open a window into your world that your spouse didn't know about, and it could bring your relationship closer. Perhaps you are privy to information your spouse was unaware of and sharing those facts could change his or her opinions. Whenever you have open discussions, it is natural and acceptable to agree to disagree: the perfect win-win situation when you have conflicting perspectives.

Examine closely the underlying causes of quarrels and how you might prevent them from happening with a heartfelt prayer. It is okay to pray when you and your spouse struggle with a topic that results in conflict that cannot be resolved. Take a break from the discussion and return to it later after a meal or sleep. Just as you wouldn't ride a bike over a twenty-four hour period without time for rest, food, and grooming, you need to do the same for your marriage. Perhaps if you stepped away from the issue that is causing turmoil, and did something fun, you might come back to the topic with a totally different perspective. What subjects have you and your spouse argued over that you are struggling to resolve? Is the topic one that you can both agree to disagree?

Dear Lord, grant me open-mindedness to accept the differences in opinions of my spouse. You created [*name*] to think, feel, and act differently, and I love you for that. Thank you for wiring his or her brain differently than mine because we will have more knowledge between us to solve many of life's difficulties. We make a great team and I feel blessed that we have the capabilities to work out issues instead of allowing them to weigh us down. Amen.

January 30

*Watch carefully then how you live, not as foolish persons but as wise,
making the most of the opportunity, because the days are evil.*

EPHESIANS 5:15–16

Nothing quells the chill of winter like warm woolen mittens. Mittens are warmer than gloves because fingers maintain their warmth better when they are in contact with each other. How do you and your spouse maintain contact with each other when myriad forces tug you in different directions competing for your time? The TV and computer compete for your time; perhaps children or caring for elderly parents vie for your attention. Limiting your resources and time with obligations and distractions will afford more quality hours to devote to your spouse. Make the most of every opportunity you have together.

Reflect on your favorite ways to spend quality time together. Perhaps you talk while you take long walks together. You might be able to devote the first five minutes of the walk to discussing "business" topics, and the rest of the time dedicate to recreation by focusing on the clouds in the sky, the birds warbling overhead, the warmth of your partner's hand in yours. On the last five minutes of your walk, plan your next outing. Even though it is winter, don't let the weather impede your plans. Walk inside a shopping mall or try snowshoeing.

Make plans to do something; they don't have to be grandiose. In fact, your plans can be as simple as building a snowman in your front yard. When was the last time you had a snowball fight with your spouse? Afterward, warm yourselves with a hot beverage and spend even more time together.

Maybe you could volunteer to provide hot meals to the homeless or work in a soup kitchen. You will feel blessed when you warm the hearts of the less fortunate through small acts of charity. Perhaps you could buy socks and mittens for the homeless in your community. Whatever you decide to do as a couple, ask God to bless those actions and strengthen you to become the best version of yourselves.

Buy a pair of mittens for your mate with a note describing how much you value spending time together walking and talking. Only you can choose the destination—make it a worthy place. Where will you go and what will you do?

Dear Lord, bless the hours in my day; make me productive and not squander one second of it. Grant me the wisdom to ascertain how to spend more quality time with my spouse. I cherish the gift of time with [*name*]. Thank you for allowing me to share my life with him or her. Amen.

January 31

The city will be filled with boys and girls playing in its streets.
ZECHARIAH 8:5

It's enjoyable watching children play in the snow. They build snow forts, have snowball fights, make snow angels, and even eat the stuff! They know how to have fun with little more than their imaginations. What prevents you and your spouse from having fun? Perhaps you once had the time, energy, and money to go out to seek entertainment, but not so much anymore.

If money is tight, seek affordable options. Look for "cheap seat" movie tickets or try going to a matinee show. Libraries sometimes hold movie nights with a wide range of activities that might be interesting to you. Home improvement stores host classes with free instructions on how to lay tile or hang wallpaper. Consider doing an inexpensive remodeling job on your home, even if it is only changing the paint color, because sometimes that is enough. Perhaps you could find an inexpensive cooking class that you and your spouse could take together. Some churches sponsor inspirational speakers or hold Bible classes. Consider attending them. Consider attending daily Mass together; it's the perfect way to begin each day in the Lord's presence. Think outside the box; you might be surprised at what you find pleasurable, because your tastes change over time.

It becomes tricky when arguments ensue after a decision cannot be reached on an activity you both enjoy. Maybe you could list all of the activities and rate them on a scale of one to ten. Perhaps you could take turns doing the pleasurable activities; that way you both win.

In the winter, some people experience cabin-fever with a tendency to go stir-crazy indoors for long periods of time. Could you invite neighbors over for a game of Pinochle, Rummy Royal, or checkers? Perhaps you could host a covered-dish supper with a small group of friends. Could you go cross-country skiing one weekend? Even if you don't know how, it's fun to learn something new. God brought you both together for a purpose; he wants you to find fulfillment and pleasure in your relationship with each other and with neighbors and friends.

Dear Lord, let me tap into my inner child and experience the joy I once had with my spouse when we were dating. Erase my inhibitions and allow me to be imaginative with all I can do to honor and please you through my marriage. Bring a smile to my face so I can warm my partner's heart with it. Thank you, sweet and loving Lord. I love you. Amen.

February 1

Will the ax boast against the one who hews with it? Will the saw
exalt itself above the one who wields it? As if a rod could sway the
one who lifts it, or a staff could lift the one who is not wood!

ISAIAH 10:15

Cooking can be enjoyable with the right tools. Cooks on television chop through vegetables like a well-oiled machine. After I bought good knives, I could too. It took less time and energy to prepare meals and it enhanced the overall cooking experience. Using proper kitchen utensils made a huge difference.

Think about the many marriage tools God has given to you: touching, kissing, holding hands, caressing. He has also given you the ability to speak in a loving and respectful manner, and listen with the goal to understand. He gave you the means to solve conflict, apologize when the need arises, how to forgive, and rebuild trust. God made sure he provided couples with many tools to choose from to keep marriages on track. The problem is that many couples don't realize they have these tools, or they use them incorrectly, or they simply opt not to use them.

Another useful marriage tool is prayer. If you have something difficult to say to your partner, try praying first. The Holy Spirit dwells within you and can enable you to think straight, speak more clearly, and listen more completely. The Lord can bring you understanding and work through conflict with your spouse and family. When life seems complicated, try praying your way through it. Ponder how reading holy Scripture passages can give insight to your relationship. Perhaps you could read the Bible with your spouse before you start your day and put your best foot forward. Prayer can set the tone for how your entire day will enfold.

Evening prayer is a perfect time to reflect on the events of your day to consider what didn't go well and how you can try to improve tomorrow. Reflecting over the happenings of the day, you might see God's hand guiding you or steering you in a direction you didn't anticipate. Maybe saying the rosary with your spouse each night before sleep would work best for your relationship. However you incorporate prayer into your day, God will bless you for it. How will you use your marriage tools to enhance your relationship and will prayer be one of them?

Dear Lord, I reach out to you in my hour of darkness and await your words to sooth and heal me. Bestow many blessings on me and grant me the courage to trust completely in you. I love you, Lord. Help me. Amen.

February 2

Thus says the LORD: Stand by the earliest roads, ask the pathways of old, "Which is the way to good?" and walk it; thus you will find rest for yourselves. But they said, "We will not walk it."

JEREMIAH 6:16

A favorite winter pastime is walking snow-covered park trails and iden-tifying animal tracks. There is an abundance of deer, rabbit, squirrels, and coyotes. Sometimes while walking through wooded areas, it's easy to get disorientated, misinterpret landmarks, and get lost.

Have you ever wandered aimlessly through life unsure or confused about where your relationship is going? Maybe you are uncertain about your job satisfaction or employment clientele, your neighborhood, or activities. When you experience feelings of uncertainty, the best thing you can do is stop searching or trying to fix whatever you think is broken, and just pray. Sit alone and contemplate your life. It's hard to sit still and welcome God's presence into your life, but only God can make total and complete sense of it. God will never lead you astray.

It's easy to get stuck in a rut, but not so easy to pull out of one because usually change is needed. Change is difficult for most people to do because it requires stepping outside of your comfort zone or doing something dif-ferent. People crave routines, even if they are not the best ones to follow. A routine offers a habit; a rote sense of structure, which can make some people feel safe; but safe does not mean secure. Security in a relationship comes with maturity and mastering the skills that knit it carefully over time, with patience and love. The only way to know for sure if you are on the right path is to check in with God on a regular basis.

One way to get direction back is to call upon God and follow his ways because they are just. Read holy Scripture and study one passage at a time; reflect on how you could emulate it in your own life. When you meditate on the written word, God will speak to you in the silence of your heart; be still and listen for his voice. What is he asking you?

Dear Lord, as I go through the motions of life, it feels hollow and pointless. Please, Lord, tell me my purpose. Give me direction. Guide my footsteps as I journey onward following your light, your way. I trust in you, good and mighty King of heaven and earth, even if I do not understand where I am going or what I am doing. I honor you always. Amen.

February 3

And the king of Israel said to Jehoshaphat, "I will disguise
myself and go into battle, but you put on your own robes."
So the king of Israel disguised himself and entered the battle.

1 KINGS 22:30

A former Army depot is sealed behind twenty-four miles of fencing in Seneca County, New York, and provides a quiet and tranquil place for the world's largest herd of white deer to roam. The deer blend into their snowy landscape making spotting one difficult.

Sometimes you can stare directly at your marriage problems but not really see them because they are unclear or they are disguised, like the white deer. An example of not seeing a problem is when your spouse avoids responsibility, putting a majority of the work on your plate instead of splitting the load with you. Or perhaps you don't have any idea what your marriage difficulties are because you think everything is fine. Ask your spouse if everything really is fine. Denial is common because it's never easy admitting it when something is wrong. Some people believe if something is wrong, they failed. Failure occurs when you don't try to fix the problem or quit altogether.

Perhaps you cannot visualize the problems for what they really are—inadequacies, mistakes, or an oversight. Maybe you are spending too much time doing chores or working long hours to provide for your family when in actuality, your partner just wants to spend time with you. Reflect on the past quality time you have spent with your partner. Even if you just go for a walk, it would allow you to reconnect, hold hands, chat while you walk, or better yet, pray while you walk. It is not good enough just to live in the same house together; you really need to have quality time together, where you are both focused on each other. Finding the right balance is critical. Contemplate the many wonderful aspects of your spouse and build off that love. Ask God to give you the courage to remove the disguise from your marriage and address whatever is component is insufficient. How can you make it better?

Dear Lord, open my eyes, kind and merciful Lord, let me see the mistakes I am making and the rules I might be breaking. Propel my feet to take me in the direction of meeting my spouse's kindnesses. Allow me to be a supportive and kindhearted life partner. Fill my heart with compassion and enable me to recognize the outstanding acts my spouse does each day to please me. Teach me to see and appreciate the underlying message of affection and reciprocate that love. Amen.

February 4

From each you shall receive the contribution
that their hearts prompt them to give me.
EXODUS 25:2

Snowshoeing burns nearly 50 percent more calories than walking at the same speed. Your metabolic rate increases because of the added weight of the snowshoe coupled with the resistance moving through snow. Exercising in cold weather and using walking poles allows you to burn extra calories. Some workouts are better than others; you usually get out of it what you put into it.

If you put more into your marriage, you might get more out of it. There are countless ways you can give more without feeling the burn that comes with exercising. You could try smiling more often to your spouse. You don't have to say a word, just smile lovingly the way you would if you were looking at the Lord. Since the Holy Spirit dwells within your spouse, remember that when you smile at your partner, you are smiling at God. A smile can warm the heart and convey a message of sincerity. See how many times you can smile at your mate today. Smiling can also pave the way for more loving gestures.

When you walk by your mate, lightly touch his or her arm or back in an affectionate gesture. Again, not a word need be spoken, yet this physical contact sends a powerful and compassionate message of love to your mate. It affects you both emotionally and opens the door for more caressing to occur. If you lack the courage to do this, remember how many people longed to touch Jesus and once they did, they were forever changed. It's possible that a simple touch could lead to an embrace. Taking seemingly small steps through these amorous gestures could melt away tensions that might have been creeping into your relationship.

When is the last time you told your spouse, "I love you"? Maybe you could write a sweet note expressing your thoughts or appreciation or buy a card that conveys a heartfelt message. If you are feeling adventurous, you could purchase two sets of snowshoes and shed unwanted pounds and get physically fit together. The sky is the limit to what you can do and all things are possible with God. Maybe you could pray for your spouse and inform him or her of your intentions. Prayers are the best gifts; they are free, take little time, and reap God's sweet rewards.

Dear Lord, help me to express thankfulness and appreciation for what my spouse provides for me, even if I don't recognize or feel it. Bless my efforts and extend a gift with good intention to restore love and harmony in our marriage. Amen.

February 5

But to you who hear I say, love your enemies, do good to those who
hate you, bless those who curse you, pray for those who mistreat you.
To the person who strikes you on one cheek, offer the other one as well, and
from the person who takes your cloak, do not withhold even your tunic.

LUKE 6:27–31

Each winter there are festivals that feature ice sculpture competitions. Some sculptures use power tools and chainsaws, razor-sharp chisels, and hand saws to cut ice. The complicated process is incredible to watch because a chunk of ice gets carved into an extraordinary art form.

What component of your marriage needs grueling work in order to transform it into a glorious union? Perhaps anger is being harbored in your relationship and you don't know how to handle it. Some people suppress their anger, which doesn't solve anything. Subduing rage is dishonest and can actually deteriorate your physical health. Are you the type to explode with anger and attack your spouse verbally? Verbal attacks are unhealthy to you, your partner, and your marriage.

Channel your fury through a workout: exercising, dancing, running, vacuuming, scrubbing floors, or cleaning bathrooms. Prayer is one of the best ways to convert anger into sincerity. Consider praying while you expend your anger physically. While you work out your wrath, God will speak to you, enlighten you, and guide you down the right path.

Anger is like depression turned inside out. Reflect on where your anger originated from. Consider if it is from your childhood or if it might be misdirected anger from another person or event unrelated to your marriage. Contemplate if your anger is from fatigue, frustration, fear, or hurt. Try to get to the bottom of what caused your irritation. When you are calm, talk to your spouse in a loving manner about what caused your anger. If you don't discuss it, the problems will resurface later.

Anger, if left unresolved, can turn into hate. Instead of allowing that, act like Jesus; be kind and tenderhearted, offering words of affirmation and congeniality and see if your spouse will respond favorably to your acts of love. Ask your partner for suggestions that could improve your relationship, accept that information, and focus on developing those areas without complaining. Throughout the week how will you handle your anger differently?

Dear Lord, help me to find and give love in the face of discontentment while I work on becoming a better marriage partner. Enable me to find healthy outlets to my anger and to understand what is causing it. Safeguard my heart in your merciful hands, sweet Lord, and allow me to see your love and follow your ways. Amen.

February 6

Like golden apples in silver settings are words spoken at the proper time.

PROVERBS 25:11

A nice hockey team dramatically improved their game by installing brighter lights over the ice arena. The players were amazed that something so unassuming could procure such positive results. What seemingly simple gesture, something as basic as flipping a light switch, could you offer your spouse to enhance your marriage?

Consider using positive language in a loving manner that builds up your partner. Using positive phrasing informs your spouse what can be done. You come across as a supportive mate by suggesting alternatives and choices. When you are helpful and reassuring, your partner will be more receptive to your input and embrace ideas that otherwise might not have been considered. Words are very powerful, if used correctly, to convey sincerity and admiration. Words also have the capability to destroy your mate and ruin your relationship; why do that when you can have an amicable marriage? Focus your words on encouragement, love, and respect. The act of showing love verbally tells your partner that you genuinely care for his or her best interests.

When you notice your spouse doing something nice, say "thank you." Sometimes spouses feel taken for granted; being acknowledged, praised, and appreciated eliminates that. Another thoughtful act you can offer your spouse is to frequently compliment him or her. Praise, given freely and sincerely, is an influential and effective communicator of love. Practice saying please and thank you, offering compliments, and speaking with respect and love. Soon, it will become a rote behavior that your spouse will appreciate hearing. Contemplate the consequences that can be anticipated after you change your language to all that is positive and kind.

Ponder ways to offer compliments, express your appreciation, and say or do something positive for your mate's well-being. Invoke the Holy Spirit to inspire you to be more reassuring to your spouse. How do you meet your spouse's emotional needs to make him or her feel secure?

Dear Lord, invigorate my vocabulary; bless every word that comes from my mouth so that my spouse understands that I am trying to acknowledge him or her with kind and caring words that uplift and enrich our union. Let the manner I speak be as thoughtful and sincere as the message I deliver. I want my marriage to be strong, and I am willing to work on it by using inspiring words of praise and recognition. I will not be blind to all of the love that has been given to me so freely and completely in the past. I ask this in your holy name. Amen.

February 7

*Everyone in the crowd sought to touch him because power came
forth from him and healed them all. And raising his eyes toward his
disciples he said: "Blessed are you who are poor, for the kingdom of
God is yours. Blessed are you who are now hungry, for you will be
satisfied. Blessed are you who are now weeping, for you will laugh."*

LUKE 6:19–21

Winter is a time of chili cook-offs where restaurants boast their best recipes and top chefs to create the best concoction. Some use a mixture of beans while others experiment with spices. When cooking the perfect chili, chefs use a blend of complimenting spices to achieve the right flavor. How do you put the spice in your relationship?

Don't limit your creative abilities to flavor your marriage. While some couples prefer just a hint of spice, others add pizzazz with heat. Their warmth and passion is conveyed by various methods of touch. When you talk to your spouse, try touching his or her hand. If you watch the evening news together, sit beside each other instead of opting for your comfy chair. As you give your spouse the mail, touch his or her hand, pat his or her shoulder, stroke his or her back or kiss his or her head as you walk by. Be creative to find stimulating ways to spark a moment of intimacy between the both of you through the power of touch.

Perhaps you could bring your mate a hot cup of tea or put a candy kiss next to his or her car keys. There are many simple but effective ways to spice up your marriage. If you prefer to spend more time putting zest in your relationship, maybe your mate enjoys an invigorating back rub or a gentle foot massage. Is there a quiet place in your home where you could pray the rosary together? Contemplate the marriage that Mary and Joseph shared and how their struggles and obstacles were overcome through their steadfast faith in God. Prayer and meditation unites you and your spouse together with God.

If you feel starved for your spouse's attention, hungry for love, longing for touch, trust in God's message that he will provide. "Blessed are you who are weeping, for you will laugh." Have faith; trust in the Lord's ways because he knows what he is doing. Be brave when you reach out to your spouse to stroke his or her arm or kiss his or her cheek. These thoughtful gestures could be the kind of physical contact your mate has been yearning for too. If this is not easy for you, consider the importance of touching Jesus. If you would you take Christ's hand, can you also take your spouse's?

Dear Lord, fill me with your endless stream of love; let it spill over to my spouse and to all of the other areas of my precious life. Take my hand and I will follow you, Lord, wherever you may lead. Amen.

February 8

For how do you know, wife, whether you will save your husband; or how do you know, husband, whether you will save your wife? Only, everyone should live as the Lord has assigned, just as God called each one.

1 CORINTHIANS 7:16–17

Many people anticipate the Super Bowl with much excitement; others only watch it on TV for the commercials, while some people could care less about any of it. What element of your relationship does your spouse like that you do not? Perhaps you don't like sports as much as he or she does.

There are bound to be differences with likes and dislikes; how you handle them or accept them determines if there will be conflict. Inconsistencies in the differences in parenting styles create much conflict in marriages. While mothers have a tendency to be overly nurturing and overbearing, men have an inclination to be inattentive, using a hands-off approach. Other marital complications can arise from spending habits; perhaps your spouse is an extravagant spender, while you are thrifty. Whatever the conflict is in your marriage, God gave you the ability to tease out ample workable solutions.

The consensus solution entails you and your spouse both giving a little to reach an acceptable agreement. For example, parenting styles could be discussed and specific actions agreed upon: Saturday afternoons there won't be any naps, or play dates will only happen for two hours each Sunday after Mass. Another solution is compromise. You each are required to give a little: you agree to spend less than fifty dollars, while your spouse saves the same amount in a vacation fund. Taking turns works well in settling disputes by allowing one spouse to watch the Super Bowl every other year. On the "off" years maybe you could go to the movies. Perhaps you could join your spouse watching the game, but the next weekend do your favored activity together. Maybe you could both abandon the game and go away on vacation; do something you both would enjoy. The possibilities are endless. Make an activity out of seeing just how many options you can consider.

God wants you to look for solutions to your conflict. The way you can achieve that is by using good communication skills and positive language. Begin by defining exactly what the problem is. Only try to fix that problem. List all solutions. God gave you an amazing brain, capable of dreaming up amazing, workable options. Draft a pros and con list for each option. Pray on it until God enlightens you. God wants you to do what is right. Put your faith in him that he will always help you. What conflict will you work on today?

Dear Lord, thank you for giving me an awesome brain and for freeing my mind to consider the infinite opportunities that exist to resolve the conflicts in my marriage. I adore you. Amen.

February 9

How long will you utter such things?
The words from your mouth are a mighty wind!

JOB 8:2

Black ice is a transparent coating of ice on the asphalt surface of the roads that is practically invisible to drivers. It makes driving conditions extremely dangerous, resulting in accidents. Reflect on a callous behavior that isn't obvious, but detrimental to your relationship. Maybe you keep it hidden from your spouse because you are not proud of it, or you are trying to improve. Are you working on becoming more truthful? Perhaps you omit certain elements believing that is not deceitful, when in fact, omission is a form of dishonesty.

Honesty is one aspect of your moral character equating to being trustworthy, loyal, fair, sincere, and having straightforward conduct. It implies positive qualities such as integrity and candor. Is there a facet of your marriage that isn't overly apparent that could undermine it with a form of deceitfulness? Perhaps you "beat around the bush" with responses to your mate, or you tell convoluted stories that confuse and bewilder him or her.

Consider what you say to your spouse or what you purposely omit from the conversations. Reflect on the body language that you use when you talk to your spouse. Are you respectful? Don't undermine your relationship by hurling insults and barbs. One "zinger" counteracts the many kindnesses that you have done for your spouse in the past. Every harsh word you speak will be like journeying over black ice on your marriage. Prevent ice from forming on your relationship by keeping it warm, loving, open, and honest.

Contemplate the root of your dissatisfaction and pray on it, finding an amicable way to converse with your spouse openly and honestly. Evoke the Holy Spirit to empower you with the strength necessary to convey your thoughts and feelings laced with peace and tranquility. Your spouse married you and wants to know the real you, not some form of who you think you should be. The real you is better than any version you can concoct. Remove the mask and reveal the real you. Use your words wisely, as if they are gifts to build up your partner and fortify your relationship. How will you speak to your partner today in truth and love, even if you feel like fibbing?

Dear Lord, build a fire of warmth within me by keeping me honest, loyal, and sincere. Let me embrace the stirring I feel and act upon it as a sign from you to continue to walk the path of righteousness. Fill my heart with a compassionate and loving vocabulary so that I can convey thoughtful messages to build a strong relationship with [*name*]. Bless my marriage and the journey we travel together. Thank you, Lord, for caring so deeply about me. I love you. Amen.

February 10

At that time I said to you, "I am unable to carry you by myself....
But how can I, by myself, bear the weight, the contentiousness of you?
DEUTERONOMY 1:9, 12

A heavy snowfall can cause a roof to collapse. Some homeowners ensure the integrity of their roof by using chemical tablets or heaters to melt snow mounds on roofs, while others use rakes to pull it down. Consider what weight is burdensome to your marriage.

Do you feel taken for granted? Perhaps you feel as if your plate is too full and you are expected to do too much. If you are experiencing feelings of resentment, that is a sign you might be doing too much. If you feel like you are drowning in obligations, reexamine them to see if they be can be divided. You cannot carry the weight of your marriage alone; it is meant to be shared. Nor should you be overly responsible by doing your partner's tasks and hoping he or she will notice and eventually appreciate your efforts and reciprocate.

Convey your feelings congenially to your spouse using "I" statements. If you are doing most of the household chores while working outside of the home and raising children, ask your spouse to split the chores 50/50, being specific with the requests. For example, say, "I would appreciate your doing the laundry after work." It's possible that your spouse was preoccupied and didn't notice your stress. Your partner is not a mind reader; you need to speak up and articulate exactly what you need done in a pleasant, well-meaning tone that is not judgmental or critical.

If you made a specific request and it was overlooked or forgotten by your spouse, provide a thoughtful reminder, remembering that you and your spouse are lifelong partners and your success depends on your partnership. If your spouse was a business partner, chances are good he or she would not forget an important meeting or overlook a major project. Your marriage is more important than a professional corporation, because your marriage is forever, bound together by God.

Be patient with the plan, for all things are good with God's involvement. God brought you together for a purpose that you may not understand today. However, in time, God may reveal it to you. Additionally, ask God to bless you with a continual stream of patience to help you throughout your marriage. How will you accept responsibility for yourself, your choices, and feelings when you feel overworked?

Dear Lord, bless my relationship, and enable my spouse to recognize the investment I make each day in my marriage without criticizing. Let me offer the sacrifices I endure to you, sweet, Jesus, who sacrificed yourself for the salvation of my sins. Amen.

February 11

Those who offer praise as a sacrifice honor me; I will let him
whose way is steadfast look upon the salvation of God.

PSALM 50:23

Early cameras were burdensome and awkward to use. Today's digital cameras are so small they can slide into your shirt pocket and are easy to use with immediate results. Reexamine your methods to determine if you are using an antiquated system that might not be effective at preserving your admirations. How do you capture your spouse's heart?

Perhaps you enjoy doing small favors for your mate such as: filling his or her car's gas tank, emptying the dishwasher, or paying the bills. These expressions of love are gifts you give to your spouse. Reflect on times in the past when your spouse provided you with favors. Did you appreciate them and thank your partner for the effort that was expended in preparing the dinner, taking out the trash, or doing the laundry or grocery shopping? Relaying appreciation can go a long way in creating a caring environment.

Often, it's easier to thank a stranger than the person we share our lives with. It's easy to thank the neighbor who shovels your driveway when you are sick and cannot do it. It's easy to thank the grocery store clerk who carries your bags to the car and then gently loads them in your trunk. God wants us to be thankful to our spouses each time a good deed is done. God doesn't want us to overlook a good turn from him or your spouse.

Thank God for the debacles in your life also. The notion might seem strange and the words might sound foreign when you say them, but there is a reason for everything that happens to you: good and bad. Perhaps you got a flat tire on your way to work; if you continued on, maybe you would have been in a car accident. Thank God for that! You might not understand the crises that you struggle through, but trust in God's ways and thank him for it all.

Ponder creative ways you can express your thankfulness to your partner while trying to gain his or her respect and affections. How do you thank God for all he gives to you each day?

Dear Lord, teach me how to be gratifying to my spouse and to you, who gives me all that I have. My life is good because of you. Thank you, Lord, for my spouse and the kindnesses that are shown to me each day. I thank you for all of the good and for the bad in my life. There is a lesson in it for me and while I may not know it or understand it, I appreciate it and trust in your ways. Thank you, Lord, for continuing to bless me even when I might not deserve it. Amen.

February 12

Then she gave the king one hundred and twenty gold talents, a very large quantity of spices, and precious stones. Never again did anyone bring such an abundance of spices as the queen of Sheba gave to King Solomon.

1 KINGS 10:10

The New York State Thruway Authority spreads a mixture of sugar beet juice and brine ahead of winter storms to avert icing on the highway. This is a creative example of using all available resources to thwart highway catastrophes in the winter. How creative are your disaster prevention methods in your marriage?

Ponder a recent fiasco in your marriage that could have been averted if you had taken preventative measures to avoid it. Accidents happen; it's a part of life. However, if your spouse feels secure in your love, a mishap can be downplayed. For example, if a favorite vase was mistakenly shattered, it might not be a major concern if others were given with an emotional value attached to them.

Maybe it's been a while since you gave your spouse a gift to say, "I was thinking about you today." Gifts have emotional value and while some are more important to some than others, they are nice to receive. An unexpected present tells your spouse that he or she is appreciated and thought about. It doesn't have to be expensive, merely a thoughtful symbolic token of your love. If your partner collects coupons, maybe you could find a coupon folder. Possibly you could buy your partner's favorite tea or beverage. Perhaps a gift card at his or her favorite store would make a nice surprise. The smallest gift could mean the most if much heartfelt thought is invested.

This is especially endearing when a spouse who doesn't enjoy shopping, selecting gifts, or who is frugal, makes an effort. When a spouse is extremely busy with work and sets aside time to browse through stores, catalogs, or the Internet to find a gift, it makes the object exceptional. Imagine how special a gift would be to someone who wasn't feeling loved or appreciated. Even if you can only offer a plate of homemade cookies, the time and energy coupled with the thought makes that a special and loving gesture. What gift will you give to your spouse this week?

Dear Lord, you have given me countless gifts over the years; I'm sorry it has taken me so long to thank you for them. You are so generous and kind to me. Specifically, thank you for the gift of life that you have given to me in my spouse and family. I am a better person today because of them. Teach me how to rise above my insecurities and be more giving to my partner. I cannot recall the last time I surprised [*name*] with a gift. Help me to be a selfless and generous partner. Amen.

February 13

I [am] the Alpha and the Omega, the beginning and the end.
To the thirsty I will give a gift from the spring of life-giving water.
REVELATION 21:6

A polar bear plunge is held during the winter where participants take a quick dip in a body of water despite frigid temperatures, usually to raise money for a charitable organization. No one expects you to actually jump in a lake, but what unusual gesture would you do to be supportive, kind, and loving to your spouse?

How many opportunities have you missed because you waited for a more convenient time, better weather, or more money? Don't fail to recognize your spouse because you thought you had forever to do it; don't wait, do it now! Taking extraordinary measures to demonstrate what your spouse means to you speaks volumes to your devotion. Consider writing "I love you" in the snow, or hanging a banner in the living room that says, "Congratulations!" Then, write a card that explains your feelings why he or she is the best spouse in the world. Do something crazy that your partner would never expect and will never forget.

Perhaps you could encourage your partner to go on a special getaway weekend with friends or go on a religious retreat. Perhaps just spending an afternoon at a spa to unwind or a gym to work out is all that is needed or desired. Consider attending morning Mass together before you start your work day. It's a special way to unite under God's watchful eye. Perhaps you could say a rosary together in honor of Mary. It only takes a few minutes, and during that precious time you have Mary's undivided attention; a perfect platform to request special blessings on your marriage. Prayers really are the best gift that you can give to each other.

What outlandish thing are you willing to do to show your partner what he or she means to you?

Dear Lord, erase the doubts that cloud my mind and show me ways to please my spouse. Lead me down the path that will create a loving home and a giving heart. I have become idle and I need your help, Lord. Lift me up so that I can be the decent and devoted partner you intended me to be. My spouse deserves a restful retreat; bring joyful ideas to me and put the means to make it happen within my reach. Thank you for always being close to me when I need you the most. I truly love you. Amen.

February 14

May I not seem as one frightening you through letters. For someone will say, "His letters are severe and forceful, but his bodily presence is weak, and his speech contemptible." Such a person must understand that what we are in word through letters when absent, that we also are in action when present.

2 Corinthians 10:9–11

Calligraphy is a style of scripted writing using a special instrument in one fluid stroke. It is frequently used to embellish formal wedding invitations. You don't have to use fancy lettering to write something lovely to your spouse. When words flow from your heart, they are beautiful no matter how they appear on paper. What message do you want to convey to your spouse?

Even if you do not think you are capable of writing a letter to your spouse, make the effort today because you just might surprise yourself. The apostles and holy men from the biblical time did not consider themselves writers, yet together their words created the Bible. Try reading Psalms and let the Lord stir your awakening conscious.

Imagine the letter you would have written to your partner when you were dating and how your feelings have intensified over the years. Contemplate all of the kind deeds and thoughtful gestures that your spouse has showered you with over the years and describe how they made you feel then and how they may have impacted you today.

Instead of getting flowers or chocolates to celebrate Valentine's Day, can you relay your thoughts, feelings, and emotions on paper and give that to your spouse? Writing letters is a lost art form with technology leading the way to quick and concise messages. Try to put forth the effort to delve deeply within, stirring your contemplations for your partner. Perhaps the task would be less taxing by imagining the Lord dwelling within your spouse. Ask the Holy Spirit to allow the words to flow through you. This testament of your love could become the best gift your partner receives. Will you buy a Valentine card in the store and simply sign your name, or will you draft a heartfelt letter revealing your deepest emotions?

Dear Lord, allow me to find and form the words to convey what I carry in my heart. Let me sift through the inadequacies and shortcomings, and dwell upon the attributes that make my spouse the loving creature you intended for me to find and always cherish. Thank you for my spouse and the love between us. Sometimes I don't always feel it, but I know it's there. Amen.

February 15

She had a sister named Mary [who] sat beside the Lord at his feet listening to him speak. Martha, burdened with much serving, came to him and said, "Lord, do you not care that my sister has left me by myself to do the serving? Tell her to help me." The Lord said to her in reply, "Martha, Martha, you are anxious and worried about many things. There is need of only one thing. Mary has chosen the better part and it will not be taken from her."

LUKE 10:39–42

Ice fishers catch fish through a hole they make in the ice on a frozen body of water. Have you tried to exercise power over an unassuming spouse similar to an angler catching a fish in winter?

Martha was busy with meal preparations, frustrated that Mary wasn't helping but instead listened to Jesus speak. While Martha wanted Mary's help in the kitchen, she also asks Jesus to persuade Mary to help her. Martha tried to control Mary. Who do you more closely resemble: Martha, desirous of controlling, or Mary, living beyond control and discovering what truly needs her concern?

Perhaps you have control issues in your marriage. Reflect on past occasions where you controlled your spouse or circumstances. Perhaps you tried to manipulate your partner's vulnerabilities to get your way. Consider subtle ways you might have controlled your partner by being overly helpful, wanting to complete a project your way, or by being totally helpless where you indirectly manipulated your spouse to do an entire project so you could avoid it. If you "surprised" your spouse with plane tickets to your favorite vacation destination, that's subtle control over your spouse unless he or she had a part in the planning. When Martha worried excessively, that was an elusive form of control she tried to possess over Mary. Reflect on times when you might have been slightly controlling of your spouse without realizing it.

Have you made attempts to please your spouse, but it wasn't satisfying? Maybe there was an element of control concealed in your gesture. Try it again, including your partner in the process, even if you do not get your own way. Marriage is a give-and-take partnership; when you stop giving in reluctantly and start giving lovingly, you will find more peace and happiness in your marriage. Acts of service require thought, preparation, and energy, not control. How will you stop being controlling in your marriage?

Dear Lord, be merciful with me as I examine my conscience and identify areas where I have controlled my spouse. Help me through this difficulty. Teach me how to be genuinely helpful and to do each task enthusiastically as an expression of love, not manipulation. Forgive me, Lord, for I am weak. Amen.

February 16

*So long as I have life breath in me, the breath of God in my nostrils,
my lips shall not speak falsehood, nor my tongue utter deceit!*

JOB 27:3–4

At this point in winter, people nearing retirement age escape the cold by flocking to Florida beaches. They are affectionately called "snowbirds." How do you keep warmth in your marriage when you are surrounded by cold? While not everyone can take trips to cozy locations, you could offer your spouse warmth in a variety of ways.

If you feel like giving your spouse a tongue lashing, bite your tongue and forget it. If you want to convey a message to your partner, do it lovingly. If you don't feel the love, pray on it in the silence of your heart, and the right words will come. It's draining to constantly listen to a nagging spouse. Maybe you don't consider it nagging, but it's hurtful to hear day in and day out. Can you hear yourself say, "Not like that," "The trouble with you is...," "How many times have I asked you to...". These statements don't build up your partner. If you feel tempted to criticize your partner, stop and pray. Ask God to reformulate the words in your head and bless you with a better message. Instead, could you say, "That's an interesting way to do that," "I love your adorable quirks," "You must be really busy. Can I help you?" These statements will warm up your marriage.

Your relationship will blossom once you add mutual respect to your vocabulary. Reflect on the statements you have said to your spouse this week. Were you courteous? When your spouse takes the time to do a chore, don't criticize the way it's done, even if you deem the task poorly completed. Don't point out the mistakes, inadequacies, or failures. If your spouse cleaned the toilet as a "gift" to you, don't complain if it's not up to your standards. If your spouse gave you a diamond ring, would you complain that the stone was too big or too small? A gift is a gift, however you want to look at it. Try appreciating the intention behind it more than the actual gift.

Another way to procure warmth in your relationship is to acknowledge or compliment your partner to colleagues, friends, or relatives at social events. Perhaps you could share credit with your partner for an accomplishment you achieved. The way you use words can build a fire of love between you. How will you stoke the fire of love in your relationship today?

Dear Lord, fill my mind with the ability to convey love to my spouse. Wash away my apprehensions and fear and sanction me with a vital message that my spouse needs to hear, or a gift that will make him or her feel my love. I ask this in your sweet and holy name. Amen.

February 17

God, you know my folly; my faults are not hidden from you.

PSALM 69:6

An instructor distributed an orange to each student and asked them to "get to know it." When the teacher took back the oranges, the kids were reluctant, wanting to keep their fruit. That sadness is what Jesus would feel if the kids abandoned him. The class was allowed to claim their original orange from a huge bowl. The students were shocked when they found their original orange, identifiable by nicks and bruises on its skin. Our character flaws and imperfections are how Jesus knows and loves us. What inadequacies or mistakes are keeping your marriage in a slump?

Perhaps you keep repeating the same blunders and don't know a better solution. If what you are doing is not working, don't keep repeating it; stop and try another approach. Pray to Jesus for guidance and answers. If you are shouting a lot, contemplate what might be causing your anger. Anger is pain trying to tell you something. Consider if your rage is saying you want to get your own way. If so, talk about it with your spouse and try to negotiate something you can both agree on. Perhaps you could take turns.

Shouting won't solve anything, but it can make matters worse. When you explode with anger, it's unhealthy and can escalate into verbally abusive language. When you feel your body responding through early warning signs such as a reddened face, tense muscles, clenched jaw, and elevated voice, think of Jesus. Take a deep breath and envision him talking to you and reminding you to stay calm and think rationally. Take a time out from what you are doing and simply pray your stress away with the Lord.

While you think your situation over, you can expend your energy by going for a jog or walk. Cry in the shower. Listen to relaxing music. Use exercise equipment. Scrub the kitchen floor. Pray while you get rid of your pent up energy. Ask the Lord to help you make sense of your fury. Consider if it originated from sadness, tiredness, fear, frustration, or hurt. After you are able to place it, you will be in a better place to work it out with your spouse peacefully.

The next time you become irritated, what will you do differently to avoid yelling at your partner?

Dear Lord, thank you for your unending stream of mercy. Allow me to extend that same compassion when my partner loses his or her temper and yells. Help us to work through our difficulties and find a place of comfort, love, and peace. Grant us the capabilities to solve problems and reach attainable solutions so that we can live together in harmony. Amen.

February 18

Therefore, you must use this money with all diligence to buy bulls, rams, lambs, and the grain offerings and libations proper to these, and to offer them on the altar of the house of your God in Jerusalem.

EZRA 7:17

I struggled to communicate with an Italian merchant until I opened my wallet. In Italy, money was my universal language. As long as I was able to exchange currency for merchandise, entrance fees, or services in restaurants, I was okay. But I had to acknowledge that there wasn't an endless supply of cash. In families, money can be the source of contention. Perhaps one person is a spender and the other a saver, which could cause friction in any relationship. Ponder recent purchases made in your home this week to see if there is a spending problem. Were superfluous items bought without need, and who is making the purchases, or do you suspect someone in your house has a shopping addiction? Do you struggle to balance the checkbook? How do you handle money issues in your marriage and how well is it working?

Compulsive shopping is a temporary balm for depression, anxiety, and loneliness, but will ultimately make a person feel worse after credit cards are pushed to the limit because of increased financial debt. "Shopaholics" shop to feel better, the way a drug addict gets high. Most are in denial about the problem even though they have clothes with price tags still on them and cannot pay their bills. Addictive behaviors tend to cluster, so if you have an eating disorder or a problem with drugs, alcohol, or gambling, you may also have a shopping addiction. Seek professional counseling because this problem will not disappear on its own, and it will spill into your marriage.

Sometimes it's essential to draft a list of "needs" and "wants" and then decide what can be purchased and what must wait for later depending on your financial situation. Only buy what's on the list. Destroy your credit cards. Only "window shop" when the stores are closed. Don't look through catalogs, don't shop online, and do change TV shopping channels. Instead, take a walk, exercise, clean your house, or pray when you experience the urge to shop.

If you question your spending habits, call out to Jesus to guide you. Consider donating the money to worthy causes or to the impoverished in your community. If you have free time to shop, contemplate volunteering in a hospital or refugee center. What improvements to your finances can you make so it won't taint the marriage that God intended for you?

Dear Lord, let love be the universal language in my marriage. While we need money to live, it won't mean anything without my partner to share it with. Let me make my spouse a priority in my life, not money. Amen.

February 19

*Draws me up from the pit of destruction, out of the muddy clay,
sets my feet upon rock, steadies my steps, and puts a
new song in my mouth, a hymn to our God.*

PSALM 40:3–4

The first time I climbed a mountain, I became uneasy when I saw hikers ahead of me attempting to traverse a massive mud hole. A shoddy rope bridge hung over it where people were carefully inching their way across. Each calculated step caused it to sway precariously as I prayed my way forward. Have you ever felt like you were stepping onto a rickety bridge to meet your partner at a halfway point in your relationship?

For two people to be a team, each member must give and take once in a while. Take turns choosing the movies or sport events by considering your partner's desires, not just your own. Maybe you could try something totally new, such as attending the theater or local school productions or taking karate classes together. Take turns selecting restaurants to dine in, cookbooks to cook from, and farmer's markets to meander through. You could share doing chores together: one washes the dishes, the other dries them. Consider volunteering together for organizations that resonate with each of you.

Sometimes marriage turns out to be full of unexpected disappointments; it's how you handle those disenchantments that determines how successful your relationship will be. Try speaking for your desires and express what you want and why, not presuming your spouse's needs. Also, refrain from attacking your spouse with demands. Realize that you might not get everything you want; however, with compromise you might get something and your spouse might also get something. Make your goal a "win-win."

Address the small irritations, such as leaving the door open or always being late, so they don't turn into big issues. Discuss them lovingly with "I" statements. The statement, "I worry about you when you are late. Please call me if you are running behind schedule or stuck in traffic," speaks of truth lovingly. Listen to your spouse's response without interrupting. Repeat it back so that it is clearly understood. Consider your options carefully, listing as many as possible before deciding without allowing your desires to cloud your judgment. Invoke God's blessing when you contemplate the best solution for your marriage. God can enable you to move forward in peace and love. What can you do to stabilize the unsteady bridges in your relationship with your spouse and with God?

Dear Lord, don't let me fall into a pit of despair. Teach me how to navigate over the problems in my life and how to build better bridges to reach my spouse. Amen.

February 20

Who fills your days with good things, so your youth is renewed like the eagle's.

PSALM 103:5

People flocked to the areas where bald eagle sightings were reported in New York state. Spectators spent hours peering through binoculars, remaining hopeful that they would spot this magnificent creature. In a remote location, when least expecting it, I saw one by simply looking up. God touches our lives with countless blessings each day, if we would look up, embrace them, and thank him. What gifts has God blessed your life with?

Ponder your talents and what you do with them, how you tap into your creativity, and how you share them with others. Perhaps you use your talents best at the workplace. Do you enjoy your job? Today's economy is having a profound impact on families. Occasionally, travel is required by one spouse in order to maintain employment, which radically affects marriages because more responsibilities ultimately fall on the spouse remaining at home. Insecurity, fear, worry, and doubt can seep into the best relationships. If your partner is meeting new people without you, voice your worries or concerns in a calm and loving manner so that you can discuss them and reassure one another. Reinforce your commitment to your spouse to be trustworthy. It's critical for both of you to avoid compromising situations and not to be overly suspicious of each other. Exhaustion and erratic schedules wreak havoc on attitudes and moods; unspoken expectations can erupt into arguments. Stay connected through online visits, phone calls, e-mails, or social-networking sites. Tuck special notes in suitcases or leave them on the nightstand for a spouse to find and reread.

Military families have experienced the emotional strain of deployment on an unparalleled scale since the end of the Gulf War. The impact on couples during long separations is concerning. Establish a support network and plan to fragment time by embracing unique opportunities for individual growth. Perhaps having more free time would be a chance to learn a foreign language, dance, or study theology. Possibly you could teach a religion class. Knowing that God's watchful eye is protecting your loved one affirms your strength to carry on in their absence.

When you are apart, how do you depend on God to sustain your relationship during that lull?

Dear Lord, wrap your loving arms around me and fill me with the sustenance I need to forge onward in my spouse's absence. Thank you for filling my days with sunshine when I know that rain is what I should be getting. I bow to you, my loving savior. Amen.

February 21

Your adornment should not be an external one: braiding the hair,
wearing gold jewelry, or dressing in fine clothes, but rather the hidden
character of the heart, expressed in the imperishable beauty of a
gentle and calm disposition, which is precious in the sight of God.

1 PETER 3:3–4

The American Museum of Natural History in New York City displays ugly-appearing rocks with interiors encrusted with jewels. How many people have overlooked something incredible, perhaps valuable, because of a plain or unattractive exterior? How often have ordinary people who had inner treasures like a heart of gold been ignored?

Consider the resources your marriage holds. Did you know that married couples are typically healthier, happier, and enjoy longer lives than those who are not married? Married couples ascertain more wealth than singles or cohabiting couples, and married men earn more than single men with similar training and experience. Married women are less likely to be victims of violent crime than single women. Married men are less likely to commit crimes than unmarried men. Marriage creates social, economic, and emotional conditions for effective parenting. Marriage changes people's lifestyles, behaviors, and customs in socially beneficial ways. Marriage has nice perks if you deliberate all of its facets.

Have you considered if your spouse is a gem or an ordinary person? Perhaps if you contemplate all aspects of his or her personality, you might find that gem you were seeking. How do you convey the importance of your partner's best qualities to him or her? Do your spouse's actions say that he or she is in love with you? Are you treated with love and care? Does your spouse act as if he or she is in love with you? Most of us judge someone's heart by their actions. Right or wrong, that's what we do. We all have minor irritations or trivial annoyances at some point; however, if you can look at your spouse and say, "My marriage is basically good," than you are truly blessed. God gave you a precious jewel in the form of your marriage. You can build it up into anything you desire; you can mold and shape it to fit your needs around God's loving touch. God made you and your partner unique with precious talents and the ability to love. Ponder ways to convey the importance of them to your partner.

Dear Lord, thank you for making my spouse a rare and valuable jewel that you entrusted to my care. Teach me to appreciate and uphold this precious gem. Bless [*name*] and keep him or her well so that we can be a dynamic couple, growing in your love and tender mercies. Amen.

February 22

Cleanse me with hyssop, that I may be pure;
wash me, and I will be whiter than snow.

PSALM 51:9

When a handyman nicked a white bathroom tile by mistake, it was challenging to disguise it with paint because there are countless shades of white to choose from. While the handyman could have masked the problem, he chose to reveal the scratch and pay the consequences. I appreciated his honesty and willingness to make numerous attempts to match the hues perfectly to conceal the crack. When something seems off in your marriage, that subtle feeling is an indication to decipher what is causing the discrepancy and seek ways to correct it. Have you sensed tension or discontentment in your relationship recently? Contemplate what might have caused it.

Everyone makes mistakes; you are no exception. It takes courage to confront your spouse and admit your vulnerabilities, your flaws, and mistakes. It's challenging to admit blunders, accept responsibility, and be held accountable for our actions; but it's necessary to do because it's a vital component of your spiritual and emotional growth. Your relationship with your spouse is constantly changing; growing; gaining understanding, tolerance, and patience; and learning from your daily experiences. Your mistakes can be your greatest gifts if you learn from them instead of allowing them to overtake, manipulate, and destroy you. Ponder what lessons you have obtained from your recent marriage slipups.

Perhaps you start arguments because you think you are right. Ask yourself if being right is really that important to you. Would you rather be happy or be right? If the mistake is minimal, don't crush your partner's feelings. Accept it as a lesson learned and move on. Maybe you prefer not to have any confrontations and instead sweep problems under the rug. Ask the Lord to enable you to initiate open dialog lovingly with your spouse to uncover his or her true feelings. Communication in the key to resolving small issues and preventing them from escalating into bigger, more complicated ones. Invoke the Holy Spirit to use the perfect words to convey your heartfelt concern to your spouse. Whatever good you do to try to improve your communication, your mate will appreciate your intentions. What small infraction has recently happened in your relationship that needs to be addressed? What will you say and how will you act?

Dear Lord, help me speak amicably to [*name*]. Help me remember that mistakes are opportunities to learn and grow. Let us work together to build each other up to become better versions of ourselves and to have the wonderful marriage that you meant for us to have. Amen.

February 23

The kingdom of heaven is like a treasure buried in a field,
which a person finds and hides again, and out of joy goes
and sells all that he has and buys that field.

MATTHEW 13:44

There are many banks in America that vie for customers' business: savings and checking accounts, credit card services, and loan opportunities. Your marriage is like a bank account. What are your transactions like: are you putting more into it or taking a lot out of it precariously? Ponder your actions this week to decide if you are building up your marriage or tearing it down. Consider the ways you have contributed to doing both.

You can build up your marriage by cordial speech, random acts of kindness, compliments, and prayers. Each time you ridicule your partner with hurtful remarks, snide comments, or undermining gestures, you destroy a piece of your relationship. If your spouse acts in a hurtful manner, say "Ouch!" It's possible he or she doesn't realize their actions are hurtful. Once your spouse realizes the infraction, it's an opportunity for your partner to apologize. When you accept this humble gift of regret, a door opens for you to unite peacefully. An apology clears a loving path for all that is good and just to unfurl in your marriage. Try to remember the next time your spouse inadvertently hurts you that an apology restores your relationship the way a BAND-AID helps a scraped knee to heal. It might not seem like much initially, but it allows the healing process to begin. Instead of retaliating, lay down your swords and move toward each other. Think of ways you can restore your marriage, not destroy it.

It is not always easy to accept an apology, especially if you suspect it might be insincere. Work to meet in the middle by stripping off emotional layers of hurt, anger, fear, regret, and desire, because underneath it is love. It might be drudgery and painful working through it, but it will be worth the effort in the end. Pray while you work through the issues; ask God to keep you strong and give you insight to continue to move forward. As you work through this difficulty, focus on the love that God filled your heart with. Concentrate on the atrocious agony Jesus endured for your sins when he was crucified. He did not quit in the middle of his suffering; he endured for the good of mankind. Can you endure your struggles for the good of your marriage?

Dear Lord, touch me with your healing powers and fill me with ingenuity to repair my marriage and prevent future dilemmas from keeping me away from you. Empower me to withstand hurtfulness and move on. Teach me to forgive, let go, and grow in your unfaltering love. You know what is best for me. I love you, Lord. Amen.

February 24

But the noble plan noble deeds, and in noble deeds they persist.

ISAIAH 32:8

Whittling is the art of carving shapes typically out of wood with a knife. Carvers use chisels, gouges, and a mallet, while whittling involves using a knife. What good or bad feature is being whittled away in your marriage? Shaving off inappropriate language can have a positive impact on a relationship, as can getting rid of a past grudge that has weighed you down or held you back like a ball and chain. You cannot change the experience; however, you can change your attitude about it by letting it go. Instead of focusing on a past hurt, dwell on the endless possibilities of your future and all you might be able to accomplish. Holding onto grudges is damaging; heal the memory so that it no longer rules your life and drives your ambitions.

Consider if you are chipping away at something you value in your marriage with a cutting behavior. Perhaps you interrupt your spouse at home or out in public, because what you have to say is more important. Honoring your partner's right to speak is akin to giving a gift of love. When your spouse listens to you, he or she is giving you the gift of time while valuing what you have to say. No one is a mind reader, therefore it's essential to listen to what your spouse thinks, feels, and conveys. If it's important to your spouse, make it important to you too. Your spouse may not want you to fix, solve, or judge; but merely desires to be heard. Perhaps you could inquire first if you are merely a sounding board or ask if feedback is wanted. Sometimes your opinion may not be asked for. What negative behaviors are you trying to thwart?

Perhaps you are sabotaging your marriage with unsuitable language, carrying grudges, and not fully listening to your spouse. Instead of tearing down your relationship with destructive behaviors, small adjustments will yield favorable results and mold your marriage into a stronger union. Simply exchange negative words for those Christ would use. Envision how Jesus would act, how he would listen, and what he would say. That may be the impetus you need to live more lovingly with your spouse.

Dear Lord, help me to make peace with the circumstances that have shaped my life. Redirect my energy and let my heart overflow with forgiveness for any past hurts that I might have caused and for sufferings I have endured. Teach me how to let go of the unrealistic expectations I have of [*name*] and accept him or her as is. Don't let me carve my spouse into the image I want. Let me embrace my mate as you created. You know best and I trust you. Amen.

February 25

Do not be friendly with hotheads, nor associate with the wrathful,
Lest you learn their ways, and become ensnared.

PROVERBS 22:24–25

An avalanche is an accelerating rush of snow sweeping down a slope which grows rapidly as it plummets. Most avalanches occur spontaneously during storms with an increased snowfall. Does your anger build up and eventually spill over like an avalanche, burying your marriage in a mound of pain and hurt feelings?

It's easy to lose your cool with your spouse because you might be frustrated by trying to correct their faults, challenge their opinions, and question their reasoning. If you want to be helpful, anger cannot be a part of it. Anger is good when asserting yourself after you have been treated unfairly; it motivates you to take a stand and be heard. However, it's important not to speak out of anger. When you feel yourself becoming inflamed, think about what you want to say. Ask God to help you speak clearly, intelligently, and lovingly to make your point without berating your spouse.

Don't get buried in your anger. Control it by recognizing early warning signs: tense muscles, reddened face, clenched jaw, or changes in your voice. Take a deep breath, close your eyes, and focus on Jesus face. If you feel overwhelmed with rage, consider taking a time-out to use up that energy by jogging, crying, vacuuming, or praying before addressing the upsetting issue. If your church offers adoration, sit with Jesus, reflect on your feelings, and meditate on the underlying circumstances that trouble you. God will never leave you in your time of need.

In an effort to have a healthy marriage, manage your anger so it doesn't destroy it. Give yourself time to digest the disconcerting situation before responding. Sweeping the problem under the rug is not an option. Because you are no longer reeling doesn't mean you should ignore it. Calmly discuss it with your partner to bring resolution to your relationship. What troubling issue do you need to discuss with your spouse?

Dear Lord, cool my anger and fill me with peacefulness and tranquility so that I can uncover the truths about myself and the problems permeating my marriage. Heal my aching heart and guide me as I work toward shaping myself into your image. Strengthen me, Lord, as I untangle a mess I have made with my life. Give me the courage to make things right again. Light my path, take my hand and show me the way. I want to walk in your merciful love all of the days of my life. Amen.

February 26

I have stretched out my hands all the day to a rebellious people,
who walk in a way that is not good, following their own designs;
a people who provoke me continually to my face.

ISAIAH 65:2–3

Shoveling snow can strain the heart enough to cause a heart attack. Even pushing a heavy snow blower increases blood pressure and heart rate. What stresses your relationship to the breaking point?

When trying to work through an issue, stick to one topic only and don't dredge up the past because those concerns might still be unresolved. You could write them down and discuss them next week, but don't complicate matters by making your troubles larger than they are.

Don't blame one another; attack the problem, not each other. Blaming escalates negative emotions, allowing the problem to become dreadful to work through. It is common to react with negative emotions when you feel threatened, even if it's only your ego that is vulnerable. Blaming can trigger your spouse's link to childhood anxiety, anger, and shame and could stem from your own emotional immaturity. Talk to your partner the same way you would to a friend.

If you are unhappy with your spouse's behavior, which might appear blameworthy, examine your expectations. If your partner is unwilling to change, even though your expectations seem reasonable, you will still be unhappy. When you are upset, ask yourself, "What did I expect?" Sometimes your expectations can feel like demands to your partner. Turn those expectations into hopes. One way to do this is by articulating it to your partner, perhaps through negotiation. If you are constantly disappointed that your spouse does not have dinner waiting for you after work, ask yourself if this is a realistic expectation. Even if it is realistic, turn it into a hope by saying, "Last week when I walked in the house after work, dinner smelled amazing in the oven. It was the best meatloaf. I hope you will surprise me like that again."

Your relationship satisfaction is your own responsibility because you are accountable for what you think, how you feel, and how you behave. God gave you both magnificent brains; put them together and work calmly, listing all solutions regardless of their feasibility. Pray on it, asking for God's intervention and guidance. Don't let disagreements turn into arguments that result in heart attacks.

Dear Lord, let me work in alliance with [*name*]. Fill our brains with your unquestionable reasoning, fill our hearts with your never ending love and mercy, and let us walk the path of righteousness. Amen.

February 27

Thus he makes the snow like wool, and spreads the frost like ash;
He disperses hail like crumbs. Who can withstand his cold? Yet when again
he issues his command, it melts them; he raises his winds and waters flow.

PSALM 147:16–18

When the wind chill factor approaches zero, frostbite becomes a hazard for anyone outside unprepared for wind and frigid temperatures. In order to prevent frostbite in your marriage, resolve conflict utilizing a policy you both establish and agree to. For example, if your spouse's family visits, he or she does the work before, during, and after the stay. You can create a policy for anything as simple as whoever is near the phone when it rings, answers it, or whoever uses the last of the toilet paper replaces it. Policies are not set in concrete and can be changed if you both agree to the modifications.

Money is often a source of contention in many marriages; therefore, having a policy in place could eliminate some of the typical struggles couples deal with. Perhaps you could agree to pool your combined salaries, then design and agree to a budget where a certain amount is saved and spent. Perhaps you could agree to consult with each other if one of you wants to spend over $100.

If one partner's need takes priority over the other's preference, that could be another type of policy. For example, if your normal routine is to take a Saturday morning walk, but your spouse has a sprained ankle, you would go to a movie instead. If your spouse is allergic to pollen, you wouldn't bring fresh flowers indoors. Another policy can be set when one spouse enjoys a particular job or has more time to do that chore. For example, one spouse might enjoy cutting the grass while the other likes to trim the edges. There are many creative solutions to using policies to prevent conflict in your marriage. Be creative and let God's love flow through you as you work on them.

It might also be sensible to establish guidelines with raising children because disciplinary matters differ between most couples. Having strategies could help you to avoid conflict. When couples disagree on a course of corrective action, a policy in place might circumvent marital discord while child rearing.

Dear Lord, melt the ice in our marriage with your warm words, thoughts, and messages of love. Thank you for putting resourceful tools in our midst and for teaching us how to use them constructively. Thank you for keeping me flexible to consider policies as a way of keeping our marriage on track. It is not always easy living with another person, so thank you, Lord, for walking this journey alongside us. Thank you for bringing us together and for blessing our union. Amen.

February 28

They pass the night naked, without clothing;
for they have no covering against the cold.

JOB 24:7

Quilting is the stitching together of layers of padding and fabric and dates back as far as ancient Egypt. Early quilts were made of leftover cloth scraps as a meager bed covering. Eventually they became decorative items that exhibited the fine needlework of the maker, often telling a historical family story. If a quilt was made chronicling your marriage, what would it be like and what would it say?

Everyone's lives fit together differently when bound together by love. How do you show your partner that you love him or her unconditionally? If your spouse has disappointed you, offer him or her grace and a steady stream of affirmations. Recall when you first met your spouse, how he or she made you feel and what you found endearing. Consider what you might have said back then and let those affirmations drive your feelings to repeat them again, even if you feel disenchanted. Weave uplifting, encouraging words into your daily conversations with your spouse, because that will bring security. When your partner feels safe and understood, insecurity decreases. Reassure your commitment to your marriage vows.

Find time to reconnect at the end of each day. When you both finish work, take a few minutes to discuss the events that shaped your day. You can have deep discussions or chatty, lighthearted conversations. The connection you establish can set the attitude for the evening. Remember that you are teammates committed to the same game, without competition or fear of preaching. Simply listen to each other; don't try to fix each other's problems unless you are asked to.

Contemplate your own private relationship with God. After prayer and meditation, don't you feel loved, protected, and understood by him? When you pray every day, you develop a sanctuary with God and cultivate a mature relationship with him, where everything is possible. Marriage is intended to work the same way. Cherish the time you connect with your spouse the same way you value your prayer time with the Lord. How will you reconnect with your spouse today?

Dear Lord, grant me the wisdom to comprehend the holy Scriptures and then apply those values and philosophies in my marriage. Strengthen me, Lord, so that I can be the loving, caring, and understanding spouse that you intended for me to be. Let my life story mimic yours. Amen.

February 29

If I speak in human and angelic tongues but do not have love, I am a
resounding gong or a clashing cymbal. And if I have the gift of prophecy
and comprehend all mysteries and all knowledge; if I have all faith so
as to move mountains but do not have love, I am nothing. If I give away
everything I own, and if I hand my body over so that I may boast but do
not have love, I gain nothing. Love is patient, love is kind. It is not jealous,
[love] is not pompous, it is not inflated, it is not rude, it does not seek its
own interests, it is not quick-tempered, it does not brood over injury, it
does not rejoice over wrongdoing but rejoices with the truth. It bears all
things, believes all things, hopes all things, endures all things. Love never
fails. If there are prophecies, they will be brought to nothing; if tongues,
they will cease; if knowledge, it will be brought to nothing. For we know
partially and we prophesy partially, but when the perfect comes, the
partial will pass away. When I was a child, I used to talk as a child, think
as a child, reason as a child; when I became a man, I put aside childish
things. At present we see indistinctly, as in a mirror, but then face to face.
At present I know partially; then I shall know fully, as I am fully known.
So faith, hope, love remain, these three; but the greatest of these is love.

1 Corinthians 13:1–13

Love is the most important gift we can give to our spouse, because where
there is love, God tells us that all things endure. If you thought the difficulties in your marriage were not worth the hassle, remember God's words:
love never fails. Jesus's message to everyone is built upon love. Therefore,
build your marriage on love. Don't build your family on money, because
money won't last. Build your marriage on the greatest of all the gifts: love.
When God calls you home someday, you will have to leave your spouse and
all of your worldly possessions behind. The one thing you can bring to heaven
with you is a heart filled with love. How will you spend your time on earth
creating love with your spouse?

Dear Lord, teach me how to release my grasp on weighty possessions
and embrace the love that you created in my spouse. Teach me to
truly appreciate [name] and sanctify our marriage as the sacred bond
you meant for it to be. Thank you, Lord, for your unfaltering and
unconditional love. Amen.

March 1

*For if you were cut from what is by nature a wild olive tree, and grafted,
contrary to nature, into a cultivated one, how much more will they
who belong to it by nature be grafted back into their own olive tree.*

ROMANS 11:24

When horticulturalists graft two different plants together, the result can
be a stronger, more beautiful plant. Vegetation that complements each
other is selected with one having an ideal root system while the other yields
more fruit. What attributes do you bring to your marriage? Perhaps your
language talents are balanced with your spouse's mathematical capabilities.
Who is more creative and who is more technical? Reflect on the many talents
your spouse provides to make your union richer and more balanced.

Contemplate what you and your partner can accomplish together that
you could not do alone. You both have the ability to create life and raise a
family. Married couples can live together more economically with tax benefits. Married couples live longer and tend to be happier. While there are no
guarantees to success, there are things you can do to attain a long, healthy,
and harmonious marriage.

Try to see the best in your partner because it helps to keep things intimate where love can be expressed and enjoyed. Romance and passion bring
couples together, but compromise and respect keep couples united. Instead
of bringing up sour topics, reminisce about the wonderful things you have
done together. Relive the love. Spend more time together getting to know
your partner's tastes, aspirations, and who they like and dislike at work,
because knowing the details of your partner's inner and outer life creates a
stronger bond.

Sometimes you have to apologize to your spouse. Keep the words "I'm
sorry" in your vocabulary and use as often as necessary. Eliminate all forms
of condescension from your relationship including: rolling your eyes, curs-
ing, sarcasm, and name calling. Keep defensiveness and stonewalling out of
your marriage. Don't be critical.

There are many areas of your married life that you can shape by trim-
ming off the negative and adding more of the positives. What areas in your
relationship require propagation? Focus on your personal strengths, and
ways you can develop them in God's love to make your relationship heartier.

Dear Lord, cradle me in your loving embrace as I put all of my hope
and trust in you. Allow me to appreciate the talents, the strengths,
and weaknesses, of our relationship. Thank you for your insight and
wisdom. I love you, Lord God Almighty. Amen.

March 2

*Finally, brothers, whatever is true, whatever is honorable, whatever is just,
whatever is pure, whatever is lovely, whatever is gracious, if there is any
excellence and if there is anything worthy of praise, think about these things.*

PHILIPPIANS 4:8

Roses are reminiscent of relationships. To enjoy the soft petals curling around each other with its unique beauty and fragrance, the thorny stem must be touched. While your marriage is akin to this magnificent flower, there are certain aspects of your relationship that have thorns that are painful to approach without caution. Is intimacy or physical touch one?

Physical touch is used globally to express feelings of emotional love to people around us. Babies who are touched and loved develop healthier emotional lives than babies left alone without it. Inside everyone is the need to feel loved, cherished, needed, and wanted. Married couples need to be able to show affection through physical embraces, hugging, kissing, and holding hands. Spouses need to care for each other and see to each other's needs. This expression of love is as multifaceted as the individual seeking it. Perhaps you are reluctant to show your love through these behaviors or are unable to interpret or accept your spouse's touch.

Touch provides information about surfaces and textures, which is a part of nonverbal communication in interpersonal relationships and is vital in conveying physical intimacy. There are several kinds of touch: positive, playful, control, ritualistic, task-related, and unintentional. Nonverbal communication sends and receives messages hoping to gain your spouse's approval or love. In appreciation touch, gratitude is conveyed for something another person has done. In the supportive inclusion touch, attention is drawn to the closeness. Affectionate touch transmits positive regard beyond mere acknowledgment of your spouse, and sexual interest is expressed through physical attraction touch. Which area of touch do you need to focus your energies on to convey your feelings to your spouse? Knowing that gardeners wear gloves to cut roses, what provisions will you use to approach a thorny matter?

God created you and the roses with love. Once the rose is cut and placed in a vase, you can focus on its features that you love the most. What are some of your spouse's endearing qualities of touch that you cherish and want to develop?

Dear Lord, thank you for making my partner good, honest, loyal, and dependable. Those merits make me strive to constantly improve myself. Thank you for bringing us together and keeping us close. With your radiant presence in my life, I can always find the beauty that is within. Amen.

March 3

The LORD is my strength and my shield, in whom my heart trusts.
I am helped, so my heart rejoices; with my song I praise him.
PSALM 28:7).

When you walked down the aisle on your wedding day, do you recall thinking how much you didn't know about your partner, or were you thinking about all you did know and admire? What have you recently discovered about your spouse? Is he or she reliable?

Trust is critical for any relationship. When you trust someone enough to share your life with them, you believe what they say. Trust is the foundation of a marriage. You tell your spouse what is important and what you expect from him or her. If they agree to honor and respect what you consider important, you will continue to trust them with your feelings and thoughts. If you are deceived, problems will ensue. If amends for the betrayal are made, you might deem your spouse trustworthy and slowly begin to trust again. Your relationship will be in serious jeopardy if your spouse lacks the understanding, consideration, and importance of honoring an agreement and protecting your trust.

Because of past hurts, many people don't trust their spouses. When someone tries to get close, they run into the wall. If the person keeps trying to get close, people with a shell around their heart sabotage the relationship. Humans want to be loved. But some people don't want the emotional risk. They prefer to engage in a semi-emotional relationship with a façade of love without risking heartbreak. You can't experience true love that way. You cannot unite with your spouse spiritually and emotionally if you won't tear down the barrier encapsulating your heart. Jesus exposed his heart to heartache to allow the disciples in. He loved them wholeheartedly even though it brought despair; he was willing to take that necessary risk. Jesus, the perfect example of unfettered love, decided that with true love you must expose your heart.

It can be unnerving to walk through unchartered territory with your partner without risking some pain, but that is what God desires. Trust that God brought you both together for a reason. Focus on the bigger picture and less on the trivial nuances of the day. Is an insignificant annoyance preventing you from admiring your spouse's finer attributes? Reflect on past occurrences where you were truly thankful for the trust and dependability of your spouse.

Dear Lord, I trust in your plan explicitly; though I do not understand it entirely, I know there is a motive for our blessed alliance with each other and with you. My life is much richer because of your divine intervention. Thank you for the gifts that you constantly shower us with, especially the gift of love. Amen.

March 4

Have no anxiety at all, but in everything, by prayer and petition, with
thanksgiving, make your requests known to God. Then the peace of God that
surpasses all understanding will guard your hearts and minds in Christ Jesus.

PHILIPPIANS 4:6–7

Have you ever seen a sleeping child in a bustling shopping center and wondered how that infant could feel comfortable enough to tune out the noise and fall asleep? The security the child feels is similar to what God wants you to experience in his love. Do you feel that same kind of comfort and security in your life with your spouse, or is your relationship in a downward spiral of burnout?

Marriage burnout is an agonizing state of physical, emotional, and mental exhaustion that afflicts couples who believe marriage gives meaning to their lives. After the realization that their relationship doesn't do that, the problem combines unrealistic expectations of a spouse and marriage with the stresses and realities of life. Spouses might feel physically and emotionally drained. Without an intervention, the marriage will deteriorate with episodes of discontentment and feelings of dissatisfaction.

Focus on the positives in your life, what you like about each other, and what a wonderful person your spouse is. Don't waste time dwelling on aversions. Show appreciation to your spouse. Say "I love you" or "Thank you for doing that for me." Praise and compliment your spouse frequently. Happily married couples talk to each other all of the time, while burned-out couples have brief conversations. Talk about pleasant topics, reminisce about fun things you did in the past, and discuss feelings and needs without judgments and criticisms. Make your marriage more exciting by mixing up routines. Balance your security, commitment, and trust with the excitement of personal and spiritual growth, the feeling that you both have the opportunity to get the most out of yourself and your life.

Marriage burnout provides a chance to reexamine your marriage, make changes, and spawn growth. Those who cope with it often emerge with a better, richer, more exciting marriage. What kind of noise and disruptions are creating havoc in your marriage? How can you tune out the commotion of the world and focus on your mate and making your marriage stronger?

Dear Lord, give me the wisdom to differentiate between what I should bring into our relationship and what needs to be excluded. Guard my heart, Lord, and keep my steadfastness in alignment with all that is good, holy, and pure. Thank you for my spouse and the life you have given to us. You have blessed me tenfold. Amen.

March 5

Life and love you granted me, and your providence has preserved my spirit.
Yet these things you have hidden in your heart; I know they are your purpose.

JOB 10:12–13

Sometimes, building a relationship is like creating a perennial flowerbed: it takes considerable thought and planning, time to select the perfect plants, purchase them, dig holes for them, and then water. After the initial work is completed, nothing more is needed except a little sunshine and water. With little attention or minimal effort, the plants grow. However, with fertilizer mixed into the soil, pruning and dead-heading, and daily watering, the blossoms are bigger and heartier. How much work do you put into your marriage?

Maybe you don't feel like marriage needs any effort, but to ensure its success it needs reinforcements the same way gardens need work to produce quality flowers. You get out of your marriage what you put into it. Even if it's difficult for you to compliment your spouse, ask God to help you convey praiseworthy words for your partner. Perhaps you noticed a tender moment between your children and spouse, or a kindness with a neighbor; compliment that. Use a friendly manner and loving tone so there won't be room for a misinterpretation of your intended message. When is the last time you told your spouse you liked their smile, hairstyle, or laugh? It's like working fertilizer into the soil around your flowers; it will make them produce bigger and better blooms.

You can shape the happiness in your marriage by making an effort to recognize your spouse when he or she does something nice. Pray that every decision you make, every compliment you offer, every task you perform, will take your marriage in the right direction. When you make a mistake, use it as an opportunity to grow and learn from it so you don't repeat it. Vow to make it better next time. Reflect with the Lord the effort you expend on your marriage. Do you go the extra mile to ensure you have a healthy and loving marriage? How do you make your spouse feel special and loved? Invest in love.

Dear Lord, you gave me life and nurtured me with constant love and care. Enable me to do that to my marriage. Teach me ways to yield a more robust relationship with the one special person in my life that I care about the most. Help me to relay my feelings, thoughts, and emotions so that love blossoms all throughout our life. Amen.

March 6

Pray without ceasing. In all circumstances give thanks,
for this is the will of God for you in Christ Jesus.

1 Thessalonians 5:17–18

Water falls freely from the sky, cleansing, hydrating, and satisfying all that is below. Every living thing needs and craves water. It's such a simple thing: hydrogen and oxygen molecules, but our existence depends on it. A drop of water is comforting and lightweight, yet a gallon of water is heavy and cumbrous to carry any given distance. What tiny element is necessary for your marriage to be successful? What is the oxygen molecule in your marriage?

Reflect on the simplest components that you must have from your spouse and ask if you also provide it. It's important to thank your spouse for the "little things" they do for you, even the inconsequential things that might have gone unnoticed for years. It's time to notice and communicate your appreciation in an affectionate way. You could say, "Thank you for taking out the trash. I hate that job and you never grumble about doing it," or "Thank you for working today; I know your job is tough." Acknowledging your spouse will make him or her feel appreciated and loved. When you miss the opportunities to thank your spouse, it becomes like the burdensome weight of water that must be carried from the well. Therefore, celebrate every worthy occasion with a smile, a hug, or a kiss, because it is better to have a loving relationship full of joyful praises than one crushed with resentments.

Consider how thoughtful you are with complete strangers. Can you at least offer your partner the same courtesies that you would extend to them or to neighbors or coworkers? Use that as a starting point. Provide kind words expressed sincerely to your spouse. Your loving messages and words of thanks could quench your partner's thirst like a cold glass of water on a hot day. What type of partner do you want to be? Think about the blessings, both great and small, that God gives to you each day. How do you thank God for them? How do you thank your spouse for all he or she does for you?

Dear Lord, transform my heart into an appreciative one, capable of recognizing and acknowledging even the smallest acts of love and kindness because it's all important. Help me to be more kindhearted to my spouse. Let me please my spouse, but more importantly, let me please you and abide by the will you have set forth for me. Amen.

March 7

Blessed is the one whose fault is removed, whose sin is forgiven.
Blessed is the man to whom the LORD imputes no guilt,
in whose spirit is no deceit.

PSALM 32:1–2

Have you ever driven down the highway and noticed the beautiful flowers alongside the road? Most of the wildflowers in New York State are weeds. The deceit is in the outer appearance. What is the perception of your marriage like? Do you put on a show for friends, family, and neighbors, or is your relationship genuinely sincere?

Lies and dishonesties pull us away from God's plan for marriage. Don't depend more on what society and culture dictates rather than what the Bible says. When you feel unhappy or resentful in your marriage or as your spouse's weaknesses show, don't let negative thoughts fester. Instead of accepting these unpleasant attributes, convince yourself prayerfully that you married the right person, the one God intended for you to share your life with. Remember that God is in charge and he knows what he is doing. Ask the Almighty to keep you emotionally and physically connected to your mate. Do not allow deceit to derail your relationship.

Movies, books, and fairy tales depict a theatrical version of what love is "supposed" to look like. Perhaps you married your partner with your own definition defined by your parents. Don't waste time comparing a fabricated definition of love with the love you are experiencing. Focus on God's greater plan for your life. God wants you to be happy, but his greatest desire is to seek and glorify him in all that we say, think, and do.

Perhaps you speak lovingly to your spouse in public, but are condescending at home. How would Jesus speak to your spouse and what would he say to you? If your relationship needs fine-tuning, what adjustments can you make? Try to communicate your true feelings to your spouse. By offering suggestions to enhance your relationship, you are moving toward achieving an honest persona. Invoke the Holy Spirit for guidance as you peel back the superficiality to expose the essence of your union. Ponder how honest you are in your marriage and how you can improve it in God's love.

Dear Lord, you created me in your image, so please sanction my genuineness in my relationship with [*name*]. Let me live, work, and play authentically in your love, to be the very best partner I can possibly be. Help our relationship to mature into one of total acceptance and love. Let our marriage be fruitful and pleasing to you. I adore you, Lord, and trust in your ways. Amen.

March 8

You shall not keep two differing weights in your bag, one heavy and the other light; nor shall you keep two different ephahs in your house, one large and the other small. But use a full and just weight, a full and just ephah, so that you may have a long life on the land the LORD, your God, is giving you.

DEUTERONOMY 25:13–16

Each spring, hundreds of fragrant lilacs blossom on trees; I always count on this enjoyable pleasure happening. When an unusually warm air mass settles too soon, it forces flower buds to form prematurely. When the normal frigid temperatures returned, the buds were destroyed. Could spending too much time with friends destroy your marriage the way the cold weather killed the lilacs? How can you balance your marriage with friendships?

In a healthy marriage, you have the right to time apart, time with your spouse, and time with your friends. If your spouse develops jealousy, try to sort out what's bothering your partner. He or she could be feeling left out or threatened by the closeness you share with friends. Examine if there are tangible explanations for the wariness or if it is used to control you. Talk to your partner openly and honestly. Reassure him or her that no one can take his or her place, but you need other friendships to balance your life. Discuss the friendships that could be lacking in your spouse's life. Deliberate options where you can both agree to have one day a week to spend with friends, another day for solitude, or days where all friends are gathered together. It can be challenging to be a part of a couple while maintaining a sense of autonomy.

When you are away from your spouse for a brief period or for extended travel or military deployment, the way you keep in touch and how you reconnect is more significant than the time of your separation. Successful couples touch base frequently through text messages, letters and cards, short phone conversations, or online visits. At the end of the day or end of the week, find some time to renew your bond. Consider rituals that you both enjoy for reconnecting before bed. Perhaps you could say the rosary together, recite special prayers, or read holy Scriptures. Whether you share a drink, a caress, or dialog, make sure that you do not overlook how important renewing your bond is for your relationship. Couples who fail to do this feel isolated from each other.

Do you depend on your marriage for security, loyalty, and longevity? Ponder ways to demonstrate to your mate that you value your pledge to each other and won't allow anything to come between you—not physical space, time, or distance.

Dear Lord, keep my marriage holy and don't let anything harm, neglect, or destroy it. Amen.

March 9

Then I should still have consolation and could exult through unremitting
pain, because I have not transgressed the commands of the Holy One.
What strength have I that I should endure, and what is my limit that I
should be patient? Have I the strength of stones, or is my flesh of bronze?

JOB 6:10–12

Trainers push athletes to work through their fatigue and discomfort with
expressions such as "no pain, no gain" and "feel the burn." Both are signs
of progress and after a while, athletes see the rewards of persistent training and dedication. Sometimes, it is agonizing working through marriage
dilemmas, but once a resolution is found, the end result will be a happier
relationship. Because couples are different people, with diverse ideas, there
will be disagreements. Some of the disagreements could be about how to
settle the disagreement. What plots the course of your marriage is how those
disagreements are handled.

You could sweep the problem under the rug, which wouldn't solve anything. Your disagreement could escalate into a vicious fight, which would
only make matters worse. The best thing you could do is work together to
find a solution that you can both be happy with. That can be accomplished
by sticking to one issue at a time. Only discuss the topic that is troublesome.
Do not drag everything else, including the kitchen sink, into the dialogue.
Leave the past in the past and don't blame each other for the struggles you
are now facing. Disassociate yourself from the problem to enable you to attack the problem, not each other. Define it and agree on the definition of the
problem. The object is not to convince your spouse that you are right, but to
find an amicable solution you can both live with.

When there are disagreements with your spouse, do you fly off the handle
or quietly sulk? Instead, use positive communication practices by replacing
"you" statements with "I" statements such as "I feel sad when you cut my
idea down without hearing me out. Will you please listen to my idea again?"
Try to be open-minded when devising and considering a list of probable
solutions. Attempt to work toward a compromise with the endurance of an
athlete. Bring God into your debating arena to be your personal trainer. With
God, anything is possible.

Dear Lord, teach me to celebrate the differences in our marriage.
Meld our abilities and talents so that we can use them to move us
through the difficulties quickly and painlessly. Bless the words we
use. Keep kindness in our hearts so that only unadulterated love can
pour out. Amen.

March 10

You shall have honest scales, an honest ephah, and an honest bath.

EZEKIEL 45:10

Maple syrup is made from sap that runs from maple trees. After the sap is collected, it's boiled down. If it's over-boiled, it will crystallize and be gritty, and under-boiled syrup will be watery and spoil quickly. There is a perfect balance between the two, and a sweet distinctive flavor is obtained under the right conditions. Do you create ultimate conditions for a harmonious marriage or are you just getting by?

Marriage needs constant balance between work and recreation in order to keep the channels of love open and communication clear. Spend time and energy addressing issues as they arise to keep them from spiraling out of control. Also, develop self-improvement techniques by dealing with the issues you brought into the marriage. These issues could be from unmet expectations or from emotional baggage and unfinished business from your childhood. Each time "triggers" opens the flood gates from childhood trauma originated from anxieties that stem from criticism, guilt that could be derived from perfectionism, anger that resulted from ridicule, resentments connected to rejection, hurt from abuse or trauma, or depression. Identify the negative childhood feelings that weigh you down in adulthood whenever something similar happens.

Avoid playing the "blame game," because it makes your partner defensive and angry and interferes with the potential of finding a win-win solution to your problems. Blaming can also conjure resentment that can destroy your relationship.

Try to understand where your partner is coming from when you disagree. Encourage your spouse to discuss his or her feelings. Listen and request clarifications that you don't understand. Encourage a curiosity for your spouse's feelings and take a special interest in caring to create an emotionally safe environment for the discussions.

How do you weigh the time you spend with your spouse versus time with your children, chores, or hobbies? Do you spend too much time on the computer? If too much time is dedicated to one task, your marriage suffers. Ensure you spend equal amounts of quality time together doing something you both enjoy. How can you include God into this balance between your recreation and obligations?

Dear Lord, help me to differentiate between all that I must do today. Don't let me become preoccupied with trivial things. Let me focus on serving you and creating stability within my home. Amen.

March 11

The spirit of the LORD spoke through me; his word was on my tongue.

2 SAMUEL 23:2

Your voiceprint has measurable characteristics that uniquely identify you. They are based on the physical configuration of your mouth and throat and can be computed as a mathematical formula. Voiceprints are used in voice ID systems for user authentication. Your voice is important and opens the lock to your partner's heart. What you say and how you say it affects your spouse's moods and attitudes. Are you cognizant of how your voice is perceived and interpreted by your mate?

One very effective way to express love is by using words that build up your partner's self-esteem, ensures him or her that you care, and that you are one hundred percent committed and will be held accountable until the end of time. The emotional desire for love needs to be met if you want your relationship to be emotionally healthy. All married couples long for affection and love. When your spouse accepts, desires, and commits to your welfare, that is security you can depend on. When you watch out for your spouse's best interests, that is love. How do you express that love?

Compliments are wonderful communicators of love. Every time you see your spouse do something nice, thank him or her and compliment the job well done. It used to drive me crazy when my husband would squeeze half a bottle of dish soap to do the dishes. Instead of complaining, I thanked him for doing the job and getting the dishes so clean. If I was living alone, I would use half the amount of soap, but I would be lonely without my mate to share my life with. Soap is a small price to pay for my spouse's happiness. Celebrate the small victories and rejoice in the love wherever you find it. Wherever there is love, God is also there. What can you do to ascertain that your voiceprint also has a heart print embedded in it?

Dear Lord, help me to speak the truth in love to my partner. Enable me to take responsibility for my half of the dialog with a loving message and honest intentions. Teach me to use my voice positively to build a stronger marriage bond and to raise my spouse to new heights. You gave me the power to build up or tear down. Remind me to use my words to lovingly, the way you talk to me. I love you, Lord. Amen.

March 12

The whole world had the same language and the same words. Come,
let us go down and there confuse their language, so that no one will
understand the speech of another. So the LORD *scattered them from*
there over all the earth, and they stopped building the city. That is why
it was called Babel, because there the LORD *confused the speech of all*
the world. From there the LORD *scattered them over all the earth.*

GENESIS 11:1, 7–9

When my mother traveled through Great Britain, she asked to use a
restroom in a Scottish restaurant. The waitress brought her into a
quiet room with a sofa and was told to rest there. Sometimes it's easy to misinterpret what is said. Other times it's subtle or there is room for a message
to be misconstrued. Does your marriage have frequent miscommunications?

A poor conversationalist will relay a message to a third person instead
of their mate. Triangles are unreliable methods of communication. Another
ineffective technique is mind reading. Unless you work for a circus or fortune
teller, don't use this method to communicate to your spouse. Using sarcastic
language by verbally acting out will cause hurt feelings and an argument may
ensue. Using disrespectful language or swearing is one of the worst communication techniques you could use. Instead, focus on healthy ways to communicate.

Be direct, clear and specific, and respectful of your spouse's feelings. It is
worthless to crush his or her spirits just to make a point. Take your partner's
ego into consideration when speaking. Use "I" statements and begin softly,
by stating something positive first. The majority of discussions end the way
they begin, so start with love, honestly, and politeness. Consider the time
that you begin your conversation: is it too early in the morning, too late at
night, or is my spouse hungry or sick? If your spouse understands better by
utilizing word pictures whereby words elicit an image, try to accommodate
that technique. If your spouse understands better by using analogies or
ratings on a scale of one to ten, use those methods. Ask nicely for what you
want. The most important part of a conversation is to ensure your spouse
understands you and your request.

Contemplate ways you can prevent miscommunications from happening
in your relationship. How can you inquire if your partner needs clarifications
without sounding condescending? God gave you the ability to include love
in everything you think, say, and do.

Dear Lord, grant me the wisdom to know when to stay silent and
when to speak up. Let me pause and reflect on the message I want
to send to my spouse. Teach me to say it lovingly to ensure [*name*]
understands. Help me to mean what I say, and say what I mean. Amen.

March 13

Put falsehood and lying far from me, give me neither poverty nor riches;
provide me only with the food I need;
Lest, being full, I deny you, saying, "Who is the LORD?"
Or, being in want, I steal, and profane the name of my God.
PROVERBS 30:8–9

After I overloaded a wheelbarrow with bricks, I was surprised when the tire popped. Something similar happens if we overload our lives. It's understandable to take on extra activities, additional volunteer jobs, another project at work, or more family obligations. What's on your list of responsibilities that is stressful? It's plausible to get so bogged down with commitments that the pressure can make you physically, emotionally, or spiritually ill.

When you feel stress, hormones stimulate nerves causing blood vessels in your brain to swell, resulting in tension headaches or migraines. Practice relaxation techniques and prayer as a coping mechanism. God will not give you more than you can carry. Call out to him in your time of need. Even little daily annoyances can cause digestive problems just as much as major life changes can. Anxiety and stress can cause heartburn, gas, and bloating. Stress suppresses the immune system, making it easier for you to get sick. Stress is the number one cause of sleep deprivation and insomnia, which can makes you irritable and anxious and impairs your ability to concentrate. When your body is stressed, it releases adrenaline and cortisol, hormones that trigger the sensation of being hungry, which explains why you might put on a few extra pounds. Research shows that most chronic back pain is caused by psychological stress. People tend to hunch over and tense their shoulder and neck muscles when they're anxious.

Can you prioritize your duties to determine what is important and what to let go of? Where does your spouse and marriage fit into the picture? Put God at the center of your life and build around that. In shifting your focus back on the Lord, your responsibilities will fall into place and be easier to manage.

Dear Lord, teach me to simplify my hectic life and center my world on you. Let me to release everything that ails me and weighs me down physically, mentally, spiritually, and give it all to you. Teach me how to let go of it and let you take over. Don't let me keep taking it back. Give me the courage to trust in you implicitly. You are the Almighty Creator of heaven and earth. You alone can carry my burdens and put my mind at ease. Thank you, Lord, for cradling me in your loving arms and enabling me to simply be. I love you. Amen.

March 14

*But God said to him, 'You fool, this night your life will be demanded of you;
and the things you have prepared, to whom will they belong?' Thus will
it be for the one who stores up treasure for himself but is not rich in what
matters to God." He said to [his] disciples, "Therefore I tell you, do not
worry about your life and what you will eat, or about your body and what
you will wear. For life is more than food and the body more than clothing.*

LUKE 12:20–23

At the National Institutes of Health, children with growth disorders have
their height measured the first thing at daybreak. At night, the discs
between the vertebrae of the spine are replenished with fluids making height
optimal every morning. During the day, the liquids squeeze out, decreasing
a third of an inch off our height. The stress of the day can leave us feeling
emotionally or physically drained. If your marriage feels drained, how can
you replenish it?

According to research, unhappy couples have compromised immune
systems, higher blood pressure, and faster heart rates. And they could be at
risk for heart disease, arthritis, and cancer. These are good reasons to alleviate
stress and not neglect your spouse. Keep open dialogue with your partner.
Instead of talking to friends about marriage problems, talk with your partner. Try strengthening your marriage by confiding with your spouse about
everyday things that are going on in your life: news at work, the children,
neighbors, or in-laws. Sharing will increase your emotional intimacy. When
stress levels skyrocket, your spouse can help you manage it just by having
someone to talk it out with.

Everyone deals with stress differently. Find activities that you can do
individually or as a couple that minimize the buildup of stress. If stress
starts to escalate, learn to deal with it appropriately. Have an outlet to your
tensions, whether it is running, exercising, cooking, cleaning the house, or
another hobby that gives you enjoyment. Most importantly, keep the lines
of communication open with your spouse.

Perhaps seeking rest through meditation and prayer could be rejuvenat-
ing. Maybe sharing an intimate meal with your partner without interruptions from television, children, or phone calls, could be revitalizing to your
relationship, or possibly taking a long nature walk is all that is needed. What
will it take to invigorate your marriage in God's love?

Dear Lord, bless our rest and reenergize our spirits. Teach us ingenious
ways reconnect and bring our relationship to a realm of new height.
Shine your generous love on us and renew our relationship. Lift us
up and hold us near. Amen.

March 15

There is an appointed time for everything, and a time for every
affair under the heavens. A time to give birth, and a time to die;
a time to plant, and a time to uproot the plant.

ECCLESIASTES 3:1–2

When my favorite plant wilted, I suspected it could be root-bound. After I repotted it with new, richer soil, the plant bounced back and thrived in its new container with additional room to expand. Occasionally, we, too, need a little space in order to grow. Even though you love your job, you still need vacation days to escape it. Even though you love your children, you still need to hire a sitter to step away for a brief duration. Even though you love your partner, you need time away from each other.

Perhaps you need a designated private spot in your home where you can exercise, tinker with a hobby, or express your creative talents in music, art, or writing. Perhaps you need a place to work or a recreational space. If your house is too small to accommodate a designated spot for you, perhaps you could take a longer bath or shower and use that time to contemplate your life challenges, possible solutions, and give you time for self-realization. The alone time that you incorporate into your life will allow you to exchange thoughts with yourself in the silent of your soul. It gives you time to reenergize, regroup, and reconnect. It could enhance your marriage and quite possibly make you a better person.

Don't wait until you feel trapped to ask for "space." When you approach your spouse, do it lovingly with respect, while being honest and specific with your request. Reassure your partner not to take it personally, that you are committed to your marriage, and your time alone will make you a better spouse. Include your partner in designing a private place. If you long for space away, perhaps time away with friends to go camping, a weekend away shopping, or time without you or the kids, then help plan it.

While it is good to include your spouse in activities, it is also good to have aloneness to reconnect with your feelings and emotions—perhaps in silent reflection, prayer, and meditation at church. Is it plausible to pray in the solitude of your car while you drive somewhere?

Dear Lord, when I am alone, remind me to think of you, talk to you, and thank you for the many gifts you have so generously given to me. Thank you for helping me to carve out quality time with my spouse and prayer time to spend with you. Teach me to embrace the quiet that fills my ears, teach me to be still and wait for you to speak to me. I am ready and eager to listen to your message and honor you all of the days of my life. I love you, Lord. Amen.

March 16

Who has laid out a channel for the downpour and a path for the thunderstorm
to bring rain to uninhabited land, the unpeopled wilderness.

JOB 38:25–26

Most gorges are formed through water erosion. Over time, waterfalls erode the rocks they topple over and gradually the water recedes, leaving a gorge behind. Water has the power to carve away land and create a vast cavernous gorge.

While it is so important to have a voice and to be heard, it is also essential to be cautious of the words used and the intended message. When you speak to your partner, are your words nasty or sarcastic? One of the worst things you can do is to speak disrespectfully. Ponder the last time you used cutting words with your spouse. Apologize when you say something hurtful, and make a plan to prevent yourself from repeating that mistake. Invoke the Holy Spirit to enable you to form loving, truthful words in your mind before you speak.

When you initiate a conversation with your spouse, be astute to timing. Wait for after dinner to bring up a precarious topic, don't start in-depth conversations too close to bedtime, and take care to have discussions when you are driving. Use a soft start by chatting about something positive first. Ease into difficult topics that need to be debated. If you are struggling to make your point, try rephrasing your words or be more specific. Use word pictures, which elicit an image your partner can relate to. Sometimes, analogies are beneficial. It is helpful to ask for what you want in a respectful manner, or grade what you want on a scale of one to ten. The way you speak to your spouse determines how receptive he or she will be: always aim for a positive route.

Consider praising your spouse in public. It can be an influential motivator to others, not just your spouse. People align their actions and their attitudes with their words. When you speak positively of someone, they trust what you say. Affirmation strengthens your spouse's best qualities, and everyone needs positive reinforcement. Athletic trainers use words of encouragement to entice clients to stick with their regimented workout. Teachers use verbal praise to inspire students to continue excelling in their studies.

How can you take responsibility of your half of the dialog this week to ensure your messages are clear and concise, created from love?

Dear Lord, remind me to be kind, gracious, and loving when I speak to my spouse. Don't let me use harsh language that can destroy his or her self-esteem. When I speak to [*name*], you are there, smiling at me, loving me, and guiding me. Use me as your instrument of grace to speak lovingly, to apologize when I slip. Amen.

March 17

Therefore, putting away falsehood, speak the truth, each one to his neighbor,
for we are members one of another. Be angry but do not sin;
do not let the sun set on your anger, and do not leave room for the devil.

EPHESIANS 4:25–27

Mushrooms appear to be unassuming fungi and are considered a healthy food because they are low in calories and high in vegetable proteins, vitamins, and minerals. They also have properties that fight tumors; and the first antibiotics were extracted from fungi. With so many wonderful elements to mushrooms, it's hard to fathom that some are poisonous. Does your marriage have many positive attributes, but a few characteristics that are toxic?

People in happy marriages have better physical and psychological health than those in unhappy relationships. There are measures you can take to augment the likelihood that your marriage will thrive regardless of the difficulties you encounter. Discuss your problems with your spouse amicably or else the marital tension and the distance between you will worsen. If you are harboring ill feelings, you need to work them out in a constructive way by using sound conflict resolution skills.

Establish ground rules that work well for you and your spouse. If you have multiple topics that concern you, write them down and rank them. Select the most troublesome difficulty to solve. Define it in a way that is agreeable to you and your spouse. The object of resolving this issue is not to blame your partner, but to find a solution that you both can agree on. Don't dredge up past mistakes; stay focused. Set your swords down and attack the problem, not each other. Use "I" statements whenever you speak to your spouse and use reflective listening skills to gain a full appreciation for the root of the problem. Be creative when listing as many solutions as possible. Even if you abhor the solution, write it down with a subset of pros and cons. After you have exhausted all possibilities, decide on one. Working through conflict is challenging. Ask the angels and saints for intervention to help you and your partner find a win-win solution to your woes. Jesus settled disputes through reasoning and love. What issue will you work on with your spouse today?

Dear Lord, enlighten me, sweet Jesus. Clear my mind of clutter and replace it with love and knowledge necessary to find peaceful solutions to my marital troubles. Teach me to focus on the solitary issue that gnaws away at my marriage foundation. Bless my spouse with patience and perseverance to work through our difficulties peacefully in your love and grace. Amen.

March 18

When he returned to his disciples he found them asleep. He said to Peter,
"So you could not keep watch with me for one hour? Watch and pray that
you may not undergo the test. The spirit is willing, but the flesh is weak."

MATTHEW 26:40–41

When Jesus went to Gethsemane with his disciples to pray before his crucifixion, he needed his trusted friends nearby because he began to feel sorrow and distress. Perhaps the disciples were clueless to the extent of Jesus's sufferings, because if they had truly known and understood, they would not have fallen asleep countless times. Jesus's frustration is palpable in this reading.

Have you been frustrated by your spouse or disillusioned when you needed and depended on his or her support, or has your spouse ever made a request of you that you were unable to honor? Perhaps you got sidetracked and forgot the promise you made. Recognize the disappointment and be honest with your feelings. If you feel something is missing in your relationship, don't disguise or ignore the emotions because it could intensify and irritate you more. Ponder what might have caused it. Disappointments arise from everyday happenings of marriage. Stay positive in reactions and expectations.

After you realize where the disappointment originated from, strive to be positive with your reactions and expectations to it. For example, I was disappointed when my husband was late picking me up after work. I was worried that he was in an accident. When I learned that he was overworked and feared losing his job, I felt sorry that I overreacted. I allowed my reactions to turn into anger, resentment, and frustration. Be open-minded and trust that the best way to combat the feeling of disappointment is to focus on the blessings God has provided. Discuss your feelings with your spouse, being receptive to open dialogue.

Your spouse has the right to be taken seriously in your marriage. If something is important to your partner, you need to take it earnestly. It's about respect of your partner individually, treating him or her as though what concerns him or her is vitally important to you also. Do you take your spouse seriously, your marriage, their hopes, dreams, and goals, too? What is significant to your mate? Has your loyalty ever been tested? Turn to God during trying moments; ask him to give you the strength you need to be successful in your marriage.

Dear Lord, I pray that you keep me grounded in your love; keep me strong in desires, and agile enough to carry out whatever is pleasing to you. Let me adore the distinctive facets in my spouse that you created. Amen.

March 19

Husbands, love your wives, even as Christ loved the church and handed himself over for her to sanctify her, cleansing her by the bath of water with the word, that he might present to himself the church in splendor, without spot or wrinkle or any such thing, that she might be holy and without blemish.

EPHESIANS 5:25–27

Have you ever wondered what kind of husband St. Joseph was? He is portrayed as a devoted and honorable man. He was obedient and accepted his marriage while it was initially confusing, because Mary was pregnant. But he trusted in God's plan even though he did not understand it completely. He moved through it lovingly and tenderly despite all of the hardships he encountered—and there were many. Each time he faced adversity, he called out to God, who provided the way for him.

Joseph endured the long and harsh journey on foot with a pregnant wife. Once they arrived in Bethlehem, there was no place for them to stay to bring Jesus into the world, so they used whatever humble and meager provisions God intended for them. Can you imagine laying your newborn infant in a manger to sleep and then allowing hundreds of strangers to show up unexpectedly on your stoop to see the child to pay him homage? Then, a dream warns them to pack up and begin another arduous journey. Joseph was obedient each time he was tested.

Contemplate the tests your marriage has endured. Think about how you acted the last time you had to do something out of the ordinary for the sake of your marriage because you felt it was God's plan. Perhaps you were chosen to bring many children in the world, or you were asked to be a foster parent like St. Joseph was. Whatever God asks of your marriage, recall St. Joseph's courage in embracing his tasks, his calling, and lead by his example.

Are you a devoted, honorable, obedient, and selfless spouse? Make St. Joseph be a role model for your family today, on his feast day. Instead of giving minimally to your relationship, try to emulate St. Joseph's generous level of providing for his wife without expecting something in return.

Dear Lord, you are the God who cares for me and the wellbeing of my marriage. Remind me to be more like St. Joseph: devoted, honorable, obedient, and selfless to my spouse. Lift me up when I feel like I am drowning in a sea of confusion. Help me to see your guiding light and to walk the straight and narrow path—the one you intended for me. I truly love you, Lord. Amen.

March 20

Yet even now—oracle of the LORD—return to me with your whole heart,
with fasting, weeping, and mourning; Rend your hearts, not your garments,
and return to the LORD, your God. For he is gracious and merciful,
slow to anger, abounding in steadfast love, and relenting in punishment.
Perhaps he will again relent and leave behind a blessing,
Grain offering and libation for the LORD, your God.

JOEL 2:12–14

Days are nearly twelve hours long at the spring equinox, and they continue increasing as springtime progresses. The spring refers to ideas of rebirth, rejuvenation, renewal, resurrection, and regrowth. What areas of your marriage need rejuvenation?

Perhaps your relationship needs improvement in order to prevent a separation or divorce. Learning how to reconcile differences to save your marriage is imperative. There are several things you can do to overcome the hurdles you face. Consider the state of communication between you and your spouse: do you avoid discussing problematic areas for fear that it will spiral out of control, or do you feel you won't be taken seriously, heard, or understood? You must commit to spending time talking about the issues you are struggling through. Set ground rules beforehand: vow to allow your spouse time to speak uninterrupted. Learn from the conversation and absorb what was shared so you can grow and become a better partner. In order for your marriage to improve, you might have to embrace self-change. Ask yourself if you have been fair, have you really listened, what have you done to work toward improvement, and are you willing to work on self-improvement to save your marriage?

Perhaps you need a "do over" for a past transgression. You can start the process by resuming respectful treatment of your partner and working toward honest and open communication. After offering an apology, make a plan to prevent it from happening again. Offer a gesture to portray your sincerity. You cannot force your spouse to forgive you; give it time. Healing can be a lengthy process. Forgiveness is a gift Jesus wants everyone to embrace. If God can be forgiving, can you forgive too?

Dear Lord, you are such a kind and merciful ruler. Transform my wretched and throbbing heart into one that forgives and loves unconditionally, as you do. You have given so much to me and I am truly thankful for it all. You afford me the opportunity to wipe the slate clean and start over. Fill my heart with love and teach me to be a kinder, gentler spouse. Amen.

March 21

Hear the sound of my pleading when I cry to you for help when I lift my hands toward your holy place. Blessed be the LORD, who has heard the sound of my pleading. The LORD is my strength and my shield, in whom my heart trusts. I am helped, so my heart rejoices; with my song I praise him.

PSALM 28:2, 6–7

Battery-powered smoke alarms beep when their batteries run low. It signals homeowners to take action. Are your batteries worn down? What warning sounds does your marriage make when its batteries are worn down?

Perhaps you hear squabbling or discontentment when your marriage is not functioning as it should be. Concentrate on developing good listening skills because it can be your salvation to a peaceful marriage. Approach your spouse with compassion in your heart to begin dialog. Your body language needs to be inviting, tranquil, and friendly. Think of Jesus and what his body stance would be like, and emulate that. Take your spouse's hand in yours when you inquire what is wrong. Look into your spouse's eyes and concentrate on the words and emotions used as you really listen. When you listen to your partner in this manner, it will make him or her feel loved. The goal of listening is simply to understand. It is not about fixing problems, deriving solutions, or judging. Allow your spouse vent his or her fears or frustrations..

Summarize and repeat back what you understand in your own words, focusing on the emotions they could be feeling. For example, you might say, "It sounds like you are really hurt that I didn't go to the office party with you." Encourage your spouse to expand on what he or she is feeling, shifting the focus away from you and onto your partner. Your spouse will appreciate the focused attention, and it could help them feel sincerely cared about and understood. After your partner gets all of his or her feelings out, ask if he or she wants your opinion or advice. Sometimes people just want to vent and don't want your input. If your spouse asks for advice, you can brainstorm solutions together by listing ideas and considering the pros and cons of each. Being a good listener can make you a stronger, more caring spouse.

Can you simply open your heart, mind, and soul to accept your spouse's words? Maybe your mate just needs to purge whatever is troubling him or her. Can you be more Christ-like and allow your partner to vent while you sit and listen?

Dear Lord, when I cry out to you, you always listen. Help me to offer that same courtesy to [*name*] so that he or she feels the glowing embers of love that burns in my heart. Teach me how to be still and listen tenderly to whatever my spouse has to say. I ask this in your sweet and holy name. Amen.

March 22

When the wine ran short, the mother of Jesus
said to him, "They have no wine."

JOHN 2:3

Jesus, his disciples, and Mary were invited to a wedding in Cana in Galilee. When the wine ran out at the reception, Mary turned to Jesus, hoping to deflect embarrassment for the bride and groom. There, Jesus turned water into wine. Think back to a recent humiliation you endured in your marriage. Did you possibly mortify your partner inadvertently? Perhaps it occurred at your own wedding, at a family gathering, or a social function with your spouse.

In your marriage, you have the right to be given the benefit of the doubt. Instead of jumping to conclusions, cut your partner slack and offer him or her an advantage promoting innocence and well-being by presuming the truth. This may not be easy to do, but remember that Mary went to an extraordinary measure to ensure no one suffered embarrassment at the wedding in Cana. How did Mary know Jesus could do anything about the wine; had she ever seen him perform miracles before? Turning the water into wine was Jesus's first miracle, and it was to prevent embarrassment of a newly married couple. Use this passage as inspiration to help you extend the same courtesy to your loved one when you are in a difficult or embarrassing situation.

Giving your partner the benefit of the doubt is an effective way to nurture your relationship. Make your goal to get along with your spouse, even when it is difficult to do so. You are not going to change your spouse; but you can change your attitude and you can improve yourself. When things seem off or you're embarrassed about something that you have no control over, simply change your attitude about it. Remember that you married your spouse with good intentions and abundant love. God brought you together for a very special reason and you cannot second-guess God.

Don't take your spouse for granted; give him or her the respect and appreciation that is deserved. When you acknowledge even the tiniest kindnesses, your partner will notice and reciprocate the thoughtfulness and respect back to you. Do you admire your partner even in trying situations?

Dear Lord, let me be as kind, gentle, and loving as you always are to me. Bless me with patience and tolerance so that I can graciously offer the benefit of the doubt to my spouse. Enable me to laugh away embarrassing moments that we live through. Allow me to rise above the challenges that we face as a couple. Bless me with perseverance to accept my spouse, warts and all, through thick and thin, because you will be walking this journey beside us every step of the way. Amen.

March 23

Then he released Barabbas to them, but after he had Jesus scourged,
he handed him over to be crucified. Then the soldiers of the governor took
Jesus inside the praetorium and gathered the whole cohort around him.
MATTHEW 27:26–27

Imagine being a spectator at Jesus crucifixion: watching an innocent man being tormented so brutally with his mother, followers, and apostles watching from the sidelines. Would you stand in the crowd and remain silent and suppress your true feelings? Witnessing a devastating event, whether it is a tornado ripping apart communities or bombs exploding in our cities, it causes anguish. How do you respond to anguish in your relationship?

What earth-shattering catastrophes have recently caused you anguish in your marriage? Are there numerous arguments in your relationship? Are they senseless, or is there an underlying cause? Do you suppress your anger or withdraw emotionally? "Stuffing" anger doesn't solve anything, but it can cause depression and can be detrimental to your physical and mental health.

By stuffing your anger you allow things to happen to you without making an effort to stop or change them. Perhaps you avoid conflict because you don't want to be "the bad guy." However, this behavior diminishes your self-worth. Don't allow your anger to build up inside you because eventually resentment could build up. Don't remain quiet and hope that your feelings will disappear. Instead, communicate your needs and desires assertively.

Contemplate what might be causing your anger. Evaluate your feelings honestly to determine if it could be sadness over a loss of something, or if it is fear, frustration, or something caused from your childhood? Ponder what your feelings are trying to suggest. Do you simply want your own way or are your marriage rights being violated? Ask the Lord to move you through your anger and identify what is causing it. After you know, you can work on resolving it in God's love.

Dear Lord, thank you for enduring the anguish during your tormenting crucifixion to save me from my sins, sweet, kind, and compassionate Savior. Carry me through the pain of my difficulties and allow me to find solutions to them. Help me to find my voice and to use it appropriately throughout my marriage struggles. Keep me strong and seeking you in all that I think, say, and do. Amen.

March 24

Weaving a crown out of thorns, they placed it on his head, and a reed in his right hand....They spat upon him and took the reed and kept striking him on the head. And when they had mocked him, they stripped him of the cloak, dressed him in his own clothes, and led him off to crucify him.

MATTHEW 27:29–31

Imagine how Jesus felt being adored one day and crucified the next. Perhaps you have felt cherished by your spouse one day and then victimized the next. Maybe there were outside elements beyond your control that were distressing to your marriage. Whether you struggle with infertility, illness, or financial hardships, these matters can be out of your realm to fix. Trust that God has a wonderful plan for you; while you may not understand it you can at least accept that these difficulties have a purpose in your life. Cling to hope that your struggles will not last forever and that God is with you throughout it all.

Ponder what other reasons could have caused your spouse to act miserably toward you. Maybe he or she had a bad day, and you suffered the brunt of misdirected anger. Instead of retaliating, offer a prayer and a warm embrace. It's possible your spouse needs your love, grace, and flexibility more than ever. Your partner could need space to sort out what is troubling him or her. Reassure your spouse that you are committed to your relationship and are willing to work it out. If your marriage feels like one big headache, take a deep breath, relax, and remember that God will not abandon you during this troubling time. Let your partner know that when the time is right, you are there to listen and be supportive.

Whenever you notice tension building, think of Jesus having a crown of thorns crushed over his head and offer a prayer of thanksgiving for the sacrifices Christ made. Whatever is holding your relationship in gridlock, let go and let Jesus take over. Ask him to bring the right people into your life to help you through your difficulty.

Dear Lord, master of the universe, take my pain. If you want me to carry it, give me the strength to endure and not become embittered by it. Thank you for lighting my path, showing me the way, and enabling me to have a respectable life. Give my spouse the courage and power to work out the difficulties that stress our relationship. Help me, Lord. I love you, sweet Jesus. Amen.

March 25

As they were going out, they met a Cyrenian named Simon; this man they pressed into service to carry his cross. And when they came to a place called Golgotha (which means Place of the Skull), they gave Jesus wine to drink mixed with gall. But when he had tasted it, he refused to drink.

MATTHEW 27:32–34

Sometimes certain events of life can seem unfair. You may have felt ridiculed, humiliated, terrified, or sullied. But none of it can compare to dragging your cross across town and then being crucified on it. What cross have you been carrying throughout your marriage? What has caused your pain and sadness?

Perhaps you have been unfaithful to your partner emotionally or physically. Perhaps a demanding job and busy schedules distance you from your spouse. Maybe you have drifted away from your partner by not sharing your thoughts, feelings, and emotions. The detachment sets the stage for an emotional affair. It begins innocently as a friendship with someone of the opposite sex, but it feels more like an intimate companionship. It excludes physical intimacy but develops an emotional closeness. If you rationalize that you're "just friends," you might be in trouble. If you daydream about this friend, look forward to seeing this person, and share personal feelings and problems, you quite possibly could be in an affair of the heart. If you believe he or she is more understanding than your spouse, if you keep secrets, exchange gifts, or spend time alone, this person has become your primary emotional confidant.

Ultimately an emotional affair creates emotional distance in your marriage. Instead of developing bonds with a new friend, reinforce your marriage bonds. If you would be embarrassed if your spouse knew about the interactions between you and the "friend," it's time to stop the affair and channel your energy back into your marriage. Nurture your relationship with your spouse the way you used to. Address the issues that caused you to go astray and ask God to keep you strong as you journey onward with your spouse. When Jesus hung on the cross, he forgave those who tortured him. Can you be forgiving? Perhaps during Lent you can hold up a cross because God conquered it. Give yourself the gift of reconciliation—a holy sacrament that can lift you up and set you back on track.

Dear Lord, shine your tender mercies on me. Lift me up, Lord, to that healing place. Fill me with your divine grace to allow me to radiate your love to [*name*]. Let me be an extension of your goodness. Amen.

March 26

*After they had crucified him, they divided his garments by casting lots;
then they sat down and kept watch over him there. And they placed over
his head the written charge against him: This is Jesus, the King of the Jews.*

MATTHEW 27:35–37

When you ponder the crucifixion of Jesus Christ, what emotions come to you? Perhaps you have feelings of profound sadness that something so gruesome happened to the Son of God. Yet woven into that same sadness is a thread of joy knowing the Holy Father sent his only begotten son to be crucified for your sins to ensure eternal happiness in heaven.

Therefore, can you find a hint of happiness hidden in the tribulations of your marriage? Maybe you can find happiness in the children you share, the smiles you wear, or the burdens you bear. Can you find solace in sharing responsibilities in the marital problems with your spouse? You are both in the relationship together taking ownership of your half of the good and bad. At least you are not carrying the entire weight alone; you divide that encumbrance equally with your spouse. Two is stronger than one. Therefore, celebrate that together you can pool your resources to resolve your difficulties.

Dilemmas make you stronger; they force you to think abstractly and respond creatively. Quandaries enable you to become more resourceful, to act more courageously, and pray more wholeheartedly. God will not abandon you throughout your struggles. He will safeguard you as you walk through raging fires and torrential storms. He will see you through it on his terms, not yours. When you suffer, you want the pain to end quickly. But God has a purpose for it: to build you up for something yet to come, to take you to a new place where he wants you to be, or something unimaginable that you cannot fathom. The one thing you must hold onto is trust in God even if it seems impossible, for nothing is impossible with God.

As a woman endures intense labor pains, she knows there will be joy in the child she gives birth to. If difficulties at work are spilling into your marriage or if extenuating circumstances of a friendship are gnawing into your marriage, step away from them and focus on fortifying your relationship with God and your spouse. If you look hard enough, you will find the love you are seeking.

Dear Lord, warm me with your love; empower me through the Holy Spirit that dwells within me to truly experience the bliss you have knitted into my life. Though I cannot see it, touch it, or feel it, I know it is there, hidden in my mixed up world. Remove the blinders from my eyes and open my heart to feel, to trust, and love. Amen.

March 27

So be imitators of God, as beloved children, and live in love,
as Christ loved us and handed himself over for us
as a sacrificial offering to God for a fragrant aroma.

EPHESIANS 5:1–2

God wants your life to be controlled by love, the same way that Christ loved us and gave his life for us. In life, sacrifices may need to be made. It could be a financial sacrifice or letting go of dreams or unrealistic expectations. Ponder where these dreams originated from to determine if they are realistic.

Question if they formed in childhood as you observed your parent's marriage, if they are cultural, or from movies, television shows, or books. Contemplate if you expect your spouse to know intuitively and to the heal wounds you may not even be aware of. It is not fair to expect your spouse to live up to the imaginary fantasies you created and have not articulated. You could face disappointment upon realizing that you are holding your spouse to an impossible standard, especially because he or she is not a mind reader and cannot mysteriously create the picture-perfect marriage you are envisioning.

Discuss your expectations with your spouse and agree which ones you can meet and have fulfilled. Embrace the challenge to meet some of your spouse's needs, even if it wasn't what you were imagining. Use it as a foundation of new personal and marital growth. It could be amusing to establish new routines ranging from when you will pray individually or as a couple to who will pay the bills and make financial investments for your future.

This could springboard into a more profound stage of your relationship: deciding when to begin a family, buy a home, manage an illness, or prepare for the empty-nest period of your lives together. By building the blocks of a solid foundation to your marriage through discovery of realistic expectations, you will reveal what's really important and what you can let go of. The process of letting go might be challenging. Think of how badly Jesus wanted to let go of his suffering and climb down off his cross, but he endured his horrendous suffering because of his unwavering love. Recall Jesus's crucifixion the next time you make a sacrifice dealing with unrealistic expectations in your marriage. What unrealistic expectation will you let go of?

Dear Lord, teach me how to be more patient in enduring sacrifices in my marriage. Help me to find the love that you put in my life, dear Lord. Let me fixate on the goodness that is present so I don't get derailed by petty grievances. You keep the embers of love glowing in my heart. Amen.

March 28

When Simon Peter arrived after him, he went into the tomb and
saw the burial cloths there....Then the other disciple also went in,
the one who had arrived at the tomb first, and he saw and believed.

JOHN 20:6–8

The concept of Jesus's resurrection is not easy to grasp, yet you believe. You do not have to actually experience it to understand, accept, and trust. You cannot see or feel your marriage bonds, yet you trust in the alliance of your union. You have pictures and symbols of your wedding but the authentic pledge is something you cannot see, but still you trust and honor it. How can you continue to depend on your marriage vows in the midst of everyday chaotic life? In a word: trust.

Couples who focus on building trust in a marriage are more likely to have a prosperous life together. Outside extraneous forces tug at marital bonds threatening discombobulation and havoc; couples need to stay focused on what really matters: each other. But how can you do that when trust is broken? Prayer can help. Open the pages of the Bible and spend some quality time deepening your faith with Christ while developing your relationship with your spouse. Perhaps you could read passages together and reflect on them.

Trust is earned slowly, mutually, and gradually through a series of small tests managing risk. It sounds complicated, calculated, and cautious, when it is in reality a process that requires a lot of time, patience, love, and understanding. When a spouse feels trust has been betrayed, disappointment, heartache, and anger can set in. You may question what else in your relationship was untrue. You may fear being hurt again, perhaps in the process of rebuilding trust with your spouse by climbing the "ladder of trust."

The injured person might feel guarded while moving out of a mistrust phase into being polite and civil toward his or her spouse, while the "wrongdoer" works toward rebuilding trustworthiness by offering respect and courteous treatment. To move up to attain a status comparable to a good friend, you need to feel more comfortable, confidant, and true to yourself. Your spouse would be more personal with committed unconditional acceptance, where your trust will be earned. If you don't have trust in your marriage, can you work through this model to gain it back?

Dear Lord, even though I do not see you, I know you are there willing
to love me with whatever weaknesses I have. Help me, Lord, to gain
trust back into my marriage. Amen.

March 29

Would he not rather say to him, 'Prepare something for me to eat.
Put on your apron and wait on me while I eat and drink. You may
eat and drink when I am finished'? Is he grateful to that servant
because he did what was commanded? So should it be with you.
When you have done all you have been commanded, say, 'We are
unprofitable servants; we have done what we were obliged to do.'"

LUKE 17:8–10

Many Eastern Orthodox Christians dye Easter eggs red, symbolic of Christ's sacrificed bloodshed at his crucifixion and the empty tomb of Jesus. Often in a marriage, one person does something without understanding the reason behind why it is done one way. Consider if you do that in your relationship. Do you take the easiest route or the path of least resistance? Is it possible that you are the more irresponsible partner in your marriage? If you are "helping" by avoiding responsibility, perhaps you can become more responsible for yourself and the choices you make. How can you be more accountable for your own feelings? Maybe you can turn over a new leaf and do more to attain self-responsibility in your home and personal life. Invoke the Holy Spirit to direct your energies in positive ways to be more liable.

Resentment can tell us what is or is not taking place in your relationship. Perhaps you feel like you have been enabling your spouse to be emotionally or physically absent by picking up the slack too often. If this flippancy reoccurs in your marriage, resentment will inevitably build. Love cannot thrive where there is irresponsibility and resentment. Marriage is built on mutual respect. One way to gain that is by holding each other accountable for the agreements you make. If you feel as though you have been doing too much, give the problem back to your spouse and do less. This will help your partner stop avoiding responsibilities. Take responsibility for yourself, your own choices, and feelings. How will you do your part to create a mutually responsible marriage?

Dear Lord, thank you for surrounding me with the shield of your love and protection. Enable me to accept more responsibility in my life and marriage. Help me to identify exactly how to be resilient while being accountable. Guide me, Lord, and show me what I need to do to keep my marriage thriving. Invigorate my spirit and breathe new life in me. I depend on you, Divine Master, to point me in the right direction and keep me in sync with your grace, mercy, and never-ending love. Amen.

March 30

*On entering the tomb they saw a young man sitting on the right side,
clothed in a white robe, and they were utterly amazed.
He said to them, "Do not be amazed! You seek Jesus of Nazareth,
the crucified. He has been raised; he is not here."*
MARK 16:5–6).

Easter rejoices in the resurrection of Jesus with a complicated history that can persuade people to reach different conclusions. Motley-colored eggs, jelly beans, and chocolate rabbits should not detract from the central meaning of the Easter celebration: that Jesus Christ has risen from the dead. What tugs at your relationship vexing you to undermine the fundamental aspects of your marriage?

Maybe it is the way you listen to your spouse. Just because you are present while he or she speaks doesn't mean your mind is attentive to what is being said. When your partner speaks, are there distractions? Is the TV on? Perhaps you are preoccupied with the newspaper or social networking sites. Do you daydream, plan a rebuttal, or do you completely tune out your spouse? Resist the urge to interrupt once your spouse begins talking. Allow your mate to express his or her feelings and emotions completely.

Communication is key in maintaining a good relationship; listening is only half of the equation. Ask the Holy Spirit to help you improve your listening techniques when you are in the midst of a conversation with your spouse. Maybe you are afraid of the message your partner will deliver because it might cause you to question your own strengths or weaknesses. Give your vulnerabilities to the Lord while you listen with an open mind to what your spouse has to say. He or she might be opening the door to a new or better path for you to travel.

Focus on your partner's face, mouth, eyes, and body stance. Think about what your mate's body language is conveying. Give your undivided attention and try to name the emotions your spouse feels. Check to ensure you got the message correctly. That will speaks volumes to your spouse on how much you care. For example you could say, "You seem really frustrated. What can I do to help?"

Dear Lord, open my ears to allow me to hear. Open my heart to allow me to listen. Open my mind to allow me to understand. Teach me to be sympathetic while I receive my spouse's words. Enlighten me to respond in a loving and charitable way. You gave me the skills to communicate, help me to use them wisely to the best of my abilities. You are my saving Lord and I love, honor, and respect you. Amen.

March 31

*We impose these commandments on ourselves: to give a third of a shekel
each year for the service of the house of our God, for the showbread,
the daily grain offering, the daily burnt offering, for the sabbaths,
new moons, and festivals, for the holy offerings and sin offerings to
make atonement for Israel, for every service of the house of our God.*

NEHEMIAH 10:33–34

If you spot a penny on the ground, would you pick it up? Albeit one cent is
an insignificant amount of money, it is worth something monetarily, and
the word "God" is written on it. If you picked up every penny you found,
you won't achieve great wealth. However, if you smiled and said a prayer for
your marriage, you could have a richer union. Perhaps if a "penny for your
thoughts" were all positive ones earmarked for your partner, you might be
able to create enough momentum to make a difference in his or her attitude.

Staying positive can be bewildering when things aren't going well at
home. Begin by expressing gratitude for all the blessings that God has given
to you over the years. Recalling these gifts might improve your state of mind
enough to cultivate more positive attitudes. Think about the food you have
to eat, the clothes you have to wear, the home you live in, the friendships you
value, and the medical care that is available to you. Think about the books
you can read and the ability to express your thoughts, desires, and emotions.
Be thankful to your spouse for the kindnesses shown to you. Words of thanks
are always appreciated and will make you both feel good.

Try volunteering in your community or church. Often, when you extend yourself in a charitable way, whatever you give, you receive twofold.
Perhaps you could do something nice for your spouse: fill up his or her gas
tank, make their lunch, or buy a favored snack. It's possible that striving to
put your spouse in a good mood will also put you in a much better mood. If
you put a price tag on your spouse's outlook, how much is it worth? Prayers
can move mountains; therefore, say one for him or her whenever you see a
coin on the ground. It might be a sign from God that he or she needs your
prayers, positive thoughts, and kindnesses.

Dear Lord, thank you for [*name*] and our life together. Thank you
for the gifts you have blessed me so abundantly with: the ones I can
see and those I can feel. Let me pray constantly in your mercy, grace,
and love. Amen.

April 1

Elijah approached all the people and said, "How long will you straddle the issue? If the LORD is God, follow him; if Baal, follow him." But the people did not answer him...."Answer me, LORD! Answer me, that this people may know that you, LORD, are God and that you have turned their hearts backs to you."

1 KINGS 18:21, 37

Each year, two adorable house finches instinctively return to the same arborvitae tree to produce a nest full of chicks. It's understandable why they return to what they know. Sometimes we do that, too, out of habit, because it's easy or familiar when handling a situation, but it doesn't always yield good results. Rote responses don't always work; sometimes it's important to bend and alter what is said or done to achieve better outcomes. Is there a routine you might vary, or a mundane behavior that you should change? Perhaps if you step away from an issue that you are struggling with, God can enlighten you to see it or approach it differently.

If you feel your relationship is stuck in a rut or if you are drifting away from your partner, take the time to reunite. You can redirect your marriage back on track by following a few simple rules. When you eat meals together, have the TV off, resist the urge to answer text messages, and don't answer the phone when it rings. Instead, use dinner time to reconnect with your mate by inquiring about his or her day. Use this time to make plans to do enjoyable things together. Maybe you can do something new and exciting such as take a cooking or painting class, learn a new language, climb a mountain, do yoga, or attend Bible study classes at your church.

Remember that you married your loved one because you enjoyed spending time together. Don't allow household chores to get in the way of your quality time. Perhaps you might consider cutting back on the overtime you spend working or the time you spend with other friends to ensure you have adequate time for dates with your partner. Maybe you could schedule a romantic weekend away. If money is tight, it might be plausible to designate one room in your home as a safe haven where you can escape the rigmarole to enjoy the tranquility of each other's company. It would also allow you a place to meditate and pray together. What measures will you take to ensure you and your spouse have quality time together today?

Dear Lord, I turn to you for direction. Help me to reunite with [*name*] and find the love that I know exists between us. Help me to fan the embers of our love and burn with the passion that we once shared. Bless the actions that I take; guide the steps that I make. Grant me the wisdom to listen to you. Amen.

April 2

Send forth your bread upon the face of the waters;
after a long time you may find it again.

ECCLESIASTES 11:1

When a friend found fifty dollars, he instinctively gave it to church. His wife lamented over the bills that were due, but he reassured her that they would be okay because God would provide. He wasn't surprised when a fifty dollar rebate arrived in the mail later that week. Likewise, in marriage, we reap what we sow; therefore, it's prudent to contemplate ways to send out good intentions and positive vibes to your spouse. Contemplate ways that you can give to your mate without expectations of reparations. Consider what small, random acts of kindness you can show to your partner.

Consider that a kind word promotes confidence in your spouse. Therefore, try to make the messages you deliver kind and thoughtful because ultimately your spouse will exude with self-assurance. Would it be possible to say, "I love you" after everything you say to your spouse today? For example, "Thank you for emptying the dishwasher. I love you," or "The television is a little loud; could you turn it down? I love you." Try positive experiments to see how your spouse responds, because kindnesses create love.

In marriage, kindness is also demonstrated through generous acts and thoughtful deeds. Love is a choice you can make by showing it freely in what you do. Maybe you could set the table and center lit candles to transform an ordinary dinner into one featuring soft conversation, loving expressions, and compliments. You might want to do the dishes, brew a pot of tea, and serve your spouse to make him or her feel special. Your marriage will be strengthened when you and your mate treat each other with love, understanding, dignity, and respect. Ponder how you can convey tenderness and concern for your spouse that will be delightful for him or her.

Try putting your spouse's needs before your own, building a relationship of mutual trust and respect, and not being rude. Even if there are no immediate outward signs of appreciation, attempt to give bigger and better gifts to your spouse. Eventually, he or she will notice. Think of something wonderful that you can do today to please your spouse.

Dear Lord, help me to reach beyond myself to build up my spouse in a big and beautiful way. Teach me how to give without the expectation of receiving. Enable me to trust in your goodness and love that everything I do for [name] will fill his or her heart with delight and that joy will enlighten my heart as well. Amen.

April 3

Then the LORD will guide you always and satisfy your thirst
in parched places, will give strength to your bones And you shall be
like a watered garden, like a flowing spring whose waters never fail.
ISAIAH 58:11

Gardeners pull weeds from their beloved flower beds attempting to keep them pristine. Yet within a day or two, the ugly weeds return. The roots must be dug out, the soil treated with poisons, and a barrier laid to prevent weeds from returning, requiring much hard work and time. What preventative measures have you taken to ensure nothing dreadful grows in your marriage?

Whatever you are unhappy with in your life could be a result of a bad habit compounded over time. If you are overweight, it could be a result of the bad habit that you overate and didn't exercise. If you are in debt, it's a result of the bad habit of overspending. A bad habit is like a cancer with the potential to spread throughout your life. The differences in successful marriages from failures are successful habits. Therefore, start creating good habits in your marriage. Do you have date nights or do you work too many hours? To instill a good habit, cut back the overtime and start planning dates. Not every date has to be dinner or a movie. A date can be a long walk, coffee at a bistro, or stargazing. Try to set the precedence for a date each week to ensure only goodness grows in your marriage. Weeds might creep in, but if you stay on top of it, it will be easier to tackle.

Sometimes bad habits are so ingrained into you that you move through them without realizing what you are doing. Interjecting old patterns frees a space for something better. One way to interrupt your pattern is to shock yourself with something that makes you laugh or interrupt it through some physical action. For example, I hung a crucifix over my treadmill to remind me not to get off of it until the timer rang. If Jesus couldn't get off the cross, that impetus pushed me to keep working out even when I wanted to quit. Are you willing to expend the time and energy to keep your relationship pleasing, lovely, and beautiful? Ponder what you can do to noticeably improve your relationship.

Dear Lord, teach me how to be more loving, even when I don't feel like it or have time for it. Please, Lord, don't let anything foul take root and grow in my marriage. Let me cultivate a wholesome relationship through planning and paying diligence to keep it worthy. I ask this in your sweet and holy name. Amen.

April 4

He arose, paced up and down the room, and then once more stretched himself over him, and the boy sneezed seven times and opened his eyes.

2 KINGS 4:35

Pollen sails through the air as the flowers bloom each spring. The higher the pollen count, the more people will suffer with allergies. Even though we can't see pollen, it's there. With a warm breeze, it slips through the screens on the windows and forms a film on everything inside the house. Allergy sufferers take precautionary measures to keep the inside of their homes clean. They might keep their windows closed and opt for air conditioning, or they may take allergy medication so they don't sneeze constantly, have watery, itchy eyes, or stuffed noses. What counteractive steps do you take to keep your marriage well and free from allergens?

Do you invite trouble into your relationship by allowing intruders to invade your home through your computer, TV, or text messaging? Spending too much time on the computer can put stress on your marriage. Whether it's through computer games, social networking sites, or a personal blog, the Internet opens a window into a fantasy world that some people escape to or can get lost in. Addictive drugs produce the same effect, which stimulates a "reward trail" in the brain that releases dopamine, the brain's "feel-good" chemical. Brain-imaging studies show the same part of the brain linked with drug addiction lights up with computer use. To help limit your time with technology, set an alarm clock, allowing only thirty minutes of computer time followed by equal amounts of time with your spouse doing something pleasurable together from reading quietly, chatting over a cup of coffee, or going on a date. Invest your time wisely by setting aside time for prayer and soulful meditation.

Perhaps you spend too much time socializing with coworkers, neighbors, or friends. Redirect your focus back to your marriage, making it a priority. Remember that your spouse is committed to you for life and will always have your back. It's best to balance your time wisely between friends, technology, and your spouse. Supercharge your relationship with prayer. Be still with your thoughts and allow the quiet to quell your trepidations. Go for a walk and gaze at the trees that surround you; God made them for your enjoyment. How will you make your spouse a priority over computer time and socializing with friends?

Dear Lord, teach me to monitor my computer time and the hours spent socializing with friends. Wash over me with your gentle wealth of knowledge and enlighten me. Keep me on the path of righteousness and allow me to enjoy the journey with [*name*]. Fill our hearts with the happiness we once knew and trusted in. Amen.

April 5

I set my bow in the clouds to serve as a sign of the covenant between me and the earth. When I bring clouds over the earth, and the bow appears in the clouds, I will remember my covenant between me and you and every living creature—every mortal being—so that the waters will never again become a flood to destroy every mortal being. When the bow appears in the clouds, I will see it and remember the everlasting covenant between God and every living creature—every mortal being that is on earth.

GENESIS 9:13–16

A rainbow is an optical phenomenon caused by the reflection of light in water droplets in the Earth's atmosphere taking the form of a multicolored arc consisting of red, orange, yellow, green, blue, indigo, and violet. Do you show your true colors to your spouse?

When you show your true colors, you are not pretending to be something you're not. God knows the real you; therefore, be genuinely the person he created you to be. Believe that you are unique and precious because God formed you with his own hand, in his image, and he doesn't make mistakes. You are God's masterpiece. Don't compare yourself with other people. Instead, celebrate who you are and who you are becoming in God's gracious love. Celebrate your God-given talents and your potential, not your limitations. Study your weaknesses so that you can develop them into strengths.

Most people show their true colors during periods of difficulty. What are your relationship struggles? Perhaps you are frustrated by trying to change your spouse. Instead, focus on self-change. Work on becoming the best version of yourself. Maybe you always need to be right. Ask yourself if the need to be right is greater than your need for marital bliss. Sometimes it's best to let the little things go. In the scheme of things, ponder if what is annoying you really matters. If it is, speak gently and kindly to your spouse. However, if it is trivial, forget having the last word. Do you really want to be a know-it-all forever? Admit when you make a mistake or that you don't have all the answers. All relationships endure in a state of flux with highs and lows. If your marriage is in a slump, what can you do to change that? Prayer is the best medicine for whatever is ailing your marriage. Set your sights on the Lord; he won't forsake you.

Dear Lord, thank you for the reminders to stay focused on you. Grant me the endurance to forge on in my relationship no matter how difficult it gets, I know you are with me, keeping me on the straight path. Lift up my marriage, Lord, the way the flowers grow after the spring showers. Strengthen me to withstand the rain so I can see the rainbow and remember your promise. Amen.

April 6

Suddenly a violent storm came up on the sea, so that the boat
was being swamped by waves; but he was asleep. They came and
woke him, saying, "Lord, save us! We are perishing!" He said to them,
"Why are you terrified, O you of little faith?" Then he got up,
rebuked the winds and the sea, and there was great calm.

MATTHEW 8:24–26

Have problems in your marriage become so difficult to manage that you feel like the disciples in the storm? When you are faced with a marital dilemma, don't automatically give in to your spouse because you are afraid that a fight will ensue. You could harbor resentment over it, exacerbating the problem. Don't run away from it or ignore it, hoping the problem will go away. It might go away temporarily, but eventually it will return in one form another. Nor should you assert any authority to gain control of the situation to get your own way. It's best to address the issue when it occurs in a calm and loving manner.

Define the problem and what is overwhelming about it. Write it down on paper. Sometimes in defining the problem, you might realize there really isn't a problem after all, just a minor misunderstanding. Defining and discussing it might resolve it or you might learn that the real problem is something altogether different than what you originally thought. Stick to the topic, and don't accuse your spouse of always behaving a certain way. Instead, build up your spouse with positive comments. For example, say "We are intelligent; we can figure this out by working together as a team." Discuss your beliefs, feelings, and expectations openly. Don't misconstrue your spouse's thoughts from his or her behavior. Instead, be direct with questions while being compassionate.

Contemplate several solutions to resolve them and draft a list of pros and cons for each, regardless of feasibility. Often seeing them on paper gives you something tangible to work with. Settling disputes requires much thought, energy, and time. Be mindful of the time you have devoted to resolving your conflict. You might need to take a break to eat or rest. Sometimes stepping away from a problem temporarily by taking a walk will revitalize you with new ideas or strategies that you hadn't considered. If bedtime approaches, you might need to set the matter aside until the next day when you are refreshed.

Pray on disputes, asking God to empower you with the wisdom to tackle each one. Like the disciples in the boat, Jesus won't let you drown in a sea of discontentment. Call out, be still, and listen for his voice.

Dear Lord, sometimes I forget that you are sailing with me and you will not let me drown. Thank you for keeping me buoyant throughout my difficulties. You are at the helm. Amen.

April 7

Trust in the LORD with all your heart, on your own intelligence do not rely;
In all your ways be mindful of him, and he will make straight your paths.

PROVERBS 3:5–6

When you contemplate everything you must do in your life, and you question how you will possibly accomplish everything, trust that you can do anything with God in your life. Instead of depending on your own capabilities or your spouse for help, rely solely on God—that his divine wisdom and power can elevate you to do unimaginable things. Trust with all of your heart even if it is beyond your comprehension. Let God lead you to where you to where he means for you to be even it seems impossible, for nothing is truly impossible with God.

Critics say marriages are in deep trouble in America, with more couples divorcing than reconciling their differences. Do not even consider divorce. Remember that God brought you together for a reason. You might not grasp what his purpose is, but by trusting in God's plan, someday you will understand when he shows you the bigger picture. Together you can work through your differences in God's love by depending on faith, trust, hope, and love.

Don't get derailed by statistics, the critics, or what your neighbors are doing. Focus on your own marriage and your faith in God that he will see you through your difficulties no matter how big or awful they seem. Don't replay old arguments or resurrect old hurts because that might blow them out of proportion and make you lose perspective on saving your relationship. Instead, assess all the options you have for dealing with your troubles. Maybe it's time to consult with your parish priest. He might be able to recommend a marriage counselor, support group, or prayer group. Maybe he can recommend books that can help you. Maybe you could attend adoration or penance services to receive the sacrament of reconciliation.

Try to remember that most marriages aren't perfect. Each person brings their own philosophies, morals, beliefs, and personal history into the relationship, which may not match their partner's. Differences are not always bad; they can complement one another, allowing each other to understand, respect, and accept differing views. Some of the differences that you once valued can eventually irritate you and cause stress, worry, or fear. Problems if left alone could fester and lead to physical or psychological problems, such as depression. Give your worries to God and trust that he will point you in the right direction. How will you rely on God subliminally today?

Dear Lord, help me to trust implicitly in you today. Let me lean on your understanding and be carried through your wisdom. Take my hand and show the way. I will follow where you lead me. Amen.

April 8

As the earth brings forth its shoots, and a garden makes its seeds spring up,
*So will the Lord G*OD *make justice spring up, and praise before all the nations.*
ISAIAH 61:11

The fresh air smells delightful in the springtime. When the morning chill lingers, the winds blow a fresh and familiar scent that seems to hug the earth and cling to our clothes and hair. When you smell spring in the air, it can make you feel happy remembering past feelings of love. Ponder ways you can recapture it and keep love lingering in your life.

Perhaps you could play favorite music from your dating days or travel back to your old stomping grounds. If that is not plausible, maybe you could have fun together the way you did when you were dating, through laughter, talking, and making an effort to please each other. Does your spouse know your desires and do you know his or hers? There might be times when you have to tell your partner what you want. It's best to be clear, specific, direct, and respectful.

To develop and enhance your relationship, express wishes in a loving way so they don't sound like demands. If your yearnings sound like ultimatums, your partner's guard could go up and it eliminates having your desires met. Remember the tone Jesus used when he spoke to people. Many couples find it difficult to ask about having a specific need met because of embarrassment, shyness, or a fear of rejection. However, within the sanctity of marriage, it would seem natural and safe for you to be able to reveal your deepest desires to your spouse.

Try to make your request reasonable. For example, instead of asking for a two-week vacation in France, suggest getting away for the weekend. Don't bombard your spouse with myriad reasons; pick one that will benefit one of you. For example, "You've been working nonstop; a getaway would help you recharge." Remember that you are worth what you are asking for. Make an honest self-evaluation by mentally organizing your thoughts beforehand so you're prepared. Contemplate the best time to make your request, smile, and be nice when asking. It is reasonable to give your spouse a way out if he or she is unable to meet your request, and don't sulk if you don't get your way. You will have other opportunities for requests. The effort you expended was not done in vain: your spouse knows your desires, and you can hope that someday he or she will fulfill them. What will you ask your spouse for today?

Dear Lord, grant me the grace to use unpretentious words to persevere when I feel unsure of myself. Enable me to recapture the passion I once felt with [*name*]. Enable me to rekindle the admirations you gave to us long ago. Amen.

April 9

So for one who knows the right thing to do and does not do it, it is a sin.

JAMES 4:17

Many people dye their hair to cover the grey. Some don't want to see the reminder of their impending old age. What are you trying to conceal in your marriage? Do you harbor feelings of resentment? Whenever you feel as though you have been treated unfairly or misjudged, you experience a strong emotional reaction. The unspoken emotions felt from your spouse's actions can transform into resentment if not released in a healthy, effective, and timely way.

Resentment thrives internally, feeding off negative feelings and emotions, which become stronger if left ignored. It can prevent you from visualizing the world from a healthy perspective. If left unresolved, resentment can be consuming and can fuel anger. Internalized anger is a ticking time bomb that can lead to abusive or self-destructive behavior.

If you are experiencing feelings of resentment, don't deny the truth. Instead, allow yourself to feel your emotions, which will cleanse you from negativity that you might be subconsciously holding on to. If your spouse hurts you, intentionally or accidentally, express your pain in a healthy manner, which enables you to let go and move onward. It requires courage to communicate your pain to your spouse because you expose your vulnerability. In doing this, you step outside your comfort zone to allow for a growth opportunity. This will free you from resentment, which will enable you to live a truthful life and help your marriage.

Forgiving is one of the greatest gifts you can give yourself because it frees you from resentments. Forgiveness destroys anger. If you can forgive, it prevents your past from controlling your future. Accept your past mistakes because it made you the person you are today. Embrace forgiveness because then resentment evaporates. You cannot control what your spouse does, but you can control how you react.

Do you feel like you are constantly picking up after your spouse? Is your partner disorganized or do you feel responsible for cleaning up his or her messes? When you notice embitterment building, it means you are doing too much, and you need to give the problems back to your partner in a kind and gentle way. In these instances you need to do less. Help your mate accept responsibility through encouraging words. Focus on taking care of yourself. Invoke the Holy Spirit to fill you with grace while you work through these issues.

Dear Lord, my heart longs to hear your voice. Teach me to be more loving, kind, and forgiving. Amen.

April 10

"Ask and it will be given to you; seek and you will find;
knock and the door will be opened to you.
For everyone who asks, receives; and the one who seeks, finds;
and to the one who knocks, the door will be opened."

MATTHEW 7:7–8

Sometimes it's difficult to ask for what you want when you have myriad explanations to remain silent. Maybe you are embarrassed or feel uncomfortable asking for something because you're not exactly sure what you want. Possibly you hope that your spouse is a mind reader. You could subconsciously believe that you shouldn't have to ask, or that it's demeaning to have to ask for something, so if you must ask, then your spouse's response becomes worthless. Maybe you don't know how to ask or are afraid of the response you will hear. You could be afraid of how your spouse will react to your request, or you incorrectly convince yourself you won't get what you want.

Perhaps you thought you asked, but the methods you chose weren't successful. You could be an indirect communicator hinting at what you want, then end up disappointed. Maybe you believe that asking for what you want is selfish, or you consider your needs to be inferior to your spouse's, so you remain silent and afraid of appearing selfish. You could be paralyzed with fear unable to ask the questions that confuse you. But to move forward, you must reach down and muster up the courage to ask because it could be the only way to get to the bottom of your problem.

Jesus says to ask and you will receive. Be nice, be honest, and ask kindly with a smile. Ask God to form the words you use. Perhaps you need to pray on the request you want to make of your spouse. Pray without ceasing. Maybe you need to alter the way you speak to your spouse in general. When was the last time you acknowledged your spouse for something he or she did? Does your spouse feel appreciated? Try affirming your spouse in front of friends or family when he or she is present. Do you share credit with your spouse for your accomplishments? Tell your children how wonderful their mother or father is. This will go a long way in laying the groundwork for a more loving relationship when you make a request of your spouse. What changes will you make today?

Dear Lord, Put the right words in my mind and in my heart so that I use them wisely with my spouse. Give me the courage to ask for things without worry, trepidation, or reprisals. Let me create an amicable foundation built on your love. I ask this of you, Lord. Amen.

April 11

"Now go, I will assist you in speaking and teach you what you are to say."
EXODUS 4:12

It's distracting to watch a TV show where the actor's voices aren't aligned to the movements of their mouths. It can be so annoying that viewers change the channel. Do you talk to your spouse on the right channel or do you long for quality conversations with your spouse where you share your thoughts and listen compassionately? Communication is vital to the success of any marriage. It's a complicated skill that requires both speaking truthfully and listening intently.

When you speak to your spouse, be mindfulness of your emotions, hopes, and desires. Read your spouse by sensing the mood, attitude, and concerns, knowing that your goal is to understand and meet your partner's needs and expectations. Your spouse will open up to you if he or she trusts you. Your trust can be earned through the right behaviors.

Communicate using simple and concise statements instead of complicated and confusing words. Focus on what you can contribute to your spouse instead of what you can get. Concentrate on your spouse's wants, needs, and desires with an open mind. Your goal is to understand what's on your spouse's mind. Try to be genuinely curious and interested. Consider substituting your ego with empathy because it may convert anger into respect and doubt into trust.

When you speak to your spouse, don't try to convert or convince his or her ideas or opinions to match yours. Instead, know what you're talking about because what you say matters to your partner. Be sure you are logical, giving specific, consistent, clear, and accurate information. Communication with your spouse is about trying to meet his or her needs, understanding their concerns, and adding value to your relationship.

Sometimes, your spouse only needs to "vent" his or her feelings. Do you offer your mate a shoulder to cry on with sympathy or do you jump in with ideas to fix problems? It is possible that your spouse wants to use you as a sounding board. First ask if your opinion is wanted before giving it. Perhaps your spouse needs affirmation of your love and devotion as he or she works through a particular difficulty. Think of how Jesus would act in this situation.

Dear Lord, expand my mind and tell me what to say, think, and do. I want to please my spouse and be a loving partner especially in times of difficulty. Enable me to be a sympathetic listener to [*name*] and meet his or her needs. Make my arms strong enough to hold him or her and to feel my affections and love. I ask this in your holy name. Amen.

April 12

*For he has faithfully given you the early rain, sending rain
down on you, the early and the late rains as before.*

JOEL 2:23

In the saying "April showers bring May flowers," there is a positive spin on
rain, which could be considered negative. How can you be more positive
in your marriage? Consider choosing to be positive. If you find yourself in
a bad situation, look for the good in it. Something good comes out of every
bad situation. If you struggle to see the good, remember that it may not be
evident right away. God might reveal the purpose later and you will have to
be patient. God has a purpose for everything he does. You might not understand it, but at least take comfort that the unpleasant situation you might
find yourself in has a reason and God will see you through it.

Try to think more positively in general and reinforce these thoughts
with positive behaviors. The more you practice being positive, the better
you become. Start by appreciating yourself, who you are and who you strive
to be: a better Christian and a better spouse. You are off to a great start by
remembering that God created you in his image: perfect. Remember all of
the wonderful attributes about yourself; they are gifts from God.

You also need to be positive with your spouse by being nice. If your spouse
is feeling down, do what you can to cheer him or her up. Maybe you could
send flowers, bake his or her favorite cookies, or write a heartfelt e-mail.
Strive to be encouraging and supportive to your spouse. Perhaps you can
contemplate all of the good attributes your spouse possesses and be thankful
for them. Focus on his or her good qualities. Is your spouse a good friend,
a loyal partner who provides a stable and comfortable home for you? How
can you be more accepting of the rain that sometimes falls in your marriage?
After rain falls, look for the rainbow that God paints across the sky for you
to enjoy; look for the flowers that grow in your relationship.

Remember to strive to be a positive person every day. When you feel
discouraged, remind yourself that it only takes one small step in the right
direction to move toward a positive attitude. Believe in yourself and in God.
He walks this journey with you and he will never lead you astray.

Dear Lord, I am thankful for the rain in my life because it makes me
appreciate the sunshine that much more. Thank you for the hardships
and misfortunes because they make me stronger and more creative to
solve problems. Thank you for some sadness in my life for it makes
me appreciate each smile I see. I love you, Lord, for giving me so many
choices in my life. Amen.

April 13

Let your speech always be gracious, seasoned with salt,
so that you know how you should respond to each one.

COLOSSIANS 4:6

While on a walk, have you heard a tweeting bird and tried to spot it? You might first look up in the sky, then to a tree, scanning the branches before checking another area. Tiny birds aren't easy to find. Sometimes it's hard to find positive attributes in a relationship. It might take a while, but it's worth the effort to identify and acknowledge the decent or admirable characteristics in your spouse.

Let your spouse know how much you appreciate him or her. Perhaps your partner is honest and loyal. Try verbalizing, "I love how trustworthy and dependable you are." That simple sentence could put the extra spring in his or her step and possibly reciprocate thoughtful comments to you fostering a loving camaraderie between you. Remember the Holy Spirit dwells within your spouse; what you say to him or her, you also say to God.

Accept your spouse with an open mind without casting judgments. While this could be challenging for you to do, it is the way you might want to be treated too. Tell your partner why he or she makes a difference in your life, even if it's something as simple as saying, "I adore your smile." Ponder what specialness your spouse has that no one else has and then convey that to him or her. It's important for your spouse to know that he or she makes your life better for sharing it and then thank him or her for being themselves. Treat your spouse with respect for his or her individuality.

Maybe your spouse has unique personality traits. Ponder those that you are proud of or appreciate. Perhaps your spouse excels at multitasking. Let him or her know how much you admire that ability. Contemplate if you could learn that skill from your spouse. God gives you opportunities each day to notice your spouse's gifts and celebrate them. Which of your spouse's talents will you recognize today?

Dear Lord, help me to identify the goodness in my spouse. You made [*name*] unique and I feel blessed that I am able to share my life with him or her. [*name*] adds so much excitement to our marriage and I am grateful for that. Teach me to appreciate, rejoice, and be thankful, for you created my partner magnificently. Don't let me take him or her for granted. I trust in your ways even when I do not understand them. I truly love you, Lord. Amen.

April 14

Hezekiah replied to Isaiah, "The word of the LORD which you have spoken is good." For he thought, "There will be peace and stability in my lifetime."

2 KINGS 20:19

Do a heartfelt introspection to determine what kind of a spouse you are. How you live at home is the true test of your Christianity. When you are at work or socializing with friends, you are on your best behavior. In the privacy of your home your partner knows your vulnerabilities and witnesses them when you are stressed, tired, or hungry. Don't give in to bad temper, laziness, sarcasm, or greediness. Instead, invite God to fill you with peacefulness, love, happiness, tolerance, faithfulness, discipline, and compassion. Contemplate ways you can ward off a bad attitude when you feel one brewing. Consider stepping outside to breath in the fresh air and thanking God for the many gifts he has given to you throughout the day. Imagine how welcoming your home would be to your partner if you could master this.

Try to cultivate a tranquil home by clearing away clutter and designating one TV-free zone for you and your spouse to reconnect in. Maybe you could light scented candles and listen to soft music while you read Holy Scripture or pray the rosary. Hang a cross, holy statues, or pictures of Jesus to remind you that you are loved and cherished by the Almighty. With a special place to pray in your home, you just might be more inclined to pray more frequently, uniting you closer to each other and to God.

Make your home a calm retreat from the stress of the outside world. Create a tranquil atmosphere by decorating the room with colors that are relaxing to you. There are many varieties of CDs of nature sounds such as crashing ocean waves, forest sounds, chirping birds, or chanting monks that you might enjoy listening to. Some people find wind chimes soothing. A small electric waterfall is visually relaxing and the sound of trickling water is peaceful. Aromatherapy could be beneficial for relaxation with scents such as lavender or jasmine. Arrange soft, cushy, chairs or sofas to add to the tranquility in your space. Serenity and stress relief offer health benefits that are your rewards for creating a calm atmosphere in your home. Identify a spot in your house today that you can transform into a stress-free place for you and your spouse to share.

Dear Lord, cool my temper, ease my stress, and fill me with your never ending stream of love. When I feel a warm breeze blow across my face, remind me that it's you. Let me be a conduit of your affection so that I can replenish my spouse when he or she is running on empty. Amen.

April 15

This is why you also pay taxes, for the authorities are ministers of God, devoting themselves to this very thing. Pay to all their dues, taxes to whom taxes are due, toll to whom toll is due, respect to whom respect is due, honor to whom honor is due. Owe nothing to anyone, except to love one another; for the one who loves another has fulfilled the law.

ROMANS 13:6–8

Everyone loathes paying taxes, yet the Bible commands it. When the Bible instructs you to show respect, honor, and love to another, you do it. God wants you to comply, even if there are times when you don't want to. Reflect on the vows you made with your spouse: to honor and love each other in good times or bad, not only when it's convenient.

God also wants you to obey the commandments. Laws were created to establish conformity, a standard of conduct, and keep society running smoothly. Contemplate the rules that you struggle to keep and pray on them. Take your direction from Christ, his teachings, and church, and not from the standards of today's world. It can be challenging to live a Christian lifestyle in a society that at times is abrasive, reckless, and hostile.

Sometimes it is only until after marriage that you begin to realize how different you and your spouse are. You might not truly know yourself until you are married. It might take your partner to help you to see yourself as you really are. Spouses share their burdens with each other hoping to encourage and build up their mate, not try to change the other. When you offer your partner the gift of total acceptance despite complications within your relationship, the best thing you can do is correct your own faults to foster your own growth within Christ's instructions.

A successful marriage takes time. It is a laborious process that requires considerable effort, patience, trial, and error. There is room for improvement in all relationships if you are willing to grow in God's grace toward the maturity of Christ who came to serve. It is important to stop being irresponsible, to cease being jealous, and not insist on getting your own way. Instead, check your ego, offer sympathy and a never-ending stream of forgiveness. The most important thing you can do as a married couple is to pray every day. What measures will you take to create an all-embracing relationship in God's love today?

Dear Lord, thank you for the vows and laws that I am bound to. It gives me freedom, yet keeps me on the straight and narrow path to your heart. Help me to be more mature, to look beyond myself and to realize the needs and feelings of my spouse. Enable me to accept the responsibility I have accepted now and forever. Amen.

April 16

*"Stop judging and you will not be judged. Stop condemning and you
will not be condemned. Forgive and you will be forgiven. Give and gifts
will be given to you; a good measure, packed together, shaken down,
and overflowing, will be poured into your lap. For the measure
with which you measure will in return be measured out to you."*

LUKE 6:37–38

D o you like presents wrapped as a big package or a small one? The best
gift you can give or get from your spouse is love. Your need for love is
one of your strongest emotional needs. When it's being met, you respond
favorably to the person providing it. Can you provide love to your spouse
when he or she is not meeting your needs? Ask God to give you the power to
overlook your short-term desires for the long-term benefits of your marriage.
Channel positive energies, kindness, and loving gestures toward your spouse
because eventually he or she will reciprocate.

When you love your spouse unconditionally, you love him or her without
reservations, regardless of circumstances. To love your spouse unconditionally, you must like yourself. To give love, you need to be content with yourself
or else your insecurities will creep in and interfere with your relationship.
Loving unconditionally does not mean to give into everything your spouse
desires. Your mate could do devastating things to your marriage. If there are
inappropriate behaviors, you could discover that your love has limitations.
Ponder if you could allow your spouse to destroy your prized possession and
not give it a second thought, or if you could relocate across the country for
them, or support their every move. If either of these are true, then you love
unconditionally.

When you are completely open and honest, you love unconditionally.
Do you allow your spouse to see the "real" you and allow them to accept
you? You have to convey your ideas and feelings to your mate. You have to
release your uncertainties to be completely in love. You cannot have a hidden
agenda or motives. Love is not something you learn, it's just something that
you do. Learn from Jesus's unconditional love how you can love your spouse
absolutely without bounds.

Dear Lord, let me be the conveyer of your loving touch to enable me
and [name] to hold onto what is sacred: our marriage bonds. Teach
me how to love unconditionally, how to give wholly and completely,
and how to patiently wait for love to find me. Thank you for wrapping
me in your endless stream of limitless love. With you, Lord, I rejoice
in your glorious love. Amen.

April 17

Who speaks so that it comes to pass, unless the Lord commands it?
Is it not at the word of the Most High that both good and bad take
place? What should the living complain about? about their sins!

LAMENTATIONS 3:37–39

In order for the average person to lose weight, there needs to be a balance between cutting calories and increasing physical activity. In order to maintain a healthy marriage, there is stability in giving and taking. Contemplate if you take more from your marriage than you give. Question if you give more to your relationship than you take.

Perhaps you criticize or complain about your spouse. Instead of verbally complaining, consider drafting a list of what is bothersome to you. Inform your spouse that you want to change into a better partner and improve your methods of meeting his or her emotional needs. Ask for suggestions on how you can improve. Focus your attention on the suggestions, concentrating on self-improving. After a few weeks, make a specific and heartfelt request from your grievance list. Chances are good that your partner will meet your emotional needs too.

Criticism creeps in when complaints are ignored. Complaints are objective statements of unmet needs. An effective complaint is one that starts softly with a request for help. Contempt is intentionally abusing your spouse verbally, emotionally, and psychologically. Contempt expresses the absence of any admiration and is delivered with insults, name-calling, and mockery. It must be eliminated in order for your marriage to survive. If you are struggling with this issue, call out to God for help.

Defensiveness is a reaction to being criticized or treated condescendingly. It's also a way of sidestepping responsibility. Consider if you might be neglecting a marital responsibility or if there is an aspect of unreliability in your relationship. If you are ignoring complaints from your spouse or failing to contribute creative solutions, those complaints can become criticisms that you naturally want to defend against.

When you stonewall, you avoid the work of maturing, either because you are unaware of your own feelings or because you are afraid of conflict. Rather than dealing directly with the issue or with your partner, you tune out, turn away, or become preoccupied with some activity or busyness. Don't stop relating to the most important person in your life—your spouse. How you handle conflict makes the difference between a disastrous relationship or a marvelous marriage. What changes will you make in your marriage?

Dear Lord, bolster me spiritually as I transform into a more generous spouse. You are my saving God and I adore you. Amen.

April 18

"You have heard that it was said, 'You shall love your neighbor and hate your enemy.' But I say to you, love your enemies, and pray for those who persecute you, that you may be children of your heavenly Father, for he makes his sun rise on the bad and the good, and causes rain to fall on the just and the unjust."

MATTHEW 5:43–45

D o you ever feel like your spouse is an enemy? Jesus wants everyone to love the people who are annoying or those who irritate you, or feel bitterness toward even if it's a spouse. It's hard not to retaliate; however, Jesus wants us to love and pray for our enemies. If your spouse hurt you, pray for him or her and in time God will help you to let go of that pain. Living with anger, hatred, and resentment is destructive and counterproductive. The sooner you free yourself from ill feelings, the better you will feel. When you have been wronged by someone, even if it is your spouse, ask yourself, what would Jesus do? And then do that.

First, think of Jesus, then start with a smile. If Jesus came to you, a smile would automatically appear on your face. You might extend your hand to touch him; therefore, touch your enemy. If your foe is your spouse, draw him or her near in a loving embrace. The ability to love your enemy comes from the Holy Spirit empowering you to achieve the impossible. Whatever your spouse did to hurt you, extinguish those thoughts from your mind and leave a resting place for God to dwell. Ask the Lord to replace any negative thoughts with pleasant, loving thoughts instead.

Pray for your spouse. Ask God to help him or her. It's easy to pray for the people in your life that you admire, but it's difficult to pray for someone who has disappointed you. Ask God to heal the hurts in their lives that motivate their evil actions. Ask God to bless them and show mercy to them. When you are with friends, instead of complaining about your unjust treatment, speak well of your spouse. Implore the Lord to enlighten you with a way to show your love to your spouse. Do something good for him or her. Even if it's the smallest gesture, it will please God and thrill your partner. If your spouse has hurt you, how will you act today with God in your heart?

Dear Lord, fill me with kindness and compassion for [*name*]. Mend my brokenness and carry my pain so that I don't have to bear it. Walk with me, my sweet Lord, each and every step of the way on the path of righteousness. Amen.

April 19

Or if an ear should say, "Because I am not an eye I do not belong
to the body," it does not for this reason belong any less to the body.
If the whole body were an eye, where would the hearing be?
If the whole body were hearing, where would the sense of smell be?

1 CORINTHIANS 12:16–17

How good would an orchestra be if there were no flutes or percussion? How good would a marriage be if one person was always away on business or military duty? It might take an extra effort to make your partner feel loved and appreciated, but one of the easiest ways to accomplish that is by saying, "I love you and appreciate you" over the phone or through online visits. You could write it in cards, letters, and e-mail. Handwritten messages require additional thought and time, but they provide a tangible reminder of your affections. Sending photographs or a care package tells your partner that you are concerned in a loving way. Perhaps you could plan a special weekend alone when you both are reunited. Say extra prayers and let him or her know about them. Sync up a time when you could pray together.

Perhaps you live with your spouse physically, but feel like you are drifting away emotionally. Make the time for each other to nurture your friendship by focusing on the things that you really like about each other. Perhaps your spouse is musically gifted. You could attend musical productions or concerts, join an orchestra, or be in a talent show. Maybe you could do something altogether different by taking an art class together or collect stamps or old post cards. Find a new hobby that neither one of you has ever explored but in which you share a mutual interest. Share your dreams with each other and make plans to make them come true. If one of your dreams is to climb a mountain, make plans to do it this summer! If you dream about your retirement, start building a retirement fund now. Experiencing something new together will allow you to see it in a fresh way while allowing you something draws your together amid life's commotion that can pull you a part.

Talk about the exciting things you can do in the future, and don't forget to talk about the fun things you did in the past. Sharing fond memories is a beautiful way to bond with your spouse. Perhaps you could look at old photographs, scrapbooks, or yearbooks. What will you do with your partner that will draw you both together?

Dear Lord, keep [*name*] safe while away from me, and keep our love strong until we can be reunited physically, spiritually, and emotionally. Amen.

April 20

Turn, turn back from all your crimes, that they may not be a cause of sin for you ever again. Cast away from you all the crimes you have committed, and make for yourselves a new heart and a new spirit.

EZEKIEL 18:30–31

Have you ever been lost? The feelings of panic and disorientation can be paralyzing. When you feel lost in your marriage, stop what you are doing and let God direct you back on track. Perhaps you started acting out of your normal character, using quip remarks, barbs, or jabs in conversations with your spouse. The moment your surroundings are unrecognizable, just stop and say a prayer. God knows who you really are and what you are made of. God can bring you back into alignment and keep you steady on the course you were meant to walk.

If you feel like you have lost yourself in your marriage, take responsibility for your own life regardless of the role your spouse plays in it. Turn this painful situation around with prayer, introspection, and self-improvement. Be honest with yourself about what you want and what you are willing to do. Create some time to explore possible passions and interests. You might want to try a new activity, such as gardening or jogging, where you can think through solutions while enjoying your alone time.

If you are used to automatically going along with whatever your mate wants, it might take a while to break that habit. For instance, you could tell your partner lovingly that you want to choose the movie. Sometimes the answer to feeling lost is relatively simple and fits effortlessly into your routine. Other times, you might need to be more patient, open, and flexible. Share with your spouse about what you are feeling. He or she might be more supportive than you imagine. As you work through this by giving yourself time and space to understand and appreciate your true self, your words and actions will be more in alignment and your marriage could improve also. What steps will you take today to be true to yourself while journeying through life with your spouse?

Dear Lord, draw me into your loving embrace and extend your tender mercies to me. Teach me how to be true to myself and my partner in difficult times. Don't let me get lost in a sea of confusion and turmoil. Let me see your light shining brightly in the midst of chaos. Guard each step I take. Hone in on me and fill me with renewed hope for a better, brighter tomorrow. Amen.

April 21

Looking around at them with anger and grieved at their
hardness of heart, he said to the man, "Stretch out your hand."
He stretched it out and his hand was restored.

MARK 3:5

A fever is an indication that something could be wrong with your health. Yelling is a sign that something is wrong in your relationship. Shouting is unhealthy and can become verbally abusive; nothing good can come from it. When you hear yourself yell, stop and think about what is causing it. Is it from fatigue? Are you overworked or not sleeping well at night? Perhaps you are frustrated about something that happened in your marriage.

If you're mad about something, you probably yell because anger creates tension. As your tension builds, you release it by yelling at your spouse. Whatever you say out of anger adds fuel to the fire because it unleashes a negative emotion that grabs your partner's attention more than any point you want to make. Your spouse will be defensive and frustrated by your outburst instead of responsive and understanding. The next time you feel angry, try a different approach. For example, "I get frustrated when I can't find the car keys. I'm not blaming you, but I'm suggesting we keep them in the same place so we always know where they are." This communicates your emotions in a way that lets you move past them, not fuel them. Keep your emotions under control, and your message will be heard. .

Excessive emotion interferes with communication. You might need to take some time alone to sort out your feelings and put them into proper perspective or pray over them. Another alternative is to take an exercise break before you continue your discussion. Exercise is a terrific stress reducer, and it easily distracts you from intense feelings. Perhaps you could go for a walk together while talking out the issue. It isn't easy to focus on problems when you are out of breath and walking uphill. You might choose to write down what you want to say. This could help convey your message more thoughtfully and lovingly. Take your time discussing something emotional. Hold your rosary beads or prayer book while you speak to remember that the Holy Spirit is with you. Try to control your feelings through prayer. Ask God to carry your pain and help you to understand where the hurt is coming from. The next time you hear yourself yell, what will you do differently?

Dear Lord, shield me from the pain that rains down on me. Protect me from the harsh words that cut deep. Be the balm that heels and strengthens me. Thank you for your never-ending stream of love that keeps me afloat and brings me to still waters. I love you, kind and gentle Lord. Amen.

April 22

Then he prayed, "O LORD, open his eyes, that he may see." And the
LORD opened the eyes of the servant, and he saw that the mountainside
was filled with fiery chariots and horses around Elisha.

2 KINGS 6:17

If sand gets in your eye, the grit is painful, causing visual difficulties; yet sand is used in eyeglass lenses to enable people with impaired vision to see. What are you struggling to see in your marriage? If your spouse is working late most nights, are you questioning his or her love and devotion to you? Perhaps if you looked at it from another angle, you might actually see the love in it. Maybe you partner is working longer hours to provide more security, healthcare benefits, or a retirement or vacation fund for you both. If your spouse seems to be wrapped up in chores, perhaps he or she wants to give you a nice home. Try to look from another perspective to find the love that is buried within the acts of service.

Try organizing the "junk drawer," the messy closet, garage, or basement. Pick a task that would make your spouse happy if he or she didn't have to do it: wash the car, the kitchen floor, the bathroom; give the dog a bath. If you see your spouse emptying the dishwasher or making dinner, pitch in and help. When you are out, call your partner to see if you can run an errand for him or her before you head home. Consider taking care of the children for an afternoon to give your spouse a break. Perhaps you could take them to the park for an hour or to a museum for the afternoon. By making the kids happy, you'll make your spouse happy. Maybe you could give your spouse an invigorating back rub or foot massage. Feeling your hands on his or her body, working out the stress of the day could be the best gift you give. Sometimes these little acts go a long way to making your partner feel loved.

Ask God to open your eyes to recognize the love that your mate is demonstrating through small acts of kindness. Consider what task your spouse did for you last week. Did you appreciate it and convey your thankfulness for it? It's never too late to go back and say, "Thank you." If your spouse feels valued, he or she just might do it again. What act of service will you do for your partner this week?

Dear Lord, if love is hidden in my marriage, let me see it, know it, and feel it. If love is disguised in chores, let me recognize it. Teach me to accept and appreciate everything that is given to me, even if I don't see it right away. I don't see you, yet I know you are there and I love you. Amen.

April 23

I sought the LORD, and he answered me, delivered me from all my fears.
PSALM 34:5

Do you have fears in your marriage that are troubling you? Having fear is a normal response to peril or the uncertainty of an unpredictable outcome. Contemplate what is driving your uncertainty or fears. The reality of marriage is that you know how to push each other's buttons or tap into each other's fears. When your spouse says or does something hurtful, you can react defensively, criticize, or shut down and withdraw. Identify your fears to prevent a vicious downward spiral and find a healthier pattern to follow. Otherwise, you will constantly revert to reacting out of fear by doing or saying anything to soothe your pain.

Consider if you fear being a successful spouse or having your partner ultimately leave you. Perhaps you fear your spouse won't accept you as you are, or will want to change and control you. Do you question if you are incompetent, not good enough, or if something is wrong with you? Maybe you fear your spouse won't be affectionate or desire you. Maybe your uncertainty revolves around how to motivate your mate to give you what you want, which is the opposite of your fears. For example, if you fear being a failure, you want success.

Eventually, fear makes you dependent on your mate for happiness and fulfillment, as you look to your spouse to fulfill your desires. God created you to depend on him. This dependency was designed and reserved for God, not for your spouse. To break out of this cycle, learn to communicate effectively with your spouse about your true fears. Instead of arguing about trivial matters, acknowledge and discuss your fears with your spouse to take the first step to healthy communication in your marriage, which can lead the way to real intimacy.

Don't be afraid to seek counseling, talk to your priest, or join a marriage support group. If you feel anxious talking to your spouse on a delicate topic that might cause conflict, give those fears to God instead of being paralyzed by them. Worry does absolutely no good whatsoever; but prayer can move mountains. God can permeate you with faith, hope, and trust. God can talk through you and work through you if you let him. Be still and listen for God's words. He will tell you what to do and deliver you from all of your fears.

Dear Lord, thank you for being the stoic presence in my life, to carry my fears, worries, and doubts so that I don't have to. Thank you for replacing them with love, happiness, and trust that with you all things are possible. Thank you for transforming my heart with immeasurable joy. I truly love you. Amen.

April 24

The sun stood still, the moon stayed, while the nation took vengeance on its foes. This is recorded in the Book of Jashar. The sun halted halfway across the heavens; not for an entire day did it press on.

JOSHUA 10:13

A sun dog is an atmospheric phenomenon that creates bright spots of light in the sky when the sun is low. It appears as a colored halo near the sun and can be seen anywhere in the world during any season. It's like a surprise gift from God to make us happy. You can give a surprise gift back to God by thinking of him, saying a prayer, and doing a kind act.

Consider doing random acts of kindness to your spouse when he or she least expects it. The sky is the limit to what you can do. Maybe your spouse would enjoy something extravagant such as sailing through the sky in a hot air balloon. Perhaps having all of their Saturday morning chores done for them would be more appreciated. When was the last time you surprised your spouse with flowers just to make him or her happy? Even if you can only afford one single rose, buy it for your partner. The kind gesture will bring a smile to his or her face and linger for the longest time inside their heart, warming them each time they think of it. It's also nice to hear the words, "I love you." When is the last time you said them?

Contemplate if you and your partner could spend a few hours each week volunteering together serving the homeless in your community. It can be more rewarding to do kind acts for the less fortunate. Include your children or other family members to educate them on ways they can serve God's people in the future. When you look into the eyes of the indigent, that is where you will see God. With so many worthy organizations vying for volunteers, enjoy the selection process with your spouse. You will be helping the community while growing together in God's love. Where will you find God today in your life?

Dear Lord, when I see tiny miracles strewn about, I smile remembering that you give me these blessings to brighten my day. Thank you for caring about my happiness. Work through me to bring joy to my spouse. Thank you for the gentle reminders to serve others as well. Point me in the right direction; the place you want me to be today. I trust in you and I love you, Lord God Almighty. Amen.

April 25

He believed, hoping against hope, that he would become "the father
of many nations," according to what was said, "Thus shall your
descendants be." He did not doubt God's promise in unbelief; rather,
he was empowered by faith and gave glory to God and was fully
convinced that what he had promised he was also able to do.

ROMANS 4:18, 20–21

When the mailman arrives at your house, do you anticipate his delivery eagerly? It might be a pile of junk mail, catalogs, or bills, but there is always the chance that something exciting will come. If you can have such hope for the mail delivery, what is your hopefulness for God within your marriage? No matter what is eating away at your relationship, don't give up on it; seek guidance from God's holy Word. Hold strong onto the Lord and pray for strength; he will give it to you to accomplish things that you never thought possible.

Just as you cannot demand your mail carrier bring happy letters and joyous cards from friends, you cannot have expectations of your spouse because it feels like demands to him or her. If you request something and your spouse refuses it, your instinct might prompt you to become forceful with a demand. The mandate intimidates with a type of punishment, not caring how your spouse feels. Ideally, there is shared power within your marriage, with you both working together to accomplish mutual objectives. However, when one spouse makes demands or threats, that is a power play. The threatened spouse strikes back, fighting fire with fire. It abruptly becomes a power struggle.

If the demanding partner lacks power to complete the threat, he or she gets punished, perhaps ridiculed. If power is equal in marriage, a battle can rage until one surrenders. The spouse making the concession feels resentment and is less likely to meet any future needs. When the demand isn't met, both spouses are embittered. To avoid this, remember that you don't have a right to control your partner, nor do you have a right to your expectations. Unmet expectations can feel like rejection. When you feel this way, ask yourself, "What did I expect?" Expectations can feel like demands to your mate. Convert expectations into hopes. Instead of demanding your gas tank be filled, say, "I would love to have a full tank of gas for my long drive tomorrow." What expectations can you turn into hopes?

Dear Lord, teach me how to convert the demands of my marriage into hopes. Give me patience to endure the wait when what I hope for doesn't come on my time schedule. Teach me how to appreciate the little gestures as signs of progress to maintain hopefulness in a brighter tomorrow. Amen.

April 26

As face mirrors face in water, so the heart reflects the person.
PROVERBS 27:19

A facial recognition system is a computer application that is used as a security measure that automatically identifies someone from a digital image by comparing facial features from a database . A random sampling of faces on a city street might reflect a smattering of similarities; however, there is no way to determine how their hearts, or their capacity to love, compare with each other. Contemplate how your capacity to love compares with your partner's. Do you love your spouse unconditionally or are there terms and situations with strings attached?

Unconditional love is the notion that you love your mate because of who he or she is, regardless of looks, actions, or flaws. Boundaries safeguard your marriage commitment and foster lifelong, healthy emotional relations while you grow with each other.

Limitations allow you to love freely while forming an understanding of what is acceptable. Open and honest communication is critical. Establishing relationship rules requires both partners to be open and honest with themselves and each other. These moments of honesty and clarity are not always going to come in the form of civil conversations or carefully negotiated lists.

Small things can make a big difference if there are thoughts and feelings involved. Your spouse wants to know that they're thought about. Maybe you could take an early morning jog before work, or sit in your backyard to drink of cup of coffee together before you begin your day. Perhaps you could take a walk together after dinner and discuss your day and make plans for the future. Maybe you could go on a date night, couples retreat, take a mini-vacation, or plan a surprise anniversary party. Show your love through thoughtful actions such as drawing a bubble bath, giving a massage, doing the dishes without complaining, or writing a love letter. Whenever you show affection, do it with an open and loving heart, not angrily or begrudgingly. Love is different for every person, and every person shows it differently. The important thing is finding what makes your partner happy. Ponder the ways you demonstrated your love to your spouse last week. Did you pray for him or her, or did you offer quality time doing something exceptional knowing your mate would appreciate it? Contemplate how you plan to show your love to your spouse today.

Dear Lord, thank you for allowing [*name*] and me to adore the matching essence of our lives and that which unites our hearts into a sanctified bond before you. Your love is reflected through our love. Amen.

April 27

Do not say: How is it that former times were better than these?...
Wisdom is as good as an inheritance and profitable to those who see the sun.
For the protection of wisdom is as the protection of money; and knowledge
is profitable because wisdom gives life to those who possess it.

ECCLESIASTES 7:10–12

Frequent flier points can be accrued and saved until enough of them earn a free ticket. Marriages have a similar system: a memory bank of accumulated tokens of appreciation earned from accrued love after doing fun things together. Without fond memories of a close relationship, we would cease to grow and mature. Also, it's prudent to remember the past to avoid repeating previous mistakes. Reminiscence therapy uses life stories to improve the psychological well-being of aging adults with the goal to maintain good mental health. There are several benefits of this therapy, including intimacy maintenance and problem-solving. Information reminiscence is celebrating the enjoyment by retelling stories from the past. It could be useful to you if you currently lack interest in your life or in your marriage. Recalling fond memories reminds you what you have to be happy about and thankful for.

Reminiscing earlier circumstances may be helpful in your marriage, especially during stressful times or for coping with change, because when you share memories, it enables you both to achieve a sense of honesty and self-worth. An invitation to the past can begin with, "What did you like most about our first date?" or "What did you like best about our wedding day?" A dinner discussion could reminisce about the time you and your mate rode bikes along a stone path, swam in a cool lake on a hot summer day, or the time you took the family to Disney World. Reliving past experiences allows you to remember what fun you had, and could prompt you to spend more time together enjoying fun activities.

Ponder what childhood reveries you wish to share with your spouse. Set aside a specific time to share memories and plan another adventure together to recapture more pleasurable conversations for the future. Through this process peace, love, and joy can be achieved in your marriage. Where will you go and what will you do with your spouse this week?

Dear Lord, thank you for the many joyful events that comprise my life. They are all glorious memories for me to recall and share with my spouse. They remind me of happier times bringing warmth back to my heart. Allow me to appreciate life with my spouse so that someday when we are much older, we can reminisce about the outings we enjoyed today. You are my generous and loving Lord. Amen.

April 28

He willed to give us birth by the word of truth that we may be a
kind of firstfruits of his creatures. Know this, my dear brothers:
everyone should be quick to hear, slow to speak, slow to wrath,
for the wrath of a man does not accomplish the righteousness of God.
Therefore, put away all filth and evil excess and humbly welcome the
word that has been planted in you and is able to save your souls.

JAMES 1:18–21

While eating a grapefruit, you might get squirt in the eye; but it's worth it to enjoy the nutritious fruit. Some might squint, anticipating the juice hitting their eye. Are there areas in your marriage where you might do something knowing it might be painful? Sometimes people make hurtful statements without realizing how it stings until it's used on them. One example is "you" statements.

Consider avoiding an accusing "you" when talking to your spouse, such as "Did you leave this room messy" or "You shouldn't have lost the car keys." When your spouse uses the "you" word, it stings like grapefruit juice in your eye. Replace the accusing "you" with "I" statements: "I feel discombobulated when the room is messy; I would love your help to clean it" or "I feel frustrated when the car keys are misplaced; would you help me look for them?" Changing the way you speak takes time and effort, but it's worth it to avoid arguments. Ask the Holy Spirit to help you speak.

If you hear yourself begin to speak with the words "you always" or "you never," stop and think before you finish the sentence. Refocus back to the problem and ask for a "do over" to rephrase your thoughts in a kinder manner. It's essential to focus on the problem, not your spouse. Be quick to hear without interrupting. Speak slowly and carefully to ensure your message is loving. And be slow to anger. This is the message the Lord wants us to live by.

Dear Lord, cool my tempers when I am inflamed. Let me think of you and welcome your loving words in my thoughts to replace my vengeful ones. Place your calming hand on my shoulder and let your tranquility seep into my bones. Convert my words to those Jesus used to keep peace. Thank you, Lord, for always being there for me in my time of need. I love you. Amen.

April 29

Once more will he fill your mouth with laughter and your lips with rejoicing.
JOB 8:21

A smile is the best thing you can wear. What good is a nice outfit if your face is wearing a frown? It's not easy to smile when your insides ache. If you feel depressed, you might feel trapped with nowhere to turn for help. Depression is a disease that can make your marriage miserable. If your spouse is depressed, it can deprive you both of emotional, spiritual, and physical intimacy. Regardless of who is depressed, have hope by taking healing steps such as reading the Bible and praying. During this time avoid making any major decisions. Instead, stick with what works: depending on God.

Depression comprises negative behaviors such as low motivation and increased irritability, which strains the marriage and can affect the victim's ability to function. Marital problems and depression form a vicious circle: depression leads to marital problems and marital problems lead to depression. Depression is an illness with the potential to negatively impact a marriage if left untreated. If this is happening to you, seek help through your parish priest or family physician who can recommend a mental health professional.

If your marriage feels unstable and there is no depression, question what is causing you to feel upset. Hurt and anger are entwined. Peel back the emotional layers to keep the hurt cycle from spiraling out of control. Question what exactly makes you feel hurt. What are you afraid of? Ponder what regrets you have and what your desires are. Lastly, state what you truly love.

When your spouse hurts you, tell them immediately. It's possible he or she is unaware that you are unhappy about a particular behavior. It's your responsibility to tell your partner what he or she does is hurtful. Begin with loving dialog, not negativity and hostility. Your spouse will be more receptive to your feelings if he or she believes your goal is to improve your relationship, not destroy it with grumbling and complaints.

Having a positive outlook is a personal choice. How can you put optimism in your heart and then share it with your spouse? Ask God to bless you and transform your attitude into a more loving one. Lean on the Lord. His love can change your life and expand your mind to new thoughts and dreams. Perhaps you can begin by seeking the sacrament of penance. Forgiveness is the antidote to bitterness. When you stand at the crossroads, choose the path of forgiveness. Let go and move on in God's infinite love.

Dear Lord, thank you for allowing me to show my great faith in you and to turn over my life to you. Help me, Lord, to carry my heavy burdens. Amen.

April 30

The wilderness and the parched land will exult; the Arabah will rejoice and bloom;
Like the crocus it shall bloom abundantly, and rejoice with joyful song.
The glory of Lebanon will be given to it, the splendor of Carmel and Sharon;
They will see the glory of the LORD, the splendor of our God.

ISAIAH 35:1–2

There are special vases designed especially for rosebuds. Most people expect the buds to bloom eventually where the full impact of the soft pedals and the flower's fragrance can be enjoyed. Precautionary measures can be taken to promote the opening of a bud by providing adequate airflow and sunlight. Is your marriage akin to the rosebud? Consider how you nourish your marriage from the stress of your job, your children, activities, an aging parent, your church, friends, neighbors, and volunteer duties. It can be problematic to nurture your spouse and relationship when you are stretched so thin from your daily obligations. Distance is created in your marriage. As time rolls on, assumptions are formed on the distance, amplifying the gap. It doesn't take much to feel isolated and resentful. Trust can break down and you can grow apart by focusing on your differences.

To prevent this from happening to your marriage, make the time to understand what is truly important to your spouse. If your partner loves gardening, check out gardening books from the library. Spend quiet time alone with your spouse every day whether it is early in the morning or before you go to bed; find a few moments where you can reconnect. Have a date night every week where you step away from the routine and stress of your day to focus on one another. Compliment you spouse every day and say "thank you" for the little things he or she does. Spend one minute kissing each day; set the timer if necessary. Hug your spouse; touch is therapeutic. Make a list of five things you would enjoy doing with your partner. Exchange lists and surprise your partner by doing an activity together from the list. What preventative actions will you take to ensure your marriage blossoms?

One way to ensure your marriage flourishes is to pray together every day. With divine intervention, you will be more successful keeping your relationship in full bloom.

Dear Lord, touch my heart with your healing powers to enable the petals of my marriage to open. Help me cultivate a more loving environment for my spouse and me to grow and nourish each other. Thank you, Lord, for bringing my spouse into my life. My life journey is sacred because [*name*] is in it. Amen.

May 1

*The Lord preceded them, in the daytime by means of a column of cloud
to show them the way, and at night by means of a column of fire
to give them light....Neither the column of cloud by day nor the
column of fire by night ever left its place in front of the people.*

EXODUS 13:21–22

Anyone who has had to work outside under the intense heat of the summer sun knows the relief felt when a cloud rolls overhead and offers a bit of shade. The short respite from the sweltering temperatures gives the sense of hope that the shade will linger, perhaps with a breeze or promise of a gentle, cleansing rain.

When struggles ensue within a marriage, it's understandable to seek a brief interval from the overheating between each other. Sometimes, stepping away temporarily offers a fresh outlook and renewed hope of solving a predicament. Try taking a break from conflict resolution to take a walk with your spouse. To reduce brain fatigue caused by arguing, take a stroll through a park. Even a tree-filled plaza minimizes stress and improves concentration. Green spaces are calming, providing a tranquil spot for quiet contemplation to allow the brain to recover from mental fatigue. Perhaps you could take a jog, play a game of tennis, or go bicycle riding with your spouse. Focusing on the enjoyment of the activity could liberate biased thinking and allow you to process your circumstances more rationally. Consider other techniques you can do to regain your composure.

Prayer is the most common therapeutic ritual in America today. Regular prayer and meditation have shown to be a central factor in living longer and staying healthy. In the midst of a quarrel, take a moment to connect spiritually with God. Ask him to organize your thoughts to resolve your marital disputes amicably and intelligently.

During an argument, contemplate how you address problems with a level head. Do you instigate quarrels or sweep them under a rug? The key is addressing them amicably with God's grace.

Dear Lord, thank you for being the center of my life, especially when there are arguments in my marriage. Thank you for stabilizing me in the midst of crisis and bringing me out of the darkness and into your radiant light. Thank you for being beside me during throughout the deluge of havoc that has been crashing through my marriage lately, and for freeing my brain cells to intelligently address it and repair my union with [*name*]. Thank you for reminding me not to sweat the little things, but to work through the big ones that can't be swept under the carpet. Amen.

May 2

*After Lot had parted from him, the LORD said to Abram: Look about you,
and from where you are, gaze to the north and south, east and west;
all the land that you see I will give to you and your descendants forever.*

GENESIS 13:14–15

Some people have a poor sense of direction, constantly questioning if
they are going the right way. Hikers use compasses and trail markers on
trees in the woods. Teenagers get directions online and either memorize the
guidelines or print out a map. However, some maps are difficult to interpret.
Global Positioning System (GPS) is a lifesaver for many people. Contemplate
if your marriage is moving in the right direction. What markers do you use to
determine if you are on the right track? Use the God Pleasing System (GPS) to
keep your marriage on target by questioning if your objectives are honorable.

All marriages endure periods of disillusionment, stress, or busyness
brought on by an illness or accident, a child difficulty, job instability or loss
of employment, finance troubles, or death of a family member. While you
are living through the external turmoil, your marriage is under duress. This
is when you should be attentive to keeping your marriage on track. When
you are entangled in a crisis, it's easy to neglect yourself or your marriage.
However, when a plane is crashing, passengers are instructed to put breathing apparatus on themselves first, then take care of their families. Don't get
emotionally run down. Take care of yourself, then tend to your marriage.

Always treat your partner with respect regardless of the turmoil you are
struggling through. Two heads together are better than one. Your spouse
can help you through a difficulty and be willing to work with you if you are
respectful. If your relationship has taken a turn for the worst, don't partici-
pate in verbal assaults. If there is abuse in any form, your marriage needs an
intervention to be resolved. Talk to your priest for guidance.

Ask God for wisdom and see how he will transform your heart and your
marriage. Disregard your human timetable when you believe your prayers
should be answered. Line up your will with God's and you will always have
hope. When needs are being met and you both have emotional fuel in your
tank, your marriage can withstand the stressors of everyday life. If what you
think, say, and do pleases God, than they are also good for your relationship.

Dear Lord, bless my marriage and the road we walk together. You
chose the best person for me to share my life with. Thank you for
being my GPS through my life and marriage. Amen.

May 3

Oracle on the Valley of Vision: What is the matter with you now, that you have gone up, all of you, to the housetops, You who were full of noise, tumultuous city, exultant town? Your slain are not slain with the sword, nor killed in battle. All your leaders fled away together, they were captured without use of bow; All who were found were captured together, though they had fled afar off.

ISAIAH 22:1–3

Have you ever glanced up at your rearview mirror to see a red flashing light? How do you cope with that panic when you are behind the wheel and realize you are being pulled over by the police? The sudden sensation of fear can prevent reasoning and logical thinking. Ponder what causes anxiety in your relationship. Are you an alarmist? Do you blow disagreements out of proportion? Invoke the Holy Spirit that dwells within and remember that God will not allow a hair on your head will be destroyed (Luke 21:18). God will bless you with tranquility, clarity, and the ability to cognitively discern what is troubling you. Perhaps you could impersonalize the issue to brainstorm an intelligent solution to overcome it with your partner.

St. Francis de Sales said anxiety is one of the greatest evils that can happen to us. Anxiety is a strong emotion that stems from the loss of trust, lack of confidence, safety, worry, and guilt. The increased level of anxiety within marriages today could be a result of the poor economy. If you have financial difficulties, that could lead to insomnia, which leads to increased irritability. Try meditating several times throughout your day, focusing on trusting God with all of your fears and apprehensions. Scriptural prayer from Psalms and in the New Testament can be particularly helpful because of the elements in building trust, a virtue that can reduce anxiety.

Anxiety interferes with marital happiness when a spouse is unable to give or receive love and cope with life's demands. Perhaps your spouse responds to anxiety by becoming controlling, irritable, dejected, or uncertain, which negatively impacts romantic feelings. If you are experiencing anxiety, talk to your doctor or priest about it. Don't remain silent; reach out to God and let his infinite wisdom guide you through it.

Dear Lord, fill me and [*name*] with peacefulness to reach a loving solution to our problems. Enable us to put our heads together to work as a team to find plausible answers and live by them in the serene lifestyle we crave. Let us think of you first when there are controversies. Don't let them morph into something when they are not. Amen.

May 4

Then our mouths were filled with laughter; our tongues sang for joy.

PSALM 126:2

Have you ever heard a snappy tune and started tapping your toe to the beat of the music? Depending on the nature of the music, it can either put you in a good mood or bring you to tears. What power music has! You also have that same influence to change your partner's mood. Ponder how you have altered your mate's disposition. What can you do to lift your spouse's spirits? If your partner is feeling blue, you could stargaze on a blanket in the backyard, build a bonfire and toast marshmallows, or watch a scary movie and share a bowl of popcorn. You could play your mate's favorite music and dance in the kitchen while your dinner is cooking or play air guitar and sing. Even if you don't know all of the words, it's fun to make them up as you go along.

Music with positive messages and happy tunes can actually make you feel more content. Melodies can alter brainwaves and elevate your mood even after you stop listening to it. Scientists have shown that classical music can improve intelligence. It increases your brain's pleasure states by boosting serotonin, norepinephrine, and dopamine. Also, studies have shown that music has biological indicators (heart rate, respiration, body temperature) consistent with emotional arousal. Music can change your brain chemistry and physical state in a matter of minutes, making it a fantastic medicine for the mind, body, and soul.

Music is mostly used for entertainment, however, it helps pass the time while stuck in traffic, and it makes a boring task less dull. Music eases exercise by creating a diversion. Music distracts the mind from unpleasant thoughts, decreasing anxiety. Soothing music decreases stress and the stress hormone cortisol. Listening to music similar to deep moods releases emotions with a cleansing effect and boosts your immune system. Upbeat dance music increases antibodies levels in your body. Many college campuses have developed curriculums for music therapy.

If music makes you feel happier, chances are good it will make your marriage better-off too. Music enhances a church service to make it richer and more spiritual. Do you and your spouse like the same kind of music? Maybe you could listen to your favorite tunes while you eat dinner and get ready for work each morning. How will you incorporate music in your daily routine?

Dear Lord, help me to incorporate music into my day. Fill me with the happiness and desire that I long for. Reunite [*name*] and me in your loving embrace. Teach us how to lay down our swords and pick up our hearts with joyful sounds of laughter. Amen.

May 5

The foolish son is ruin to his father, and
a quarrelsome wife is water constantly dripping.

PROVERBS 19:13

Have you ever walked any distance with a tiny pebble in your shoe? It is mind-boggling how something so tiny and seemingly harmless can cause so much discomfort. Many people cannot endure it. They must stop and shake it out in order to continue on. Consider what tiny nuisance has caused turmoil in your marriage. Perhaps you have nagged your spouse about something unimportant. Nagging is faultfinding, continually complaining, demanding, and unrelenting. Nagging can create a vicious cycle: the more you nag, the more your spouse withdraws emotionally and physically.

Nagging is counterproductive. Even though your complaints may be valid, it makes your spouse resentful, defensive, and disrespectful because it's perceived as criticism, so your spouse will probably tune you out. If you nag, your partner might feel attacked personally making him or her feel inadequate. Don't blame, demean, or manipulate. If your partner doesn't adhere to his or her end of the bargain regarding household chores, do not cave in and do them. Your mate must absorb the consequences of the mess. Give the problem back and only be responsible for yourself, your choices, and feelings.

If you have been picking up your spouse's slack, you might be feeling resentful. Share your feelings with him or her in a congenial manner by sticking to the issue at hand. Don't preach, teach, or lecture. Keep your statements concise and refrain from making ultimatums. Avoid using, "You always," "You never," and "You should." Your partner would probably prefer to hear, "Would you please help me make the bed?" When your spouse does make the bed, express your appreciation. Contemplate what other options you might experiment with in order to resolve your issue. Consider hiring someone to help around the house. If you still cannot make progress with shifting responsibility back to your spouse, is it possible to overlook it or put it into perspective for the greater good of your relationship? Can you reexamine the irritant for what it is and perhaps even find some endearing qualities in it?

Dear Lord, thank you for making [*name*] with so many charming characteristics that I adore. Give me the strength not to let them get under my skin. Help me to see him or her as the delightful partner you intended me to share my life journey with. I love you, Lord, and trust in your ways. Amen.

May 6

How long will you afflict my spirit, grind me down with words?

JOB 19:2

In building a deck, I was overzealous nailing the floorboards down. A few nails were whacked in the wrong spot. When they were pulled out, several holes remained in the wood and I was angry with myself for leaving visible mistakes. Something similar happens when harsh words are spoken to a loved one: an empty hole remains in their heart. Have you said unkind or insensitive words to your partner? Contemplate loving ways to rephrase a message you want your spouse to hear. Invoke the Holy Spirit to scramble the cruel words and rearrange them with a loving meaning. Let Jesus be your role model.

When you are conversing with or frustrated by your partner, it can be taxing to spot your spouse's strengths, because you are too focused on the deficits. Practice noticing the good attributes, the finer qualities, the subtle high points, and mention them. That soothes any irritation, and the source of frustration seems insignificant compared to his or her many good qualities. For instance, "I admire how quickly you can accurately assess a situation." Embrace the realm of optimism and cultivate within your heart an attitude of gratefulness. Eliminate the need to criticize, complain, or point blame because it's counterproductive. Thrive off the positive sentiments toward your spouse, and the covenants you made to him or her will influence how you approach and resolve differences. Ungratefulness by you or your mate can seriously hamper the happiness of your marriage; therefore, it is vital to develop gratitude.

Some topics are more complicated to discuss than others: in-laws, finances, and sex. One of the most sensible things to do is begin your discussion with prayer. This blessed habit can transform your marriage as you include the Holy Spirit to guide your conversation. Hold a holy medal or your rosary beads as a physical reminder to avoid any pitfalls. While it's good to resolve issues affecting your marriage, your relationship is more important than the topic you want to discuss. Your spouse is your life partner. Don't lose sight that your agenda is to please God first. What topic will you discuss with your mate next, and how will you keep your conversation on track in God's love?

Dear Lord, let ugly words, tainted with hurtfulness, vanish before they leave my mouth. Teach me to wait patiently and calmly before I deliver any message to my spouse. I only want sweet and loving words from my heart to fall on [*name*]'s ears and live in his or her heart. Instruct me, Lord; I want to learn to be more like you. Thank you for giving me the ability to change. Amen.

May 7

But now ask the beasts to teach you, the birds of the air to tell you.

JOB 12:7

Each spring, robins sweep across the lawns searching for little twigs and snippets of string to build a nest with. The birds work tirelessly, and within a week it's complete. Ponder what seemingly insignificant gesture would build your relationship into a more solid union. Perhaps you could offer respect; it is at the core of your ability to attain acceptance, achievement, and contentment. When there is respect in a marriage, the integrity of the relationship remains intact. Your marriage needs both love and respect in order for it to be truly successful.

If you do not feel loved, you will treat your spouse disrespectfully. If your partner doesn't feel respected, he or she will be unloving to you. It's another vicious cycle that is challenging to break—but it can be done by catching yourself in the old, unhealthy pattern, and replacing the response with love and respect. Even if you make an insensitive remark by mistake, stop midstream and ask for a do over. Your partner will respect that you are trying to improve. Eventually, your spouse will stop mid-sentence and catch mistakes and work to improve for you. The transition phase might feel awkward initially, but the positive changes can bring your marriage to a higher level of respect.

Solicit your spouse's opinion and include the input in a decision that you would have made alone in the past. It's perfectly acceptable just to listen or be a sounding board. The goal of listening is to understand. Acknowledge how appreciative you are of his or her strengths, naming the ones you admire most. Believe in your spouse, and help his or her dreams to come true. Tell your partner that you need him or her in your life. You might think it is a given, but spouses still like to hear it. In social situations or family gatherings, speak well of your spouse. During times of conflict, speak respectfully to him or her even if you disagree. It's okay to disagree because you are two totally different people, with differing backgrounds and opinions. You are not supposed to agree all the time. Just remember to be respectful and affirm your love for him or her while reflecting back the words communicated to you. This will enable your spouse to feel heard when you disagree.

If your spouse does nothing to improve, you can still choose to self-improve. If you are the one to make positive changes in your marriage, your relationship will begin to move in the right direction and eventually your spouse will come aboard. What changes will you make today?

Dear Lord, let me always be honorable with good intentions every day of my life, starting today. Amen.

May 8

Sarah then said, "God has given me cause to laugh,
and all who hear of it will laugh with me."

GENESIS 21:6

Laughter is infectious; it is more contagious than a yawn. When humor is shared, it unites couples and increases their happiness and intimacy. Laughter also triggers healthy physical changes in the body. It can strengthen your immune system, boost your energy, diminish pain, and protect you from the damaging effects of stress. Humor brings more than biological benefits to a husband and wife; it helps you cope with trivial nuances and even with the tragic. Researchers reveal that couples with a sense of humor are less likely to burn out and be depressed and will enjoy life and their marriage more.

Every system in your body gets some exercise when we laugh. Twenty seconds of laughter is better for your cardiovascular and respiratory systems than three minutes on a rowing machine. By laughing heartily, muscles release tension and neurochemicals, which create similar feelings to what joggers know as a "runner's high." With health benefits supporting the importance of laughter, it's understandable for the need to be more lighthearted.

Avoid poking fun at sensitive issues, such as your partner's weight, family, or profession. One of the best ways to cope with stress is through laughter because it makes things more tolerable. The most beautiful therapy that God granted you is the ability to laugh; it's like a sedative without side effects and it doesn't require a prescription or involve money. If you and your partner have had a particularly rough day, laughter will melt away the tension and bond you both together. If your spouse comes home from work stressed, find something amusing to lift his or her spirits. Buy a pair of funny glasses with a big nose and crazy mustache to wear, or change your hairstyle into something absurd for the evening meal to make your spouse laugh. Buy a few funny movies to watch or a joke book to read when your spirits are low. Invite friends over to share a few giggles or play a card game.

Take humor seriously. Everyone has a unique sense of humor; your spouse is no exception. Discover his or her funny bone and tickle it every day. God gave you this gift to bring merriment into your marriage. Reflect on the level of happiness in your relationship. How can you increase it? Perhaps you could eliminate something that is causing you unhappiness, or set it aside temporarily while you both do something to lift your spirits. Try to smile more today because that is contagious too.

Dear Lord, take my pain and sorrow, my worries and predicaments, and crumble them into the gusting wind. Hold my heart in the palm of your hand and fill it with love and laughter. Amen.

May 9

They surrounded me like bees;
they burned up like fire among thorns;
in the LORD's name I cut them off.

PSALM 118:12

To someone with a bee sting allergy, it's perplexing how something so miniscule can trigger a dangerous anaphylactic reaction that could potentially be deadly. Some of the smallest things can also end a marriage. Contemplate what began as a small issue that has escalated into a much larger problem that could destroy your marriage if you don't resolve it. If something has been bothering you for several months, don't keep sweeping it under the rug; address it before it intensifies. If you attack the problem and not the person, you will be more successful at finding an amenable resolution.

While you might have learned not to sweat the small stuff, petty annoyances can get under your skin and fester into stumbling blocks in your marriage. It's important to resolve the issues straightaway without nitpicking or nagging. Experts say that it usually isn't the bothersome issue that's the problem; it's what the action represents. It's not about the dirty clothes left on the floor beside the hamper; it's what happened with your father. Dig deeper when you evaluate an irritation with your spouse. God gave you the ability to be rational and to contemplate the best way to handle frustrations.

Pick your battles. Let the little things slide and see how that goes. When you release annoyances, it means you appreciate that you and your partner are different. If he or she cooks using every pan, utensil, or surface in the kitchen, leave and let him or her cook their way. The most important thing is preserving your union; not fretting over the way your spouse peels the carrots. However, if some action is keeping you up at night, it's best to discuss it in a loving manner and bring it to closure.

Fortunately, it doesn't take much to turn a relationship around, putting life back into balance. What small gestures can you offer your spouse that signifies your dedication to solving your relationship concerns, no matter how trivial they seem?

Dear Lord, enlighten me, Lord; tell me what I must do to keep my relationship running smoothly. Teach me to ignore insignificant frustrations and address issues that could disrupt my marriage. Teach me how to swat away one annoying bee so that I am not faced with an entire swarm. Amen.

May 10

With that, Pharaoh took off his signet ring and put it on Joseph's finger.
He had him dressed in robes of fine linen and put a gold chain about his neck.

GENESIS 41:42

One universal tradition is the wedding ring, which dates back to the ancient Romans. The roundness of the ring represents eternity, symbolizing that a union should last forever. It was once believed that a nerve ran directly from the "ring" finger of the left hand to the heart. Reflect on the way you felt when your partner slid that ring on your finger the first time. Consider if the sight of your wedding ring conjures a feeling of warmth and fondness. You received the sacrament of marriage and had your union blessed by God. Contemplate what fused and strengthened your bond for life. Was it the circle of trust or something else? With so many years after your wedding, what can you do now to infuse your marriage with more love to ensure that your marriage does last forever?

Make your marriage a priority. In the throes of day-to-day life, set aside time to reconnect with your spouse; not to unload your burdens on his or her shoulders, but to accept his or her troubles and embrace the good and bad that comes with a marriage. When you recited your marriage vows that you accepted your partner for better or worse, you could be living through one of those low points. Remember from the prayer of St. Frances: it is in giving that we receive. By giving your time, energy, and love to your spouse during a low period of your relationship, you will reap much love in return.

When you make it a precedence to spend time together, you share thoughts, feelings, emotions, and experiences. The shared experiences bind you emotionally to your spouse. Try doing something out of the ordinary: a hot air balloon ride, horseback riding, salsa dancing, or something to make you happy and give you material to talk about for years to come. One of the worst things you can do is spend too much time away from your spouse. Distance does not make the heart grow fonder; sometimes it turns cold. The more entwined your lives are, the closer you will feel to your mate. God brought you both together for many reasons; one is to enjoy each other. What enjoyable activity will you do with your spouse this week?

Dear Lord, Flood my soul with your spirit, and renew the bonds of our marriage. Shine your grace upon me. Teach me to be kinder, gentler, and more loving than I ever thought possible. Amen.

May 11

Spikenard and saffron, Sweet cane and cinnamon, with all kinds of frankincense; Myrrh and aloes, with all the finest spices.

SONG OF SONGS 4:14

A delicious salad dressing consists of three ingredients: ketchup, brown sugar, and vinegar. The pizzazz is from the mixture of spices used. What spices do you bring to your marriage? Some spices are hot, subtle, pungent, robust, or sweet. After combining flavors, a totally different taste can be attained. When you and your spouse began a life together, methods of cohabitating were combined: decorating, housecleaning, laundry, cooking, and banking. Perhaps there were similarities with several approaches to certain activities. Combining furniture is often difficult when you have different decorating styles. Which amalgamations were smooth with your transition and which were unpalatable? Reflect over new activities you can try together to enhance your relationship with more zest. God provided spice so that your life would not be mundane.

Marriage can be regarded as a business partnership of running your home which entails keeping financial records, house and car maintenance, shopping, laundry, cleaning, cooking, and childcare. If the business runs smoothly, there is more tranquility in your home. But if the bills are not paid, the car isn't working, dirty laundry is piled sky high, there is nothing planned for dinner, and the kids need rides to youth group, then frustration grows, misunderstandings surface, and conflict ensues. Conflict over domestic duties is second to conflict over money in a marriage. When it comes to chores, asking for help implies the responsibility of the task belongs to you. In actuality, chores should be a shared obligation. Studies show that women feel more sexually attracted to partners who share chores. One way to spice up chores is to do them together as a family, while not being overly critical if the task is not done to your satisfaction. Try cleaning to lively music or whistling while you work; it makes chores more enjoyable.

Establish a time when you all stop working to do something fun. It's important to spend as much time relaxing as you spend doing errands. God didn't unite you to spend all of your free time together doing tasks. Take time to praise him as well. How will you add spice to your routine chores?

Dear Lord, as I reflect over my ordinary existence, nudge me toward the spices that can enhance my life with my partner. Thank you for reminding me that my life doesn't have to be average. I can shake things up a bit with your guidance and limitless love. Amen.

May 12

*In the sixth month, the angel Gabriel was sent from God to a town
of Galilee called Nazareth, to a virgin betrothed to a man named Joseph,
of the house of David, and the virgin's name was Mary.*

LUKE 1:26–27

When Mary agreed to be Joseph's wife, she had no idea what she was getting into or how complicated her life would become. She maintained her faithfulness to God while honoring her husband, an older man that she barely knew. Imagine the questions Mary must have harbored while journeying to Bethlehem with Joseph. Do you question the journey you are on with your spouse? Trust in God's plan for you. He brought you both together for a reason, and while it may seem incomprehensible, have faith and continue onward. Think of Mary when you feel lost or hesitate sharing the path with your spouse. Pray to Mary when you don't understand and doubt your destination. She will send her son to walk with you as she watches out for you, as any mother would.

Imagine how Mary felt when she gave birth to Jesus: she didn't have her mother to help or comfort her. She was in an earthen manger surrounded by animals and she made the best of that less-than-perfect situation with eloquence and loveliness. Contemplate what inadequate situations you have been in with your spouse. When you find yourself in dire circumstances, think of Mary and petition her for grace to help you through it. Remember that after Mary made the long journey to Bethlehem, she gave birth to our Savior of the world, then, God asked more of her. She had to continue on to Egypt with the infant Jesus. When you least expect it, God might ask more of you too. Don't question the Almighty because he knows your life plan. Trust in God that you will make it through your difficulties, just as Jesus, Mary, and Joseph made it through theirs to arrive safely in Egypt.

Your marriage bonds can be stressed if your family is growing to include children. It can be exhausting and worrisome, a combination that can be toxic to the romantic relationship that made you parents. Work on your relationship and it will pay off. Children bring more chores, obligations, and annoyances to your home life. Bringing home a newborn or newly adopted child might mean an influx of visitors to your home too. Think about the visitors Mary welcomed after she gave birth to Jesus. She welcomed shepherds, kings with camels, and myriad wanderers. Mary lovingly shared the Christ child with each person who passed by. What aspect of your life will you consider changing to match the Virgin Mary?

Dear Lord, on Mother's Day, I honor Mary for looking down upon me.
Amen.

May 13

Hatred stirs up disputes, but love covers all offenses.

PROVERBS 10:12

Why are some plants easier than others to grow? Daisies grow like weeds. Daylilies require minimal effort, but roses are temperamental. A rose bush needs considerable primping, but the blooms are worth the extra work. Ponder what aspect of your marriage requires extra attention. Consider if there is any lingering hurt in your relationship. Do you forgive too easily, too often, or not enough? Do you struggle with holding grudges?

A common grudge outside of marriage is anger toward your parents for past hurts or a grudge against a friend who wronged you. It affects your marriage when you complain to your spouse about grudges because they gnaw away at you. They sap your energy as your thoughts sour. You need to move on. The destructive grudges are those within your marriage because they are pent-up, cloud your interactions, and cause defensiveness. If old grudges still affect you, discuss them with your spouse. There are numerous explanations why people hold grudges: immaturity, some things are unforgivable, some people are bitter, some people have ego or control issues, or some are waiting for an apology.

Forgiveness is a gift you can give to yourself and your spouse because it frees you from the pain and encumbrance of a grudge. Also, forgiveness is a process that begins with respectful treatment toward each other. It's easy to hold onto a hurt, perhaps for inflicting pain on you. It's conceivable to withhold love or hold onto resentment that turns into bitterness or hatred over time. Why is it so hard to forgive? In order for your spouse to behave differently toward you, he or she needs to know about the infraction. To love your partner fully and completely, you must release the toxins of bitterness, sadness, or regret.

Who facilitates honest and open communication in your marriage? If you are the wrongdoer, contemplate ways you can offer an apology with a plan to repair your union. If you are the injured person, remember that you are entitled to your grief, but eventually let it go to achieve inner peace. Perhaps the best place to begin this process is at confession. Talk to Jesus first; he will enlighten you.

Dear Lord, comfort me during this difficulty. Heal my hurt and empower me with your tender mercies so that I can resume an amicable relationship with [name]. Propel us through the reconciliation process unscathed. I trust you and love you. Amen.

May 14

My son, to my wisdom be attentive, to understanding incline your ear,
That you may act discreetly, and your lips guard what you know.

PROVERBS 5:1–2

To make cutting the grass enjoyable, I make patterns with the lawn mower as I go. I might mow horizontally one day, vertically or diagonally the next time. Sometimes, I revert back to the last pattern because it was fresh in my mind. In marriage, we often backslide to a particular behavior because it's familiar, and change is difficult. In developing good listening skills, it's critical to eliminate any distractions, not be preoccupied, or not develop a rebuttal until after all of the information has been heard.

When listening to your spouse, be mindful of defense mechanisms that can prevent you from truly appreciating the intended message being delivered to you. The most common are blaming or rationalization to your partner for some action. Projection of your thoughts hinders listening and denial stops it. Perhaps you have the habit of tuning out your partner, which involves the processes of selective attention and selective perception. You hear only what you want to hear and screen out what you don't. Often, what your spouse says and what you hear are two totally different things. Therefore, you are required to listen intently with your heart, mind, and soul.

Listening helps prevent minor problems from becoming enormous ones. The goal to listening is to understand what's being said, not to fix or judge. Listening allows you to gain knowledge from your spouse about topics, ideas, and people. Listen for the meaning beyond the words. It will make your spouse feel respected when you show an interest in his or her problems, ideas, thoughts, and opinions. Effective listening skills enable you to solve problems and resolve conflict in your marriage. Once you understand your mate you can agree or disagree, and try cooperatively to clarify thinking, seek solutions, and resolve conflict. Listening also reduce tension by allowing your spouse an opportunity to "clear the air."

Effective listening can strengthen your marriage. How can you be a better listener? When your partner listens to you wholeheartedly, does it make you feel important and loved?

Dear Lord, grant me the ability to hear whatever is troubling my spouse with open ears, an uncluttered mind, and a receptive heart. Help me to understand and not formulate opinions, suggestions, or solutions. Let me show my depth of caring by simply listening and caring about the words spoken and the message revealed. Amen.

May 15

For the birds of the air may carry your voice,
a winged creature may tell what you say.

ECCLESIASTES 10:20

The Northern Mockingbird imitates other birds, animals, and mechanical sounds such as car alarms. While the impersonations sound authentic to humans, they don't fool other birds. Contemplate whether or not what you say to your spouse is credible, or if you are mimicking someone else. Are your words believable? Do you tell your partner what he or she wants to hear, or do you speak from your heart with truth and love?

Use clear, specific, and direct means of communicating to your partner. When you speak, don't be brutally honest. Honesty is not an excuse to be mean; however, it's important to get to the point. One way to be direct is to take responsibility for your choices and thoughts. You have to be able to say, "This is what I want." Above all, be respectful. To be effective it will help if you aren't critical, negative, or condescending.

It's easy to get caught up in drama. Before you do, ask yourself if it is really important, or could you be overreacting. By mulling it over before addressing the issue allows your emotions to be calm. There are many ways you can get off track. Regardless what your spouse says, don't get derailed. Return to the topic if either of you veers off course. Timing is crucial when bringing up a sensitive topic. Don't wait until the nightly news is over to have an in depth discussion with your partner about the way he or she balances the checkbook. In general, it's wise not to have heavy conversations while you are driving, hungry, or tired.

If you want to discuss a topic that elicits an emotional response, try using a soft start to the conversation by saying something positive first. For instance, "Honey, you know how much I love your mother, but she often overstays her visit. Can we discuss limiting the number of days she stays with us? I prefer to have a houseguest for three days." Whenever you speak, use "I statements." What "red flag" words elicit an emotional response to your spouse: money, in-laws, or sex? Jesus spoke kindly and compassionately to those he met. Think of Christ and replicate his style and grace when you speak to your spouse.

Dear Lord, before I open my mouth to speak, let me pause to reflect on the message I want to deliver. Help me to be more Christ-like with my words and actions. I want my spouse to feel my love while understanding the thoughts I need to convey. Amen.

May 16

And all spoke highly of him and were amazed
at the gracious words that came from his mouth.

LUKE 4:22

The appendix is a useless appendage that doesn't present problems unless it becomes inflamed. Acute appendicitis requires surgery and if left untreated, a ruptured appendix could cause death. What seemingly insignificant aspect of your marriage gets overlooked? Ponder how often you flatter your spouse. Why not compliment your partner regularly? Consider the tensions of your mate's typical workday, the many pressing burdens that you aren't privy to, or the unspoken adversities that have crushed and broken his or her spirits. When sorrows burden your spouse's soul, the right words can be freeing, making an enormous impact on your relationship if used appropriately. If you don't know what to say, ask the Holy Spirit to enlighten you. God made your spouse extraordinary; notice those special features and thank God too.

You can build up your spouse with a few simple words of praise every day. It takes little time and effort. Why not start today to convey your admirations to your spouse? Marvel over your spouse's smile, how infectious it is, and compliment that. Notice how beautiful the intricate colors of your partner's eyes are as the windows of the soul and compliment them. Praise him or her in front of your children, family, coworkers, friends, and neighbors. You can complement him or her on social networking sites. Think of the many different ways you can say "I love you." You could praise your partner for providing financial and emotional support to you throughout your marriage. You could praise him or her for a task that was recently completed, even if it was as simple as doing the dishes or something complicated such as tarring the driveway. Consider the last time you thanked your spouse for a job he or she did around the house. Notice what chores get done without prodding. Then recognize and show appreciation for them.

You could encourage your mate to try something new, such as joining your church choir, complimenting their ability to sing. Inspire your spouse to reach for something that you know they want to accomplish, but lack the confidence to do alone. Each time you flatter your spouse, you reinforce how lucky you are to have married that wonderful person. How will you be complimentary to your partner today?

Dear Lord, thank you for allowing me the privilege of praising my spouse each day. Thank you for allowing me to see [*name*]'s beauty and to articulate it in a pleasing way. You blessed me with a wonderful partner and I want to relay it more often. Keep the loving words flowing, Lord, like a lazy river with nothing to do except be lovely. Amen.

May 17

The great testings your own eyes have seen, and those great signs
and wonders. But the LORD has not given you a heart
to understand, or eyes to see, or ears to hear until this day.

DEUTERONOMY 29:2–3

Is a half glass of water half full or half empty? In reality, it is entirely full with half water and half air. How you perceive things determines how your life unfolds. Contemplate what you have viewed in a positive manner last week versus what you viewed negatively. Convert all of your perceptions optimistically through prayer. God is in everything you see, feel, say, think, and do; but you have to look for it. Seek the Lord's loving touch when you are faced with complicated decisions that test your discernments. Are you questioning your vulnerabilities around your marriage?

Some older adults maintain good health and are active senior citizens, while others appear to rapidly decline with medical problems. While genetics could be a factor, positive thinking may play a major role. You have a choice about the way you think; therefore, choose to focus on something positive or a thought that makes you happy. Focus your energy on positive thinking and reasons to feel hopeful because it could help you feel better. If you struggle to think this way, dwell on the preciousness of the Lord. Focus all of your thoughts on Jesus's face, his eyes, his smile, and his love for you.

Life is full of ups and downs. There will be times when you experience rough patches of negativity with feelings of disappointment in your marriage. However, with God in your life, he can erase the negativity for nothing is impossible with God. Through prayer, you can strive to stay positive while the Lord guides and motivates you onward. Ask God to desecrate any lingering pessimism.

Believe in God and take a chance on him helping to turn your life around and put the focus back on him and all that is good, right, pure, and holy. Perhaps you and your partner could visit religious places together: shrines, churches, and places of apparitions and miracles. Such spots could empower you to embrace positive thinking throughout your entire life, making it richer and happier. How will you thank God for the many blessings he has given to you including the power to think positively?

Dear Lord, allow me to seek you first in all I do. Sometimes I forget that you are with me and all I have to do is call out to you and you will ground me and show me the way. You are my saving God, you are my salvation. Amen.

May 18

And forgive us our debts, as we forgive our debtors;
and do not subject us to the final test,
but deliver us from the evil one.

MATTHEW 6:12–13

Sometimes I cannot remember what I had for dinner the night before; but I never forget past mistakes. Are you like that or do you know someone like that? Some people can forgive but not forget. Forgiveness is challenging, especially when an apology is lacking. Try to be courteous and strive for honest communication without being self-righteous. If you were injured, grieve, and then let it go. Nothing good comes from hanging onto hurt, but much can be gained from moving forward. Strive for inner peace. Forgiveness is a healing process that takes time. We are human; therefore, we all make mistakes.

Remember that you will make mistakes, too. When you find yourself on the other end of forgiveness, you will want your spouse to treat you with the same respect that you offer him or her now. Contemplate a clearer and a healthier understanding of yourself because that will help you to understand your spouse better. When you accept the erratic ways you think, speak, and act, you can appreciate more fully how your spouse thinks, speaks, and acts.

If you have forgiven your spouse for an offence, you are not letting him or her off the hook while you suffer from their transgression. Also, you don't have to go back to the old relationship where the offense could be repeated. Instead, work to change that situation, to improve it during the forgiveness process, then to let the bitterness go while remembering your rights to healthy boundaries. It is complicated because you should still hold your spouse accountable for their hurtful actions. However, even if your partner does not repent, you still need to forgive because it is about your attitude, not their action. It might take some time, but that is okay.

When thoughts of past hurts occur, it's what you do with them that really matters. If you realize that you are focusing on a past offense, ask the Lord to help you through it. Forgiveness begins with an intellectual decision. The emotional part of forgiveness occurs after you are able to let go of the resentment. Emotional healing may take time after you forgive.

Maybe you need to forgive yourself. If you turn to God seeking his forgiveness, you can trust that you will get it. Attempt to be as merciful as the Lord. Forgiveness is a gift.

Dear Lord, wash away my sinfulness; cleanse my soul and wipe the slate clean so that I can move onward to shine brightly to everyone. Teach me how to be forgiving, as you always are. Soften my heart, Lord. Amen.

May 19

Those who traveled the roads now traveled by roundabout paths.

JUDGES 5:6

When you drive, do you like to listen to talk shows or music on the radio? Regardless of the distance you travel, you could choose to keep the radio off and pray. Why not invite the Lord to journey with you? Perhaps you could begin by asking God to keep you safe while you drive, and then open your heart and pour out the contents while you listen for his voice. God wants to hear from you; he is eager to listen. Why not use the silence in your vehicle to make a connection to the Lord? You might be surprised by the notions he puts in your head. Whatever weighs heavy on your heart, give it to God. Perhaps you could talk to him while you take a walk. You might find his presence washes over you in the sunshine that bathes you in warmth. Amazingly enough, the Lord will journey every path you take; you just need to trust that he is there.

God needs to come first in your life and be the center of your marriage. If you can put God first in your marriage, everything else will fall into perfect place. When God comes first, you will be more willing to be generous, kind, loving, and patient. You will have a better marriage because each day you will be striving to be more Christ-like. Try to love your spouse unconditionally the way Christ loves you. Let the marriage commitment you share with each other be reminiscent of the depth of Christ's love for you. Jesus gave his life for you and will never leave you. Love your spouse with that same intensity, that same unconditional love that God has for you.

When you worship and pray together, you merge on a soulful plane of intimacy that other couples don't know and enjoy. By talking about God together, whether it comes naturally or through reading Holy Scriptures together, you are actually encouraging each other to grow in God's image. Pray about your marriage, your children, your finances, or about any decisions you must make. Praying about making decisions together based on God's will enables you to have more confidence in everything you do, because you are involving him in all you do.

Before you start your day, rise a little earlier to accommodate prayer time with your spouse. It's like putting your best foot forward, setting the tone for the entire day on a glorious level of trust. While your spouse travels, works, does chores, or gives presentations, pray for him or her. Ask God to bless him or her with the right words to conduct the business set before him or her. You will be amazed at the power of prayer.

Dear Lord, guard me as I journey onward. You are my shield and protector, keeping me out of harm's way. Amen.

May 20

You changed my mourning into dancing;
you took off my sackcloth and clothed me with gladness.
PSALM 30:12

Dancing builds strength; increases flexibility; and promotes weight loss, cognition, and psychological well-being. When you're dancing, there is a mind-body connection that doesn't happen when exercising on stationary equipment. Dance your way to gladness. Think of possible times throughout your day when you could dance for a few minutes. When you are alone in a restroom, break room, or kitchen, shake it up a bit to get your blood pumping. Even if you feel silly and look a little crazy, it will make you smile and lift your spirits. If something so simple can put you in a good mood, it might rub off on your spouse and prompt him or her to dance with you. Locate the song you danced to at your wedding and relive it. Find that happy place within, enjoy it, and make it grow.

Dancing stimulates a desire for healthy living and romance. The type of dancing you do doesn't really matter; all styles are beneficial. Dancing with your spouse creates another way for you to connect with each other. As you dance, your eyes meet, your bodies are close, and the rhythm of the music sends your spirits soaring. Dancing is like a long and wonderful hug that requires the two of you to work together as a team while it builds your self-esteem. It's an activity that requires you to pay attention to one another and communicate both verbally and nonverbally so that you're not stepping on each other's toes all night. Dancing lessons and going out dancing provides enjoyable alone time for the two of you, where you can step away from your children, jobs, obligations, or stress from everyday life.

If you look for a reason not to dance, you are sure to find one. Instead, let go of any desire to be a perfectionist, and allow yourself to just enjoy the experience and fun of it. Accept that as you learn how to dance with your spouse, you both may be a bit clumsy. In time, you will be more graceful with one another as you learn to move together with the music and rhythm of life.

Dear Lord, thank you for giving me the ability to dance and put a spring in my step. You lift me up when I feel down. You shake me up when I need it most, and fill me with the jubilation from loving and honoring you. Amen.

May 21

A sharp two-edged sword came out of his mouth,
and his face shone like the sun at its brightest.

REVELATION 1:16

Reflective material was invented to create a tape that could reflect a car's headlights at night and make it glow. This ingenious discovery thwarted numerous accidents. Have you identified certain behaviors that impede disasters in your relationship? One way to avoid marital discord is to master healthy methods of communication. While there are endless poor ways to communicate, the most commonly used is expecting your spouse to be a mind reader. Unless your spouse has a crystal ball or telepathic skills, this method is detrimental to your relationship. Another ineffective style of speaking is referred to as triangulation: telling a third party what you want your spouse to know. Have you ever told a coworker, friend, or relative something you should have told your mate directly? It is unproductive and should be avoided. Swearing, speaking disrespectfully, and acting out sarcastically are other fruitless ways to converse.

Instead of using improper methods that can sabotage your marriage, develop keen skills that will propel your relationship forward. Try asking your spouse for what you want in a clear and direct manner while being respectful. For example, say, "I would love to eat out tonight," instead of, "I'm so tired from working all day; the last thing I want to do is cook in a hot kitchen. Why is it left up to me to cook each night? That's not fair!" Sarcasm will escalate into an argument with hurt feelings. When you sense disrespect building, say a prayer. Ask God to fill you with the right words to convey your feelings.

Some spouses use analogies because they are one of the most effective ways of getting your message across. Analogies help your partner accept a complicated concept and apply it to something in life that's easy to understand. Using word pictures is a helpful skill that elicits an image. For instance, your spouse could be strong like a rock. Another successful communication tool is to scale something of importance to you from one to ten. For example, "It is important that you attend my company picnic with me. On a scale of one to ten, this is a ten." Rephrasing is a method that allows you to be more specific in getting your point across. It behooves you to use the many useful communication skills that are available. What poor method of speaking will you transform this week?

Dear Lord, erase the negativity that builds within and replace it with all that is pure and holy. Fill my mouth with loving words that convey everything that resides in my heart. Thank you, Lord. Amen.

May 22

Isaiah replied, "This will be the sign for you from the LORD
that he will carry out the word he has spoken:
Shall the shadow go forward or back ten steps?
2 KINGS 20:9

Early road signs were milestones, giving distance or direction. What signs give direction in your marriage? Do you pray for direction or "wing it?" A resource of the Catholic tradition is spiritual direction. Do you have a spiritual advisor? A spiritual advisor is akin to a trusted friend who can enable you to see yourself and your relationship with God. How can you make your primary role in your marriage to help one another get to heaven? Perhaps you could attend Bible classes together and discuss it throughout the week, or you could read passages together before bedtime. Try to find a way to incorporate prayer with your spouse into your daily routine so that you don't put your own needs and desires ahead of the spiritual needs of your spouse.

Does your parish offer eucharistic adoration throughout the week? Consider spending time alone with the Lord when you can meditate and focus on him. Adoration can draw you more profoundly into the mystery of Christ's presence in the host and fortify your bond with Jesus. It also allows you to express your love, gratitude, and respect for Christ. Your spiritual life can be strengthened when you sit with Jesus, even for a short while. Taking time for adoration enables you to slow down in your busy and stressful day. God hears your prayers wherever you are; however, if you visit him in the Eucharist, you will obtain an abundance of grace. Before you can love your spouse, you first must learn to love God through contemplation of his love by gazing upon him in the Eucharist. During the time spent with him in contemplation, you gain nourishment that provides the grace and the strength to go out into the world and be fruitful.

Contemplate ways you and your spouse can be fruitful. Consider praying for those who have no one to pray for them, perhaps prisoners, nursing home residents, or people mentioned on prayer lists. Perhaps you could make a donation of blood to the Red Cross or bring a bag of groceries to a food pantry. Clean out your closets and donate a portion of it to the poor. Maybe you could make and distribute sandwiches to the homeless in your community. By performing acts of service with your spouse, you will grow closer to each other, to your community, and church family. What changes will you make in your schedule this week to spend time with the Lord?

Dear Lord, bless my relationship with you and my spouse. Help me
find a way to unite prayerfully while walking in a spiritual direction
toward you so that we spend eternity in your kingdom. Amen.

May 23

Trustworthy are the blows of a friend, dangerous, the kisses of an enemy.
PROVERBS 27:6

Constructive criticism provides valid opinions about someone else using positive and negative interpretations. In collaborative work it is a valuable tool in sustaining performance standards. Consider how well you receive constructive criticism from your spouse. Do you think there is an underlying thread of hurt causing the words, or is he or she genuinely looking out for your best interest? Perhaps your spouse is being an overly critical nag. Some people become defensive when receiving constructive criticism even if it is given in a spirit of goodwill. Perhaps criticality is a trigger emotion from your childhood, being raised by perfectionists. Take time in prayerful reflection to uncover where your feelings have originated and what you plan to do with them.

Throughout your marriage you will have complaints about your spouse that need to be expressed. First consider if your grievance is something you can overlook or tolerate. Not every shortcoming needs to be vocalized. However, if there are legitimate circumstances that warrant voicing your concerns, do it cautiously because no one wants their faults pointed out to them. If a criticism is presented in a caring, beneficial manner, a positive response is likely to happen. Therefore, it is prudent to be mindful of the time and place to initiate the conversation, while keeping your frustration under control. If it is not convenient to talk immediately after a negative behavior has occurred, say a prayer and wait for a more appropriate time and place when another setting provides the best opportunity of your comment being heard.

Be mindful not to phrase criticism that will invoke a defensive response. Imagine if the tables were turned; how would you want to be approached and spoken to? Ask God to influence your intentions, motives, mind-set, and attitudes. Try to approach the confrontation with humility and confidence while maintaining a positive regard for your spouse. Reassure him or her that you love, respect and esteem him or her regardless of any mistake. This way your spouse will feel safe with you, moving forward in your marriage in genuine mature love. The next time you criticize your spouse, what changes will you make in the way you speak, the words you use, or the love you invoke?

Dear Lord, my spouse must truly love me to confront me with issues that stir my emotions. I don't know what to do with my feelings. Help me, Lord, to sort it out and deal with it in your loving grace. Give me the stamina to grow and become the wonderful partner you intended me to be. Amen.

May 24

LORD, let me know my end, the number of my days,
that I may learn how frail I am.
To be sure, you establish the expanse of my days;
indeed, my life is as nothing before you.

PSALM 39:5–6

The gastrotrich lives only three days before it dies. These worms are vital to aquatic food chains by consuming various bacteria, microalgae, and protozoans. They play an important role in explaining the history of life and relationship of organisms despite their short life. To God, your life is a mere flash, yet you act as if your days are unlimited. Life is short. Do you act as if you will live forever? Do you waste time and spend money as though you are immortal? Do you shop for things you don't need, but want, and still buy? Do you have more clothes than you will ever wear? Do you buy stuff with little regard to the attachment of it? If you die tomorrow, will any of your stuff matter? You cannot take any of it with you when you go to heaven, so why do you clutter your life with it all now? Have you put off a vacation because next year would be better? What if you don't have another year?

Because your days are numbered, make each moment count. Take your spouse in your arms today and say, "I love you," and mean it because there might not be a tomorrow. Smile lovingly, give compliments, words of encouragement, and warm hugs. Each day is a gift from God. What you do with it is your gift back to him. Ask the Lord what you can do with the precious time he has given to you. In the silence of your heart, ask God what his intentions are for you. Are you afraid that you might fail? There is a purpose in everything you do if you simply trust in the Lord. Give your pressing concerns to God and allow him to carry your worries.

Release all of your shoddy excuses to stifle doing something magnificent with your life because it is so short. Whatever it is that you think you should be doing, begin now by doing it passionately and brilliantly. Fan the glint of the burning embers into a roaring flame. Regardless of what it is, start today. How will you begin to enjoy the life God has given to you?

Dear Lord, let me walk through this life by making a difference and an impact on this world. You have entrusted me with the gift of time; don't let me squander it. Fill my days with your presence in my life. Let me see you in my spouse and the strangers I meet on the streets. I trust in your plan for me, Lord, no matter how long or short it is. Amen.

May 25

While the morning stars sang together and all the sons of God shouted for joy?
Who shut within doors the sea, when it burst forth from the womb.

JOB 38:7–8

Why are certain sounds so relaxing? Some people love listening to it rain, while others enjoy hearing ocean waves. Whether it's the lilt of chirping birds in springtime, summer night crickets, or a crackling fire in autumn, everyone yearns for a particular sound. Does the sound of your partner's voice stir your awakening conscious? What is it about your mate that you are fond of? Dwell on the positive qualities that fill you with peacefulness, happiness, and love. Tell your spouse how those attributes make you feel. The Holy Spirit dwells within you, so invoke him every day to enable you to put your best foot forward while walking the path of righteousness with your spouse and enjoying the sounds along the way.

Some characteristics that researchers have found in successful marriages are positivity, empathy, commitment, acceptance, love, and respect. Consider how you foster optimism in your marriage. Contemplate if you are playful and affectionate with your spouse or if you need to improve that area of your relationship. Take joy in each other's achievements and understand each other's perspective by putting yourself in their shoes. Successful marriages involve commitment to each other and the relationship. If you are truly dedicated to making your marriage successful, it is more apt to be a lasting relationship. With that level of dedication, you might have to make sacrifices for the sake of your marriage. Consider what recent sacrifices you have made for the good of the relationship.

A basic characteristic of a healthy marriage is acceptance of each other. Ponder if you accept your spouse for who he or she really is, and not who you wish they could be. If you try to change your spouse, you could be met with a confrontation. Change occurs when your spouse respects and accepts the differences. An essential component of marriage is love and respect for one another.

As life becomes complicated with obligations and demands, your relationship could suffer. It is easy to grow distant as you bounce from one activity to another, but make an effort to stay close to your partner and don't neglect the romance that once came so easily. Reconnect each day with prayer. The connection you have with the Lord will spill over into your marriage and that love will strengthen your marriage and make it withstand the test of time. What characteristics of your marriage do you find endearing?

Dear Lord, fill my ears with the pleasantries you created for me to hear and love. Let me listen for your sweet voice beckoning me to continue on the course you established for me. Amen.

May 26

For nothing will be impossible for God.

LUKE 1:37

How many times have you felt like quitting? Have you wondered if your marriage is on the brink of failure, and you don't know how to save it? If you feel lost, stop what you are doing, and turn to God. He will find you and help you to climb out of the hole you are in because nothing is impossible for God. He will shine his magnificent light down around you, illuminating your path. He will guide you to the right route, the one he wants you on. Take one baby step at a time and move forward toward God.

Trust in God with all of your heart, mind, and soul—in all of his marvelous ways. If you second-guess your circumstances, pray louder, harder, and more steadfast. Say any prayer that comes to mind, or simply talk to Jesus as if he was in the room with you, because God is always with you. The Holy Spirit dwells within you and a band of angels encircle and guard you. With such a mighty force you can only be propelled forward. Trust in God to help mend your difficulties. He alone can save you.

Sometimes you have to endure hardships. During difficulties God will be there beside you. When everything seems right in your world, it's easy to get caught up in it and forget the Lord. However, when you are at your lowest point, you remember to call on him. Maybe God's response is, "I am with you; lean on me, and you will survive and thrive." Because God created you, he knows you intimately, even all of the hairs on your head. He has unimaginable love for you. God isn't always going to make your paths easy, but he will make them straight. He wants what is best for you even if you can't see it. The problem is how you define what is best from your perspective. God's definition of what is best is when your happiness comes from him despite your circumstances. Will you be strong enough to hand over your difficulties to God and trust implicitly in him?

Dear Lord, help me, Lord, God, and savior. Help me to find my way out of this dark place that has engulfed me. Shine your guiding light around me to comfort me and alleviate my worries. God, what do you want me to learn and see here? Help me to come to my senses, to learn, see, and be the person you created me to be. Amen.

May 27

*When he made a count of those of twenty years old and over, he found
that there were three hundred thousand picked men fit for war, capable
of handling lance and shield. He also hired a hundred thousand valiant
warriors from Israel for a hundred talents of silver. But a man of God
came to him and said: "O king, let not the army of Israel go with you, for
the LORD is not with Israel—with any Ephraimite. Instead, go on your
own, strongly prepared for the battle; why should the LORD hinder you
in the face of the enemy: for with God is power to help or to hinder."*

2 CHRONICLES 25:5–8

Memorial Day was established to remember the fallen soldiers who served
to preserve freedom for America. Many people visit cemeteries and
memorials to honor those who died in military service. Perhaps you or your
spouse was an honorable service member in the Armed Forces. How do you
handle the separation and the time you have together on leave?

The sacrament of holy matrimony is honorable, yet it faces challenges
for military families during and after deployment. Service, especially during
wartime, can weaken the matrimonial bonds and family life. Post-traumatic
stress is a major factor contributing to the hurt that some marriages experience. Many soldiers have disturbing memories, nightmares, and flashbacks.
They may have witnessed the death of friends and comrades. Many have experienced close-range explosions that caused concussions with undiagnosed
brain injuries. Some soldiers feel detached and unable to love as they once
did. Many experience sleep difficulties resulting in increased irritability and
outbursts of anger which greatly impact their family life.

After dealing with the hardship of separation, soldiers are reunited with
a spouse who seems distant or foreign to them. Tension can result from the
simplest situations of everyday life. Misunderstandings are common. The
communion of life, which describes marriage, suffers considerably. Many
service members believe they have not changed, or they blame their marital
discord on their partner. If your relationship feels like a battleground, focus
on the Lord through prayer and meditation. Cry out to God for help when
you are fighting on the frontline of your relationship. God will not leave you
in times of trouble. God alone can get you through anything no matter how
bad the situation seems. Have faith in God.

Dear Lord, I take refuge in you; protect me from the dangers that
surround me. Painful words cut into me through me like swords on
a battlefield. Release me from the snares that have entrapped me. You
see my afflictions, you know my distress. Rescue me, dear Lord, and
keep me safe in your unfaltering love. Amen.

May 28

"Do to others whatever you would have them do to you."
This is the law and the prophets.

MATTHEW 7:12

It's easy to give to those we love. The challenge comes when God says we must give to those we are not fond of. During troubling times, that difficult person might be our spouse. After a heated argument with your partner, do you feel like bringing him or her tea with chocolate covered biscuits? Probably not, but you could offer a genuine smile, a warm embrace, a prayer, or the offer to listen wholeheartedly to your partner to try to resolve any conflict. The ability to truly listen and understand is a gift; one that you would want your spouse to give to you when the tables are turned.

Bite your tongue to stop yourself from saying something you might regret. Don't allow your conversation to spiral out of control and turn into an argument. Instead, listen intently to the words your spouse uses and contemplate the message he or she is trying to deliver. The lack of communication in marriages today is a leading cause of divorce. If your spouse doesn't listen to you, you can feel frustrated, angry, and hurt. Additionally, your health can be compromised. Contemplate if poor communication skills were inherited from your family. Was your partner raised in a family where siblings didn't listen or were incapable of expressing themselves? You and your partner can change those habits. Don't let communication problems take you down a destructive path.

In order to listen completely, make eye contact with your spouse. Don't be tempted to look out the window, at the TV or newspaper, stop filing your nails, or finishing up a chore. As difficult as it is, listen without interruptions. If this is a problem, allow your spouse to hold an object that represents a microphone to remind you to remain quiet; concentrate on simply listening with an open mind. Don't jump to conclusions or be judgmental. Show your spouse how much you care by exerting an extra effort to comprehend what he or she wants to share with you. Disengage your defense mechanisms to blame, rationalize, or deny. Humbly accept the words, acknowledge the emotions, and relay your interpretations of it, because that's how you want your partner to listen to you. Pray before you respond, especially if it's an emotional reaction.

Dear Lord, thank you for keeping me calm amidst the storm of words and for allowing me to embrace the message and appreciate the message my spouse wants me to hear. Thank you for enabling me to truly listen with my mind, heart, and soul. I love you. Amen.

May 29

Let them curse it who curse the Sea, those skilled at disturbing Leviathan!
JOB 3:8

Turn on a TV to be bombarded with foul language and immoral acts. People drop the "f-bomb" in casual conversation, numb to its offensiveness. Jesus warns that the use of abusive language will lead to judgment so it's prudent not to become immune to it. When tempers flare, are you tempted to use bad language with your spouse? Do your words border verbal abusive? Jesus knows the words that roll off your tongue originate in your heart. Keep your heart pure by filling it with kindness. If you carry your heart like a treasure, heavy with love and adoration, there is no room for bad language. Speak to your spouse with respectfulness. Deliver messages directly, mindful of clarity, and precision. If words fail you, ask the Holy Spirit to fill you with the perfect words.

If you resort to screaming and swearing at your partner, the respect and foundation of your marriage will quickly deteriorate. No one should treat their spouse this way. Disrespectful treatment is akin to bullying while trying to dominate and control their partner. Whoever resorts to this type of behavior usually has low self-esteem and needs to develop proper communication skills. Without changing your response to the treatment, the bullying will continue. People can control their temper. Some spouses continue to control their partners because their spouse allows them to get away with it. Talk calmly to your spouse that you will leave the next time they behave in a disrespectful manner. However, if the bullying continues, make sure that you do leave. Go for a walk, take a hot shower, or walk through a shopping mall until tempers cool. When you return home, discuss with your spouse the importance of respectful treatment in your relationship. Seek counseling from your parish priest or a marriage counselor.

Remember that when you talk to your spouse, the Holy Spirit dwells within them. What you say to him or her, you also say to God. Therefore, make sure each word is good, kind, noble, and pure. Treat your spouse the way Jesus would expect you to. Ask him to bless your words, actions, and thoughts. If your thoughts are laced with anger and hatred, ask God to take them away and replace them with those that are caring and loving.

Dear Lord, bless my heart with purity, respect, and devotion so that the words that form can only reflect the love that I feel. Don't let a seed of doubt, worry, or regret take root. Pluck it out allowing glorifying songs of praise to roll off my lips. Amen.

May 30

"Whatever you bind on earth shall be bound in heaven;
and whatever you loose on earth shall be loosed in heaven."

MATTHEW 16:19

At some point we have all been hurt by someone we love. It might have happened yesterday or long ago. The pain and memory still exist. Is there a rift between you and your spouse? You can drown in self-pity. Instead, free yourself from the grudge you've been dragging like a ball and chain. Don't be burdened with the weight of a past hurt when you can be free to love again. It's a choice you can make. Work to change the feelings by striving for inner peace; not dwelling or approving of the hurtful behavior. It's mind over matter.

Each time the painful act enters your mind, pray. You can achieve this by frequently repeating the Our Father, focusing on "forgive us our trespasses as we forgive those who trespass against us." Imagine the advice Jesus might offer you about this predicament. Throughout the Bible, you can read passages on forgiveness and love. Read them often to reinforce the behavior God desires of you. Receive graces through confession that will empower you to begin the process of forgiveness.

Remember that forgiveness is a process that takes time, patience, and understanding. If you are struggling to comprehend it, ask God for enlightenment. Resume respectful and courteous treatment, striving to achieve honest communication despite your hurt feelings. Reflect on the importance of your goal, which is to achieve reconciliation. If you committed the offence, you cannot demand forgiveness. Apologize with a plan so that your spouse knows you genuinely will strive not to repeat this mistake. Then work to repair any damage done because this nice gesture will show your partner that you mean what you say. Maybe you could take your spouse to a show he or she really wanted to see or buy a much loved CD or DVD.

If you were the injured person, refrain from self-righteous behaviors. Grieve the sadness and then let it go. Heal the memory so that it doesn't take over your life. Accomplish this by doing something for yourself to feel better about yourself and your life. Take a yoga class or find a way to release your creativity. Paint a picture of your feelings or write a poem about it. Your spouse may not be ready to apologize; you may have to settle for self-soothing until he or she is ready. Your responsibility is to yourself to achieve internal harmony. Forgiveness is a gift you can give to yourself and to each other. It is a healing process that requires work. In time you will cling back to your spouse remembering that what is bound on earth shall remain bound in heaven.

Dear Lord, fill me with the will to be forgiving, the means to carry it through, and the resolution to bring me peace. Amen.

May 31

"Master, it is good that we are here."
LUKE 9:33

Have you ever wondered if you married the right person? It's natural to second-guess decisions you make throughout your life. However, God brought you and your spouse together for a special reason; one you might not realize currently, but might understand later. Don't question God's methods; instead, trust in them completely and be thankful for them. Reflect on what drew you and your partner together initially. Draft a list of the attributes you found endearing in your partner when you first met and compare it to the charming qualities of your spouse today. Take a moment to be thankful for them; they are gifts from God. It's important to be thankful for the gifts you have been given. When was the last time you thanked your spouse for something he or she did for you?

Ponder three things you are thankful for today: perhaps your good health, a job, your family. If you are thankful for your spouse, relay that to him or her. When couples express gratitude for each other, they feel more loving. For each negative interaction with your spouse, you need five positive, loving, caring, or playful interactions to counterbalance it. The next time you feel like relaying a snide remark to your partner, remember that you will need to provide five affectionate exchanges to bring your relationship back on the same level of closeness.

In an effort to strengthen your marriage, give your partner three new compliments each day. Researchers have discovered that gratitude can lead to healthier behaviors, more positive relationships, and improved overall health including better sleep and a happier mood. Thankful people are calmer and more energetic. Practicing gratitude will allow all that is beautiful in your relationship to flourish, and it can modify your perspective, expand your horizons, and deepen your love.

If gratitude transforms your relationship with your spouse, imagine what it will do to your bond with God. Consider showing appreciation to God for all he has given to you. Count your blessings and thank God for each one of them. When will you take the time to thank God each day for the gifts he gives you?

Dear Lord, thank you for bringing [*name*] into my life. You knew exactly what and when I needed him or her to become a part of my family. Every day I receive countless gifts that you give to make me happier, richer, and completely blessed with your unending love. I love you. Amen.

June 1

It comes forth like a bridegroom from his canopy,
and like a hero joyfully runs its course.

PSALM 19:6

At a Special Olympics game, a runner neared the finish line in a footrace he had trained for months hoping to win. As he approached the end of the sprint, he slowed, turned around, and ran back to his friend, held her hand, and they crossed the finish line together. Wouldn't it be nice if everyone did this in all of our everyday life races? How do you lift up your spouse when he or she is down? Perhaps your spouse needs some quiet time after work to reflect on the day before facing the challenges of home life. Maybe your spouse needs you to be a sounding board to vent after a rough day at the office. Be supportive to your spouse's needs, then, he or she will be more open to hearing about your day. Instead of dwelling on satisfying your needs, make your spouse's needs a priority.

Do you have a tendency to turn situations into competitions? Everyone likes to win. You might compete with colleagues and friends over accomplishments, kids, and appearances. Consider if you compete with your spouse. Ideally, you both need to be on the same team, where your spouse wants what's best for you and vice versa. Sometimes spouses compete, but they are not cognizant of it. It ranges from who is the better parent, who has the better career, who makes the most money, or who is the better cook.

The rivalry is derived from normal drives and some insecurity. Consider your insecurities about your own abilities, because the more you have, the more competitive you will be. Talk about your lack of confidence to ensure you don't become angry and allow it to be destructive in your marriage. Some competition is normal providing you keep it in perspective. Emphasize your spouse's strengths and attributes. Try to bring out the best in each other and your marriage will thrive.

Do you think you work harder than your partner? Keeping score in a marriage is detrimental to the union. It escalates into resentment. How can you both get on the same team and win life's battles together? Include God in your races, because only then will you start winning.

Dear Lord, come into my life and be the balm that heals our competitive wounds. Enable me to align with [*name*] in everything we do. Help me not to turn every little thing into a battle or competition. Bring me to the place of tranquility and peacefulness. Thank you for enlightening me and showing me how to make my marriage stronger and more loving. Amen.

June 2

The kingdom of heaven is like a merchant searching for fine pearls. When he finds a pearl of great price, he goes and sells all that he has and buys it.

MATTHEW 13:45–46

Not all pearls are real. Imitations have very poor iridescence and are sold as inexpensive jewelry. A genuine pearl is produced when a tiny speck of grit is introduced into the oyster's mantle folds and a sac forms around it. That pearl will have a unique luster. If you rub it on your front tooth and it feels gritty, the pearl is real. Do you feel the need to test your marriage to ensure it is genuine? Ponder your sincerity to your spouse and marriage. Do you produce grit in your relationship? God doesn't want your marriage to be unhappy. God approaches marital problems from the perspective of how to fix them, not on how to dissolve them. God encourages husbands to treat their wives with understanding so that their prayers will not be hindered.

If there's conflict in your marriage, usually women want to talk about it while men prefer to withdraw. For many men it's uncomfortable discussing relationship problems because they feel like they are not measuring up. During arguments, cortisol, a stress hormone, is released and can linger in your system for hours in men and up to several days in women. Before you can communicate with words, try to connect nonverbally through touching, doing projects, sports, or hobbies together because genuine intimacy occurs when you're not talking. Allow your words to blossom from the bonding, because once you feel connected, you can talk more easily.

Compassion is vital to the success of your marriage. Try to be cognizant of your spouse's point of view. Therefore, during an argument, as difficult as it may be, reach out to your partner. To address the hurt entwined with your anger, devise a signal, such as a hand gesture, to keep disagreements from spiraling out of control. Find a way to convey to your partner that he or she matters more than whatever you're upset about. After one person makes the gesture, the partner will feel the impact, even if the anger is high at that moment. You must decide if your relationship is more important than whatever annoys your partner. Give your spouse positive reinforcement instead of criticizing him or her, and you will see big changes in your relationship.

How can you become more like a real pearl: very rare, fine, admirable, and valuable? Reach out to God's authentic love. He will help you stay focused on what is truly important in life.

Dear Lord, teach me how to be more honest and sincere to [*name*]. Let me live in a morally sound relationship, bound by the love you meant for us to share. Amen.

June 3

Go to the ant, O sluggard, study her ways and learn wisdom;
For though she has no chief, no commander or ruler, She procures
her food in the summer, stores up her provisions in the harvest.

PROVERBS 6:6–8

A nts are social insects who operate by working together to support their colony. Their success has been attributed to their ability to modify their habitats, tap resources, and defend themselves. Ant societies have a division of labor, communication, and an ability to solve complex problems. Ponder how you can facilitate your marriage roles more effectively by working together. How can you modify your surroundings to make them more harmonious? Are there any resources in your church that you can tap into? Perhaps there is a Bible study group or lecture series you both could attend. If tiny ants can solve complex problems, what are you and your partner capable of? Ask God to keep your mind clear when resolving marital issues.

It is essential for you and your spouse to work together as a team in order to juggle the many challenges, demands, and obligations life presents. By possessing good communication and negotiating skills, couples who work together drop fewer balls and are happier overall. Reflect on the type of emotional space you and your partner have created in your marriage. Ensure that it permits open and honest communication where you both can express your feelings and opinions. Allow for the negotiation of all rules, roles, and responsibilities in your relationship. This will eliminate any power struggles which can be the source of contention in some marriages. Mastering the skill of negotiation in your marriage will encourage navigating through issues to amicably agree on solutions. This will require time, patience, and much cooperation. Be respectful of your partner while you work through difficulties.

Keep love centered in your relationship as you work through a problem. If you approach a topic with love and concern, it will likely end well. Be mindful of your emotions and tone of voice when you approach a touchy topic with your spouse. Don't allow resentment toward your spouse to build. Approach issues with love and concern, but do it in a timely manner. An important way of building trust is to bring up issues sooner rather than later. What topic have you contemplated discussing with your spouse?

Dear Lord, thank you for the reminders to keep reinforcing my marriage. Each time I see an ant, I remember the abilities you gave them. If they can carry off a crumb twice their size, I know I am capable of great feats too. Hold me in the palm of your hand and keep me safe while I balance my life and marriage. Amen.

June 4

My soul is downcast within me; therefore I remember you
From the land of the Jordan and Hermon, from Mount Mizar,
Deep calls to deep in the roar of your torrents,
and all your waves and breakers sweep over me.

PSALM 42:7–8

A pool of water at the top of a waterfall can appear unassuming a distance from the drop. However, as you approach the waterfall, there are signs of trouble ahead. There could be a plume of mist, a current, and a mighty roaring as the water tumbles over the cliff. Are there signs that your marriage is in trouble? Perhaps there is something you can sense or feel. Question if your comfort level has changed and you no longer care to look nice for your partner. Ponder if your spouse's personal appearance and hygiene has declined, signaling that one or both of you are unhappy in the marriage.

Consider if you seek out distractions from your marital problems. If the television is on constantly; you bury your face in the newspaper or a book; or you are absorbed in crafts, projects, or sports; or have something else that requires your attention, there may be a problem. Perhaps you spend countless hours together in the same home, or run errands together, but rarely have meaningful conversations. Living in silence is a symptom of marital problems. Another sign that your marriage is in jeopardy is a decline in physical affection.

Perhaps you feel scrutinized and criticized by your partner, and nothing you do is pleasing to him or her. Maybe you are yelling, creating a hostile environment. Is it misdirected anger? Ponder what underlying issues could be causing the marital discord. Maybe you are arguing over the same subject repeatedly. Your marriage could be stagnated if you are constantly arguing over the same issues. Turn to God and give your turmoil to him. Ask him to bring the right person into your life to help you sort through the problems to find amicable resolutions. You may need the assistance of your parish priest or a professional marriage counselor to help solve your problems. If you sense you are about to tumble over a waterfall, get out of the water. If you sense trouble, get help. Call out to the Lord for guidance. He will never let a hair on your head be harmed.

Dear Lord, envelop me in your love. Melt my tensions and guide me down the path of righteousness. Wash away my iniquities, Lord, and shine your divine grace around me. I love you, sweet, amazing, Lord. Amen.

June 5

You are my lamp, O Lord! My God brightens the darkness about me.
2 SAMUEL 22:29

Why do moths find porch lights so irresistible? Some scientists believe that moths are disoriented by bright lights, not attracted to them. They use the moon to orientate themselves at night, like a reference point. The artificial lights are brighter than the moon, and it confuses them. What is confusing in your marriage? Perhaps it is personality differences. How can you use them to your advantage?

Personality differences can affect compatibility, cooperativeness, and intimacy. The same traits that initially attracted you and your spouse together could seem like character flaws that interfere with how well your marriage functions. It's fruitless to try to change your spouse to be just like you. God made you unique with your own particular style and personality patterns. No one style is better than the other. Your differences from your spouse are an expression of your God-given diversity. Contemplate how you can avoid an entanglement in power struggles of trying to change your spouse when your own way seems best?

Can you focus on similarities instead? It is worth assessing your personality matches to better understand yourself, your partner, and how those styles affect your relationship. Identifying similarities and differences enables you to understand the dynamics of your marriage, but generosity toward each other is vital to personality compatibility. View your differences as gifts from God. If you concentrate on your partner's strengths, you can appreciate and not criticize. No personality style is better than another.

Reevaluate your reference point; put God in charge of your life and the way it enfolds might become clearer. Do you have dark spots in your marriage caused from personality differences? Let God shine his light on your marriage and guide every step you take.

Dear Lord, your radiant love warms me to the core. Thank you for guiding my footsteps and for being my constant beacon of hope. You brighten the gloom that lurks and threatens me in the dark corners of my relationship. You make sense of all the misperceptions in my marriage and enable me to work through each one. Thank you for making me in your image while blessing me with true uniqueness. Amen.

June 6

Knowing their hypocrisy he said to them,
"Why are you testing me? Bring me a denarius to look at."

MARK 12:15

Have you seen "trick" birthday candles that are nearly impossible to blow out? Manufacturers add magnesium to the wax. Once the candle is blown out, the magnesium gets hot enough to ignite the paraffin vapor, which makes the candle burn again. What element keeps reigniting issues in your marriage? Ponder what topics are too hot to discuss. Do you use tricks to test your spouse? Consider what subjects elicit emotional responses in your marriage. Some touchy subjects that cause conflicts are those involving in-laws, friends, siblings, and children. Perhaps you can resolve those issues by trying to work through them thoughtfully, lovingly, and prayerfully. Contemplate what secret ingredient God blessed your marriage with that can be used to keep your flame of love alive and burning brightly despite subversions.

The first step is to acknowledge that there is trouble in your marriage. No one likes to admit a problem, but it's better than the alternative: sweeping it under the rug and hoping it will disappear. Ignoring it will give it room to grow. Talk to your spouse about the problem and work toward a solution you both agree on.

God wired you with emotions and feelings that respond to a variety of issues, some being negative and some being positive. Reactions to your current circumstances may provoke anger or be overwhelming. Regardless of the emotions, make an effort to be in control. Emotions are inadequate of intelligent reasoning. Instead of allowing an emotional response to command your choices, use your brain. Consider what information you have been storing in your brain. If the knowledge you gather is immoral, it's not going to be useful. Think about the type of television you watch, the content of the books and magazines you read, and then consider filling your knowledge reservoir with what is virtuous and just.

Do you get angry due to hurts or frustrations? Anger is a secondary emotion that requires a response. You can choose either pain or peace. If you stuff anger, it festers and eventually erupts like a volcano. The key to your anger is to reflect on it instead of allowing it to control you. Delay your anger by assessing what caused it. Define why you are angry and you will defuse it. If your spouse has caused you the frustration or the hurt, accept that no one is perfect. Forgiveness is a prerequisite to love.

Dear Lord, let your love permeate my soul so that everything I think, say, and do is derived from kindness. Let me be a better spouse, more thoughtful and selfless. Amen.

June 7

Either declare the tree good and its fruit is good, or declare the tree rotten and its fruit is rotten, for a tree is known by its fruit.

MATTHEW 12:33

Throughout my childhood, there was an apple tree in the yard. As kids, we climbed it, swung from its branches, rested under it, and ate the apples. Eventually, it was chopped down and burned in the hearth, warming us throughout the winter. The tree gave 100 percent to my family. What percentage do you put into your marriage? You get as much from your marriage as you put into it. Reflect on what areas need the most work right now. If you want your marriage to thrive, you need to give 100 percent regardless of what you get from it. Don't have the attitude that you will only do "your part" if your spouse does his or her part. God never intended for marriage to be opportunistic where you only give to get.

Base your marriage on unconditional love, where you give 100 percent regardless of how much effort your spouse puts in. Love isn't based on calculations and impartiality. Was it fair that Jesus paid a debt he did not owe with his life? No, but he did it anyway because he loves us. Love is not always fair. Frequently people divorce because they grow tired in their relationship and want out. They think the grass is greener elsewhere but it rarely is what they thought it would be. You can't run from your marital discord, but it pleases God when you work to improve your relationship and try to change. Many people seek excuses to run, avoid, or quit. Marriage is not an agreement, it's a lifetime commitment—a vow you made to each other blessed by God.

There will be good times and bad times in any marriage. Concentrate on ways to improve. For example, if your spouse says something annoying, can you not take it personally? Could you consider that he or she might be overtired or overworked? Perhaps he or she didn't mean what was said and spoke out of frustration. Instead of allowing one thoughtless phrase to unravel your relationship, can you calmly say, "I know you are tired, but that statement was hurtful," and continue to love your spouse unconditionally? Your attitude is essential to have equality in your relationship. God gave you the ability to be fair in your marriage. How can you exercise that skill to enhance your blessed union?

Dear Lord, teach me to appeal to my spouse for fairness in our relationship. Grant me the wisdom to be objective, focusing on resolving our problems peaceably and respectfully. Amen.

June 8

For the love of money is the root of all evils, and some people
in their desire for it have strayed from the faith and
have pierced themselves with many pains.

1 TIMOTHY 6:10

Gold has been used as money because it is portable and can be divided into smaller units without destroying its value. It can also be melted into bars or recoined. Most of the world stopped making gold coins as currency as countries switched from the gold standard due to hoarding during the Great Depression. Ponder if you are obsessed with money. The more you work, the more money you make. The more money you make, the more "stuff" you can buy. Consider where saving or spending fits into your marriage.

Perhaps when you were first married, you and your spouse had the same approach to managing your finances. Consider if your approach was successful or if it needs an adjustment. It can be stressful if you are not living in the same style you were used to. Who is managing your marital assets? If you are the chief financial officer and something goes wrong, your spouse can blame you for mistakes. If you go into debt, you may wonder how it happened. You and your spouse need to be on the same financial page so that you both understand what you can and cannot afford. It needs to be a joint effort so that when you are faced with a major purchase, such as buying a home, you both understand what is involved monetarily.

Financial challenges that children pose can be daunting, especially when it comes to saving for college educations, emergencies, or retirement funds. Every now and then, stop to reevaluate your financial plan. If you don't have one, start now. Some couples have different approaches to spending and saving their money, which can cause arguments and resentment to build. It's worthwhile to sort out your fiscal plan now to avoid unpleasant surprises later. Over time, you might encounter financial issues that you didn't foresee, or you may reconsider your goals and how money affects them.

While money is important, it's just one aspect of your relationship. Don't make it the focal point of your marriage. Try to manage your finances with an open mind while strengthening your bond by doing things that don't involve money. Consider volunteering with the impoverished people in your community. When couples get involved in worthy projects, they discover another aspect of their relationship that tightens their marriage bonds without dragging money into it. What can you do as a couple to strengthen your union?

Dear Lord, help me to stop focusing my life around money, and start looking for you in the underprivileged in my community. Amen.

June 9

A time to rend, and a time to sew.

ECCLESIASTES 3:7

As a bride began to walk down the aisle, the lace hem of her dress ripped. Her face reddened, her voice quivered, and tears welled in her eyes. The bride's mother pulled a needle and thread from her purse and immediately stitched the fabric together, saving the day. Imagine a tool as miniscule as a needle and thread sparing drama if it's used correctly.

How difficult is it for you to apologize after you were wrong? It might be easy for some people to say "sorry," but the apology must accompanied by regret, or else the words are meaningless. It is essential to state specifically what the wrong was using honest and open communication and not offer excuses. Don't expect a reciprocal apology. Concentrate on the apology and follow it up with a plan so that it won't happen again. Present a nice gesture to demonstrate to your spouse that the offense will not be repeated. One way to repair your relationship would be to write a poem or letter to show your partner that you truly mean what you say. Offering an apology allows your spouse an opportunity for peace through forgiveness, which is a gift. Forgiveness is a healing process that takes time and cannot be demanded or rushed because it suits your needs.

Some people resist admitting when they are wrong or have caused hurtful or inappropriate behavior because they consider it a weakness. Instead, accept responsibility by saying "I made a mistake, and I'm sorry I hurt you." If your partner continues to repeat the offense, the apology loses its effectiveness. While some spouses can apologize, they forget to ask for forgiveness, which is humbling. When you ask for forgiveness, it implies your commitment to your marriage with a desire to put things right, wipe the slate clean and start over. Everyone makes mistakes because God created us human. Because you are imperfect, you have the ability to right your wrongs. Apologies can restore a broken relationship. If your marriage grows out of a love, friendship, and forgiveness, it has a greater chance of success.

What areas in your marriage need mending, and what tool do you plan to use to fix it? Perhaps a kind word or loving touch would help. Contemplate in the Lord's wisdom the problem areas that you need to address with a repair and then reinforce it later, so that it won't unravel later when you are dancing.

Dear Lord, help me to recognize the tools when they are needed. Even if the skills are new or the experiences are untested, erase the doubt that clutters my mind. Fill me with insight and wisdom to know when a repair is needed. Give me the courage to persevere and let me rest in your endless love. Amen.

June 10

You mountain of God, mountain of Bashan, you rugged mountain,
mountain of Bashan, You rugged mountains, why look with envy at the
mountain where God has chosen to dwell, where the Lord *resides forever?*

PSALM 68:16–17

At a trailhead, hikers cluster around the sign-in box to double-check their gear before ascending a mountain. Their excitement is palpable. Soon the climb yields tired, achy muscles, and sore feet. Sometimes the path becomes difficult to follow: mud holes and creeks to traverse, treacherous inclines, boulders to climb over, or inclement weather rolls in. At the summit, the magnificent view is worth it. Ponder if you navigate through your marriage similarly to hikers using God's help. Are you expending too much effort traversing the danger zones, or are you plodding the course carefully, pacing yourself with prayer, using the proper gear to keep your vision focused on the top?

Throughout your marriage you will experience difficulties such as financial, career, or parenting decisions. Perhaps you could seek advice from friends or neighbors with insignificant matters. However, more complicated issues such as serious illness, infidelity, or addictions could benefit from the counsel of your parish priest or a professional counselor. The key is to do something about the problems that are burdening you. Ignoring them and hoping they disappear is not a viable solution.

Everyone experiences bumps along the marriage road because building a life with another person is not easy. It's like climbing a mountain: exciting and beautiful, but problems are likely along the way. Nevertheless, the journey is worthwhile, especially when you can enjoy the rest and the view at the top.

Perhaps you have questioned if your love is real or even fallen out of love and considered giving up. Like mountain climbers check their gear and reinforce their efforts with specific tools, you can minimize adverse effects in your marriage with the right methods, tools, and by reaching out to the Lord. Nurture your relationship by attending an enrichment program or Bible studies at church. The answers to life's mysteries are in the Bible. With guidance, it's possible to enrich your married life by filling up on the glories of God. The Lord walks with you wherever you go. How will you enrich your marriage expedition?

Dear Lord, bless my journey by giving me the means to overcome the obstacles in my path. Remind me along the way, through my difficulties, how important this climb is. Help me to enjoy the excursion as I forge onward eager to reach the top with my spouse in your loving mercy. Amen.

June 11

My lover put his hand in through the opening:
my innermost being trembled because of him.

SONG OF SONGS 5:4

A drum is capable of any beat the percussionist desires. Your heart has a rhythm of its own, yet something else gives it a special beat. What makes your heart beat a certain way? Is it a hobby, activity, or something special you do with your spouse? Consider what it is about your spouse that makes your heart throb. Reflect on those wonderful effects and be thankful for them. Ponder what lovely things you can do to make your mate's heart skip a beat. Does he or she enjoy spending time quality together giving your undivided attention so that he or she knows just how much you care? Perhaps you could go out on the town, see your spouse's favorite movie, or have a picnic in his or her favorite spot. God wants you to seek pleasure in your partner's company and in God's eternal love.

Think back to the days when you and your spouse were getting to know each other. What sticks out in your memory that you will always cherish? Perhaps it was something as simple as holding hands, candlelight dinners, or talking and laughing the night away. Regardless of how long you have been married, it's important to keep romance in your relationship.

Schedule dates the way you once did. It doesn't really matter what you do, but how you do it. In other words, don't spend the night discussing stressful topics such as the kids' problems, insurance fiascos, bills, or jobs. Use this special time to reconnect with each other the way you used to. Be affectionate to your partner through physical touch, even if it's only holding hands. Talk about the dates you once had, what made them special, and either do something similar or completely different by creating new opportunities for fun. It's important to step away from the daily grind and escape in each other's love by finding ways to fan the passion. Maybe you could attend a county fair, take a brewery tour, or take a hot air balloon ride. The quality time you spend together is the important thing. What date will you plan this week?

Dear Lord, help me to overlook the problems that build up around me and focus on the pleasing aspects of my relationship with [name]. Let me find refuge there with him or her and dwell in the love you created. Help me to set aside the complexities of life and step away from it so that I can reconnect with the person you brought into my life. Amen.

June 12

*Or is he chastened on a bed of pain, suffering continually
in his bones, So that to his appetite food is repulsive,
his throat rejects the choicest nourishment.*

JOB 33:19–20

Pain is an unpleasant sensory and emotional experience associated with tissue damage. Some pain is unbearable and can be exhausting, making sufferers feel desperate. Are you experiencing pain in your marriage? Perhaps that is causing exhaustion or the feelings of nervousness or fear. Contemplate the underlying causes of any possible marital discord or discomfort. Often uncovering the root of the problem is painful, but then you can work to resolve it. If you are attempting to sooth yourself by over-indulging in food, shopping, gambling, flirting, drinking, staying out late, or spending too much time on the computer, that is a warning sign that your marriage is in trouble. Stop those behaviors by asking God to help keep you strong.

Shift your focus away from you and emphasize strengthening your marriage bonds instead. Connect with your partner and communicate openly and honestly about what is eroding your foundation. Polarization is not an option; try to migrate to the middle to meet your partner. Peel away the emotional layers of hurt, anger, fear, and regrets to uncover you and your spouse's desires. It's like peeling an onion: it will make you cry in the process, but it's worth it to do. God will be with you as you work through this process.

Begin by completing these sentences: "I feel hurt because...," "I feel angry because...," "I am afraid that...," and "I wish that..." Sometimes, it's a simple miscommunication that spiraled out of control and once you understand the problem, you can contemplate and negotiate the options to make things right. Avoid the temptation to retaliate or insult your partner with zingers. The goal is to resolve your marital discord, not make it worse. Pray for enlightenment as you work through these issues, no matter or big or small they are. Are you building up your marriage or tearing it down?

Dear Lord, help me as I struggle to uncover the problems that are causing me such heartache and disappointment in my marriage. Let all of my thoughts, words, and actions be of you. With you, I can do anything. Amen.

June 13

*"May we learn what this new teaching is that you speak of?
For you bring some strange notions to our ears;
we should like to know what these things mean."*

ACTS 17:19–20

There is the YMCA, the PTA, and a million other abbreviations you need to know to understand society's messages. Some abbreviations are difficult to interpret. Are there abbreviations in your marriage that are challenging to read? Perhaps you have misconstrued your partner's body language or tried to be a "mind reader." Have you ever yelled something through the house to your partner when he or she was in another room? Communication is vital in any relationship; therefore, speak to your spouse in the same room, making eye contact. Avoid sarcastic tones, disrespectful language, and telling someone else what you want your spouse to know. Instead, focus on direct, clear, and courteous communication.

Sometimes you might need to be more specific to make your point, so be open to using analogies or rephrasing your words. It is helpful to use statements such as "I prefer to do this today" or "I wish we could do that." Some people favor a soft start, which entails saying something positive first and also ending on a positive note.

While speaking is the best way to communicate, many couples are constantly giving out signals that are easy to pick up. For example, your family can usually tell when you are stressed, relaxed, happy, or sad. It might be unnecessary to say anything to convey a message accurately based on the way you act; be mindful of the nonverbal signals you emit. It can be mind-boggling to sift through all of the information bombarding you, such as facial expressions, signals, vibes, and body language. Ask God to help you manage the information and keeping the doors to communication between you and your spouse open. Keep talking because that is how you make progress in your relationship. Ask the Holy Spirit to empower you with the right words to be understood and for patience to strive to improve your communication skills. What message do you need to convey to your spouse?

Dear Lord, when my words are carefully thought out and arranged harmoniously in my heart, they can make a world of difference to my spouse. Don't let me take shortcuts with my speech, but instead use my words lovingly to build up, praise, and seek to understand. Amen.

June 14

A tester for my people I have appointed you, to search and test their way.

JEREMIAH 6:27

When the American flag hangs on a pole, snapping in soft winds, a gentle breeze can ripple the entire thing. For the flag to be tested, it must be subjected to weather. How is your marriage tested? Perhaps the wind that causes ripples in it comes from your mouth in the form of words.

Words have the power to hurt, soothe, inspire, and stop you from certain actions. Learning and developing the best language to strengthen your marriage takes time and diligence. There are many words that couples should strike from their vocabulary because they are damaging to your marriage. Avoid using the word "never" as it suggests hopelessness. When you say, "You never cook for me," you're expressing to your spouse that there is no hope for change. It's an uncompromising phrase that states finality instead of listening, compromising, and establishing approachability. Avoid using "always," because it implies inflexibility and righteousness. It's an all-or-nothing phrase, which does not promote understanding or healing. Stop using the word "but," since it infers manipulation with deceitfulness. The use of "but" contradicts whatever was said before. It nullifies your message and converts a positive statement into a negative one. It does not build trust, credibility, or intimacy.

Do not attack your spouse by name-calling or using obscenities, because it will cause irreparable damage to your relationship. Also, there is no place in your relationship for condemnation or contempt. Suggesting divorce as an option has the potential to kill your marriage; using it as a technique to control your spouse creates anxiety and despair. It's not conducive for effective communication, conflict resolution, problem-solving, or intimacy.

Instead, ponder loving and effective words to use. Pray about them and ask God to bless the message you want to convey to your spouse. Generate a kind-hearted objective rather than one that is hurtful or controlling. Find words that create intimacy. Try phrases such as "It would mean a lot to me if you would speak softly because when you do, I can concentrate better because I feel loved." When you hear yourself use these words that are detrimental to your marriage, stop speaking and ask your spouse to rephrase your thoughts in a positive way. Let the gentle breeze that blows through your marriage elevate it with love, mutual respect, and prayerfulness. When you live to please and serve God, tests will not be necessary.

Dear Lord, fill me with hopefulness to rise above my trepidations and anxieties. Let me wait patiently without demands, expectations, and tests. Amen.

June 15

Be still before the LORD*; wait for him. Do not be provoked by the prosperous,*
nor by malicious schemers. Refrain from anger; abandon wrath;
do not be provoked; it brings only harm. Those who do evil will be cut off,
but those who wait for the LORD *will inherit the earth.*

PSALM 37:7–9

Many homes are equipped with fire extinguishers in the event of an emergency. What do you have as a precautionary measure to avoid a disaster in your relationship? Consider how your anger management skills are. Do you have an effective means of controlling your anger? You can channel rage by burning the energy through delving into a project. You might consider painting away your anger, planting a tree, swimming it out, or playing a video game. Physical exertion is a superb method to expunge your temper.

When you feel angry, consider what it's trying to tell you and where it's coming from so you can prevent it from reoccurring. Could it be from a childhood experience or is it misdirected anger from another person or event? Is it rooted in feelings of hurt, invalidation, frustration, fear, anxiety, helplessness, hopelessness, inadequacy, or guilt from a childhood memory? These are trigger points. After you realize your trigger points, take a time out and say, "This is how I responded to what you said. Is that what you meant?"

It's important to discuss small issues because resolving conflict is far better than reacting. Thinking about the anger before acting on it is like a fire extinguisher on flames. Instead of counting to ten, say a prayer and let God help you control your temper and direct your thoughts making them clearer. This is a healthy way to deal with issues, by learning from them, healing, and moving on. This is a lengthy process that requires patience and understanding. Your valuable marriage is worth more than any conflict you encounter. Keeping your priorities in line by putting your marriage first reminds you to be willing to work through any marital discord because it is fixable in God's love.

When you and your spouse yell at each other, you are not going to accomplish anything except maybe get angrier. When you recognize the need to do things differently, you will realize that you have accomplished something in your marriage. What topic do you need to address with your spouse today?

Dear Lord, keep me calm through this calamity with your healing touch. Let your tranquility pour over me and be absorbed to the depth of my soul so that I react in your love. Amen.

June 16

As a father has compassion on his children,
so the LORD has compassion on those who fear him.
For he knows how we are formed,
remembers that we are dust.

PSALM 103:13–14

When I got married, I knew my man would make a good husband, but I had no idea what kind of father he would make. I had to trust in God that when the time was right in our marriage, parenting would come to us second nature as a gift from the Lord. On Father's Day, take a moment to consider how fatherhood has affected you. Perhaps you are a father, or you have a father who raised you, or you lacked a father figure in your life. All three scenarios yield different outcomes in your life: some with positive results, some with mixed emotions, and others with negative consequences. Focus on the positive experiences; the ones where you felt loved or could offer a copious supply of unconditional love.

Regardless of the circumstances connecting you to a father, you have always had God the father in heaven safeguarding your every step. Earthly fathers try to safeguard their children too; however, sometimes because of their infallibilities and struggles, they fail or don't measure up to our expectations. Being a father is not an easy task and there are no instruction books telling men what to do or how to do it. Sometimes they act using their head, while other times they make decisions using their hearts.

Jesus's foster father, St. Joseph, loved and nurtured his son to the best of his abilities. He provided for him, kept him safe, and taught him carpentry skills. However, at a certain point, God the father would take over and lead Jesus through his life journey. Imagine what it was like for Joseph to raise Jesus knowing he was God the son. Ponder if you love your own children much the way Joseph loved Jesus.

Trust that God the father created you and adores you with unlimited unconditional love. He watches over you, guides you, and protects you the way a shepherd oversees his flock. He knows what is in your heart, how many hairs are on your head, he knows all of your flaws, and he hears every prayer you say. You have a glorious father in heaven who holds you in the palm of his hand. Contemplate how blessed you are to have such a magnificent father.

Dear Lord, thank you for your unfaltering, infinite supply of love, mercy, and blessings. When I feel low, I think of you and how much you love me. Then I am instantly filled with your radiant affection. Thank you for guarding each step I take and for each breath I make. I love you. Amen.

June 17

He ordered those who could swim to jump overboard first
and get to the shore, and then the rest, some on planks,
others on debris from the ship. In this way, all reached shore safely.

ACTS 27:43–44

When you jump into a pool of water, one of two things can happen: you can sink and drown, or you can swim and go somewhere. Jumping into marriage is similar: relationships fail or they thrive. Ponder which category your marriage in. If you are not the best swimmer, you might stay in the shallow end or use floatation devices. Likewise, bring tools into your relationship to keep you buoyant and ensure your success.

Use kind and respectable speaking and listening skills when trying to resolve conflict. Avoid blaming each other for problems because it only makes matters worse. If you both blame each other, you both will suffer. People, places, or things do not run your emotional life; you are responsible for your own doings. By the power of God within you, take ownership of your feelings and reactions. You are human and allowed to make mistakes. If you forgot to pick up milk on the way home, say, "I forgot. I made a mistake." You are not going to remember everything all of the time. Additionally, your spouse is allowed to make mistakes too! The courtesy you give to your partner is the same politeness you can expect in return.

When you take responsibility for your actions and feelings, you will have a fulfilling life. God allows you to be in control of your life and to make decisions whether they are right or wrong. Life is about choices. If you choose to make honest and healthy, God-centered choices, then your life may be easier. However, if you make poor and irresponsible decisions, your life could become derailed. Your life is defined by the choices you make. Whenever you are faced with making an important decision, regardless of how big or small it is, ask God to guide you through it.

Another tool to use while resolving conflict is to stick to one issue without dredging up past arguments. Using your God given wisdom, define the problem intelligently and challenge your creative side to derive many possible solutions. Attack the problem, not your spouse. Together you can accomplish anything. God is always with you, especially in times of trouble; call out to him in distress. He will help you.

Dear Lord, rescue me from the conflict surrounding my marriage. Enable me to use the talents you gave to me. Save me, Lord, from this fury that burns within. Cool my tempers, fill me with wisdom, and strengthen me to resolve my woes. I trust in your goodness and mercy. Amen.

June 18

Then the richest of the people will seek your favor with gifts.

PSALM 45:13

The word "free" conjures an alluring excitement, beckoning your curiosity to perhaps want it. There is something thrilling about getting something for free. Ponder how you put exhilarating thrills in your marriage. When is the last time you gave a gift to your spouse when you were not celebrating a birthday or holiday? Make an ordinary day spectacular by presenting your mate with a trinket that will say that he or she is special, something that says you noticed and you care. Giving gifts is a complex and important part of human interaction, which helps to strengthen your marital bond. You, as the giver, reap the biggest emotional gain from giving a gift. Giving gifts is mentioned in the prayer of St. Frances: it is in giving that we receive.

Gifts are important. When Jesus was born, the three wise men brought gifts to give their king. They were symbolic, tangible, and valuable. You don't have to search for an extravagant gift, but give one that has significance and worthiness to your partner. Find an object that can be held onto and cherished. Consider what symbol possesses emotional value to your partner, and then try to obtain it for your spouse. A gift doesn't have to be expensive; it could be something free like a robin's egg that fell out of a nest or a pretty stone you found. Perhaps you want to buy something frugal such as a packet of seeds to plant your own garden together. Whatever you think your spouse would like, that is the present you need to get. God has filled the world with myriad things for you to choose from.

Contemplate another type of gift that could be thrilling to your spouse: the gift of service. If your partner loathes cleaning the bathroom or cutting the grass, could you do it as a gift? Maybe your spouse has too many chores to do. Consider doing something to be helpful or pitch in and do the chores together. Your mate will notice and be grateful. What gift will you give to your mate this week to say you care?

Dear Lord, remind me to give gifts to [*name*]. Help me make the perfect selection to let him or her know how much I care. Thank you for the gifts you give to me each and every day. You give me the air I breathe and the warm sunshine that brightens my world. You fill my ears with the lilt of songbirds and the toll of church bells. These things some people take for granted, I notice and thank you for them all. You are such a kind and generous Lord. I love you. Amen.

June 19

Those who lie on beds of ivory, and lounge upon their couches; Eating
lambs taken from the flock, and calves from the stall; Who improvise to
the music of the harp, composing on musical instruments like David,
Who drink wine from bowls, and anoint themselves with the best oils.

AMOS 6:4–6

When children disobey, occasionally parents use a "time-out" to give them a moment to reflect on their naughty behavior. Can you find a quiet place to reflect on all of the good things that are happening in your marriage? If something wonderful is happening, why not keep it going? Instead of dwelling on what is not working, emphasize the importance of what is working well and build on that. What works in your relationship? Perhaps you have assembled an even split of household chores. Can you also take turns planning dates and recreational activities? While it is good to work, it is also essential to play and pray together. Establishing a routine for prayer is one of the best things you can do as a couple. But it's also essential to incorporate fun in your relationship too.

Maybe you had fun while you were dating, but now that you're married you have so many obligations and chores that you rarely have time for enjoyment. The demands of your jobs, children, and running a household can take a toll on your marriage. Try to include play in your life because when it is all work, stress can build and become problematic, especially in a wearisome economy when couples are working longer hours or holding down several jobs. The notion that finding moments to be alone together to have fun is not an indulgence; it is imperative.

When you feel stressed, the last thing you want to do is go out and do something fun together as a couple. If you are unsure what fun means anymore, it may require some thought to decide what you both enjoy doing as a couple. It is essential to go out on a date. Consider a walk through a nature center, explore a museum, or build a birdhouse. Find something that you both enjoy and remember that it doesn't have to cost a lot of money. But make sure you view this as an investment in your relationship, so if it does require some money, it is money well spent. The same goes for your time. What could be more important than investing in your marriage?

Researchers have noted that when couples share new and exciting activities, they are associated with better relationships. Because the correlation between fun and marital happiness is high, what will you plan to do with your spouse this weekend for entertainment?

Dear Lord, help me to establish a healthy balance of work, play, and prayer in my marriage. Amen.

June 20

I will rejoice and be glad in your mercy, once you have seen
my misery, [and] gotten to know the distress of the world.

PSALM 31:8

Sometimes, it hurts to rip off a bandage quickly, but there are other ways
to remove it without much pain. Some stretch the surrounding skin and
gently pick it back slowly and carefully. Wetting a bandage can loosen the
adhesive making it fall off. Ponder what methods you use to resolve hurtful
moments in your marriage.

When your spouse hurts you, tell them immediately. Maybe he or she
didn't realize you were hurt; it's your responsibility to bring it up in a loving
manner without sarcasm. That way you can evaluate and discuss where your
feelings originated from. The important thing is to have an amicable dialog
to prevent it from escalating into a full-blown argument, and always pray
on it. Everything works better when prayer is involved.

If the hurt wasn't a simple misunderstanding, identify what caused it.
Then, talk to your partner about it. Even though it might seem small, explain
that you are still holding onto it. Acknowledging it allows you to take steps to
letting it go and moving on. Listen to your partner, without interrupting, to
hear his or her point. After you listened and understand his or her perspective, take a turn speaking to your spouse. After you both have really listened
and understand each other's point of view, let go of your hurt. Many times
hurt stems from a miscommunication because when you're hurt, you don't
check with your partner if you heard him or her right. By checking, you are
building trust by giving him or her the benefit of the doubt that the hurt was
unintended. Deal with hurt promptly when it is small and easy to resolve.

Some degree of hurt is inevitable in every relationship, but acquiring
the skills to manage it will make a vast difference in how you feel about
yourself, your spouse, and your marriage. It's an easy method to keep your
marriage thriving. Contemplate what is causing restlessness in your marriage. If there is a past hurt that you need to address, pray to the Lord to give
you the courage to talk to your spouse about it. Filled with the Holy Spirit
and graces from God, take the first step forward to resolving hurt. How will
you open your dialog?

Dear Lord, my feelings get hurt so easily; help me to understand why
that is. Keep my temper cool and let peace, love, and joy run through
me while I discuss my feelings with [name]. I want to dwell in your
infinite wisdom every day of my life. Amen.

June 21

*Everything indeed is for you, so that the grace bestowed in abundance
on more and more people may cause the thanksgiving to overflow for the
glory of God. Therefore, we are not discouraged; rather, although our
outer self is wasting away, our inner self is being renewed day by day.*

2 CORINTHIANS 4:15–16

When your stomach growls, you probably crave a snack to quell your
hunger pangs. Is your marriage starving for quality time or quiet time
together? What kind of "healthy snack" can you give to your relationship
to enhance it? Set aside time each day to provide nourishment to your soul
through prayer. Maybe you could wake up a few minutes early and spend
that time praying with your spouse in bed, asking God to watch over you and
bless you throughout the day. Try standing outside in the fresh morning air
with your spouse, holding hands while meditating in silence. Look for opportunities to connect emotionally and spiritually with your partner and God.

If you feel that prayer is important but don't do it regularly, this would be
a good time to incorporate it in your everyday life. Prayer unites you spiritually with God. Jesus said, "For where two or three are gathered together in my
name, there am I in the midst of them" (Matthew 18:20). Prayer unites you
into agreement with each other as you place your petitions before God. Prayer
unites your hearts for one common end: to ultimately help get your spouse into
heaven. When you are communicating from your heart to God, you are sharing
what is in your heart with your spouse. What is so special about prayer is that
you reveal your deepest longings by saying things to God that you would never
say to each other in conversation. Prayer establishes deeper companionship.

Try to pray humbly with your spouse, communicating your needs to
God. Then you will grow in a spiritual unity resulting in a deeper relationship. If you lack camaraderie in your marriage, prayer is an excellent way
to establish it and intensify it. The closer you get to God, the closer you will
get to your partner. Holy Scripture says that when a believer prays he or she
will be built up as a result.

You will never find the time to pray with your spouse; you have to make
the time by getting up earlier each day, taking time before going to bed, or
fitting it in after mealtime. Take television time or computer time and give
it to God. Start with ten minutes and pray for your marriage. Thank God for
your spouse and request his help with whatever you are struggling with. Ask
God to heal your marriage. What are some other issues you should pray about?

Dear Lord, instead of focusing on outer worldly distractions, I want to
focus on renewing my inner self, nourishing my soul and spirituality
around you—my lifeline, my sweet, amazing Lord. Amen.

June 22

*Naomi then said, "Wait here, my daughter, until you learn what happens,
for the man will not rest, but will settle the matter today."*

RUTH 3:18

Have you waited patiently in a long line of cars in a traffic jam or behind a train passing by, or were you frustrated and angry to be thrown off schedule by an unforeseen delay? Waiting can be challenging. Have you waited in a doctor's office or emergency room where it seems as if time was standing still while you waited for a dreaded diagnosis?

If your marriage doesn't feel like it is progressing, your life is stuck, as in a waiting room filled with noisy TV shows and outdated magazines. If anxiety paralyzes you from changing your situation, you are in a waiting room. Perhaps there is hurt and you can't make it stop, you are in a waiting room. What is holding you in a waiting room, preventing you from having a meaningful marriage that God intended for you?

Perhaps you are waiting for your marriage to improve. Sometimes, the amount of time you wait, the agony involved, and the will to continue are stressing because you want the pain to end. How do you handle the inconveniences and irritations of life? It's hard to wait for an answer, a test result, and the outcome of a situation. Perseverance during such times is essential. When you had hoped for an "ideal" marriage, but found yourself in a different kind of relationship, don't give up on it. Endure and persist when times are troubling because you will be rewarded by strengthened bonds, a true commitment, and greater understanding. Love is patient and kind; it endures all things and never ends. Pray for patience persistently and turn your problems over to God. Trust in the Lord's plan for you, whatever it is.

The exercise of acting patient might enable you to cope with life's many challenges. Patience is like a muscle: the more you use it, the stronger it gets. Consider the way you act and how it impacts the way you feel internally. Patience can give you peacefulness and tranquility while you endure. Patience is necessary especially when you are in the midst of trials and tribulations. When things don't go your way, or when someone hurts you, think of how Jesus would act. What would Jesus say to you?

Dear Lord, replace my tension with tolerance. Replace my dread with longing. Fill me with hopefulness and fortitude to be patient in my marriage. Strengthen me, Lord, so that I continue to work on my relationship with [name] and make it the blessed and holy union that you intended it to be. Thank you for all you continue to do for me. You are such a loving and patient God. Amen.

June 23

Remember how for these forty years the LORD, your God, has directed
all your journeying in the wilderness, so as to test you by affliction, and
to know what was in your heart: to keep his commandments, or not.

DEUTERONOMY 8:2

S hips look impressive docked in a harbor. They become remarkable once
they are tested out at sea, riding the powerful ocean waves, tormented
by torrential storms. Your marriage might appear notable to acquaintances,
friends, and colleagues, however, only you know if your marriage has been
tested and how stable it really is. Ponder what tests your marriage has endured
lately. Perhaps a recent vacation didn't go as planned, leaving your relationship
more stressed than you started. Tests are meant to measure the stability and
capability of your union. If you identify a problematic area, work on improving
it and devote time to prayer and reflection. God is the primary stabilizer in
your marriage; let him in and ask for his help, guidance, and never-ending love.

Try putting your spouse's needs before your own. This selfless act will
demonstrate to your partner your level of commitment to your union. Don't
wait for love to happen—work at it. Discover what floats your spouse's boat
and then do that. If your partner loves flowers, plant them around your home.
If your spouse loves to take a morning jog, lace up your sneakers. If your
spouse loves spaghetti, learn how to make it and serve it often. Sometimes
the little things go a long way in making your partner happy.

Don't overlook the obvious: make your marriage a priority over your
careers. Your job does not define you, and you are not married to it. While
employment is important, your marriage outranks the job. One way to do
this is to have a budget and stick to it. Try to spend less than you make and
avoid debt. Also, don't get overcommitted in your careers. This will enable
you to have more time to enjoy together doing things you both love to do.
Prioritize your marriage over your children. Kids will eventually grow up
and leave, but your marriage will continue.

Incorporate discipline in your life to avoid mistakes that could end your
marriage. Don't be tempted to cultivate relationships with people of the opposite sex. Always nurture your faith, because that will create order for other
areas of your life including your marriage. When you took your marriage
vows you agreed to keep that covenant sacred. Therefore, have confidence
that even when marriage is difficult, you will persevere. How will you work
to improve your marriage?

Dear Lord, strengthen my marriage to endure the tests of time and
tribulations. Empower me with the necessities to reunite us and grow
in your love and mercy forever and ever. Amen.

June 24

As for you, do not seek what you are to eat and what you are to drink, and do not worry anymore. All the nations of the world seek for these things, and your Father knows that you need them. Instead, seek his kingdom, and these other things will be given you besides. Do not be afraid any longer, little flock, for your Father is pleased to give you the kingdom.

LUKE 12:29–32

Have you ever buttoned a sweater incorrectly? If you fit the first button into the first hole of your sweater, all the other buttons will fall into their proper place. However, if the first button is misaligned in the second hole, your sweater will be uneven and won't look right. It's a matter of putting first things in first place and keeping priorities straight. Your marriage can be lopsided by putting your job, friends, sports, hobbies, or another individual before your spouse. Ponder if you have your marriage priorities appropriately aligned.

It might appear daunting to find time to nurture your marriage amid the hustle and bustle of life without neglecting your other responsibilities. Develop rituals that are easily repeated, well matched to your personalities, and significant for you both. They may not be convenient, but they are essential for maintaining a healthy emotional connection.

Set aside time to pray as a couple. Even if it is only one prayer you say together at night before you go to sleep, do it. Over time you might decide to say a decade of the rosary together. Find time to talk without interruptions from the TV, phone, computer, or children. Maybe you could talk after dinner and before dishes. Don't talk about tasks that need your attention. Instead, share your dreams and ideas with your partner. Maybe make a bucket list. Each time you meet, greet your spouse with a hug and a kiss because it will help nurture your relationship. And don't forget to say goodbye with affection. You might be in a hurry as you are running out the door, but it only takes a few seconds to touch your spouse's hand, smile, and wish him or her well. Try to make creative message rituals by leaving notes, texts, or e-mails for each other. If it is possible, try to go to bed at the same time because it is nice for a couple to end their day together. Perhaps you can take a few minutes to physically reconnect with a hug and a kiss, and let each other know you love them. How will you make your marriage a priority?

Dear Lord, let me not overlook my spouse and take him or her for granted. You have given me a valuable gift and I want to start expressing my gratitude for it. Remind me, Lord, to stop and recognize all of the things he or she does for me each day. Amen.

June 25

"Blessed be the Lord who has given rest to his people Israel, just as he promised. Not a single word has gone unfulfilled of the entire gracious promise he made through Moses his servant."

1 KINGS 8:56

Buying a home requires a deposit as a promise to make payments faithfully. It tells real estate brokers that you are serious about being a homeowner and that your word to continue making payments is sincere. Consider the promises that you have made to your spouse. At your wedding, you vowed to love, honor, and respect your partner in good times and bad and in sickness and in health in the presence of God. Perhaps you are experiencing a low in your relationship right now. Focus on the declaration you made to your spouse to be committed to your union until death. The vows created a moral, legal, and spiritual commitment to each other meant to unite you both together in rough patches. The pledge was meant to comfort you that your spouse would stay with you throughout the difficulties of life and not bail when times got tough. You chose to make a long-term investment in your relationship spiritually, emotionally, and financially.

A commitment blessed by God validates to your spouse that you consider him or her indispensable regardless of the circumstances. However, after the honeymoon, when reality sinks in, you understand that the integrity of the promise is tested by sickness, financial struggles, and problems. Your vows bind you together to make you stronger during life's storms. When you are at odds with each other, you will always have that one thing in common—that you will not give up on your spouse no matter how you feel at the moment. Your marriage vows, that sacred promise you made to each other will be your safety net as you stumble on your journey through life.

God provides a reinforced safety net around your blessed union. God has promised that you can have a relationship with him through Jesus Christ. He has promised that he will never leave you, and to bring you to heaven when you die. God will make good on his promise because he sent his only son, and by his death and resurrection, he purchased your salvation. God's promise gives a sigh of relief that you are in good hands. Reflect on the promises that you have made to your spouse. How will you depend on them today?

Dear Lord, thank you for the promises you made to me. Help me to remember them when I get angry with my [*name*]. I want to honor my vows today and always. Amen.

June 26

Instruct them further: "Do this. Take wagons from the land of Egypt for your children and your wives and bring your father back here. Do not be concerned about your belongings, for the best in the whole land of Egypt shall be yours."

GENESIS 45:19–20

Bacteria can be both good and bad. Without it you would die, but some bacteria could actually kill you. Good bacterium digests your food and lives on your skin and in your mouth. They also protect you against bad bacteria. If a large amount of bad bacteria gets into your body, you can get sick and possibly die. Similar to bacteria are possessions, which can be both good and bad to a relationship. In small amounts, possessions are fine, but large amounts, as in hoarding, are detrimental to living conditions and marriages.

Hoarding can wreak havoc on marriages by causing stress, resentment, and anger. While saving possessions can be acceptable if done in moderation; it becomes disruptive to family life when it's done to the extreme. Consider if you can let go of unnecessary belongings to free up your life. Letting go of them can help your self-esteem and enable your marriage to flourish.

Hoarders collect large amounts of seemingly useless items, which causes significant distress to family life. It can weaken your marriage, and cause such severe cluttering that your home no longer functions as a practical living space. If you think you have stress in your marriage caused from a cluttered home, it's time to clean house and get your life back on track. You can do this by sorting the stuff into four piles: one to keep, a second to donate, one to sell, and another to throw away. Find a local charity that would benefit from the items you have a surplus of. Have a giant garage sale; use the money you earn to organize the rest of your home. The positive motivator necessary to break the bad habit of hoarding is saving your marriage.

Improve your marriage by focusing your energy on your spouse's needs instead of your own. If it's important for your partner to have a clean and organized home, consider providing that as a gift to him or her. Take a look around your home today and question if you are responsible for the clutter. If so, ask God to empower you with the strength and know-how to get the task completed. If your spouse is responsible for the majority of the mess, have a heartfelt talk with him or her about it.

Dear Lord, help me to stop placing so much importance on materialistic objects. Teach me to be stronger than I have been in the past and place my life in your hands. Amen.

June 27

Now the one who has prepared us for this very thing is God,
who has given us the Spirit as a first installment. So we are always
courageous, although we know that while we are at home in the body
we are away from the Lord, for we walk by faith, not by sight.

2 CORINTHIANS 5:5–7

Have you ever wondered about the difference between a fiddle and a violin? Essentially, the instrument is the same; the main differences are the type of music played and style of playing. Both styles are incredibly difficult to play, regardless of what genre is being played. The musician has total control over that.

Ponder who has control in your marriage. If it is shared mutually, you are on the right path. However, if you are more controlling in your relationship, work on relinquishing it. Opt to master self-control, because you do not have a right to control your partner. If your partner is too controlling over you, assert your right to take it back. You and your spouse need to steer the ship together.

Consider if your spouse is overly helpful by doing everything his or her way, or is your spouse helpless, forcing you to take over? Does your spouse surprise you with outlandish purchases that you feel should be made jointly? Is your spouse overly sensitive or worries excessively, forcing you to constantly step in and take over? Whether control is obvious or subtle, be aware if it exists so that you can prevent it from reoccurring in your marriage. The important thing is to let go of expecting your spouse to change and work on self-change. Don't expect your spouse to make things better; you need to develop yourself. You can only change yourself.

Hopefully, your spouse will respond positively to your self-improvement and make some changes of his or her own. If your spouse doesn't follow your example, you are still better off. Any new skills that you acquire will increase your happiness and effectiveness in your marriage. Consider what category you fall into: too controlling or being controlled. What steps will you take today to assert yourself in your marriage?

Dear Lord, empower me with the strength I need to stand up for myself and take control back of my life. Teach me how to be more assertive with my spouse, and then give me the courage to be successful in carrying out whatever it is I need to do. Fill my head and heart with your love, so that I walk the path you have designed for me. Amen.

June 28

Be sure of this, that no immoral or impure or greedy person, that is,
an idolater, has any inheritance in the kingdom of Christ and of God.
Let no one deceive you with empty arguments, for because of these things
the wrath of God is coming upon the disobedient.
So do not be associated with them.
EPHESIANS 5:5–7).

The Slinky is a steel spring toy created in the 1940s. It stretches and can bounce up and down. It's notorious for travelling down steps end-over-end as it stretches and reforms itself on its own. Once it starts gravity keeps it moving until it reaches the end of the stairs. Ponder if you have been guilty of bad-mouthing your spouse to coworkers, friends, or family. With a momentum similar to the Slinky, once you start, you don't stop. Badmouthing your spouse adds to the list of secrets you keep from your mate while it tells others how little you respect your partner.

Don't unload issues about your partner on your children or ask them to take sides. It's very important that your children love both parents. Children feel hurt when someone says something bad about a parent, even if it is the other parent saying it. Instead of complaining to outsiders by focusing on negative attributes, dwell on the positive aspects of your spouse. If your friends discuss their spouses' flaws, be sympathetic, but don't add to the conversation about your partner. At friendly gatherings or family functions, take every opportunity to praise each other openly.

It's ruthless to bash your spouse in public, but it's also destructive to your marriage to suffer in silence. Nothing gets accomplished by withholding your true feelings. You can also risk building up a wall of resentment. Set aside a time to talk when both of you are relaxed. In a loving manner, tell your mate how you honestly feel. Start praising your spouse each time he or she makes a small change, such as putting dirty dishes in the dishwasher instead of piling them in the sink. Your spouse might begin to work hard to earn more compliments. It's more loving and more effective.

God knows everything that you do: good or bad. Focus your energies on doing what is honest and moral. Always strive to build up, not tear down. How will you build up your spouse today?

Dear Lord, take evil thoughts out of my head and replace them will only pure thoughts of you. Fill me with your never ending love so that only it flows out of my mouth when I open it to speak. Thank you, Lord, for allowing me to be imperfect and then teaching me ways to improve. I love you. Amen.

June 29

*Let us approach with a sincere heart and in absolute trust, with
our hearts sprinkled clean from an evil conscience and our bodies
washed in pure water. Let us hold unwaveringly to our confession
that gives us hope, for he who made the promise is trustworthy.*

HEBREWS 10:22–23

Newlyweds wear sparkling diamond wedding rings, while longtime married couples have rings that show wear and tear. There might be nicks or scratches on the bands, and the stones are often encrusted in crud. A jeweler could buff out the abrasions and clean the stones with a mild detergent making them beautiful once again. Over time, relationships get enveloped with muck. What has corroded your relationship? Perhaps you have dealt with irresponsibility issues concerning decisions. Ponder what it would take to address it and begin self-responsibility. Instead of saying, "I don't care" or "whatever," contemplate how the decisions impact you and your relationship.

Consider how you can start accepting accountability for your own choices. The decisions you make define you. How have you benefited from that in your marriage? Sharing values with your partner and trying to discern God's will when making ethical decisions are critical. Throughout your marriage you and your spouse will make myriad moral decisions on major accounts. Making a moral decision includes prayerful reflection, conversation, and evaluation before reaching a conclusion.

Start with prayer by opening your heart and mind to God. Then, ask for the grace to follow his will. Gather information to make a well-informed decision. Read articles in magazines or websites. Consult trusted friends, family, or advisors who can enlighten you about the issue. If a decision involves you and your spouse, reach a consensus that satisfies you both.

Be open to reevaluate the decision after some time has passed, or if the outcome wasn't as you anticipated. Having prayed and carefully weighed the pros and cons make an amicable decision agreeable to both of you. By agreeing to reassess your situation, it helps keep the lines of communication open, which means you won't be locked into that decision forever. There never is one clear choice; there are always other options. Making a moral decision includes weighing your options and arriving at the best solution possible at the time. Have faith in God that he will steer you in the right direction. Always make God a part of every solution. What decisions are you praying on?

Dear Lord, be with me as I deliberate over decisions that swirl through my head and heart. Help me to focus on the right choice; the one that is your will. Help me stay focused and to embrace all that you intended for me, whether I like it or not. I love you and trust you. Amen.

June 30

Like an apple tree among the trees of the woods, so is my lover among men.
In his shadow I delight to sit, and his fruit is sweet to my taste. He brought
me to the banquet hall and his glance at me signaled love. Strengthen
me with raisin cakes, refresh me with apples, for I am sick with love.

SONG OF SONGS 2:3–5

Picnics are a wonderful way to celebrate the summer by gathering family around food outside in the fresh air and sunshine. The only unwelcome component is insects. Sweet-smelling foods such as desserts and fruits attract bugs. Sweet words are attractive in relationships. By selecting kinder, gentler words, and delivering them with a softer, caring tone, your mate will be more amiable. How often do you use nice words with your spouse? Maybe you don't put much thought into the words you say, but if you start using more cordial language with your partner, he or she will notice and respond accordingly. Reflect on the tone you use when you talk to Jesus. Remember that God is in each one of us, including your partner. The next time you speak with him or her, remember that the Holy Spirit resides in your spouse. Talk to your partner with the same love in your voice that you would use to speak to the Lord.

Consider when you last gave encouragement to your spouse or spoke with an inspiring manner. Perhaps your spouse is experiencing trepidation about a project at work or embarking on a new life journey with weight loss or breaking a bad habit. Think about how much he or she would appreciate your encouraging words. When you offer supportive words spoken in a loving tone, it is like a gift to your partner building him or her up.

Have you ever acknowledged your spouse to friends, colleagues, family, or neighbors? Maybe your spouse has accomplished something noteworthy; consider affirming him or her publicly. If you were successful in an undertaking, credit your spouse as well. Perhaps you could write a loving message in a card. There are many ways you can build up your spouse with words. Let your imagination run wild.

Often, a spouse isn't looking for a grandiose display of affection. Sometimes, a modest validation is all that is necessary. You can accomplish this by listening wholeheartedly and repeating back a few key words, which tells your partner you care about what he or she has to say. How will you use words to lift up your spouse?

Dear Lord, infuse me with your sweetness so that loving words form in my mind and roll off my tongue. Let me please my spouse with only heartfelt messages. Remind me, Lord, to strive to use moving words to gladden your heart and soul. Amen.

July 1

May wheat abound in the land,
flourish even on the mountain heights.
May his fruit increase like Lebanon,
and flourish in the city like the grasses of the land.

PSALM 72:16

Have you seen the miniscule size of poppy seeds? It's perplexing that something so tiny can grow into something so tall, graceful, and beautiful. An ounce of kindness, as small and insignificant as it may seem, could be like the poppy seed and turn into something larger, greater, and lovelier than you ever imagined. Do you use cutting words to make a point? If you cut your partner down, you will undo all of the kindnesses that you worked on all week. Opt to use loving words to make a point because it will be better received and appreciated.

What seemingly inconsequential gesture could you offer your spouse to bring a smile to his or her face? Could you send an e-mail just to say you were thinking about him or her today? What kind word or compliment could you give? What if you commented on their beautiful eyes or smile? Maybe you could praise something they did, like take out the trash so you didn't have to. Contemplate your spouse's strengths and compliment them. Your partner won't feel taken for granted if he or she knows that you notice, you care, and are appreciative. The more you compliment your spouse, chances are good that he or she will praise you too.

Consider if there are small deeds that you could do to make your partner happy, even if it is something as simple as setting the table or folding a load of laundry. Such an act requires some thought and effort. They are an expression of love. Think about what your last expression of love was. Ponder what doings you can see to this week. Consider what Jesus would say for you to do. Sometimes, falling into a pattern of contributing positive deeds, comments, or concerns can blossom into something quite extraordinary. What kind gesture will you show your spouse this week?

Dear Lord, give me the courage to say sweet, gentle, and endearing words to my spouse. Put ideas and notions into my heart and mind, fostering a pattern of richness between us. Teach me loving ways to be thoughtful, kind, and compassionate to the person I committed myself to. Allow me the opportunity to show my spouse through an expression of kindness just how much he or she means to me. Thank you, Lord, for bringing this wonderful mate into my life. I love you, sweet Lord. Amen.

July 2

The clothing did not fall from you in tatters,
nor did your feet swell these forty years.

DEUTERONOMY 8:4

My husband's solution to fixing most things is by using duct tape. His motto is: if something is broken, duct tape it. On a long hike in the woods, I developed annoying and painful blisters on my feet. Bandages were not helpful. My husband proposed I duct tape cotton balls over the sores, and his comical suggestion worked. Do you set rules on how to clean the house or fold clothes? How open-minded are you in working out solutions with your spouse? Are you receptive to his or her suggestions? What can you do to become more flexible in conflict resolution in your marriage? Ponder in God's eternal love, what you can learn from your spouse's resourcefulness.

When you face a confrontation with your spouse, how do you typically respond? Do you give in because you would rather give up than fight, or do you flee hoping the problem will take care of itself? Some people assert their authority to gain control of the situation and get their own way. All three are poor solutions. Instead, focus on the problem, and don't accuse your spouse of behaving a certain way. In fact, strike the words "you always" or "you never" from your vocabulary. Those words only put your spouse on the defense. Instead of trying to resolve an issue "my way" or "your way," strive to achieve "our way."

Sometimes arguments arise because concerns disguise the real problem. Consider what attitudes are stirring your behavior so that you can decipher what the fundamental dispute is. Don't be a mind reader. Discuss your beliefs and expectations openly and honestly with your spouse so that you can get to the bottom of the problem. Don't try to interpret your spouse's thoughts. You do not know his or her thoughts because you are not inside their head. Instead, ask direct questions. As you work to resolve conflict, talk about circumstances and behavior. However, do not attack your spouse's character. Remember that your relationship with your spouse is the most important thing, not "winning" an argument, because when one of you "wins," you both end up losers. Love does not keep a record of wrongs. Jesus wants you to be forgiving, able to admit your mistakes, and quick to move on. Think about how you will incorporate these suggestions in your week.

Dear Lord, teach me to bend without breaking. Enable me to be more willing to hear my spouse's recommendations and not criticize or find fault with them. Allow me to be more approachable to try other methods to improve my marriage. Melt away my stubbornness and let me learn from my spouse's ingenuity. Thank you for giving me such a cleaver mate. Amen.

July 3

And Jesus advanced [in] wisdom and age and favor before God and man.
LUKE 2:52

Mountain climbers know the best thing they can wear is good boots. They seek certain qualities in them: waterproof, rugged, supportive, and durable. Inexperienced hikers might not realize that good boots are not efficient without top-notch socks. Ponder if you are expending energy trying to fix one area of your marriage, but a different component of it is also lacking. Are you focusing too much on your spouse's weaknesses, but not examining your own? Are you fixing the way you speak to your spouse while allowing your body language to backslide? Tone and body language are essential to master if you want productive conversations with your spouse.

If your partner shouts, "Come here" with anger written all over his or her face, your knees might buckle as you shuffle cowardly near. You might not even move, depending on your level of fear or the force of the command. If your partner crosses his or her arms over their chest, stares blankly at you and says with an even sternness, "Come here," you might wonder what you did wrong. If your spouse leans near, smiles, and whispers softly, "Come here," you might expect a warm embrace and a kiss. The same two words are used, but it was the body language and tone that conveyed the most powerful message. The balance of the nonverbal information is the largest part of the message that gets transmitted. Ponder how you communicate even when you aren't using words.

The most effective communication is when all three elements of face-to-face communication are aligned with each other: tone, nonverbal gestures, and words. Examples of body language ranges from facial expressions, the way you stand or sit, gestures with arms or hands, eye contact or lack of, breathing rate, coughing, flushing, or fidgeting. You can mimic your spouse's body language when you want to show support for them. It reaffirms that you are part of the same team, no matter what else is happening. How do you juggle multiple communication elements? Ask God to give you the strength to stay true to your desires and master non-verbal gestures to be a successful communicator.

Dear Lord, make me more efficient at repairing coinciding problems within my marriage. Give me the necessary wisdom to amicably decide what I need to do and how to do it in your good graces. Shower me with your steadfast love because with you anything is possible. Amen.

July 4

*The Lord G*OD *has given me a well-trained tongue, That I might*
know how to answer the weary a word that will waken them.
Morning after morning he wakens my ear to hear as disciples do;
*The Lord G*OD *opened my ear; I did not refuse, did not turn away.*
ISAIAH 50:4–5

Richie Havens was a performer at Woodstock. When one band was unable to make it to the stage, Havens continued singing while strumming his guitar, even though he already played every song he knew. That's when he improvised with a song he made up on the spot called "Freedom." Ponder if you have ever been in a situation where you had to think quickly and act spontaneously. How did that circumstance work out?

Perhaps your spouse's family arrived at your home for a surprise visit and even though you were unprepared, you were able to accommodate them spur-of-the-moment. How did this make you feel? Sometimes when people are put on the spot, their best comes out of them, as in the case with Richie Havens. Extroverts thrive with people surrounding them and they actually get reenergized by it. However, introverts don't respond the same way. They are met with a bag of mixed emotions, caught somewhere between happy to see family and wishing they would all disappear. Consider which category you and your partner feel the most comfortable in.

Your home is your castle; it's the one place where you and your partner establish and enforce the rules. While it's nice to have visitors, you should be the one inviting them, arranging a schedule that works best for you. You deserve to have people be courteous and call before they visit. It can be difficult, if not impossible, to turn family away. But in order to set a precedent that a phone call is required before ringing your door bell, you have to set boundaries and limits that you and your spouse both agree on. Also, you should let people know how you feel about their unannounced visits. The worst thing is to have misdirected anger toward your spouse. After the company leaves, discuss how you will handle this situation in the future.

Perhaps you have a pesky neighbor who peaks his head in your front door at the worst possible moments. If you welcome them with open arms you are setting the state for it to continue happening. It's understandable to want to be a good Christian, polite, kind, and welcoming—the way Jesus would be. You don't have to invite a neighbor in. Say you are in the middle of something and ask if they could come back. The next time someone shows up unannounced at your home, what will you do?

Dear Lord, teach me to be compassionate to visitors who show up on my doorstep. Did you send them to me because you knew I could help them? Amen.

July 5

For the king had ships that went to Tarshish with the servants of Huram.
Once every three years the fleet of Tarshish ships would come
with a cargo of gold, silver, ivory, apes, and monkeys.

2 CHRONICLES 9:21

At a distance from the shore, sailboats appear to drift aimlessly through the water. Yet the captain at the helm holds the course firmly, watching the crew on deck work the jib sails as they billow with wind, feeling the boat's power as it cuts through the water. You have to actually be in the boat to know exactly what is happening. Ponder if you are distantly removed from your marriage either by working too much, watching too much TV, spending too much time on the computer, or participating in too many activities? What is drawing you from your spouse? How can you reconnect with your partner and make him or her a priority? What if you both began your day with prayers before getting out of bed? When your marriage flows easily, everything in your life feels right. Prayer might get you off on the right foot.

Like the tides ebb and flow, your marriage does too. Perhaps the fluctuations are caused by changes with your job, sickness, financial difficulties, rebellious children, or aging parents. If you feel disappointed, disillusioned, or discouraged, those feelings could be based on serious marital issues, but other times they originate from insignificant things that might get turned from molehills into mountains. Knowing this is a part of marriage might help you through it. Otherwise, you might believe that your marriage is doomed because of distorted negative thoughts and dwelling only on the bad times. Therefore, try to recall happy times from your past: a good meal at a nice restaurant, a funny movie, or a nature walk that you both enjoyed.

A ship cannot be tested docked in the harbor. It is in the open sea that its durability and worthiness is established. During rough weather, you wouldn't abandon ship in a seaworthy vessel. You sail onward. If the tide gets rocky, you hold on tight. When all is going well, you sit back, relax, and enjoy the ride. Embrace the reality that your marriage could be like a ship where you learn to adjust your sails accordingly. What will you do today to ensure your relationship is a smooth ride?

Dear Lord, help me to ensure that my marriage sails on the right course. Guide us through smooth waters while I adjust the sails of my life to make my relationship my main concern. Neglecting you or [*name*] is not an option. Amen.

July 6

*Should you not fear me—oracle of the LORD—should you
not tremble before me? I made the sandy shore the sea's limit,
which by eternal decree it may not overstep. Toss though it may,
it is to no avail; though its billows roar, they cannot overstep.*

JEREMIAH 5:22

On a Florida beach, my dad built large sand sculptures using nothing more than sand and ocean water. He worked for hours while spectators congregated, astounded that something so grand could be made of something so trivial and miniscule. What are some tiny treasures in your marriage? Is it making your spouse smile after a long day? Perhaps it's doing a chore, good deed, giving an unexpected gift, a compliment, or an affectionate hug? God gave you the ability to build upon the small elements in your relationship. If a tiny granule of sand can hold back the ocean, imagine what your marriage will be like if you build off the meager resources of your relationship.

God gave you life, a priceless gift that has more worth than anyone can comprehend. It comes with many opportunities to experience its greatness with the partner God wanted us to our share life with. Have you thanked God for all of it, including the interactions with your spouse? Actively seek out the tiniest treasures in your life and be thankful for them and God will surely give you more.

Thank God for your spouse, even if you don't feel attracted to him or her right now. Thank God for his or her life and ask God lift the darkness that has possibly settled between you. Cradle his or her hand in yours, feeling the softness of his or her skin. Remember what it was like when you first held hands. Thank God for that too. Sometimes you have to search to find the treasures hidden in your marriage, but they are there. Some are miniscule, like the grain of sand used to build a sand sculpture, but God doesn't want you to overlook even the simplest of gifts that he gives to make your marriage sacred.

Spend some quiet time today reflecting on the many gifts God has blessed your marriage with. Focus on the similarities and know that they are not a coincidence. God meant for you to be joined as one to enjoy life together, to build each other up, and hold onto each other when the seas are rough. What tiny treasure have you overlooked in your spouse?

Dear Lord, help me to find and touch the gentle, loving, and compassionate side of [*name*] and build upon it every day. You have given me the remarkable capacity to love without limit. Amen.

July 7

Yes, a day approaches, a day of the Lord approaches:
A day of dark cloud, a time appointed for the nations.

EZEKIEL 30:3

Have you ever watched the clouds float slowly across the sky and spotted an identifiable object in them? Nephelococcygia is a term used when people find familiar objects within a cloud. Watch the moving clouds to see if you can decipher any recognizable shapes. You and your spouse may look at the same cloud and see two totally different things. Ponder if you look too deeply into your relationship for something that may not be there. Perhaps you are hopeful that your partner will change and develop your viewpoints, feelings, or emotions. Do not try to change your partner; you can only change yourself. God made your partner a unique individual just as he created you with quirky characteristics that no one else has.

The personality differences between you and your spouse can affect compatibility, emotional support, cooperativeness, and intimacy. Some of the traits that initially drew you together could later appear like flaws that need fixing. Identifying similarities and differences will enable you to better understand the dynamics of your relationship. Make a conscientious effort to see your differences as gifts to make your union stronger. When you concentrate on your partner's strengths and complimentary style, you can appreciate and affirm rather than criticize. No personality style is better than another.

Consider if you overuse comfortable personality patterns. If you do, your limitations become more obvious. For example, the more sociable partner becomes overbearing or the introvert may appear withdrawn. While you like your preferences, consider maturing within your basic style for the sake of your marriage. Any effort to curtail the overuse of a pattern preference brings harmony to the relationship.

How can you be more accepting of your partner's personality traits? Maybe you could look for the positive aspect in the traits that are opposite to yours. If your partner is overly frugal, accept his or her ability to save for a comfortable retirement that you can both enjoy. Did God bring you both together to balance each other out? Contemplate putting a positive spin on your spouse's characteristics. Which of your spouse's personality traits will you be more accepting of?

Dear Lord, expand my mind to see [*name*] hidden talents, personality traits, and distinctiveness. Allow me to find the endearing qualities that I once accepted and help me to cherish them. Amen.

July 8

*Then Isaiah said, "Bring a poultice of figs
and apply it to the boil for his recovery."*

2 KINGS 20:7

The banyan tree provides much more than nutritious figs; the sap is used to treat skin irritations, bark and leaf buds arrest bleeding and treat dysentery. The tree's roots are used for dental care, as a pain reliever, and are considered beneficial in the treatment of female sterility. Ponder how you can make your marriage bands beneficial to the many different aspects of life. Has your spouse cared for you during an illness? Contemplate what special features have a beneficial significance to you and your mate as a couple.

You have a vow that binds you together, like an insurance package that your partner will not leave you when you hit a rough patch. The vow reaffirms that you will work out your problems, no matter how complicated they seem. You and your spouse are stronger as a unit than an individual. You can meld the good aspects of your relationship and make them stronger, and completely eliminate detrimental aspects that could undermine your marriage. You have the ability to make more money as a couple because married men typically make more money than single men. Being married enables you to be healthier and live longer lives. Also, married men have more sex than single men.

You have a live-in friend who will make your happy moments richer and carry your pain when it is too heavy to bear alone. You have a home that you both can create around your own combined styles, where you feel safe expressing yourself. You have a built-in friend who will provide honest feedback and encouragement. Your spouse has your back and together you can write the next chapter of your life to be whatever you want it to be under God's direction and love. You could live alone, but God brought a wonderful partner into your life to share it, enhance it, sculpt it, beautify it, and fortify it.

Contemplate how you can celebrate companionship with your spouse. What can you learn from him or her? How can you help each other to perfect a much desired skill? The good Lord brought you together for a reason. Trust in God that he will reveal his plan to you in due diligence.

Dear Lord, thank you for my spouse and for giving me the ability to love beyond all reason. Thank you for allowing me to appreciate our differences, to embrace them, and build upon them. You are the answer to all of my prayers. I love you, Lord. Amen.

July 9

Thus says the LORD: The people who escaped the sword find favor in the wilderness. As Israel comes forward to receive rest, from afar the LORD appears: With age-old love I have loved you; so I have kept my mercy toward you. Again I will build you, and you shall stay built, virgin Israel; Carrying your festive tambourines, you shall go forth dancing with merrymakers.

JEREMIAH 31:2–4

In the Hawaiian Islands, Polynesians welcomed and entertained newcomers with a hula dance. They used hand movements to signify aspects of nature, such as swaying palm trees in gentle breezes, a wave in the ocean, or a feeling or emotion accompanied with graceful hip movements to tell a story. Ponder what story your marriage is trying to tell.

Is there something you need to do to change the course of your relationship? Perhaps you are becoming too materialistic. Draw your focus away from money and acquiring objects. You might be accumulating things because you have a void somewhere in your life. But this is like trying to hold Hawaiian sand in your hands; the reality is much of the sand will slip through your fingers, leaving you grasping at nothing. Consider filling that hole in your life with something more fulfilling because you cannot buy happiness.

Focus on enriching your marriage. Emphasize spending quality time with your partner, doing fun activities together. Take a long bike ride together, explore a new area, or travel to a destination that beckons you. Perhaps you and your spouse could focus on providing a service to others in your community. Consider volunteering in a food pantry, planting a community garden, or teach at-risk teens to play musical instruments. Volunteer to be a youth group leader or teach religion. Find a worthy cause that speaks to you and your spouse and fill the void in your life by making the world a better place.

Instead of filling yourself with objects, try a personal challenge of running your first race, or training to run a marathon. Perhaps you always wanted to go back to school to get a degree, or maybe you have always wanted to change your career. Fill your head with as much knowledge as you can. Your brain is like a magnificent sponge trying so soak up as much as humanly possible. What do your actions say about the type of marriage you have? Contemplate recent behaviors and devise a plan to improve them. Jesus story can be studied in Holy Scriptures. How will you build your life around the Lord?

Dear Lord, elevate my marriage and help me to make it into the best possible union. Bless my efforts. You have set my course in action and I will follow your ways. Thank you for reinforcing my love and devotion to you and to my spouse. Amen.

July 10

Wherever it flows, the river teems with every kind of living creature;
fish will abound. Where these waters flow they refresh; everything
lives where the river goes. Fishermen will stand along its shore
from En-gedi to En-eglaim; it will become a place for drying nets,
and it will abound with as many kinds of fish as the Great Sea.

EZEKIEL 47:9–10

After waiting ten minutes at a favored fishing spot, there was a nibble on the line. It was exciting to reel in a big one. The moment the fish was in the boat, I tossed the line back in to see if I could catch another one. I didn't want to change the lure or my methods; I wanted to keep a good thing going. After one successful accomplishment in your marriage, don't you want to stay in that good place a while longer with your spouse and keep a good thing going? All marriages go through cyclical patterns.

Contemplate if you have more highs than lows in your relationship. One way to keep your marriage on a high note is to notice the worthy actions of your spouse and comment on it lovingly. After your partner cuts the grass, say, "Wow, the lawn looks great! Thank you for making our home look nice. You must be really tired." By noticing and commenting on it, you make your spouse feel cherished. A simple "thank you" goes a long way to lifting his or her spirits. A successful relationship depends not just on how partners divvy up the household chores, but also on how they express gratitude.

If you get stuck doing certain household chores while your partner is oblivious to the piles of laundry, harmony can be found in the way you thank your mate. Regardless of whether you are doing a chore that is perceived as "just doing his or her job," some expression of gratitude should be made. When your spouse feels appreciated, there is less resentment over any imbalance in labor. Even if all you can offer is a small expressions of gratitude that will make a significant difference in your relationship. Express appreciation for work your partner does, even if it doesn't meet your standards or if you don't like the way it was done. Whoever does the job decides how s or he wants to do it. How many times do you thank your spouse each day?

Dear Lord, bless my success and enable me to keep more highs than lows in my marriage. I want to be a loving and grateful spouse by thanking [*name*] each time a chore is done. Teach me to be more adaptable and open-minded. Amen.

July 11

Put on then, as God's chosen ones, holy and beloved, heartfelt compassion,
kindness, humility, gentleness, and patience, bearing with one another and
forgiving one another, if one has a grievance against another; as the Lord
has forgiven you, so must you also do. And over all these put on love,
that is, the bond of perfection. And let the peace of Christ control your hearts,
the peace into which you were also called in one body. And be thankful.

COLOSSIANS 3:12–15

Epoxy resins require a mixture of two inert components that form a third chemical if the two are mixed exactly. The final product is a precise thermosetting plastic used in the construction of aircraft, automobiles, boats, and myriad applications where extraordinarily strong bonds are required. Ponder how strong your marriage bonds are. Consider if it is durable enough to withstand any storm as long as you together are like the epoxy resin mixture.

Perhaps you broke the circle of trust in your relationship. What can you do to mend it and make your bond more resilient? Perhaps you could make incremental steps toward rebuilding trust by providing respectful and courteous treatment to your mate and making him or her feel safe. Call out to God for reinforcement during this transition. Set aside time for honest and open communication with your mate. During dialog you may discover that there was an imagined betrayal of trust. An imagined betrayal can be just as destructive as a real one.

If you think your spouse's silence points to a loss of investment in your relationship, your trust is threatened. Imagination is enough to threaten your trust. Do you suspect that your spouse's business trips are a cover for an extramarital affair? When you do, trust quickly evaporates and your imaginings implies that your trust has been lacking. If your decision to trust is steadfast, you don't question your partner's trustworthiness.

In discussing the situation with your partner, don't shift the blame. Apologize with a plan to show that it will not happen again. Repair your relationship with a nice gesture to tell your mate that you mean what you say. If you were the injured person, grieve, but then let it go. As impossible as it seems, forgive each other and move on. If you want your marriage to grow, you have to commit yourselves totally to each other once again by starting over. Who needs forgiving in your marriage?

Dear Lord, allow my marriage to be stronger than any man-made element. Let us withstand the tests we encounter in life. Teach me how to be more energetic and trusting. Bring us to a place of happiness and love. Amen.

July 12

Your lips drip honey, my bride, honey and milk are under your tongue.

SONG OF SONGS 4:11

Honeybees have been around for millions of years and are incredible insects: they pollinate flowers and make honey. Honeybees also have the ability to sting; once they do, they die. Marriages have existed so long they predate recorded history. They provide security and the opportunity to procreate. While marriages can fail, they can also succeed. Ponder what attributes to your marriage successfulness. How can you accentuate the positives and deemphasize any negatives?

Don't allow discussions to begin inhospitably with criticism, sarcasm, or contempt because it will likely end negatively. Criticizing your spouse's character with "You are inconsiderate not to call," will lead to an unpleasant argument. Instead, bring a specific complaint to your partner. As an alternative say, "I'm frustrated that you had to work late again because dinner got overcooked while I waited and worried." The argument might end well if your spouse doesn't feel that his or her character is under attack.

Contempt is the most damaging because of the intention to hurt by using cynicism or sarcasm. Contempt can also be subtle with mean looks. The minute this happens in your marriage, stop and pray. Ask God to fill you with the love you need to communicate amiably with your spouse. Make a conscious effort to promote a culture of fondness and admiration for each other. It's natural to want to defend your position when you are blamed or attacked, especially if you think it's unjustified. However, defensiveness is counterproductive because it leaves your spouse feeling unheard, and the discussion polarizes. Take responsibility by listening and trying to understand your partner. Do not disengage from the discussion by stonewalling because it exacerbates the problems. Invoke the Holy Spirit to enlighten you to find the right words to convey what you are feeling to your spouse. Rely on God's wisdom to abolish negativity in your marriage.

Reflect on past events and experiences that drew you closer to your spouse. How can you do similar activities to keep the optimistic momentum going? If one aspect of marriage was ineffective, how can you change or adapt it to make it more productive? Remember that God is with you and will help you in every step you take.

Dear Lord, empower me with the wisdom and competencies to interject heartfelt solutions to the weak areas of my marriage. Teach me to squelch any possible troubles from erupting in a loving manner. Bless our relationship, Lord; make us fruitful, loving, and secure. Amen.

July 13

Two are better than one: They get a good wage for their toil.
If the one falls, the other will help the fallen one. But woe to the solitary person!
If that one should fall, there is no other to help. So also, if two sleep together,
they keep each other warm. How can one alone keep warm?
Where one alone may be overcome, two together can resist.

ECCLESIASTES 4:9–12

S olomon first describes the economic benefits of marriage: two are better than one because they earn good wages for their work. Couples who
pool their assets can live more economically together. Even the Internal
Revenue Service recognizes the advantage of this by giving tax breaks to
married couples. Also, two people can normally complete a task faster than
one person, whether it is cutting the grass or doing the dishes. Sociologists
agree that married couples are more financially stable and prosperous than
those who are unmarried.

Isn't it nice to know that in times of trouble, when you slip and fall, there
is a spouse who will pick you up? Solomon notes that marriage adds to our
security and health. If we stumble, our partner helps us up. It even insures
that we have heat. Married couples have each other to look after if one gets
sick. Reflect on the last time you were sick. Was your spouse there to take
care of you?

A spouse is there to provide practical help. Married couples have someone
to be with so they are not alone in this world. You have someone to share a
meal with, to converse with, to pray and worship with. Solomon implies that
married couples can share in managing their home and in the division of
labor. It's comforting that we don't have to do everything ourselves.

After God made Adam, he didn't want him to be alone so he created Eve.
God knew from the very beginning that two are better than one. How happy
are you that you are married and have someone to sleep beside each night?

Dear Lord, thank you for [name]. He or she is my best friend and my
family. You couldn't have chosen a better mate for me to share my life
with. We work well together saving for our future. I know in times
of trouble I can depend on my spouse to have my back. He or she
provides deep and loving warmth in times of cold and loneliness. Help
me to be as good and loving and caring as he or she is to me. Amen.

July 14

For over all, his glory will be shelter and protection: shade from the parching heat of day, refuge and cover from storm and rain.

ISAIAH 4:6

A squirrel was devouring kernels of corn on my deck, too busy to notice the storm that blew in. He crouched beside the house using his bushy tail covering his head as a furry canopy until the storm passed. When storms blow through your life, what kind of umbrella provides sanctuary to your marriage?

Seek sanctuary with God before you try to find it in your marriage. Without the Holy Spirit's guidance and strength, your efforts are simply inadequately human. The more you uncover the Lord, the closer you grow toward each other. The triangle analogy has God at the top with spouses situated in opposite bottom corners. As each person moves closer to God at the top, they shorten the distance between the two of them. Therefore, the best chance of finding sanctuary in marriage comes when you and your partner work on your relationship with Christ. Even if only one spouse appeals to God, the odds of finding such tranquility in your marriage improve significantly. For the unbelieving husband is made holy through his wife, and the unbelieving wife is made holy through the brother (1 Corinthians 7:14). One of you needs to be pursuing God to find genuine sanctuary in your marriage; but both of you striving to include God in your relationship is ideal.

Consider how you can possibly put God first in your marriage. Begin each day, the moment you open your eyes, by thanking God for giving you another day to live beside your mate. If you wake up together, why not pray together before starting the day? When you shower, thank God for the clean water that washes you. Many people around the world have to jump in a river; you have a private bathroom to groom in. Before you eat breakfast, pray over your bowl of cornflakes. While many people pray before dinner, why not pray before all of your meals? If you are the only one, pray aloud. It won't be long before others in your home follow suit.

On the way to work, opt to drive in silence, meditating on the beauty of God. As you stand in line waiting to buy a cup of coffee or a newspaper, say a quick prayer for your spouse. When you wash your hands, say another prayer. Each time there is a mindless lull at work, use that time to pray, to move closer to God, to reach him at the top of that triangle. He is there, just waiting for you with open arms.

Dear Lord, thank you for providing so many opportunities for me to connect with you through each day. You are my loving God, my savior, my king. I adore you. Amen.

July 15

Blessed be the God and Father of our Lord Jesus Christ,
the Father of compassion and God of all encouragement,
who encourages us in our every affliction, so that we may be able
to encourage those who are in any affliction with the encouragement
with which we ourselves are encouraged by God.

2 Corinthians 1:3–4

A rocking chair has two curved bands attached to the bottom legs. It contacts the floor at two spots enabling the chair to rock back and forth in a soothing and gentle motion. These chairs are calming because when the occupant doesn't rock, the chair finds the center of gravity, allowing an ergonomic benefit with the person sitting in a relaxed position and angle.

Ponder what tool enables you to find your center of gravity to keep you in a relaxed and tranquil state. Perhaps reading Holy Scriptures brings you to that sacred place. It's necessary to continue learning about who God is. Some people devote their entire lives to studying and seeking wisdom from it. One thing you can always count on is that the truth of Scripture will guard your heart and fill your mind with all that is honorable and sage. Allow the words in the Bible to influence your life and marriage for the better by understanding God's remarkable ways.

Another easier way to find your center is simply to talk to God the way you would speak with a friend. God is all-powerful and omniscient; he actually knows what you will say even before you do. God desires to have a close relationship with you. Find some quiet time alone where you can sit with the Lord and listen to his voice. To do this, you must turn off the TV, close the newspaper, and walk away from all technology. Perhaps you can sit outdoors under the shade of a tree and simply be still and meditate on Jesus's face as he prayed in Gethsemane, a garden at the foot of the Mount of Olives. Perhaps this relaxing time spent with the Lord, will bring rejuvenation to your life and marriage.

Also, make God the center of your marriage. God created marriage, and he provided the rules to live by. When you put God at the center of your marriage, seek his will in everything, not just your egotistical ways. Love will guide your relationship; your desire will be to respect and please each other, not just to satisfy yourself. What will you do to put God at the center of your life and your marriage?

Dear Lord, thank you for being at the center of my life, for keeping me grounded, and lifting me up when I needed it the most. I love you, Lord, God Almighty. Amen.

July 16

"If your brother sins [against you], go and tell him his fault between you and him alone. If he listens to you, you have won over your brother. If he does not listen, take one or two others along with you, so that 'every fact may be established on the testimony of two or three witnesses.' If he refuses to listen to them, tell the church. If he refuses to listen even to the church, then treat him as you would a Gentile or a tax collector.

MATTHEW 18:15–17

A dumpster dive saved an old dresser from its demise. With a lot of elbow grease and hours of sanding, several layers of paint were stripped off, nicks and scratches were buffed out, and a gorgeous solid wood piece of furniture remained. With a light stain and polishing, it was returned to its original glory. I never imagined such a treasure could be found under all of that ugly nastiness.

Consider if life's trials and tribulations have added layers of grime, malice, and offenses to your mind, body, and soul. It can hide your true inner beauty, unable to let your loveliness shine through to your spouse. One of the best things you can do to get yourself back on track is to go to confession. Until you are open with your partner regarding failures you will remain burdened by them. Jesus entered this world and preached about the forgiveness of sins. Jesus did not down play sin or rationalize it. Yet, he forgave continually, just as he wants you and me to do. Jesus wants sinners to realize their offenses, to repent, and to be reconciled.

When Jesus appeared to the Apostles, he breathed on them filling them with the Holy Spirit. God allowed the apostles to breathe new life into the souls of contrite sinners. That is when Christ established the sacrament of penance appointing the Apostles ministers of it. Confession has always been a practice of the church, it is a sacrament given to us by Christ where the Lord showers us with grace.

When was the last time that you made an honest examination of your conscience, reviewing the commandments and the Church's teachings? Consider going to confession to obtain the healing grace from the sacrament of penance.

Dear Lord, wash away my sinfulness. I am so sorry for my offenses. Please, forgive me and take pity on my soul. Give me the strength to turn away from sin in the future and live an honest and noble life. I truly want to be more Christ-like in all that I think, say, and do. I love you, kind and merciful Lord. Amen.

July 17

Jesus Christ is the same yesterday, today, and forever.
HEBREWS 13:8

Weather changes from day to day. One day it might be bright and sunny, warm and beautiful, but the next day could be chilly and gloomy. People also are constantly changing. Today you might wake up on the wrong side of the bed feeling irritated, but tomorrow you might wake up jubilant and celebrate all of God's gifts. Life continually changes, yet the one thing that will never change is God's love. He never changes; God is the same today as he was in the past and will be in the future.

Ponder how you have changed since getting married. Perhaps you were shallower than you are now, putting the needs of your spouse before your own. Contemplate if you have changed in an undesirable way. How has your spouse changed? People change and sometimes they don't always change for the better. Do you sleep in instead of attending Mass during the summer months? Perhaps you have neglected yourself, your spouse, or God. Do you pray as much as you used to? God calls us to repent and change our evil ways. There is always room for improvement.

Whatever your life experiences are thus far, you were able to do because of God who provides everything: strength, courage, and will, to carry out his plans. You might have an idea about what you want to do with your life, but unless it is God's will for you, it won't happen the way you think. Surrender your life to the Lord. Pray to accept God's plan for you and slowly you will change the way the weather does. Ask God to work them into your hearts to face your limitations, see the need for change, and then do it. You don't have to face your fears alone; you have God with you who will guide each step you take. Do God's work, whatever it is.

Dear Lord, I am a lump of clay in your hands. Mold me into what you desire for me to be. Give me the endurance to accept it and bear the heat when you test me in the kiln. I know that test will strengthen me to endure future tests of time. I am capable of anything you set out for me because I trust you emphatically. I love you, Lord, God Almighty, creator of heaven and earth. Amen.

July 18

Do you not know that the runners in the stadium all run in the race,
but only one wins the prize? Run so as to win. Every athlete exercises
discipline in every way. They do it to win a perishable crown,
but we an imperishable one. Thus I do not run aimlessly;
I do not fight as if I were shadowboxing.

1 CORINTHIANS 9:24–26

Magnets are objects with an invisible magnetic field that attracts the opposite forces of other magnets while it repels like poles of other magnets and pulls metal materials such as iron and steel. Ponder the opposite personality differences between you and your spouse, especially those that initially pulled you together when you were dating.

Perhaps your spouse is a musical fanatic, playing a variety of instruments while understanding the rudiments of rhythms and beats, whereas you merely enjoy listening to certain genres on your mp3 player, but lack an interest in actually playing an instrument. Maybe you have a photography hobby, but your partner uses his or her phone to snap pictures. Perhaps your spouse is an athlete, but you are a marathon runner. Consider how you can merge your interests. Become a student of your partner's curiosities. Having a leisure pursuit with your spouse can open a window into a new world of pleasure and recreation for you both to enjoy.

Look at the similarities you have with your partner first and celebrate that you both love to hike, by planning to climb a nearby mountain. When you find pleasure by participating in a mutually enjoyable activity, you can branch out by trying to learn a sport, hobby, or recreational doing that thrills your spouse. Maybe you have always wanted to learn how to golf, but never had an opportunity before.

Celebrate that the variances in your character because it can be areas of growth for the both of you. If your spouse is social, learn from him or her how you can become more personable. If your spouse loves entertaining, learn how he or she can pull together a party effortlessly. Perhaps with the skills you learn, you could enjoy entertaining as much as your spouse.

How can you accept and appreciate the differences in your spouse's personality? Call upon the Lord to enable you to find the good in those things that separate your spouse's characteristics from your own.

Dear Lord, open my eyes so I can see the good in my spouse and grow to adore the variances between us. Enable me to embrace them, learn from them, and become well-rounded. Teach me to celebrate our personality differences as a gift from you, sweet, and loving Lord in heaven. Amen.

July 19

*But at a birthday celebration for Herod, the daughter of Herodias
performed a dance before the guests and delighted Herod
so much that he swore to give her whatever she might ask for.*

MATTHEW 14:6–7

When is your birthday and how is it celebrated? Perhaps you have large groups of friends over or go out to a favorite spot. There might be a quiet festivity with family members at home; maybe a cake with a cherished gift. Birthdays can conjure up disappointment and unfinished childhood issues. Ponder if you have been disappointed with a birthday at some point in your life. Ponder if there is an inner child who wants to feel special on that day. Perhaps your childhood birthday celebrations were overshadowed by other events, causing you to feel that you missed out, or maybe you were spoiled and feel entitled to get your own way.

Reflect on past birthday disappointments and how they flavor your feelings associated with birthdays and future celebrations. Do you punish your spouse by sulking or withholding affection? How do you act when you are not a top priority on your birthday? Do you wonder about your birthday weeks ahead, speculating what your spouse will do for you? If your spouse forgets or doesn't plan, you can choose not to interpret the disappointment as a fatal issue. Instead, make your own birthday party. Birthdays present opportunities to move through painful disenchantment intensified by early childhood experiences. Acknowledge them, and then let them go. Leave them in the past and vow to make future birthdays special for yourself.

You live with yourself longer than you live with anyone else. You know yourself better than your spouse knows you. Perhaps you could buy yourself a gift! Instead of being disappointed by getting a blender two years in a row, accept the thought that went into it and don't make a mountain out of a molehill. Maybe your partner loathes shopping and a blender was the only thing he or she could think to buy. Focus on the bigger picture instead of retaliating, punishing, or withhold love. Focus on the fact that God allowed you to be born because he loves you and has very special plans for you. Choose love and compassion to guide your life. Stop for a moment and consider all God has given to you on this day: sunshine, a warm breeze, birds that sing in the trees. Look at each little thing as a birthday gift from God.

Dear Lord, thank you for giving me life. Thank you for each day that you give to me, each smile that I see. Thank you for the clean air I am able to breathe, and for the comfortable home I live in. Thank you for the clean water I can drink and for each and every little thing that you put in my path today. I am truly thankful. I love, Lord. Amen.

July 20

Therefore the LORD will give you meat to eat, and you will eat it,
not for one day, or two days, or five, or ten, or twenty days, but for a
whole month—until it comes out of your very nostrils and becomes
loathsome to you. For you have rejected the LORD who is in your midst,
and in his presence you have cried, "Why did we ever leave Egypt?"

NUMBERS 11:18–20

Have you ever walked down a buffet line and piled a mountain of food on your plate, more than you are capable of eating? Why not stop eating when standing next to a table filled with delicious foods? Ingestion analgesia defends eating from ending, regardless of how unpleasant you feel when your stomach is stretched to capacity. Basically, you suppress the painful feedback when your brain releases endogenous opiates. Scientists have discovered that the reaction to pain is diminished when eating tasty foods, like chocolate. You can become insensitive to the pain of overeating.

Consider if you have become insensitive to incessant bickering in your marriage. Bickering not only hurts your marriage, but it can hurt your health too. Stress slows the production of pro-inflammatory cytokines, which are protein molecules essential to your body's healing process. After an argument, cytokines may elevate more than is healthy, which has been linked to a variety of age-related diseases. The issues that trigger bickering may seem insignificant, but when fights keep resurfacing, the amount of resentment and hurt feelings fill your marriage with negativity and eat away at your quality of life. Also, recurrent quarrels can mean there are deeper, unresolved issues.

Do you and your partner have reoccurring fights? When you are engaged in conflict, it's not easy to step away from it. If you are winning a fight, it means your spouse loses, but in marriage, you are on the same team. Regardless of who "wins," you both lose with residual anger festering enough to flare up the next fight. However, when the next time arises, ask to discuss the matter with your partner calmly. Don't blame your spouse. Instead ask, "What happened?" Speak with a composed, inquisitive tone, keeping the anger and frustration out of your voice. Your goal is to find out what really happened in a loving manner without making any assumptions. Your spouse's explanation needs to be acknowledged and used to establish a compromise. You and your partner should have several possible solutions. And if you're not going to do something you agreed to, you must inform your spouse in advance. The next time you feel inclined to bicker, how will you control yourself to resolve it once and for all?

Dear Lord, teach me moderation, patience, and kindness so that I stop bickering. Fill me with the love I need to work out my conflict in a congenial manner with compromise. Amen.

July 21

Though you scour it with lye, and use much soap,
The stain of your guilt is still before me, oracle of the Lord GOD.

JEREMIAH 2:22

S oaps are made with two major ingredients: fats and a strongly alkaline
solution. A complicated yet delicate chemical process transforms the key
ingredients into the bar of soap that you wash with every day. The earliest
record of soap-like material dates to 2800 BC in ancient Babylon. Think
about how many times throughout the day you use soap to cleanse yourself.
When you feel clean, don't you feel better physically?

Experts say if you cleanse your mind of toxins, your physical health could
also improve. Spiritual cleansing therapy rids you of negative emotions, depression, sadness, and drug and alcohol addiction. Rejuvenate your mind every
day with the positive affirmations of prayer because that nurtures you with
hope, faith, and encouragement. Prayer every day lifts you to a higher place
and tells God that you are seeking his spiritual counsel; that will enrich your
heart. If negativity surrounds you, simply say, "Lord, if these thoughts are
not from you, take them out of my head. I only want to have loving thoughts
of you." Imagine gazing into Jesus's eyes, touching his hand, and feeling his
love and all negative thoughts will disappear. Try meditating by focusing
only on Jesus's face in the stillness of your mind and the quiet of your heart.

Have you considered cleaning your soul? To rid yourself of sin, confession
is a great way to wipe the slate clean and start over. Begin with prayer and
meditation that involves humbleness and humility. He may grant what you
ask for if that is his will. Or, if it is not his will, he will answer you by saying,
"No," or "Not now, maybe later." There is also another possibility that God
has given you the means to solve your own dilemmas, and he wants you to
fix the problem yourself. Quite often, prayers are answered in the manner
that God knows what is best for you, not what you think is best for you.
There are many different ways you can pray. It basically involves talking to
God. However, you can also find God by reading the Bible. How will you
cleanse your heart today?

Dear Lord, let me hear you in the stillness of my being. I have quieted
my heart and I want to hear your voice. Speak to Jesus, and tell me
what you want me to do. I will obey, even if I don't like the words I
hear. I know that you know what is best for me. I trust you and your
plans for my life. I love you, sweet merciful, Lord. Amen.

July 22

"Be on your guard! If your brother sins, rebuke him; and if he repents, forgive him. And if he wrongs you seven times in one day and returns to you seven times saying, 'I am sorry,' you should forgive him."

LUKE 17:3–4

Why do paper cuts hurt so much when they're minuscule? Paper cuts can be surprisingly painful because the skin on fingers isn't very strong against shearing forces and is easily cut. Also, fingers have more sensory receptors that get stimulated when injured. In a shallow cut the pain receptors are exposed to the air, ensuring continued pain.

Ponder what is causing continued pain in your marriage. Is there a reoccurring hurt? Because hurt and anger are entwined, it's vital to unravel them to get to the bottom of the injury. When you feel hurt, inform your partner by saying, "Ouch!" It's possible that he or she didn't know they were inflicting pain on you. It could be a simple misunderstanding that could be easily resolved.

To find the bottom of your emotional pain, first look under the anger to learn why you feel it because that will explain why you are hurting. Sometimes it's hard to know what to do about your pain but if you don't do anything, you can drift apart. The key is not to sweep your pain under the rug, because then your pain can build up onto past hurts and before you know it there is a huge pile that you cannot ignore. You need to deal with it.

Acknowledge that you contributed to a part of the pain in your relationship and together you and your spouse will work to resolve it. Confess the offense and seek forgiveness in order for the hurt to be healed so that you can both move on. Even if you might dread trying to resolve your conflict, avoiding it will be more detrimental to your marriage. Take a step toward solving your problems opening with prayer and then dialog. Ask the Holy Spirit to empower you and keep your intimidations away.

The fear of failure can affect your communication responsiveness. If you avoid resolving your hurt, you allow it to fester. Strive to achieve an emotional closeness to your spouse through open and honest communication, by sharing ideas, and doing things together. If you are harboring regrets about past hurts, how can you take that first step to getting your marriage back on track?

Dear Lord, help me! I'm hurting and I don't understand the complexities of my life. Let it unfold in a more congenial way. I will sit with you today in your peace, love, and joy, while I listen for your voice to bring me clarity. I truly love you, Lord. Amen.

July 23

Who among you is wise and understanding? Let him show his works
by a good life in the humility that comes from wisdom.
But if you have bitter jealousy and selfish ambition in your hearts,
do not boast and be false to the truth.

JAMES 3:13–14

New York City has cracked down on street vendors selling "knockoffs" at rock bottom prices. Unscrupulous merchants sell anything from phony designer handbags to watches. Police work tirelessly to stop the counterfeit trade. Have you ever struggled to differentiate between a real or fake watch? Have you ever been deceived in your marriage by something less-than-genuine?

One of the most respectful things that you can do for your spouse is to be honest with him or her. Why lie when Jesus wants his followers to be truthful? There are many different forms of lying: deception, false pretense, and withholding information. In marriage the best thing you can do for your partner is to always speak the truth. Being equipped with the truth, no matter how difficult it may be to grasp, is far better than being deceived and learning the truth later.

Trust is critical for any relationship to thrive. In trusting your spouse, you share your life, your hopes, and your dreams with that special person; because he or she does what they say they are going to do. You learn to trust someone based on what they say, what they mean, and what they do. Trust is the foundation that holds a marriage up and keeps it strong. Strive to safeguard all that is sacred to him or her. Ponder how trustworthy you are to your spouse.

People lie for a variety of reasons. Someone might lie to hide something. Or someone could lie because it works for them. Liars believe they won't get caught or they think they have a right to lie. Habitual liars lie because of a deficit of conscience, to justify their behavior, or manipulate so that they become the victim. Liars turn the tables, making themselves look good and others look bad.

If you dishonor your spouse by violating an agreement, you will have serious problems. If you make amends for your betrayal, your spouse might determine you to be trustworthy, and slowly begin to trust you again. If you don't seem to understand the importance of honoring an agreement, and the importance of protecting his or her trust, your relationship will fail. Put your faith in God that you can work toward total trustworthiness with your partner.

Dear Lord, help me to surrender unto you. Allow my heart to be full of honesty and dependability. Allow [*name*] to lean on me, trusting that I will be a source of love and respect. Amen.

July 24

Home and possessions are an inheritance from parents,
but a prudent wife is from the LORD.

PROVERBS 19:14

U sed dryer sheets have many other uses than keeping your clothes soft and free from static cling. They can be used as dust cloths of nearly any surface, they repel bees and other insects from your picnic areas, and you can scrub your showers to remove soap build-up and mineral deposits. Who would imagine so many benefits come from one product? What are some benefits of being married? Take a few moments to reflect on your own relationship to consider benefits you have enjoyed.

Sociologists suggest that married people have better health physically and mentally, and live longer than those who are unmarried. Married couples eat healthier foods, and when feeling unwell, they recognize symptoms, seek treatment, and recover more quickly without complications. One study suggests that marriage enhances the immune system, making sicknesses less likely. Spouses are intimately aware of and affected by the choices their spouse makes. Married couples watch out for each other and encourage healthier choices and activities such as taking walks. They also take better care of themselves and avoid risky behavior. Another health benefit comes from the emotional support couples give to each other, especially if they are recovering from an illness.

Married couples are less likely to develop mental illnesses. Married people have lower rates of depression with half the probability of developing a psychiatric disorder. Divorce and separation are associated with a much higher risk of mental illness and depression. Married people consider themselves happy. The health benefits experienced by married people don't exist in other types of intimate relationships.

Sometimes, the benefits are not visible on the surface, or you might not put much thought or energy into uncovering it. You might have to examine your relationship with your spouse, scrutinize, and search for the beauty before you can see it, feel it, and appreciate it. After you peek into the corners of your relationship, you will agree that the institution of marriage as a whole is good for you. Marriage involves much give and take throughout each day. For everything you take, give twice as much back. What will you give to your spouse today to let him or her know how important he or she is to you?

Dear Lord, bless my marriage. When I got married, I had no idea how many benefits there would be for me because of it. Now that I know, I am truly grateful that you brought this lovely person into my life. Thank you, Lord, for everything. Amen.

July 25

*Should you not fear me—oracle of the LORD—should you not
tremble before me? I made the sandy shore the sea's limit,
which by eternal decree it may not overstep.*

JEREMIAH 5:22

B lack Sand Beach is found on the Big Island of the US state of Hawaii. The black sand is actually made of basalt that was created by lava flowing into the ocean. When I stood on black sand with my eyes closed, it felt like any ordinary beach. The moment I opened my eyes, I realized I had something truly special.

Consider what unusual characteristic makes your spouse irresistibly captivating. Quite possibly, with your eyes closed, he or she is just an ordinary person, but if you really look hard enough, you just might find some unique characteristics in your spouse that are especially appealing to you. Maybe you have overlooked this specialness because you have been absorbed in your job or perhaps you and your partner have drifted apart. Focus on the loving attributes of your partner that you once found endearing.

If you struggle to identify a fond feature of your spouse, think back to when you were dating. What special feature drew you both together? Consider what charmed you then. Open your eyes and search for those delightful qualities that are still present in your spouse. Don't allow your relationship to become average or dull. Instead, hold it up to a higher plane. Don't stop making special efforts for each other; tell your spouse what you love about him or her.

Consider changing your indifference to your appearance. Your spouse may struggle to see you in a romantic or exciting way if you don't pay attention to your dress and personal hygiene. Make an effort to look attractive for your partner. Deliberate if your spouse could long to hear words of love from you. Who doesn't appreciate being told how much they're loved and cherished? Ponder how you can share your hopes, dreams, and secret thoughts with your spouse. This connection will be more meaningful if conveyed with affectionate touching. Physical closeness communicates different feelings and provokes different sensations. Make a special effort to find time to be alone with your spouse. After you put effort into enhancing your relationship, you will see the treasure in your spouse that you knew was there all along. How will you improve your marriage today?

Dear Lord, let me experience the love with [*name*] that we once shared when we were newly married. Let me revisit that special place and draw upon the gifts that you built into our relationship. Thank you for the many blessings in my life. Amen.

July 26

For I fear that when I come I may find you not such as I wish,
and that you may find me not as you wish; that there may be rivalry,
jealousy, fury, selfishness, slander, gossip, conceit, and disorder.

2 CORINTHIANS 12:20

The summer provides greenery in the leaves on the trees, the grass under our feet, and many plants, flowers, and vegetation. God has a purpose for it all. Do you believe that everything has a purpose? Then consider what the purpose is for poison ivy. It is important to the ecosystems it is in. Some caterpillars munch the leaves, while the small white berries found on the plant feed birds and small animals. The tangles the vines form serves as shelter because most animals are not affected by the irritants in the poisonous oil emitted by the plant.

Contemplate if there are characteristics of your marriage that are similar to poison ivy. It might be difficult to detect, but when the burning itch settles in, you know exactly what has happened. Perhaps the irritating features were dragged into your marriage with residual emotional baggage unknowingly from unresolved childhood issues. Everyone has some degree of unfinished business from their childhood. Whenever something comparable to those experiences occurs now, and you react similarly, there could be an unmet need from your childhood. Perhaps you felt that you were not listened to as a child; you have a need to be heard, understood, and known. Consider how you react now when you believe you are not being heard by your spouse.

Almost everyone grows to expect certain things: the way your children behave, the way your spouse treats you, the way your family and friends act. Even you have varying opinions of those expectations that were created during your childhood based on your home life and upbringing. The expectations can cause problems if you don't keep them as a lower priority than the person you are expecting something from. For example, if you are expecting your spouse to be affectionate every day because that need wasn't met in your childhood, and you are making that need more important than your spouse, and you might act irrationally or handle it poorly.

Expectation difficulties occur because two people want two different things. In trivial circumstances, you can both create a new standard. When you have an agenda that includes your spouse and he or she has a different idea, learn to release your expectations entirely without holding grudges. Contemplate the last time you had an argument over something that was an unmet expectation of insignificance. How will you handle it in the future?

Dear Lord, let me learn from childhood experiences and create better ways to live with my spouse. Thank you for all your gifts. Amen.

July 27

What I do, I do not understand. For I do not do what I want, but I do
what I hate. Now if I do what I do not want, I concur that the law is good.
So now it is no longer I who do it, but sin that dwells in me. For I know
that good does not dwell in me, that is, in my flesh. The willing is ready at
hand, but doing the good is not. For I do not do the good I want, but I do
the evil I do not want. Now if [I] do what I do not want, it is no longer I
who do it, but sin that dwells in me. So, then, I discover the principle that
when I want to do right, evil is at hand. For I take delight in the law of God,
in my inner self, but I see in my members another principle at war with
the law of my mind, taking me captive to the law of sin that dwells in my
members. Miserable one that I am! Who will deliver me from this mortal
body? Thanks be to God through Jesus Christ our Lord. Therefore, I myself,
with my mind, serve the law of God but, with my flesh, the law of sin.

ROMANS 7:15–25

I thought a flower's fragrance was pleasant when it blooms. A Sumatran
plant, native to the slopes of the Barisan mountain range in western In-
donesia, blooms once every seven to ten years. The rare blooming lasts fewer
than forty-eight hours and stinks like a decaying body. Though repulsive
to most humans, the rank scent allures Sumatran carrion beetles and flesh
flies, which help pollinate it.

Reflect on the rare traits that make your personality beautiful, like a
flower, and other mannerisms which might be foul. While there are no bad
personalities, some habits and behaviors can be less healthy and less likable.
Everyone has unique likes and dislikes, strengths and weaknesses. What's
right for you may not be right for your spouse. What's right for your spouse
may not be right for you. By understanding your personality and other
personality types, you can better understand your assets and fallibilities.

Do you always view the world through the lens of your unique personality style? Do you value characteristics that you perceive in yourself? If you
consider yourself "organized" and you see someone different in that respect,
you might describe them as disorganized because they lack a quality you
have. Reflect on the characteristics that differ between you and your spouse.

The Myers-Briggs Type Indicator was published in 1962 by a mother-
daughter team that emphasizes the value of personality differences. Do you
have particular inclinations in the way you interpret your experiences? What
preferences influence and inspire your interests, needs, values, and motivation?

Dear Lord, you influence me with your warming love. You inspire
me by your actions which are done with love. My interests are created
through you. Amen.

July 28

Even if it were true that I am at fault, my fault would remain with me;
If you truly exalt yourselves at my expense, and use my shame as
an argument against me, Know then that it is God who has dealt
unfairly with me, and compassed me round with his net.

JOB 19:4–6

While it's difficult to exercise daily, there are other activities you can do to burn extra calories that are more productive than jumping rope. You can burn nearly 180 calories by cleaning your house for an hour. Even while sleeping eight hours at night, you burn approximately 500 calories. Praying burns one calorie per minute. Every activity uses energy; the more you do the more energy you burn. Contemplate if you need to be doing more for your marriage. Reflect on the quality time you spend together. Is it enough? Consider if you could do chores together as a way of spending more time together. With the two of you working together, the work will be finished in half the time.

Do you need to do more around the house? Consider if you avoid responsibility. If your spouse is acting resentful, that is a sign that things are not right. Using "I" statements, ask your partner what you can do to be more helpful. Be mindful not to be accusing, give excuses, or cast blame. Pick up the slack and offer the suffering to the Lord.

If you make a mistake, take responsibility for your actions. You are allowed to make mistakes because you are human. Admit the mistake, apologize, and start over. Take a good look at yourself and see how you can change your actions to handle similar situations appropriately in the future. If you want to be viewed as a worthy spouse, have initiative in your marriage. When you notice that something needs to be dealt with, step forward and do it. Stepping forward to handle a difficult situation is admirable. If you are uncertain about what to do, ask God to bring the right person into your life who can help you. Ask God to give you courage and strength. Solicit advice from a consultant while being mindful of your principles. Question if you need to do more to help our around the house, help your spouse, or help your marriage. Where will your efforts help out the most?

Dear Lord, grant me self-discipline, honesty, and integrity to do more for [name]. I'm afraid of being criticized, Lord. Help me! I want to be a good spouse, helpful, kind, and loving. Transform me into the person you created me to be. Thank you. Amen.

July 29

Let mutual love continue.....Let marriage be honored
among all and the marriage bed be kept undefiled,
for God will judge the immoral and adulterers.

HEBREWS 13:1, 4

There are many treasures of Italy; my favorite is the Blue Grotto. It is a small cave on the coast of the island of Capri. When sunlight is reflected on the water through the tiny opening, a majestic blue reflection illuminates the cavern. Many visitors travel there, but never experience the incredible boat ride into the captivating iridescent blue waters of the cave.

Consider how long you have been married and ask yourself if you have experienced true, mature love. When you are together because you want to be, you have a mature love. It's more than a commitment; it's respect built off friendship, acceptance, and emotional support. Mature love comes with working together and growing together as a team. Mature love is like the Blue Grotto; not everyone experiences the true joy of it. Consider how your love has evolved over time.

Marriages transition from three stages of growth: the early years have romance, the middle years that are associated with parenting have disillusionment, and the latter years have mature love. Marriage is a process; it evolves over time. As soon as the honeymoon is over and the passion wanes, realization leads to disappointment and conflicts, which makes this a difficult period of adjustments as you and your spouse accept each other for who you really are.

The rebellion stage is where you both want different things and self-centeredness surpasses the interests of the marriage. Maintaining love throughout this difficult stage is crucial. Rebellious thoughts are often met with anger and frustration which results in defiant actions such as infidelity. Marriages become more complicated as careers advance and children arrive.

In the cooperation phase, marriage works like a business. When you attain the empty-nest stage, there is time to appreciate each other again as lovers and friends. In the explosion phase, either you or your spouse might be faced with a major life-changing event like a job loss or health problems that could affect your relationship for an indefinite amount of time. Your marriage could be a source of solace as you work through life's challenges. Marital happiness skyrockets after several decades of sharing your lives together. This mature love stage perpetuates living in the present, not the past. What stage is your marriage in and how can you keep it on course throughout all of the stages?

Dear Lord, don't let my marriage journey get derailed by the complications of life. I value [*name*] and desire living in the mature love stage of marriage. Please, Lord, help us get there. Amen.

July 30

*Let loose the fury of your wrath; look at everyone who is proud
and bring them down. Look at everyone who is proud, and
humble them. Tear down the wicked in their place, bury them
in the dust together; in the hidden world imprison them*

Job 40:11–13

Yellowstone National Park has the world's largest collection of geysers. A geyser is a spring characterized by water and steam erupting turbulently. Geysers are located near active volcanic sites where surface water trickles down to reach hot rocks. The subsequent boiling of water results in the geyser effect, known as a hydrothermal explosion, of hot water and steam spraying out of the geyser's surface vent. Does your marriage have explosions of anger and frustration?

Extreme anger is a major source of marital stress. Understanding and resolving it is important for good health and happiness in your relationship. Conflict and anger in your marriage is associated with increased blood pressure and compromised immune function. When you feel anger, ask yourself if it is appropriate, excessive, or misdirected.

If you are upset, the immediate intense anger can be damaging your relationship. Instead of exploding with anger, reflect on what is causing your feelings. Perhaps you could take a walk and burn up the excessive energy that you are trying to control. On the walk you can think about the anger. Question if it could be sadness, fear, or hurt. Try to get to the bottom of it to determine what the anger is trying to tell you and whether it is appropriate or not. After you understand it, ask if your rights are being violated or if you just want your own way. If you want your own way, you will have to discuss it with your partner and try to work out an agreeable compromise. If your rights are being violated, assert yourself and stand up for what you believe in. For instance, if your partner is refusing to allow you to go to Mass, that is a violation of your right to worship.

It's also wise to examine if the anger is from fatigue, hunger, or if it is misdirected. If I am tired or hungry, I know I am more reasonable after I have eaten or rested. Reevaluating it will help you to see the anger for what is really is. Scrutinize your anger to see if it could be misplaced from your childhood. Taking a good look at anger before reacting on it is always a safe bet. It gives you time to understand it and discuss it more calmly with your mate. The object is to work it out, not explode like a geyser.

Dear Lord, keep me calm when I want to explode with anger. Teach me healthy ways to resolve my conflict so that I don't hurt my marriage. Amen.

July 31

Now you are wrecked in the sea, in the watery depths;
Your wares and all your crew have fallen down with you.

EZEKIEL 27:34

The doldrums are calm periods where wind fades, trapping sailboats for days or weeks. It occurs where the Atlantic and the Pacific Ocean merge with a low-pressure air mass created from the heat of the equator. Ponder if your marriage is in the doldrums. Contemplate ways you can kick-start your marriage and get it back on track. Do you want to quell the dullness and bring it back to dynamite? Pray about where the monotony originates from so that you can do something about it. God does not want your married life to be stagnated; he wants it to be fulfilling, worthwhile, and rewarding.

It's important to make time to have fun with your spouse, because the bond that you develop during good times will help you through the rough patches. King Solomon offered sage advice: "Enjoy life with the wife you love, all the days of the vain life granted you under the sun. This is your lot in life, for the toil of your labors under the sun" (Ecclesiastes 9:9). How can you make time to have fun with your spouse?

With hectic work schedules and other obligations, make sure to schedule time for fun in your appointment book or calendar. Perhaps you could declare one night of the week "date night." If you don't plan it, chances are good that it won't happen because something else will come up. Take turns planning your fun and have an open mind to try new activities. You never know how much you will enjoy a new activity until you try it.

Plan to spend time with other couples. Create a meal club where everyone brings a dish to pass while taking turns hosting the dinners. It's inexpensive, practical, and fun to socialize. Perhaps you would enjoy playing cards or board games with neighbors. Another great place to interact with other couples is church.

Dates don't have to be expensive. Go on a picnic, take a long bike ride, hike through a nature center, and build a bonfire in the back yard. The objective is to step away from work, drama, and stress. Make an ordinary day a special one with your spouse to enjoy the little moments in life, because often they turn out to be the best. Spending quality time with your partner is just as important as anything else you do for your family. How will you play your way to a healthier and happier marriage?

> Dear Lord, remove the boredom from my marriage. Help me to appreciate fun moments with my spouse. Bless the time I take to play, laugh, and relax. Thank you for your infinite wisdom and love. Amen.

August 1

Everything that he undertook, for the service of the house of God
or for the law and the commandment, was to seek his God.
He did this with all his heart, and he prospered.

2 CHRONICLES 31:21

A graceful butterfly flutters through the air close and then drifts off in the distance; imagine God floating nearby like that throughout each day. Children playfully attempt to catch butterflies in nets, but their quickness is no match for them. The elegant insects glide quickly out of reach. Be still and watch the butterfly land near. Sometimes, it's important to simply be still in a relationship instead of always trying to move it in one direction or another. Are you overcommitted with outside activities? What issue have you been attempting to change? Seek God with all of your heart; he will guide you in your marriage so that it flourishes.

Take time to slow down, be still, and contemplate Jesus. Remove every thought that pops into your head, and replace it with Jesus. Focus on his face and give five minutes of uninterrupted time to him. Resist the temptation to ask questions or fill the silence with idle chatter. Give the Lord your heart, mind, and soul where everything in you is about God. If your mind wanders off with the butterflies that drift by, bring yourself back by saying, "Jesus." He won't leave you. He will be glad that you devoted this brief time just to him. It is in those quiet moments that Christ will speak to you. Stop and listen.

New studies are showing that the best way to get more done is to spend more time doing less. Take short breaks throughout your day to reflect and meditate, even if it's for five minutes, because in the long run it will boost your productivity, job performance, and your overall health. You cannot make more time in the day, but you can increase your energy by taking short breaks to reenergize. Every 90 minutes your body inches its way into a fatigued state. Your body gives you signs to stop and take a break, but you override it with coffee or other drinks infused with caffeine, or body's natural stress hormones. Will you take more breaks to stop, reenergize, and listen to the Lord's voice?

Dear Lord, I place my difficulties in your hands. Help me to solve them and move on. Teach me how to stop chasing things that I cannot catch and focus on listening to you instead. Remove the distractions in my marriage and let me concentrate on your master plan. Amen.

August 2

Listen to me, my child, and do not scorn me; later you will find my advice good.
In whatever you do, be moderate, and no sickness will befall you.

Food is something we must have in order to survive; without it, we die. Too little food causes life-threatening diseases. However, if we consume too much food insatiably, we overtax our bodies, inviting diseases such as high blood pressure and diabetes that can ultimately cause our demise. The key is moderation. Ponder what is slanted too much in your marriage, making it lopsided. Do you work too much; could you be a "workaholic?" Consider if you are working too hard as a way to escape from a bad relationship or to avoid working on repairing your marriage or mending your personal strife.

What can you do to get your life in balance? Contemplate harmonious ways to incorporate more stability in your relationship. Instead of nagging, share in a positive manner what your spouse has missed by working late. Don't criticize your spouse for bringing work home or for not being there for you and your children. Try to think about the job security and the financial stability that your partner is providing. Curtail your spending on items or services you could do without.

Stop enabling your spouse's desire to work longer hours by holding dinner for him or her. Don't reschedule family activities and then complain about it afterward. If your spouse decides against going with you, go without him or her. If you had planned to attend a movie, take the children anyway. If you had intended to spend the weekend away, take the children and go, remembering not to do it maliciously. Look for activities that your spouse would enjoy as a way of encouraging him or her to work less. Attempt to set boundaries; if your partner agreed to play a round of golf, ask that the cell phone be turned off. Schedule shorter events you both could attend. Maybe your partner could attend half of a party. Set aside quiet time each day to pray about it with your spouse and brainstorm solutions that are acceptable to both of you. Ask God to intervene.

Dear Lord, bring my marriage back into symmetry. Teach me to be open-minded, to compromise willingly, and be more tolerable. Make my heart malleable to accept the changes I must make. Walk with me, Lord, and guide each step I take. With you, I can rest assure that I am heading in the right direction. Amen.

August 3

I will give you a new heart, and a new spirit I will put within you.
I will remove the heart of stone from your flesh and give you a heart of flesh.

EZEKIEL 36:26

Craftsmen convert a piece of leaded glass by cutting deep grooves into it to create a crystal heart paperweight. Something plain and ordinary is transformed into something quite remarkable. When the crystal heart is held to the light, it refracts the light, creating a barrage of tiny sparkling rainbows. Have you ever considered this object's similarities with your own heart having deep grooves cut into it by life's injustices? Perhaps they were wounds inflicted by your spouse or unavoidable circumstances. Ponder how you possibly contributed to it or allowed it to happen. How did you forgive and overcome them with the heart God made for you? When raised up, those gashes will transform you into a more beautiful person, sprinkling subtle rainbows to those you love.

Jesus understands heartbreak. The week before his crucifixion, townspeople adored him. Soon their adoring chants turned to jeers. Even the apostles couldn't stay awake and pray with him. One of his "friends" sold him out for a bagful of coins, while other "friends" denied him. Who hasn't experienced heartbreak? Through the pain you have felt, something remarkable has occurred. Jesus perfected you with a resurgent type of power to rise above your suffering, shake it out, turn it inside out, and learn from it. Take a good look at your pain and consider what God wants you to learn from it. Are you a stronger person today because of it? Has it transformed you in some way? Is it possible that your heartbreak has made you more compassionate, more loving, and more accepting of other's shortcomings and imperfections?

Don't allow pain to hold you as a captive prisoner. You have the ability to break free. Nothing is impossible to overcome and move on as long as you have God with you. Instead of placing chains around you that strap you to past mistakes and struggles, free yourself from them. Don't cling to negative comments. Instead, ask God to take away those evil thoughts and comments and replace them with God's pure love. Study the problems you are faced with and ask God to tell you where it is leading you; is it God's will or are you going the wrong way? Ask God to guide your footsteps.

Dear Lord, melt my heart in your indelible love to enable me to withstand the inequities that I have endured. Help me to rise above them and be more loving to my spouse and family. Transform my heart to love beyond its capacity. Amen.

August 4

Indeed, goodness and mercy will pursue me all the days of my life;
I will dwell in the house of the LORD for endless days.

PSALM 23:6

In sports arenas around the globe, enthusiastic fans fill the stadiums wearing their team colors and shirts, waving flags, or toting paraphernalia with a high degree of spirit. What are you most proud of in your marriage? Perhaps it's the number of anniversaries you share. How do you demonstrate to your mate that you are honored to be married to him or her? Does your spouse know that you are proud of your commitment and devotion to him or her? Reflect on ways you can show your high degree of spirit to your marriage through God's grace.

Anniversary celebrations rejoice in the continuation of your love for one another throughout the years. Each one deserves to be celebrated in a memorable way because when you do, it is a renewal of your commitment. If you saved the top layer of your wedding cake, share it with each other, or recreate a small version of your wedding cake while reminiscing about the splendor of your wedding day. Talk about the most special part, any humorous aspects or mishaps that made your day unforgettable. Maybe you could recreate a meal similar to the one you served at your reception.

Perhaps you could go away for the weekend to commemorate your anniversary like a mini honeymoon. It provides you with an opportunity to assess where you have been and where your relationship might be heading. Getting away allows you both to renew your commitment to each other in a special location. Perhaps you could attend a marriage enrichment workshop sponsored by your church or a marriage encounter weekend on your anniversary.

If you are celebrating a big anniversary, maybe you could consider renewing your vows or having a party. Maybe you would want to celebrate with a special bottle of champagne. One couple spent their anniversary delivering one red rose to each resident in a nearby nursing home. Another couple makes a donation to a charity to honor their years together. Regardless of what you do, remember that the important thing is that celebrating your anniversary together reinforces that you are making your marriage a priority. When is your wedding anniversary and how will you celebrate it this year?

Dear Lord, allow the Holy Spirit to work through me to show my partner how much [*name*] means to me. Help me to make it a priority to convey my feelings every day. Don't let me get caught up in the day-to-day grind that I overlook the most important person in my life. Thank you for always being there for me, Lord, to keep me on track and live a just and honest life. Amen.

August 5

Will the ax boast against the one who hews with it?
Will the saw exalt itself above the one who wields it?
As if a rod could sway the one who lifts it,
or a staff could lift the one who is not wood!

ISAIAH 10:15

I have walked in woodlands without a walking stick hundreds of times and was fine without it. However, after I used one, I truly appreciated its worth. It facilitated balance, provided support, cleared brush aside for easier footing, tested mud, and offered reassurance in defense against snakes and wild animals. Is there a tool that could improve your marriage without you realizing it because you have never tried it? Have you considered marriage counseling through your church or priest? Have you thought about attending an adult Bible class together? Ask God to reveal the tool your marriage might benefit from.

It takes a lot of thought and work to build a successful marriage. It requires deliberate plans while you actively pursue the construction. Don't allow daily activities to take priority over it, because when the building stops, "status quo" settles in. Keeping an eye on building your relationship will make it fun and productive. You and your spouse are on the same team working toward a complete sharing of heart and soul, mind and body. If you find yourself bickering about trivial things that don't matter, drop it. Don't overreact; but respond. Think about why you react in certain ways and plan ahead how you handle it the next time it happens. Have the mantra: "I choose us."

Another important thing you can do is put words of honor and devotion into his or her heart. Let your spouse know how much you appreciate about him or her by affirming many of his or her positive traits and talents. Ask God, who sees the best in everyone, to reveal to your heart constructive qualities you can affirm. Share your time, your thoughts, and interests. Time spent together fosters a connection opportunity. Remember that in order to have a history together it must be built one event at a time. Consider doing that this week with daily contact either emotionally, mentally, physically, or spiritually. Consider how you can do that starting today.

Dear Lord, be the crutch my marriage needs. Expand my heart to be more open to working through stubborn issues that I am reluctant to deal with. Be my beacon of hope and guide me to the restful place where [name] and I can flourish and worship you all of the days of our lives. Amen.

August 6

Because of laziness, the rafters sag; when hands are slack, the house leaks.
ECCLESIASTES 10:18

M y niece drove a car for two years without doing anything more than pumping gas in it. She was surprised when a thick plume of smoke billowed out from the engine, choking the car to a standstill. She was flabbergasted to learn that the car needed preventative maintenance. Ponder what anticipatory upkeep you give to your marriage to keep it running smoothly. Do you only do the bare minimum because you are swamped with household chores, work, or volunteer obligations? Could you say "no" to others and put your spouse first? Can you ask for outside help with your ancillary tasks to free up time for your partner? Instead of feeling resentful, ask your spouse for help. Consider if you are over-responsible or irresponsible. If you are overly responsible, you need to do less and stop enabling your spouse to do less. If you are irresponsible, you need to do more and start taking ownership of issues that involve you.

It has been said that it is better to be the right marriage partner than to have the right partner, because you can only change yourself. You may want to change your partner, but the truth is that you can only change yourself: your feelings, reactions, attitude, and how you relate to him or her. If you feel neglected and emotionally empty, turn to God to fill you up. Always remember that God loves you, and he is eagerly awaiting you to invite him into your life. Lean on the Lord. He will hold you upright and guide you down the chosen path. Open your heart to receive God's love. Don't even try to live your life your own way because God has a true plan for you. Welcome God in and allow him to weave his love throughout your life and your marriage. God is the endless source that you can always draw from. Ask the Lord to fill you with the wisdom you need. God will not let you down.

Dear Lord, help me to give more quality time to my spouse, who is deserving of my love and attention. Teach me how to be a more productive worker, to multitask, or ask for outside help so that I don't get overwhelmed. Walk with me, Lord, on this journey and help me to trust in your ways. Amen.

August 7

Hezekiah asked Isaiah, "What is the sign that the LORD will heal me
and that I shall go up to the house of the LORD on the third day?"
Isaiah replied, "This will be the sign for you from the LORD that
he will carry out the word he has spoken: Shall the shadow go forward
or back ten steps?" "It is easy for the shadow to advance ten steps,"
Hezekiah answered. "Rather, let it go back ten steps."

2 KINGS 20:8–10

Stories have circulated that log cabin quilts were used as signals in the Underground Railroad to help slaves to reach a safe haven. Certain quilt designs were used to inform runaways what they needed to do to reach freedom. These signs were essential information. Don't you wish you had signs in your marriage to tell you what to do? Perhaps there are signs, but you are too busy to notice, or maybe you see them but can't interpret them.

One sign of trouble is when you feel as though you no longer have anything in common with your spouse. If that should happen, try engaging in meaningful conversation with him or her. Reflect on past times where you had fun together. Set a date to do something similar or try to do something totally different, like go whitewater rafting or fly fishing.

Another red flag is when you feel like every action is being scrutinized or criticized by your partner. Tell your spouse that you don't appreciate being criticized and that you won't tolerate such behavior. If your spouse nags, that makes you defensive, disrespectful, and resentful. Nagging can be perceived as criticism; therefore, your spouse may ignore you. Don't blame, demean, or attack your spouse. Take responsibility for yourself and your chores and obligations.

Does your partner keep information from you about his or her career, personal problems, or achievements? If your partner is sharing information with a friend instead of you that is a red flag that your marriage is in trouble. Prompt communication between you and your partner in an attempt to rebuild trust in your relationship. Do you hide with your face buried in the newspaper or a book, or are you constantly on the computer or watching TV? If you always have something else to do, that may be a problem. Arguing constantly over the same subject is another red flag.

You may need a professional marriage counselor to get your relationship back on track. If you don't know where to turn, talk to your parish priest. Draw upon God's strength and infinite wisdom to see red flags in your relationship. Through quiet meditation God will tell you what to do.

Dear Lord, I turn to you with a heavy heart and troubled mind. Nourish my soul, Lord, and help me to find the peace and tranquility that my marriage is desperate for. Pave my way with your love. Amen.

August 8

A mild answer turns back wrath, but a harsh word stirs up anger.
The tongue of the wise pours out knowledge, but the mouth of fools spews folly.
PROVERBS 15:1–2

Rabbits in arctic regions are white in the winter to blend in with the snow, and in summer and autumn they turn brown to blend in with woodlands. This method of camouflage protects them against predators such as the fox. What is your defense against anger in your marriage? Ponder if you suppress it quietly or if you explode in a rage. Many people respond the way their parents responded in their childhood homes. Consider if you emulate your parents' behavior because it's a healthy response that deserves continuing. Many people rely on responses that were learned as children. The responses can serve as constructive or destructive behavior. Identifying what makes you angry can help you improve coping methods. What matters is what you do with your anger: stuff it, explode, or deal with it constructively. The success of your marriage may depend on how you cope with your anger.

Successful anger management can mean the difference between marital joy or misery. Do you recognize early warning signs such as changes in your voice or jumpiness? Ponder healthy ways you can channel anger. The best thing you can do when you feel angry is pray. Step away from your anguish to spend quiet time with God for a few moments. He will quell your animosity and fill you with the peacefulness you were longing for. Then you will be able to speak intelligently and calmly to your spouse with the words the Lord put in your head and heart.

If you notice anger growing, those feelings should be expressed calmly and lovingly in words. You might need to go for a walk first, but that time will allow you to reflect on any underlying issues that may have triggered the anger.

It is necessary to express and acknowledge anger, but never to verbally attack each other. Could you develop a "no yelling" policy during angry episodes? That would eliminate your spouse's defensiveness or retaliation. If you both can express anger serenely, you will be better equipped to know why there is anger.

Dear Lord, the moment I am incensed, let me step away with you. Cool me, Lord, and remove the redness in my face. Replace the quiet with your comforting messages that I need. You are my saving grace. Amen.

August 9

Each one must examine his own work, and then he will have
reason to boast with regard to himself alone, and not with
regard to someone else; for each will bear his own load.

GALATIANS 6:4–5

When people plan their summer vacations, they want sunny days, not cloudy with rain. People crave the warm sunshine. While sunshine makes people happy, it can also be dangerous. Too much sun on unprotected skin can cause painful burns or possibly skin cancer. How can something that feels good cause such trouble? Ponder if you reap the rewards of your relationship while putting very little into it. Are you an irresponsible partner in your marriage, creating havoc because of something you don't do? Contemplate how you can do more while demonstrating your ability to be held accountable.

Perhaps you pretend to take responsibility for your actions but secretly blame your partner. Ponder a difficulty that you had in the past. Did you hold your partner more responsible for the problem? You can improve your relationship through accountability. Examine the reasons why you blame your partner.

Your spouse needs to be able to rely on your truthfulness, your dependability, and consistency of your actions. The foundation of that trust is accountability. In a healthy marriage, partners encourage, support, and help each other. If either partner is acting in an unhealthy way, it's the other partner's obligation to hold him or her accountable. Don't punish or judge, or try to force him or her to stop or change the unhealthy behavior. You are not responsible for what your partner says or does. Your role is only to point it out. What your spouse does with it is his or her problem.

In marriages affected by addiction, accountability is vital. If you are a recovering addict, your spouse's need for accountability is not a punishment for your illness. Your spouse needs proof that you are correcting your behavior, improving yourself, and following through on your commitments. Accountability can protect you from isolation, pride, and sin. To protect you from the traps of temptation and weakness, tell your spouse about them and ask him or her to keep you accountable. This responsibility means asking your spouse to make honest observations and to give honest advice and evaluations. In the silence of your heart, ask if you or your partner has a problem with addiction. Ask God to bring the right person into your life to help you. The first step to recovery is admitting there is a problem.

Dear Lord, give me the courage to be more responsible in my marriage, to help my spouse, and my fellow brothers and sisters in my community. Amen.

August 10

Yes, it approaches, a day of darkness and gloom, a day of thick clouds!
JOEL 2:1–2

Have you ever noticed dark clouds approaching and assumed a storm was imminent? Anticipating a storm necessitates preventative measures be taken like closing the windows, gathering ornamental objects, covering lawn furniture, and protecting potted plants. If you think a storm is brewing in your marriage, what preemptive actions do you take? Perhaps you can invoke the Holy Spirit to formulate loving ways to convey your feelings to your partner. Ask God to put the right thoughts in your mind, the perfect message in your heart, and the best method to deliver them.

Begin by using "I statements." Perhaps you could use a soft start-up to ease into the conversation. Bring up grievances in an unbiased, less harsh way. Complaining is an ineffective means of communicating. Say what your spouse has done incorrectly, emphasizing what he or she could do right. Speak using a calm voice and loving tone. Imagine how Jesus would speak and use that tone. State your request clearly, firmly, and politely.

It is essential to time your discussions appropriately. Don't hit up your spouse the moment they walk in the house after a long day at work. Waiting until your spouse has had some time to unwind and relax is more suitable. Don't begin a conversation if your spouse is hungry or tired. Giving feedback to your spouse in an effort to change behavior is a delicate process. Be sensitive to your spouse's feelings when you begin speaking to avoid a defensive reaction. Your spouse will embrace the feedback positively with good results if you "sandwich" positive statements at the beginning and conclude with an encouraging optimistic ending.

Another valuable technique to initiate dialog is to use "red flags" when speaking about a topic that elicits an emotional response. If you need to discuss sex, money, in-laws, or any topic that could stir up emotions, the red flag would prepare your spouse for that type of a conversation. An example of that might be, "I need to talk about finances today because the credit card bill arrived. Would this be a good time to talk?"

Maybe using an analogy would be beneficial or rate your message on a scale of one to ten. Before you talk to your spouse, remember that God is always with you. Ask the Lord to bless your words and intentions. What strategy will you use to initiate a conversation with your spouse this week?

Dear Lord, help me speak tenderly to [*name*]. Enable me to suppress the anger that is festering and convert it into love instead. Teach me to converse quietly, kindheartedly, and tranquilly so that my spouse doesn't feel threatened. Amen.

August 11

Then God said, Let the earth bring forth every kind of living creature: tame
animals, crawling things, and every kind of wild animal. And so it happened:
God made every kind of wild animal, every kind of tame animal, and
every kind of thing that crawls on the ground. God saw that it was good.

GENESIS 1:24–25

Cottontail rabbits have made my yard their sanctuary. There are ample hiding places behind trees and shrubbery, with sufficient food sources for all of the critters to share. A menacing hawk occasionally terrorizes the bunnies, chickadees, and other wildlife. Ponder what threatens the refuge you created with your spouse. Perhaps you are struggling with change. Routines are comfortable, but they can become a rut.

Think about the last big change you made. Was it leaving single status to become a married couple? Maybe it was leaving childless status to become a parent. Perhaps it was leaving the world of employment for retirement. Perhaps the change was beyond your control, such as your health status was altered to patient.

Even if some of your life changes were planned, making adjustments is critical when confronted with a major life transformation. You create a "new normal" based on modifications to your routines and schedules. How do you adjust to a new normal? You have to move beyond the infinite differences between "what was" and "what now is" by trusting in God's plan for you. There is a reason for everything that happens regardless of whether or not you see it or appreciate it. Trust that God is with you and will not abandon you when you need him most. God will give you the tools you need to be successful in your transformation. He will bring the right people into your life at just the right time: it is no coincidence.

Allow your heart to adjust first, because while it will continue beating, it often expands easier than any other part of the human body, especially when it conforms to love. Look for the love in your new normal, remembering that it takes time to adjust. Remember back to a time of adjustment when you got a new dog or cat; you might have chosen the pet accepting the differences in your home. However, it's more difficult when something happens that is beyond your control. If possible, ride the wave and let it go where it must because you have God with you to keep you strong. Don't worry about what tomorrow will bring. Just focus on each day and trying to find and celebrate the love in it. God puts love into everything. You just have to look for it. It's also helps you to overcome fear or pain because God won't let it linger forever. Time moves you onward and teaches you to accept and someday embrace.

Dear Lord, help me through the transitions of my life. The new stages
are difficult to embrace. Be with me and keep me strong. Amen.

August 12

For if I were to send you to these, they would listen to you. But the house of Israel will refuse to listen to you, since they refuse to listen to me.

EZEKIEL 3:6–7

Building the Panama Canal was one of the largest and most difficult projects ever undertaken. The shortcut made it possible for ships to travel between the Atlantic and Pacific oceans in half the time it previously took. Ponder if you can delve into a hefty project to improve communication by eliminating disagreements and other behaviors that sabotage your relationship.

A challenge every married couple faces is dealing effectively with differences in their spouse. The differences could be small disagreements, but even they can build up over time and strain your marriage. When confronted with a difference in opinions, remain calm, remembering to focus on the problem, not your spouse. Find a safe place for honest communication. Don't initiate a conversation while your spouse is brushing his or her teeth, washing the dishes, or changing the oil in the car.

To voice your concerns, begin by expressing your interests, needs, concerns, desires, and fears, and allow your spouse to do the same without any interruptions. Only focus on one issue at a time. If there are several issues, write them down and agree to address them later. Use this time wisely, not to blame your spouse or call names. Instead, treat your spouse with respect and work together as a team to resolve your disagreement.

Developing a structurally sound set of reflective listening skills will enable you and your spouse to communicate more efficiently. It requires full concentration; do not try to rehearse in your head what you want to say next. Your goal is to understand the message your partner is trying to convey. When it is your turn to speak, repeat what you think you heard, and accept feedback from your spouse. You are agreeing with your partner, you are merely trying to understand his or her point. Name the emotion your partner uses: you seem frustrated or sad. Check out what you think you heard your spouse say. Reverse the roles, allowing your partner an opportunity to listen to you. It takes practice, but the reward of feeling loved by your partner will be worth the effort of listening to him or her. When you and your spouse master the art of reflective listening, you will resolve your disagreements amicably and save a boatload of time. What kind of listener are you?

Dear Lord, give me the patience to fine tune my listening skills. Help me understand, love, and appreciate my spouse. Amen.

August 13

We are writing this so that our joy may be complete.
1 JOHN 1:4

Handwriting is a person's individual style of writing. Everyone has different handwriting; even identical twins have differences. What is your partner's cursive penmanship like? Is it endearing when you see it and do you recognize it from others? Think back to when the last time was that you wrote a love letter to your partner. Could you write a heartfelt note to your spouse describing his or her finest attributes? Remind your partner about their unique characteristics that you were initially attracted to. How can you build off the talents you adore about each other? Can you see God's hand guiding you both together?

Today it is rare to receive a handwritten letter, but that is why you should do it. A thoughtful passage will tug at the heartstrings because the words are from your heart. A love letter is a treat for the senses because your spouse can see your handwriting, feel the paper, perhaps imagining the sound of his or her voice reading it. Even without the scent of perfume or cologne, the sweet words from your loved one can be read over and over again. If your spouse bought you a knickknack you might forget about it by the end of the week, but a love letter is much different. Each time you reread it, you can experience the same wonderful, amorous feeling all over again.

Maybe the practice of writing a one-page love letter detailing why you think your sweetie is special will become easier after each one you write. Could you possibly write one letter each month? The writing exercise might become second nature after a while and propel your spouse to write a few letters to you too. It is a simple romantic notion that can do wonders for your relationship if you can put forth the time and effort knowing how much it will please your spouse.

Perhaps you could initiate a tradition of writing letters to your parents or children, which could serve as a heartfelt gesture that could become a keepsake. This task doesn't take much time and costs little, but reaps many rewards. Can you write a small love letter to your spouse today?

Dear Lord, I have forgotten about the qualities that I first found adorable about [*name*]. Let me make a list of the many talents he or she has so that I can refer back to it with a loving and grateful heart. Thank you for bringing this wonderful person into my domain to share my life journey with. I love you, Lord. Amen.

August 14

You have been born anew, not from perishable but from imperishable seed,
through the living and abiding word of God, for: "All flesh is like grass,
and all its glory like the flower of the field; the grass withers,
and the flower wilts; but the word of the Lord remains forever."
This is the word that has been proclaimed to you.

1 PETER 1:23–25

Most gardeners know that plants need the dead parts cut off in a process called "deadheading." This technique is good for plants because it prevents them from going to seed. Also, it allows them to conserve energy, concentrate on root development, and grow overall. Delphiniums and weigela shrubs can rebloom if deadheaded after the first bloom has finished. Consider if there are aspects of your marriage that need to be trimmed off. Are you a controlling person? Do you need to be in control of most aspects of your family life? Ponder how you can relinquish some of that power to your spouse or children.

Control needs to be shared in order to have a healthy relationship. If you make all of the decisions, that implies your spouse is incompetent. Your spouse may feel resentment or a lack of respect. If there is a control problem in your relationship, you might have difficulty relinquishing some of it or asserting your needs. This could be a result from your upbringing and not something you would ordinarily think about. A continuing desire for control or to get your way on most things could be connected to underlying insecurities traced to your early childhood experiences.

If you are a control-oriented spouse, try to be more accepting of your partner's ideas, thoughts, and feelings. Solicit more influence from your partner because that will make him or her feel validated, appreciated, and loved. If modifying your behavior is too overwhelming, talk to your parish priest or seek counseling to resolve insecurities. Perhaps you and your spouse need to be more tolerable of each other's differences. You might have to set aside any unresolvable differences for a while because couples don't always agree on everything. Maybe there is one topic that you have to agree to disagree on. Quite possibly after some time has lapsed, you might revisit it and reach a compromise. Marriage compels couples to have realistic terms regarding their needs. Marriage works best if you find ways to support yourself when you and your partner can't agree. This means tolerating some differences without the need to change your partner. Can you settle for controlling your own thoughts, ideas, and emotions?

Dear Lord, help me to only control myself today. Stop me from trying to control [*name*]. Teach me how to love unconditionally. Amen.

August 15

*A great sign appeared in the sky, a woman clothed with the sun,
with the moon under her feet, and on her head a crown of twelve stars.*

REVELATION 12:1

In Catholic churches around the world, the Assumption of Mary into heaven is a feast day celebrated on August 15. When Mary's time on earth was complete, God brought her body into heaven because she was purely perfect. Mary was the only one to be conceived without sin. No other person on earth has been perfect since Jesus and Mary. Take comfort in knowing that you are not expected to be perfect. Because you are human, you will make mistakes. Therefore, your marriage will not be perfect either.

Making mistakes is a part of life and making progress. Own your mistakes, take responsibility for them, and think about them. Ask yourself what you have learned from them and how you can keep from repeating them. You are going to make mistakes throughout your life because you are not perfect; some of those mistakes might be very painful. Give yourself permission to be human and to accept that you will make errors, accept the consequences, and grow by becoming a better person as a result of them. Because you and your spouse are human, neither of you are perfect, so don't expect perfection in your marriage. Make allowances for being human: you get tired or hungry, are overworked, stressed out, and have personal or family illnesses. Forgiveness is key in your marriage. When you say, "I'm sorry," mean it and then don't repeat the action. Learn from it and grow.

Try to find humor in awkward moments because it could enable you to smile as you roll with the punches. Laugh at the little mistakes in life, reserving any drama for genuine catastrophes. Give each other the benefit of the doubt. You are building your marriage on a foundation of trust, loyalty, and dependability. Many couples fight over the craziest things, mostly doing chores. Pick and choose your battles by letting little things go. Ask yourself if a little irritation is worth fighting over. Where do you encounter the most frustrations?

Share responsibilities around your home, allowing your partner to do chores however he or she wants to do it, even if it is not the way you would like it done. Find the joy in doing chores together because you are together. Celebrate the happiness that your spouse helps do some of the chores. If you were living alone, you would be doing all of the chores yourself. Set aside quality time to reconnect with your partner each day to reflect, cuddle, and share each other's company. God made you uniquely human, full of fragilities knowing that you do not have to be perfect.

Dear Lord, thank you for creating me in your image. I love you, Lord. Amen.

August 16

The wise heart turns to the right; the foolish heart to the left. Even when walking in the street the fool, lacking understanding, calls everyone a fool.

ECCLESIASTES 10:2–3

The summer is the perfect time for outdoor concerts, keeping in mind the flexibility that is necessary for both the performers and the audience. The community clusters in their canvas lawn chairs under the open sky for a few hours of merriment. The venue could be a grassy park, a woodland setting, or seaside. Some people are not bothered by the weather, outside noises, or insects, while others detest it. Many things could go awry because of numerous elements that factor into the success of a concert are beyond anyone's control when a makeshift stage is used. And yet, the shows go on, but many don't attend outdoor concerts because they prefer an auditorium.

In your marriage, many things can go wrong too. Ponder the factors that erode your marriage bonds. What if you love outdoor concerts but your spouse loathes them? Perhaps your spouse is a sport enthusiast but you are a bookworm. When you were dating your spouse, the personality differences between you didn't impede your relationship or warm feelings toward each other. After a few years the same traits you once thought were endearing are now annoying in your marriage. Avoid trying to change your spouse. God made you unique with your own particular style and something about that drew you together.

Reflect on your own personality style and how it impacts your marriage by identifying similarities and differences. It is key to your compatibility to see your differences as gifts. Focus on your spouse's strengths because it's better to appreciate it than to criticize it. There are no good or bad personality traits. Think about the personality trait that you are the most comfortable with. If you overuse it, your limitations become more blatant. For example, the introvert may become a recluse. For the good of your relationship, develop maturity within your style. Therefore, the recluse would make an effort to attend an outdoor concert and not complain about the bugs or raindrops. That would increase your own personality balance and bring harmony to your marriage.

God created everyone with a need for a relationship that is so strong that it compensates for personality differences. Different personality traits offer complementary resources for handling all of life's challenges. Use them to your benefit to make your union stronger. What personality trait of your spouse would you like to learn to embrace?

Dear Lord, enable me to be more tolerable of my spouse's unique personality traits. Help me to learn from them, to stretch to meet it and grow in the process. Thank you for all you do. Amen.

August 17

*Then she said to him, "How can you say 'I love you' when your
heart is not mine? Three times already you have mocked me,
and not told me where you get your great strength!"*

JUDGES 16:15

Sometimes the bite of a mosquito is subtle and you may not realize you've
been bitten until the next day when there is an itch and a welt. Sometimes
in marriage, you feel the hurt the day after you have been injured. Maybe a
secret was revealed and you needed time to reflect on it.

Betrayal hurts because your marriage is built on a promise that your
spouse will always be true to you. Because your spouse has behaved properly
in the past, you wouldn't have a reason to believe that betrayal could happen,
but when it does it stings much more. A betrayal destroys trust and creates a
likelihood that things you once believed in may not be as they seem. Betrayals are psychologically traumatizing, as if your world has been a lie. Trust is
essential in your relationship and for a happy, meaningful life.

You can work through broken trust and repair your relationship, but
it is a long, arduous process. The good news is that your marriage will be
stronger as a result. It's vital to take responsibility when you make a mistake,
especially if you were the one who was betrayed. Within the depth of your
heart, contemplate how you have contributed to a betrayal. If you struggle to
see it, ask God for enlightenment. After establishing mutual responsibility
for the betrayal, another aspect to rebuilding trust is recapturing a sense of
control. The control comes in doing something to improve your marriage
by allowing sincere amends to be made. It is damaging to your relationship
to talk about the unfaithfulness nonstop. Step away from it using a positive
distraction, even if it's to take a brief walk in a park or get ice cream.

Evaluate your capacity to forgive your partner. Forgiveness is thread
throughout the Bible. Lean on the Lord during this difficult period. Question if
your partner is genuinely motivated to change. After a betrayal, it's acceptable
to check phone records and e-mails for reassurance in your partner's loyalty.
Relying on stability between what your partner says and does is essential to
rebuilding trust. It takes much time and prayer to work through the process
of rebuilding trust because wounds can heal and you can recover. It requires
a willingness to believe that the future may not resemble the past, and it can
be even better. Do you have the courage to work through a betrayal?

Dear Lord, carry my pain and guide each step I take in rebuilding
my relationship with [name]. Even though I can't see the light at the
end of the tunnel right now, I know you are there, always at my side.
Help me, Lord. Amen.

August 18

They shall not hunger or thirst; nor shall scorching wind or sun strike them;
For he who pities them leads them and guides them beside springs of water.
I will turn all my mountains into roadway, and make my highways level.
See, these shall come from afar: some from the north and the west,
others from the land of Syene.

ISAIAH 49:10–12

E veryone anticipates vacations with great enthusiasm, despite knowing that they can be stressful when something goes awry. Maybe the flights were overbooked, your luggage was lost, or the weather was bad. Maybe you got a flat tire or became ill or got injured. People still take vacations knowing there could be a problem around every corner. When you got married, did you think your relationship would be stress-free, or did you know that there could be problems around every corner? Trying to be successful in your career while raising children and doing household chores is not easy. Ponder how you plan to prevent problems from occurring in your marriage. Sometimes the smallest things can derail a day.

Try incorporating a few stress-prevention techniques into your daily routine. Reconnect with your spouse every day, even if it's only ten minutes before you begin your day or before falling asleep at night. Share how much you appreciate each other. Say a prayer together to thank God for the many blessings he gave to you throughout the day. Make a "to do" list and prioritize each item. Try to delegate some of the tasks to your children or hire someone to help manage your load. Perhaps you need to hire someone to cut your grass or run errands. Look at a calendar and plan ahead to take a vacation. Maybe take a mini-vacation closer to home, or trade homes with a relative, giving you a free place to stay while you explore a new location. Consider taking a personal day with your spouse midweek to enjoy some quality time together. Even if you spend the afternoon in the back yard gardening together, it will be good for you to work beside each other in the fresh air and sunshine.

Start saying "no" to things you don't have time for. Be true to yourself and your spouse. If there is something that sounds interesting, consider doing it with your spouse. Take turns scheduling a weekly date nights. Dates don't have to be extravagant, just quality time where you can reconnect with your partner and have fun together. How will you reduce stress in your life today?

Dear Lord, teach me to free my stress and anxieties. Remind me to relax and smile more and depend on you for my strength. I love you, Lord, and depend on you to keep me on track. Amen.

August 19

The king was shaken, and went up to the room over the city gate and wept.
He said as he wept, "My son Absalom! My son, my son Absalom!
If only I had died instead of you, Absalom, my son, my son!"
Joab was told, "The king is weeping and mourning for Absalom,"
and that day's victory was turned into mourning for the whole
army when they heard, "The king is grieving for his son."

2 Samuel 19:1–3

On breezy days, neighborhood children run in a nearby field flying motley-colored kites. While watching the wind lift them up, I thought about how God does that to us: keeps us afloat, raising high above our difficulties, tethered on a line connected to him. As you struggle through difficulties in your marriage, it's comforting to know that you have God with you to raise you up above them. What are you currently struggling with? Perhaps you have recently lost a parent, relative, or close friend. Are you grieving the death of a loved one, the end of a relationship, or the loss of a job or your health?

God can help you heal. Remember that he is holding onto you, the way a child holds onto a kite. Write yourself a note that says, "Trust in God," and put it in a place where you will see it throughout the day. Be extra kind to yourself and remember that grieving takes energy. Surround yourself with friends who are sympathetic and will listen to you and take care of you. God can heal you through the love of others. Give yourself time to grieve by getting in touch with your feelings. Give yourself permission to cry. Jesus cried; he understands the need to cry. Ask God to turn your grief into gratitude. Read Holy Scripture and find comfort in the words written on the pages. Through the power of the Holy Spirit, God will heal your grief, and use it for good by having a new meaning for your pain.

Contemplate the activities you once enjoyed doing and then actually do one of them even if you don't feel like it. There is something therapeutic in doing something that once brought you pleasure. If you used to do yoga, wear comfortable attire and work your way through it, permitting yourself to be slow or clumsy. Give yourself credit for trying. Eventually your joy will return. Talk to yourself with positive language. Say something like "Jesus loves me, I can do this." While you work through your activity, you can pray or continue talking to God, asking for help to keep you strong. Remember that the pain will not last forever. Each day will be better than the last. Everyone grieves differently; there is no right or wrong way to grieve.

Dear Lord, carry me through this pain and wipe away my tears with your loving caress. Build me up and forge on to do your work, whatever it is. I trust you, Lord. Amen.

August 20

For this very reason, make every effort to supplement your faith with virtue,
virtue with knowledge, knowledge with self-control,
self-control with endurance, endurance with devotion,
devotion with mutual affection, mutual affection with love.

2 PETER 1:5–7

Fireflies dot the evening sky with random spurts of light emitted from their miniscule abdomens. They are winged beetles that chemically produce either a yellow, green, or pale red light from their bodies in an attempt to mate or attract prey. Think back to when you were a child; did you ever try to catch fireflies? Consider that random spark of light visible in the darkness of the summer evening sky. Is there a tiny spark of love in an otherwise darkness of your marriage? Consider what caused that flash and how can you feed it to grow into something bigger and better in your relationship?

Call your spouse or send a text just to say hello. You can spark your marriage by recapturing the same feelings you had when you first dated by doing little gestures of kindness throughout the day. Enrich your marriage with tiny surprises, like the flash of the firefly. Say "I love you" more frequently. Even though your spouse knows, hearing those three simple words can mean so much. Tell your spouse how handsome or beautiful he or she is. Try complimenting his or her smile or their new haircut. While you're at it, say "Thank you" for all of the little things they do throughout each day. What could it hurt to say "Thank you for working today?" Thank your spouse for making dinner, cleaning the house, doing the laundry, cutting the grass, doing the grocery shopping, or whatever chore they do. It's nice to be noticed and thanked for the tiniest of things.

Perform little acts of kindness: pack a lunch for work, leave notes on his or her laptop, empty the dishwasher without being asked, walk the dog or clean up after a pet, give a back rub. Surprise your spouse with a nice meal or a small gift. Find something that you think your spouse will enjoy and buy it. If he or she likes flowers, buy them every now and then. If there's a particular magazine or ice cream he or she likes, get it the next time you're at the grocery store. How will you put a tiny spark of love in your marriage today?

Dear Lord, show me how to be more thoughtful in words and actions. I want to be a kind and thoughtful spouse. Tell me what to say and do. I trust in your ways. Amen.

August 21

"When the crop grew and bore fruit, the weeds appeared as well.
The slaves of the householder came to him and said, 'Master, did you
not sow good seed in your field? Where have the weeds come from?'
He answered, 'An enemy has done this.' His slaves said to him,
'Do you want us to go and pull them up?' He replied, 'No, if you
pull up the weeds you might uproot the wheat along with them.'"
MATTHEW 13:24–29

Everyone has their own methods of keeping weeds out of their gardens. I put a layer of cardboard, then leaves, with mulch on top. Neighbors use black plastic and mulch, which works too. Some people dig weeds out by the roots, while others use chemicals to keep their flower beds pristine. There are many effective ways to keep weeds out. The commonality among gardeners is that no one wants weeds in their gardens. In families, no one wants problems in their marriages. The best solution to keeping arguments out of your relationship is using effective communication. Even with the best dialog and listening skills, one key issue that is prevalent in many relationships is money woes. Ponder if you have money disputes with your spouse.

Do you and your partner agree on how much to save or spend? Do you make the financial decisions or is that done jointly? What is your method to managing money? If your method isn't fruitful, it's not too late to make a budget. If you have tried in the past and failed, consult with a financial planner. Decide on a certain amount to save, an amount earmarked for bills, and an amount for both of you to use without accountability. Whether its $10 or $100 per week, you can spend this amount on whatever you want. In tough economic times, financial stress causes more stress and conflict than things unrelated to money.

Sometimes, couples argue about finances when it's actually the result of relationship neglect and money becomes a weapon. Have you ever used your spouse's spending habits as ammunition when it would hurt the most? Has your spouse spent money to get even regardless of your agreed upon rules? Sometimes, resentments get played out with money. Consider if you have made a reckless purchase to seek revenge on your spouse. Perhaps you could seek help resolving your relationship issues and as a result, fix your financial difficulties too. Make communication a priority about your spending while acting responsibly and making decisions together.

Dear Lord, teach me to be smart about money, to use it wisely and be thankful for all that I have. Teach me to be more appreciative of the things money cannot buy: love, kindness, truth, and respect. Thank you, sweet Lord, for all you give to me each day. Amen.

August 22

Enjoy life with the wife you love, all the days of the vain life granted
you under the sun. This is your lot in life, for the toil of your
labors under the sun. Anything you can turn your hand to,
do with what power you have; for there will be no work, no planning,
no knowledge, no wisdom in Sheol where you are going.

ECCLESIASTES 9:9–10

The energy an object has, due to its motion, is called kinetic energy. Where do you get your energy from? Some people find that working consistently with their life mission will alter the way their energy works: you can work much longer and harder and feel energized rather than depleted. Are you in sync with what you are doing? Eating certain foods, not getting enough exercise or sleep, or consuming too much coffee or sugar will alter your physical energy.

People, actions, and thoughts that are charged with emotion make a stronger impact. Feelings and emotions bring your thoughts to life, making them yield some effect in the world, similar to the way electricity enables appliances to work. Both electricity and thoughts need some sort of energy to make them work and produce results. Consider what thoughts you had today that you did nothing with, and compare them to the thoughts that you put into action.

Change in your life—whether it is grief, mental or physical illness, or relationship distress—can take a tremendous toll on emotional energy. When you're energized, you're able to do more, be more, and give more. Ponder how you can get energized. Dehydration can cause fatigue, so consider drinking more water each day. Also, incorporate physical exercise every day because it boosts your mood by releasing endorphins, lessoning your stress. Try to eat healthy foods at regular times. Consume protein, such as almonds or Greek yogurt, to deflect fatigue because it provides more long-term satiety.

If you find yourself yawning excessively, it probably means your body craves oxygen. Sit up straight and take a few deep breaths, holding it in a few seconds before exhaling. After a few minutes of doing this, you should feel revitalized. If not, take a break by leaving your work area. If possible, go for a short walk outside; look at the vegetation, breath in the fresh air, enjoy being bathed in sunlight. If you are not responding to any of these tips, your body might be craving rest. A twenty-minute catnap might be enough to invigorate you. Close your eyes and envision Jesus smiling at you lovingly. Focus on his face, his peacefulness, and ask him to fill you with tranquility.

Dear Lord, bless my rest and fill me with the energy I need to complete my tasks today. Amen.

August 23

Take the finest spices: five hundred shekels of free-flowing myrrh;
half that amount, that is, two hundred and fifty shekels, of fragrant
cinnamon;…five hundred shekels of cassia—all according to the standard
of the sanctuary shekel; together with a hin of olive oil; and blend them
into sacred anointing oil, perfumed ointment expertly prepared.

Exodus 30:23–25

What do you think when you smell freshly cut grass, gingerbread in the oven, or popcorn at the movie theaters? Researchers have discovered that certain scents can reduce stress-induced muscle tension. Studies reveal that fragrance is powerful enough to reduce stress. Aromatherapy items are booming in the marketplace with research endorsing stress-relief claims in the products. What stress reliever do you use in your marriage?

Research demonstrates that touch reduces stress. Take some time throughout the day to touch, whether it's to hold hands, casually caress one another, embrace each other, or kiss. Touching your spouse releases levels of oxytocin, a naturally produced calming chemical that lowers blood pressure. Touching your partner lovingly throughout the day is a powerful communicator of love and can lead to increased sex.

God covered your body with tactile receptors so that each time you are touched lovingly by your spouse, it registers in your brain as a pleasurable experience. Your fingertips are extremely sensitive, as are the tips of your nose and tongue. Consider how you can touch these areas to give maximum pleasure to your partner. You could give your mate a massage, a more sensual way of reducing stress. Consider a foot, shoulder, temple, or back massage to help loosen up tight muscles. Try making the massages erogenous by using scented oils and fragrant candlelight. Serving your spouse through a massage will help you reconnect and lower stress levels.

Heat is another great stress reliever because it loosens tight muscles. A nice warm bath with candles and soft music might melt tensions from the day. Try stepping in the shower with your spouse to wash his or her back. Bathing together is a sensual way to touch while giving attention to your partner. Sometimes, just listening to your spouse talk about the stress of his or her day is enough because he or she knows that you truly care. What would your partner like from you the most to erase the stress from his or her day?

Dear Lord, let me be Christ-like to [*name*] when he or she is stressed from a long day at work. Fill me with patience to listen and be a sounding board. Give me the mindset to caress his or her anxieties and tension away. Let me be the one he or she clings to and give me the strength to endure. Amen.

August 24

Settle with your opponent quickly while on the way to court with him.
Otherwise your opponent will hand you over to the judge, and the judge
will hand you over to the guard, and you will be thrown into prison.

MATTHEW 5:25

When people buy a home, they make a list of their "must haves." They must have so many bedrooms and bathrooms, some want garages, others want a finished basement. Real estate agents stress the importance of location. There are so many factors to consider when buying a house. There were many factors to consider when you chose your mate: were there religious differences, interracial differences, cultural differences, or age differences? Maybe you had subtle differences that were easy to manage or put in perspective. Learning how to manage differences respectfully can make your marriage stronger.

Marital differences are not inadequacies. If you and your spouse are different nationalities, blending the two traditions and cultures gives you a richer, fuller, and better-rounded union. Whenever you spot a difference, first think how you can embrace it and make it a part of your marriage. Another option is to choose not to point out a difference. Choosing to love your partner may prevent things from ever becoming issues.

Remember that differences can add richness and depth to your marriage if you choose to embrace them. The first thing you could do is identify your differences using the Myers-Briggs Type Indicator Test. It identifies how you approach the world using introversion or extraversion. Extroverts draw their energy from being with people; with introverts, people wear them out. When couples love one another, they help their spouse get what they need. Consider if you would prefer to stay home and read, but your spouse needs to connect with others to remain emotionally healthy. Similarly, your spouse can't socialize every night or you will burn out. Because of love, your spouse chooses to stay home so you can recharge.

The Myers-Briggs test also explains how you gather information using either intuition or sensing. It categorizes how you make decisions using feelings or thinking and it pinpoints how you approach structure using judging or perceiving. Don't resent your differences, instead, celebrate them. Together, you have more tools to help you through life. You weren't attracted to your spouse by accident. God brought you both together because he knew precisely what you needed to realize your full potential. Do your differences provide a broader spectrum to approach your spouse, family, or friends?

Dear Lord, thank you for making [*name*] and I so different because we balance each other out. Thank you for giving us so many tools to work with. I have been richly blessed and I thank you for it all. Amen.

August 25

But I will call this to mind; therefore I will hope: The LORD's acts
of mercy are not exhausted, his compassion is not spent;
They are renewed each morning— great is your faithfulness!
LAMENTATIONS 3:21–23

You can't always tell a book by its cover. The picture on the jacket might be alluring, the title might be intriguing, but it isn't until you begin reading that you can truly tell whether or not it is good. It's easy to form expectations based on little information or slight observations, not only with books, but people too. Consider if you have unrealistic expectations of your spouse.

Have you formed assumptions about the way you think things "should be" in your relationship based on your childhood experiences: the way your parents interacted, the books you read, or the movies you watched? Perhaps your expectations are unconscious. Does your spouse know your expectations? If you have unrealistic expectations that your partner does not know about, he or she can't possibly fulfill them. Your spouse is not a mind reader. Therefore, they will be unsettled and unmet.

Unsatisfied expectations feel like rejection; your reaction may begin at disappointment which then might turn to hurt. After you feel hurt, anger settles in, which could lead to an argument. Once you are angry, that fury is unleashed on your spouse in the form of punishment. Without realizing it, you make your spouse pay for not meeting your expectations. These phases transpire on an unconsciousness level. It is impossible to change something that you are oblivious to.

Ask yourself if you have a right to your expectations. If your rights are being violated, then, yes, you do have a right to them. You have a right to worship God. You have a right to vote for whatever candidate you deem best to run the country. You have a right to your safety and privacy. However, if you just want your own way, then you do not have a right to those. You do not have a right to tell your spouse where he or she will work. You do not have a right to tell your mate what chores he or she will do at home. Those things need to discussed and mutually decided upon or negotiated. Sometimes, expectations can feel like demands to our partner; turn them into hopes. Help one another to grow in your marriage through prayer and service. Have you had expectations coming into marriage that your spouse exceeded?

Dear Lord, help me to mature and release any unrealistic expectations I had of [name]. Enable me to bend without breaking and try to meet some of [name]'s expectations that are within my realm. Help us, Lord, to do your will today and every day. Amen.

August 26

*Then God said: Let the earth bring forth vegetation: every kind of plant
that bears seed and every kind of fruit tree on earth that bears fruit with
its seed in it. And so it happened: the earth brought forth vegetation:
every kind of plant that bears seed and every kind of fruit tree
that bears fruit with its seed in it. God saw that it was good.*

GENESIS 1:11–12

Have you ever walked through the produce aisle in a market and wondered how to pick good vegetables or fruit? A watermelon might look perfectly fine on the outside, but disappointing after slicing it open to find it wasn't ripe. What can you do with an unripe watermelon that tastes bad, especially when you had your heart set on it? How do you deal with disappointments in your marriage?

Hidden in your disappointments are life lessons, which can be seen as opportunities to make greater strides in your journey of faith. Embrace disappointment knowing it possesses a strategy necessary for reclaiming something you have lost. Trust that God has a wonderful plan for your life; you might view the value of carrying those afflictions differently. Every test that you endure is measured with the grace to bear it and power to be blessed by it. Give your troubles, disappointments, and disparity to God, because he will do something wonderful with it. Life can be difficult and disappointments can weigh you down, but know that it won't last forever. At the right time, God will guide you through it and give you the strength to endure and see it through to completion. Just hold on to Jesus, maintain your faith, and believe in him who provides everything you need.

Your circumstances don't define you. Your job doesn't define you. Your spouse doesn't define you. God defines you. Don't become disillusioned by life's trials and tribulations. Don't let them keep you from fulfilling God's purpose for you here on earth. You may not understand it completely, but God has an amazing plan for you to be fruitful, joyful, and experience God's true love. When you don't know what to do in your disparity turn to the Lord, ask him to shine a renewed light on a fresh perspective. Spend time with God, praying, meditating, and reading Holy Scripture. How do you fuel your faith during difficult times?

Try to be good to yourself while considering your vulnerabilities throughout any disappointments your encounter in life. God walks with you.

Dear Lord, thank you for granting me a wonderful life. Thank you for reminding me that nestled inside each disappointment is a gift waiting for me to discover it. Thank you for giving me hopefulness to hang on during my difficult moments. I love you, Lord. Amen.

August 27

Notice how the flowers grow. They do not toil or spin. But I tell you,
not even Solomon in all his splendor was dressed like one of them.
If God so clothes the grass in the field that grows today and is thrown into the
oven tomorrow, will he not much more provide for you, O you of little faith?

LUKE 12:27–28

Ubiquitous tulip bulbs, the size of a golf ball, look unassuming. They are planted in the autumn and take root straightaway. Then they root slowly throughout the winter months where the cold temperatures stimulate them to sprout in early spring. As climate temperatures increase, the tulips start to grow and eventually bloom into a beautiful flower. It's astounding that by burying an ordinary bulb in the ground and expecting it to grow during the frigid winter months, under piles of ice and snow can actually grow into a beautiful flower. But that's exactly what happens. You have no control over it after it's in the ground. It is surrendered into God's care for growing and maturing into a flower.

Sometimes, it is overwhelming knowing how many things can be wrong in your marriage, but like the Bible passage, Jesus reminds you to do your best and leave the rest in God's hands, the same way the flowers grow. You can plant a tulip bulb in the ground and let all kinds of weather beat down on it, but God will take care of it. God reminds you that he takes care of the flowers and he will take care of you—just have faith in him. Consider what "bad weather" has been beating down on your relationship. Sometimes, when you find yourself in a bad way, stop what you are doing and pray. If whatever you are doing isn't working, think what Jesus would want you to do and then do that. Jesus wants you to be loving, forgiving, kind, and generous.

Married life is like a chain of problem-solving possibilities. The way you respond to problems will either lift you up or break you down. God wants you to use your problems to create something better. Like the bulb in the ground during the winter; some people might think the harsh weather will kill the plant. In reality, the bulb craves that period to develop and grow. Many people fail to appreciate how God wants you to use your problems for good, and they miss out. Instead of resenting a particular problem that you might be dealing with, consider for a moment what benefits it might actually bring to your life.

Dear Lord, thank you for good and the bad that you give to me. I don't always know the purpose for it, but I trust in your miraculous ways. Each time I see a tulip bulb, I will remember that there is a purpose for the problems in my life, and I will thank you for them. I truly love you. Amen.

August 28

Then the heads of the families, the tribal commanders of Israel,
the commanders of thousands and of hundreds, and those who had
command of the king's affairs came forward willingly and contributed
for the service of the house of God five thousand talents and ten thousand
darics of gold, ten thousand talents of silver, eighteen thousand
talents of bronze, and one hundred thousand talents of iron.

1 CHRONICLES 29:6–7

The Micronesian island, Yap, located in the Pacific Ocean, is notable for stone money. Its doughnut-shaped disks range from twelve feet in diameter to 1.4 inches. The value is based on the size and its history to obtain them. What are notable characteristics of your marriage that you value? Perhaps it is the mutual respect you have for each other. How can you use that element to enhance weak features that need improvement?

If your marriage is satisfying, your relationship is probably built on positivity, empathy, commitment, acceptance, love, and respect. If your marriage has too much criticizing, demanding, name-calling, and holding grudges, your relationship is bound to suffer. Ponder the ways you foster positivity in your marriage. Consider how affectionate you are with your spouse and whether you could do more. Reflect on how well you listen to your partner. Do you express joy in your partner's achievements? Contemplate the level of enjoyment you feel when you spend time with your spouse.

In order for your marriage to be successful, you both must be committed to the relationship. If you both are dedicated to making your relationship work, it will. You might have to make sacrifices or compromises for the sake of your marriage. Consider who is making the most sacrifices in your marriage. For a relationship to be healthy, it shouldn't be one-sided, because marriage is a series of give and take with you both being on the same team.

Reflect on the level of acceptance you have for your spouse. If you accept and respect him or her for who they are, without trying to change them, your marriage will be more secure. One component that must be present in your marriage is love. Love brought you together and will keep you together over the years, through good times and bad. Therefore, it is wise to have a reservoir of love in your marriage to draw from during periods of difficulty that come from the complexities of life. No matter how complicated your issues might be right now, don't neglect each other or the romance that drew you together. What aspect of your marriage is the most valuable to you?

Dear Lord, thank you for reaffirming the noteworthy components and making you our precious focal point. You are larger than life, and are invaluable to our success. Amen.

August 29

If you find honey, eat only what you need,
lest you have your fill and vomit it up.

PROVERBS 25:16

Honey is the only food made by an insect that is consumed by humans and includes all the substances necessary to sustain life, including enzymes, vitamins, minerals, and water; and it's the only food that contains pinocembrin, an antioxidant associated with improved brain functioning. Honey has some medical value for healing wounds and burns and is also used as a cough suppressant. Has it occurred to you that your marriage possesses all of the essential components for it to be successful? You need to realize this, identify, and use them. God gave you all of the skills and tools: a brain to rationalize, plan, and fulfill your desires and dreams, and a heart to love totally and completely. It's more meaningful to call your spouse "honey" knowing how valuable it really is. Do you appreciate how precious your mate is? Ponder ways to acknowledge your partner's sweetness.

You could give a jar of honey to your spouse explaining how valuable he or she is. Maybe you could make a dessert with honey and explain the importance of it to him or her. Perhaps you could sing a song that uses the word "honey" in it to your spouse or write a poem. You can determine how playful you want to be. The important thing is to convey to your partner how cherished he or she is to you.

You are the only one who can make your mate the highest possible priority on earth. God is your number one priority in heaven and your first priority is to get to heaven and help your spouse to get there too. However, on earth, your responsibility in marriage is to ensure your spouse is at the top of the list, before children, parents, and friends. Ponder if your mate is at the center of your world.

For romance to thrive in your marriage, your spouse must feel safe from physical, financial, social, emotional, and spiritual harm inside your marriage. How do you cherish your spouse, caring and helping him or her to feel safe in your love?

Dear Lord, thank you for providing the crucial elements necessary to build a better marriage. Thank you for the chance to correct the wrongs and make them right. Thank you for knowledge you pour over me and allowing me to put everything into action. Amen.

August 30

Nicodemus said to him, "How can a person once grown old be born again?
Surely he cannot reenter his mother's womb and be born again, can he?"
JOHN 3:4

When the Monarch butterflies flutter through the summer flower gardens, their beauty and gracefulness is admired by many. While admiring them, who remembers they originated as an ugly wormlike creature? While you might have dreadful aspects of your marriage, it is worth noting that they can be transformed into something quite marvelous. Perhaps your marriage lacks good communication; those skills can be acquired, learned, and developed over time.

First, try to improve your listening skills, remembering that your goal is to understand. While it might be tempting to tune out your spouse, or prove a point to settle a dispute, your only goal should be to understand your spouse. When you listen to your partner, it makes him or her feel important and loved. In order to accomplish this, turn off all defense mechanisms. Don't blame, criticize, or stonewall. Don't interrupt, interject a rebuttal, or rationalize. It is not your responsibility to try to fix or judge. Your job is to hear your partner out because listening strengthens your relationship.

Find a quiet and comfortable place to talk. Turn the TV off, walk away from the computer, and sit facing each other. Hold your spouse's hand to reassure him or her that you care about what is on his or her mind. Pay close attention to the verbal and nonverbal language. When your partner pauses, name the emotion you believe he or she feels. For example, "You seem really frustrated." Then repeat back by paraphrasing what you believe you heard your spouse say. For instance, "Are you saying that…" If your spouse says it was not accurate, ask for a clarification of the message that was incorrect. Remember, the goal is understanding, not agreement with the message.

You could ask your spouse if he or she wants any feedback or your opinion. Your partner might want to use you as a sounding board and not want any advice, so ask before you speak. If your input is requested, begin with a positive remark and never attack. Use "I statements" to express your feelings in an amicable manner without any exaggerations. Resolve to be respectful while being direct with your spouse and stay focused on the subject matter. Take turns speaking and listening with love and mutual respect. Try to improve those skills to strengthen your marriage. God will bless you while you speak and listen to each other.

> Dear Lord, thank you for the reminders that I can enhance the soft
> spots and troubled areas in my marriage. Bring the perfect people
> who can help us into our lives. Amen.

August 31

Likewise, you husbands should live with your wives in understanding,
showing honor to the weaker female sex, since we are joint heirs
of the gift of life, so that your prayers may not be hindered.

1 PETER 3:7

Why is the chestnut surrounded by a spiny, prickly outer covering? The annoying burrs are so painful to touch that harvesting them must be difficult. Some might reconsider their worth until they taste the delicious nut, which is even better when it's cooked. In this case, it's best not to judge the nut by the external appearance. Have you considered why God made the covering of that nut so hard to get to? What else has God made difficult for you to get to?

Consider if you wear a façade. What is the outer appearance of your marriage like; does it have prickly burrs? Ponder if it is a true reflection of your relationship. What can you do in God's grace to focus on what's important in your marriage?

Perhaps you and your spouse are considering expanding your family to include children. Do you both want them, or are they not coming to you as easily as you hoped? Whether you are struggling with infertility or over fruitfulness, the decision to add children to your relationship can be stressful. The momentous decision cannot be made lightly. Many couples feel ambivalence when trying to decide whether or not to have a child. Trust in God's plan for you. Only God knows whether or not you will have children, and whether they will come to you biologically or through adoption. God is in control. While it is good to make plans, don't fret over them. Relax in God's loving embrace.

Look for the positive aspects of your relationship right now regardless of whether or not you have children or are in the process of adopting them. What kind of parent do you think you will make? Do you need this time to prepare for parenthood? Dwell on the miracle of life that God offers you. Celebrate it as you pray and reflect on Mary's role as a parent. She was so young and inexperienced and yet she bore and raised Jesus Christ.

Dear Lord, Peel away the outer layer of roughness that masks the true inner beauty of my marriage. Help me concentrate on making the core of our journey through life together the most meaningful and purposeful and thriving the way you created us to live. If you bless me with a child, I accept. If you have other plans for me, I accept that too. I trust you, Lord. Amen.

September 1

May the God of hope fill you with all joy and peace in believing,
so that you may abound in hope by the power of the holy Spirit.
I myself am convinced about you, my brothers, that you yourselves are full
of goodness, filled with all knowledge, and able to admonish one another.

ROMANS 15:13–14

A school bus is specifically designed to transport students to and from school and school events. The first school bus was horse-drawn. When you drive and spot a bright orange-colored school bus on the road, you know exactly what it means: students are either coming or going to school. There are other buses on the road, but you have no idea who is in them or where they are going. When kids hop on a school bus, they know exactly where they are going. Do you know where your marriage is going? Marriage is an ongoing progression of learning about your spouse and how to best accommodate and tolerate your differences so that you can feel satisfied and develop mature love for each other. When you experience mature love, you are able to achieve a more meaningful connection with your spouse. Strive to cultivate mature love realizing that it requires hard work but is worth the effort.

Mature love necessitates treating your spouse lovingly, even if you don't feel like it. The reward maintains a deeper emotional connection through intimacy with your partner. It also maintains better likelihood of an endearing friendship and a life-long relationship. Mature love consists of a combination of intimacy, passion, and commitment.

The intimacy you experience matures over time, enabling you to converse openly about your hopes, dreams, and fears. Maturity provides healthier problem-solving skills enabling you to make logical decisions together, leaving emotions out of it. Mature love sanctions passion with romance with profound commitment. Mature love couples are inspired to remain faithful and loyal to each other. Ponder if you treat your spouse reverentially, talk positively about him or her, and support your spouse's endeavors. Can you achieve this level of commitment by focusing on what's best for your marriage?

Dear Lord, thank you for the happiness, peace, and joy that you have provided in my marriage. Thank you for the security, and erasing any anxiety and fear that I once felt. Help me to continue to grow, develop, and change into a better, holier version of myself. Thank you for believing in me and entrusting [*name*] into my care. Amen.

September 2

You shall not exploit a poor and needy hired servant, whether one of your own
kindred or one of the resident aliens who live in your land, within your gates.
On each day you shall pay the servant's wages before sun goes down,
since the servant is poor and is counting on them. Otherwise the servant
will cry to the LORD against you, and you will be held guilty.

DEUTERONOMY 24:14–15

Labor Day is an American holiday that celebrates the economic and social contributions of workers. It is a symbolic end to summer, marking the return to school for many students, and retailers have expansive sales. Ponder what Labor Day means to you and how you plan to celebrate it. Maybe you have been unemployed or unhappy with your current job situation. Perhaps you have been passed over for a promotion or changed positions altogether. Whatever your line of work is, find the silver lining in it. Perhaps you can be thankful for the financial security that it has provided to your marriage.

Have an open and frank discussion regarding your financial situation. Just because you have a trusting nature, don't rely totally on your spouse to make all of the financial plans without your input. Be involved in creating a family budget, deciding on an amount that can be spent without spousal permission. You might want to hire a financial planner to help you create a budget and teach you how to invest your savings for your future retirement, your vacations, or your children's college educations.

With the nation's struggling economy, many couples discussed preexisting debt, but not a plan to repay it. Finances can be difficult topic to discuss. Consider if you have hidden expectations, assumptions, and resentments about finances. Reflect on how much money your spouse must earn before you worry about his or her paycheck and whether or not the bills will be paid. Have you set guidelines and boundaries for your financial decisions?

Marriages have some degree of fragility to them. Financial harmony is critical for freedom, power, respect, security, and happiness. Do you realize the importance that money has in your relationship? How can you learn to define guidelines for money management in your marriage?

Dear Lord, help me to master the skills of financial harmony in my marriage for I know in the long run, it will also strengthen my marriage bonds. Help me to understand the value that [*name*] places on money. Keep me employed, dear Lord. And if it is your will for me to experience unemployment, give me the strength to endure and move on to the next stage of life that you want me to experience. Thy will be done. Amen.

September 3

Make seven, or even eight portions;
you know not what misfortune may come upon the earth.

ECCLESIASTES 11:2

Many people prepare for the winter by canning fruits and vegetables. Some people store jars of jam or pickles, while others stock up freezers with containers of soups, blueberries, strawberries, corn, peppers, and zucchini. It's hard work to make extra portions of food for later, but worth the effort during a harsh winter. Likewise, you can build up a marriage reservoir of good intentions, kind gestures, quality times spent together, laughs, warm touches, compassionate words, prayerfulness, and smiles. During difficulties, it's nice to be able to draw from this enormous emotional tank of goodness. Put forth the effort to constantly build up your marriage reservoir because it's like a cushion that cradles you when you fall. Instead of being snarky, just stop and be caring like Jesus. Each time you act like Christ, your tank doubles in size.

Contemplate good gestures you could do to build up your emotional tank. When is the last time you told your spouse "I love you?" Those three simple words, spoken longingly, give sustenance to your relationship. Say them often. Think of other compliments your spouse might like to hear. Does your spouse have a nice smile? When is the last time you told him or her? Do you encourage your spouse to try new approaches to attempt a new sport, learn a new language, or musical instrument? Perhaps you could try talking in a loving manner to your spouse using positive body language and touch. Caress your partner's arm the next time you have a conversation. Kind words and touch don't cost anything but mean the world to your mate when done out of love.

Instead of having extravagant date nights, try spending quality time together in a way that costs very little. Take a long walk wearing a pedometer to measure the miles you cover. See how long it takes you to cover the seventy-five mile trek that Mary and Joseph walked to reach Bethlehem. Take a nature walk through a park or sit on a park bench and have a conversation with God. Volunteer to serve sandwiches to the homeless in your community. Granted, these are not typical "dates," however, when God calls you to see beyond the parameters of your home, are you willing to say, "Yes, Lord, I will?"

Dear Lord, keep me from making myriad withdrawals from my marriage reservoir. Pick me up, Lord. I'm as deflated as my marriage and I don't know where to turn. I look to you for answers. Fill my mind, my heart, my soul with the love I desperately need. Amen.

September 4

Wives should be subordinate to their husbands as to the Lord.
For the husband is head of his wife just as Christ is head of the church,
he himself the savior of the body. As the church is subordinate to Christ,
so wives should be subordinate to their husbands in everything.

EPHESIANS 5:22–24

Grocery store shelves are chock full of nearly identical products that are packaged differently, making it complicated for shoppers to decide between them. The generic products look the same, but cost much less in a plain label. Is it worth it to buy "no name" products in an attempt to shave money off the weekly grocery bill? When people look at your "marriage label," what do they see?

Consider if you expect your spouse to pick you up when you're down. Are you truly one with your partner? Occasionally, do you purposely dress in the same colors or styles of clothes when going out together? Is your spouse responsible for his or her own growth and development? Do you and your spouse have different friends doing activities that don't include the other? Contemplate if your spouse is your only source of love and comfort. There are many different types of relationships in the marriage spectrum that work. Perhaps you need to do what works best for the both of you.

Examine your marital foundation. Consider if you and your mate are really good friends, taking vacations together as well as apart. If your partner becomes ill, can he or she count on you to be there? Ponder if you strive to meet your partner's needs before having your own met. Society mandates that couples find a quick fix to their marriage woes by immediately taking medication or getting counseling. Before seeking an easy solution, turn over any difficulties to God. Put God in the center of your marriage by reading holy Scripture, reflecting over the passages, and putting them into use in your daily lives together. Set aside time to pray as a couple, making a spiritual connection before a couple connection.

Your primary goal is to help your spouse get to heaven. Instead of fretting over dressing alike, consider if your actions are good, moral, and just. Allow God to direct your marriage. What area of your relationship is giving you the most difficulty and can you draw on God's love to see you through it?

Dear Lord, sometimes my marriage feels so bland that I honestly don't know if we are on the right track. Help me, Lord, to stay focused on you and to have a healthy and holy marriage. Amen.

September 5

For as a young man marries a virgin, your Builder shall marry you;
And as a bridegroom rejoices in his bride so shall your God rejoice in you.

ISAIAH 62:5

A windshield wiper is a long rubber blade attached to a mechanical arm that is used to remove rain or snow from a car's windshield. Almost all vehicles, including trains, planes, and boats, use them. Consider what the best tool is that you can use in your marriage. In order to get what you want from your marriage, you need to first become the best spouse that you can possibly be. If you focus on what you want to take from your marriage, your partner might react negatively to focusing on him or her. Your spouse is more likely to react to kind and loving behavior full of compassion and support. Behave like the partner you most want to be. Do not try to change your spouse. The only person you can change is yourself. Think back to when you first decided to marry your partner. Did you love him or her exactly as they were?

When it's pouring outside, it's difficult to see through the raindrops. Windshield wipers make it easier to see where you are going. Ponder where your marriage is going. Is it heading in any particular direction or just rambling along with your cruise control set always driving through one rain storm after another? If you are uncertain about where you and your spouse are headed in your relationship, the most powerful tool that you can use to help you to see your way through any storm is prayer. Use God as your windshield wiper! Call out to him for guidance; he will answer.

Invite your spouse to pray with you for guidance. Begin by holding hands and talking to the Lord as if he was standing beside you. Say whatever is in your heart, leaving room for your spouse to interject his or her thoughts, feelings, and emotions. Remember that the Holy Spirit is in you, and take a few moments to reflect on his almighty power within to guide you throughout the day. Trust that God brought you together for a reason. Ask God for enlightenment on what that reason is. Ask him to guide you both toward it to fulfill God's work. When your prayer is complete, seal it with a kiss, and plan to reconnect each day in prayer. God will eventually reveal his plan to you.

Dear Lord, come to us in our stormy relationship and shield us from the torment we are enduring. Shine your light on us and allow us to see the direction you have chosen for us. Teach us to trust in your implicitly. I love you, Lord. Amen.

September 6

Above all, let your love for one another be intense, because
love covers a multitude of sins. Be hospitable to one another
without complaining. As each one has received a gift, use it to
serve one another as good stewards of God's varied grace.

1 PETER 4:8–10

When I was a student, my teacher used chalk on a blackboard. At the end of the lesson, she wiped the blackboard clean with a felt eraser, leaving a faint trail of her handwriting behind. At the end of the day, the teacher washed the board with a wet sponge, which cleaned it entirely. After an argument with your spouse, do you feel a ghost of the quarrel lingers behind? Consider the way you handle disagreements. Sometimes couples overreact and say things they regret later. If you think this might happen, postpone your discussion until you have had time to consider everything, put it perspective, and pray about it. Think about potential solutions and don't dwell on your hurt. Don't allow your feelings to overtake you so that you can't see the bigger picture: your marriage. All relationships have issues to sort out, remember that your spouse and your marriage are worth revering.

Sometimes loving your spouse means letting him or her be right. When you decide to marry your partner, you agree to live with him or her for the rest of your life. You agreed to take your spouse for better or worse, in good times and bad. Therefore, you will have to forgive each other many times over the years, so you need to perfect your ability to forgive.

The first step to achieving forgiveness is to relinquish the desire to retaliate. Resume respectful and courteous treatment to each other. Remember that the most important thing is your spouse and your marriage. If your spouse hurt you, the best gift you can offer is forgiveness without self-righteousness. Grieve and let it go, the same way the teachers washes the slate board clean with a wet sponge. If you injured your spouse, apologize with a plan to show that it won't happen again and offer a kind gesture of appreciation for the forgiveness. You can ask for forgiveness, however, you cannot demand it. Wipe the slate clean, and start over. Forgiveness takes time and is the best gift one spouse can give to another.

You may need to ask God for help letting go of the hurt. God can heal and help you to forgive from your heart. Trust God to give you his strength and love.

Dear Lord, help me to be more forgiving in my marriage, and in my life. Empower me to live the life you have called me to. Thank you for being such a kind and merciful Lord. Amen.

September 7

*The husband should fulfill his duty toward his wife, and likewise the wife
toward her husband. A wife does not have authority over her own body,
but rather her husband, and similarly a husband does not have authority
over his own body, but rather his wife. Do not deprive each other, except perhaps
by mutual consent for a time, to be free for prayer, but then return to one
another, so that Satan may not tempt you through your lack of self-control.*

1 Corinthians 7:3–5

Stretching is good for your body by keeping your muscles warm and limber. If you have been sedentary, your muscles get tight; stretching can help you move about easily and ease pain and soreness after any physical activity. Stretching enables you to increase your range of motion. It reduces tension in your muscles and relaxes your body and your mind. When you feel tranquil, life is better overall. Stretching isn't the only physical activity that is good for your body.

Have you considered the emotional and physical benefits from engaging in sexual activities with your spouse? It boosts your self-esteem, improves posture, offers pain-relief, keeps spouses connected emotionally, and increases your level of commitment to each other. It also has a therapeutic effect on the immune system, fosters a positive attitude on life, makes couples less irritable, reduces depression, promotes calm, relieves stress, and helps people sleep better. That's not all! It lowers your cortisol level, the hormone that triggers fatigue and cravings. It reduces your risk of heart disease, gives you better bladder control, improves digestion, delivers healthier teeth, and increases circulation, enabling you to remember more, while producing chemicals in the brain to stimulate the growth of new dendrites. Having frequent sexual relations with your spouse reduces feelings of insecurity, makes your skin healthier, and builds your resistance against colds and flu. You can burn about 200 calories during thirty minutes of active sex.

God amazingly created the human body to reap so many benefits from marital conjugation. God created humans in his own image, with human sexuality a part of it, remembering that all he created is good. The way you express love to your spouse in a mutual self-giving, that sexual activity in which you are united with your partner is deeply personal and sacred between you both. The marriage bond, the forming of one heart and soul, is a sign of love between God and humanity.

Dear Lord, thank you for creating my body so beautifully in your
divine image. Thank you for designing this holy temple for the Holy
Spirit to dwell. Amen.

September 8

I belong to my lover, and my lover belongs to me;
he feeds among the lilies. Beautiful as Tirzah are you,
my friend; fair as Jerusalem, fearsome as celestial visions!

SONG OF SONGS 6:3–4

Swans form an exclusive bond that lasts for numerous years, sometimes for life. Their loyalty to their mate is legendary and the image of two swans with entwined necks forming a heart has become a universal symbol of true love. Humans believe they are faithful; however, nearly half of all marriages end in divorce, with marital infidelity as the primary cause. Being faithful can be difficult, but it's critical to be committed to your spouse.

You and your spouse vowed to be faithful to each other, have trust in one another. Consider the boundaries you have established and stay within the parameters to earn more trust. Your actions depict that you have a solid relationship, which will be a source of security when times get rough. If you never give your spouse a reason to doubt you because of your credible history, you won't have anything to worry about.

Cherish your responsibility to your spouse. You are accountable to him or her; remember your promises and commitments. Your spouse may request that you "check in," which could annoy you. If you are to be prosperous as a team, consent to sacrifices, remembering that it enables your spouse to trust you. It will keep you close, building fidelity and faith while honoring your commitment.

What if someone tries to seduce you? Explain that you are in a happy marriage with no intentions of hurting your spouse. Then, leave. The next time, take your spouse. If the problem persists, leave that situation or group. If it is work related, seek a transfer. If it's a group of friends, stop visiting the places where you run into this person.

If your spouse starts working late or frequently goes out with colleagues after work, restrict this habit. Ask your spouse to bring the work home or take you with him when socializing with teammates. Review your future plan with your spouse on a regular basis. Review your bucket list and make sure you are knocking items off together, doing fun and exciting things as a couple. Keep your married life thrilling with unexpected treats, outings, and surprises for each other. How will you maintain your commitment to your spouse?

Dear Lord, remove the temptations that beckon me to stray. Draw me back to you, dear Lord, and to [*name*]. I want to be an honorable, dependable, faithful spouse until I take my very last breath on earth. Amen.

September 9

*Remind people of these things and charge them before God
to stop disputing about words. This serves no useful purpose
since it harms those who listen.*

2 TIMOTHY 2:14

Chemists in Cornell University's viticulture program advise against chilling red wines because the cooler temperatures heighten the harsh flavor of the naturally forming tannic acid instead of the fruity grape. Are harsh or cruel words spoken in your marriage that leave a bad taste in your mouth? Perhaps you were overly critical or caused hurt feelings that led to arguments. Words can make or break a relationship depending on how they are spoken. If they are used warmly and with great love and good intentions, it can conjure much happiness. How can you prevent yourself from using ruthless words and rephrase them to deliver a caring message instead? It pleases God and your spouse when you put forth an effort to speak in a loving manner. Every new day you and your spouse must decide how you will talk to each other.

An essential component of a healthy marriage is mutual respect, which is evident through encouragement and support. Provide ongoing praise, even in the smallest of ways. Notice the small things your spouse does and compliment him or her. Maybe you have taken for granted how often your spouse drives. You could remain silent or say, "Thank you for driving so I could relax." It's such a simple thing, but it will set a positive tone for the rest of the day. You could take it one step farther by saying, "I feel safe and secure when you're behind the wheel. You are an excellent driver!" There are myriad ways to lift your spouse's self-esteem that will strengthen your marriage. You could go another step farther by offering to drive your spouse the next time, presenting your spouse an opportunity to relax.

Words are gifts you can offer your spouse. The best part about giving compliments as gifts is that eventually you will feel so richly blessed that you will begin to adorn your spouse with accolades as well. This will ultimately nurture a loving atmosphere between you both. Start out small, work your way up, and practice this often. God used words to communicate with us to encourage us how to live a blessed life. Can you do the same?

Dear Lord, fill my heart and mind with the perfect message and the means to deliver, it so that I foster a harmonious relationship with my spouse. Allow sweet words to roll off my tongue. I love you, Lord, for nurturing me. Amen.

September 10

Be sure of this: if the master of the house had known the hour when the thief was coming, he would not have let his house be broken into.

LUKE 12:39

As autumn approaches, squirrels scamper across the lawns, frantically collecting and burying nuts for the winter. Their desperation is palpable. Contemplate some things you can do preventively to prepare for your future with your spouse. Like the busy squirrel, could you fortify your relationship with abundant love, or do you have emotional wounds and disappointments that lead you to feel broken, without a clear path?

If your heart is filled with sorrow and your emotional state is related to the struggles in your marriage, have hope that God will hear your cries. God will be with you as you work to strengthen and rebuild your marriage. God is calling you to marital intimacy built on selflessness, trust, and respect. God wants you to spread grace as you love your spouse unconditionally the way God loves you. Invest in love in order to heal. Your well is not empty; you just need to lower the bucket deeper.

Deepen your faith together through daily prayer. Savor the good times in your marriage to draw upon them for strength during moments when you do have difficulties. Remember that things were not always troublesome. Turn to God during episodes of crises. He will never leave you and he will guide you through turbulent times. Let God light your path.

Contemplate if you are in a God-oriented marriage. If you are, establish boundaries to preserve quality time spent with your spouse. Search for reasons to come together rather than excuses to remain apart. Examine your list of activities that you need to do. With endless days of activities come infinite weeks of busyness. You might be disappointed when intimate encounters don't magically happen. Consider spending more time together as a way to marital intimacy. Perhaps you could splurge on artesian cheeses or fruits that you have never tried. Could you have a themed dinner once a month? Consider doing something different that would be interesting and enjoyable. Maybe you could start tonight with a harvest dinner and prayer of thanks for your heavenly bounty.

Dear Lord, be my beacon of guidance through this darkness in my life. Help me, Lord, to strengthen my friendship with you and with my spouse. Nourish me, Lord, with your steadfast love so that I have the endurance to forge onward in my marriage filled with respect, admiration, and thoughtfulness. Amen.

September 11

Therefore, we who are receiving the unshakable kingdom should have gratitude,
with which we should offer worship pleasing to God in reverence and awe.

HEBREWS 12:28

When two airplanes crashed into the twin towers in 2001, our world was shaken. The world we thought we knew had changed in an instant. Has something gone terribly wrong in your life changing you forever? Maybe you had no inclination or maybe there were signs of trouble, but you misread them. Whatever brought you to a disheveled state in your marriage, remember that the Lord is always with you. No matter how bad things may seem, God will not abandon you. With God, anything is possible, so include him in your plans.

After the September 11 tragedy, the world united to show respect, to provide aid and comfort, and to help with the recovery and grieving. If people can come together in the face of such a disaster, think of the possibilities that can transform your relationship. Bolster your faith, trust, and hope in the Lord, with constant prayer. Remember than when you cry, God is there to catch your tears. His arm is around you, guiding your step. You are not alone in your struggle. God is in the clouds, the sun, and the soft breeze that blows across your face. He is in the birds whose sweet songs fill your ears. He is in the squirrels that scamper beneath your feet delighting you. He is in the strong trees that you rest under. Your omnipresent Savior is just one heartbeat from you.

Persevere in your trust in Christ. With him, you can endure hardship and accept the discipline of the Lord. Strive for peace and holiness during this time, carefully avoid any bitterness and resentment. Give reverence to God overflowing with praise and respect because that will generate your behavior. Open the Bible and read until your mind cannot absorb another word. Allow prayer to help you develop reverence. Pray harder than you ever have before. God hears you and he will answer you. He might answer you straightaway by saying, "Yes, I will give you what you ask for right now." Or he could say, "Yes, I will give you what you ask for, but you must wait for it," or he might say, "No, that is not what I want for you." Either way, he will respond; you might not like his answer, but he will reply. Let go and let God. Can you do that today with whatever is troubling your heart?

Dear Lord, sweet ever-loving Lord, carry my troubles so that I don't have to. Take them into the palm of your hand and fix what is broken and tell me how to live now that everything has changed. Tell me what to do, dear Lord. Tell me how to act, what to say; bless each word that you put in my head. Amen.

September 12

I prayed: "LORD, God of heaven, great and awesome God, you who preserve your covenant of mercy toward those who love you and keep your commandments. May your ear be attentive, and your eyes open, to hear the prayer that I, your servant, now offer in your presence day and night for your servants the Israelites, confessing the sins we have committed against you, I and my ancestral house included.

NEHEMIAH 1:5–6

Dentists encourage patients to brush their teeth for the same time it would take to sing "Happy Birthday." Instead, say a Hail Mary. Think of all the quiet moments you spend waiting, whether you are standing in a grocery line, standing in the shower waiting for the water to warm up, on hold using the phone, waiting for popcorn to pop, or at a red traffic light. Use tiny moments for prayer. Offer up the prayers as gifts to God, or maybe you want to use those moments to pray for your spouse or your marriage. God is only a short breath away. You can murmur his sweet name, conjure Jesus's image in your mind, and simply dwell on his divine face. While it's good to establish a set time for prayer and spiritual reflection each day, it's also good to think of the Lord randomly throughout the day.

Praying with your spouse creates oneness and intimacy in your marriage. Prayer unites you both spiritually before God. It joins you in agreement with your partner as you present your petitions before the Lord. Both of your hearts are aligned toward a common goal requesting God's intervention. How glorious to be of one heart and one soul before the Lord!

Prayer requires a humble heart and willingness to bear your soul honestly before your mate and before God. Consider if you are willing to acknowledge your weakness to your spouse. Praying together squelches any pride or haughtiness. When you know your mate's heart and problems, it binds you as one. Prayer can deepen your communication, which is essential in marriage. Praying together with your spouse is the invitation to see the inside of his or her heart. When you pray you speak on an intimate level to God revealing things you might never say in casual conversation. Prayer allows you to see who your spouse truly is. Prayer establishes deeper companionship and closeness than ever before. The closer you get to God, the closer you will get to one another.

Dear Lord, Hear my prayers. Be the cement that holds our bricks of love together. Build up my marriage, Lord, as I send petitions to you, fill me with love, joy, peace, kindness, goodness, faithfulness, gentleness, and self-control. I ask this in your holy name. Amen.

September 13

In peace I will lie down and fall asleep,
for you alone, LORD, make me secure.

PSALM 4:8–9

If you or your spouse snore, chances are good you both wake up cranky. This common occurrence has an impact on marriage. Sleep centers conduct studies to evaluate how a husband's sleep apnea impacts the wife's quality of sleep. One sleep center noted that couples with sleep apnea have a high divorce rate. Can marriages be saved by treating sleep apnea? Getting a good night's rest is imperative. How well do you and your partner sleep? If you have sleep issues, it might be throwing your marriage off-kilter.

There are many things you can do to improve your sleep. Eating well-balanced meals throughout the day is a good start, and eliminate caffeine from your diet after lunch. Exercise around 4 PM even if it's only a brisk walk around the block or spend fifteen minutes doing jumping jacks in the living room. In the early evening, turn off the computer, dim the lights, and drop the temperature of your bedroom. Read the Bible and pray before you get into bed. If you have worries, write them down and plan to talk to God about them in the morning. When you close your eyes dwell on Jesus's face.

If your spouse is snoring, wear earplugs. If that doesn't work, sleep in another room; the moment you wake in the morning, rejoin your spouse to cuddle before beginning your day. The snoring spouse should consider seeking medical attention and an evaluation for sleep apnea. Don't ignore this problem and hope it will go away. This type of problem can only deteriorate. Sleep apnea is a potentially life-threatening condition. There are several medical causes that could be responsible for snoring and it's important to determine if there are any underlying causes.

Approach the topic as a mutual "couple" problem to solve together. Remind your spouse that you want to sleep together, but you also need to get a good night's sleep. Offer to help find a doctor and go to the appointment together. There are options for you both to consider. The key is to work through the process lovingly, not angrily or begrudgingly.

Maybe there is something else keeping you awake at night unrelated to snoring. Perhaps you are worrying about something. Nothing good can possibly come from worry. Don't waste your time worrying; instead, pray. A lot of good can come from prayer. Share your worries with the Lord and ask him to help you. There isn't anything God can't do if it is in his plan. What is keeping you awake at night?

Dear Lord, take my weary head and give me rest. Take my worries and give me peace. Take my heart and fill it with your love. Amen.

September 14

Take up a melody, sound the timbrel, the pleasant lyre with a harp.
Blow the shofar at the new moon, at the full moon, on our solemn feast.

PSALM 81:3–4

The harvest moon is the full moon closest to the autumnal equinox. Nature makes the full moonrises unique. When a full moon happens near the autumnal equinox, it rises about thirty minutes later for several days before and after the harvest moon because its orbital path makes a narrow angle with the evening horizon. That angle results in shorter-than-usual rising times between successive moonrises around the full harvest moon. These early evening moonrises make the harvest moon special. Ponder what is special about your marriage. During times of difficulty, you might forget about the positive aspect of your relationship. However, it is good to think about them and thank God for them because your marriage is a gift.

Marriage changes your lifestyles and habits in ways that are personally and socially beneficial. Marriage is a place of growth and development. Contemplate what areas you have grown and matured personally from being married. Do you feel more secure being able to depend on your spouse? Statistics show that married couples can live more cheaply than singles and are healthier with more security and safety than singles. Also, it is noted that children do better when they live with their own married parents.

Perhaps the best gift you have received from your marriage is your children. Maybe you weren't quite ready for children, but God blessed you at the right time—his time. Perhaps your family grew through adoption. However your family expanded to include children, know that it was God's intention for you. He will equip you with the right skills and tools to raise your family, so include God. Do you consider raising a sickly or disabled child a gift? As one might look for the joy of a rainy day, know that there is happiness in parenting a disabled child. The rewards are different than those that come with a healthy child, but they are rich in blessing. Families with disabled children experience challenges; however, if given support they are as vibrant as families with healthy children. Many families with special-needs children feel they have been blessed with a closer relationship. They have more compassion, tolerance, patience, sympathy, are more flexible, and selfless. It's important in every aspect of your married life to always search for the special factor hidden in it. There is one; what is yours?

Dear Lord, open my eyes to see the good that is hidden in my marriage. Don't let me focus on all that is wrong. Let me dwell on the good, the loving, tender aspects. You have given me countless gifts. Thank you for each and every one of them. I truly love you, Lord. Amen.

September 15

On this occasion Solomon and all Israel with him, a great assembly from Lebo-hamath to the Wadi of Egypt, celebrated the festival before the LORD, our God, for seven days. On the eighth day he dismissed the people, who blessed the king and went to their tents, rejoicing and glad of heart because of all the blessings the LORD had given to David his servant and to his people Israel.

1 KINGS 8:65–66

A harvest festival is an annual celebration that occurs near the main harvest of a given region. They feature feasting with foods from local crops in addition to contests, music, and dancing. Consider to what degree your marriage is like a harvest festival? Does it have merriment and joyful laughter? If not, it's up to you to find a way to tap into your spouse's funny bone and tickle it to bring laughter, fun, and enjoyment back into your relationship.

One of the best ways to do this is to reminisce about funny past events, silly occasions, or hysterical behaviors. Chances are good you will laugh as you relive them. Watch funny movies and talk about scenes that you found particularly funny. Watch home movies or drag out old family picture albums. Don't be afraid to laugh at yourself. Play games with friends or your children. Ask your spouse to tell you a story about their most embarrassing moment. Laughter relieves tension and stress, lifts your mood, enhances your creativity, and boosts energy. Who wouldn't want it?

If a disagreement arises in your relationship, humor can lighten things up a bit and restore a sense of connection. Used carefully, some lighthearted humor can diffuse tension, opening a chance for shared fun and intimacy. It lets you make your point without hurting your spouse's feelings. Be more spontaneous with your spouse by sharing laughter, because it lets you escape from inflexible thoughts and behaviors, allowing you to identify the problem differently to find a creative solution. Let go of inhibitions and allow laughter to run through you, freeing you to express whatever you truly feel. In a playful setting you might hear something differently and be more tolerable to learning something about yourself that you otherwise might not be able to do.

Develop and embrace a playful side now. Don't worry about how you might look or sound to your spouse in an attempt to be funny. Chances are good that your spouse will appreciate your effort. The more you joke or laugh, the easier it gets. Create an inside joke that only you and your spouse will understand. It doesn't have to be much to recap a funny incident and will usually make you both smile. When you both are the only ones "in" on a joke, it creates intimacy bringing you closer together.

Dear Lord, thank you for blessing me with a good nature and the ability to smile and laugh. You truly are an amazing God. I love you. Amen.

September 16

When he entered the house, the blind men approached him and Jesus said to them, "Do you believe that I can do this?" "Yes, Lord," they said to him. Then he touched their eyes and said, "Let it be done for you according to your faith."

MATTHEW 9:28–29

Ladybugs go dormant once the temperatures begin to cool but come out on warm autumn days. They will go anywhere for a smidgen of warmth. They will invite themselves into your home if there's a way in. If your relationship runs cool, do you withdraw from your spouse, only getting near when he or she is warm and affectionate? One way to warm up your marriage is to show your partner your playful side. When something strikes you as funny, lean in, touch his or her arm, or give a gentle and spirited nudge. Laughing is much more enjoyable when you both experience the humor and delight in each other's joy.

Touching creates a comforting and calming atmosphere between you both, building trust while deepening your intimacy with each other. A romantic and caring gesture, such as touching your spouse's face, will make him or her feel loved. Run your fingers through your partner's hair, lean in and kiss his or her temple. Grab your spouse's hand when you are walking together or relaxing on the sofa while watching the nightly news. When your spouse least expects it, kiss his or her hand while still holding it. If your spouse does something you adore, let him or her know that you enjoy and appreciate it. Also, don't be afraid to remind your partner of what you need.

Remember the importance of cuddling because it is mutually affectionate. Try to cuddle a few minutes before getting out of bed each day. Set your alarm clock ten minutes early to allocate time to reconnect by cuddling. It's expressing love and understanding nonverbally while promoting bonding. Touch is so important. Jesus miraculous touch changed the lives of everyone around him. When he passed by, strangers flocked around him, hoping to touch his garment. Jesus's touch was healing, loving, and caring. Can you make your touch that way too?

Check with your spouse regularly to know what is working and what needs improving. This opens the door for honest communication and prevents issues from building up. Find out what is your spouse's preferred way of being shown love is. It could be surprising to learn that it is something different than what you've been doing. To make your marriage the best it can possibly be, always be willing to work at it.

Dear Lord, let me reach out to [*name*] and bring warmth back into our relationship. Let my hands be instruments to transmit your unconditional and never-ending love. Amen.

September 17

Have among yourselves the same attitude that is also yours in Christ Jesus,
Who, though he was in the form of God, did not regard equality with God
something to be grasped. Rather, he emptied himself, taking the form of
a slave, coming in human likeness; and found human in appearance,
he humbled himself, becoming obedient to death, even death on a cross.

PHILIPPIANS 2:5–8

Many people say you cannot compare apples and oranges because they are two different fruit. Yet they have so many similarities: they are both round, they have seeds in their centers, they grow on trees, they are tasty and nutritious, they have approximately fifty calories each, they make great snacks and are easy to grab and go. People might have different outer appearances, but have more in common than originally imagined.

Instead of focusing on your spouse's differences, celebrate the uniformities. Think about the things you had in common that attracted you together in the beginning of your courtship. Maybe you work in the same field or like the same types of music. Perhaps you are both athletic or enjoy traveling, experiencing new foods and exciting lifestyles. Do you and your spouse share the same religion or do you have different religious beliefs?

As difficult as it may be, acquire the same attitude that Jesus had when he came to earth as a man. You are called to the same humility that Jesus displayed while on earth. He looked out for his own interests including the welfare of others. Jesus refused to selfishly cling to his rights, privileges, and favored position as the Son of God. Instead, Jesus set that aside to come to live as a man, to die for your sins, and be your Savior.

Contemplate what selfish tendencies you can let go of. Perhaps you golf with your friends more than you spend time with your spouse. Consider cutting down the time you spend away from your marriage and devote more time to doing things you and your spouse can mutually agree upon. Instead of callously clinging to rights and privileges you think you deserve, safeguard the best interests of your spouse. Regardless of whether he or she likes oranges or apples and you prefer something else, with humbleness, seek the common ground between you. How will you bridge the gaps in your likes and dislikes?

Dear Lord, squelch my haughtiness and enable me to find joy in the differences I have with [*name*]. Thank you for making us different and allowing us to have different personalities. While I thrive individually, I want to grow in my marriage. Teach me how to find and enjoy the common grounds between us. Amen.

September 18

When Joab had come near her, the woman said, "Are you Joab?"
And he replied, "Yes." She said to him, "Listen to what your
servant has to say." He replied, "I am listening."

2 Samuel 20:17

A megaphone is a handheld device for the purpose of amplifying someone's voice. When someone speaks through the narrow opening, the sound is increased through the wide opening. It directs the sound in the direction the horn is pointed. Marriages don't come with a megaphone because you don't need a device to hear your spouse when he or she speaks. Your spouse has the right to be heard. You might not like what you are hearing, but he or she has the right to tell you what he or she thinks, feels, and believes. You need to listen. You don't have to agree with what is being said; you only have to listen and understand the message being conveyed.

When couples listen to each other empathically, they cultivate a closer connection. If you listen to your spouse defensively, distance is created in your marriage. When you actively listen to your partner, concentrate on what is being said without interrupting. You may not interject your thoughts and feelings until after your spouse has delivered the message he or she meant for you to hear. While your spouse speaks, make eye contact and ensure that your body language and facial expressions shows you're interested. Try to focus on your spouse's words, feelings, and emotions.

Sometimes it's difficult to listen without reacting. Breathe slowly and try to remain calm. Ask the Holy Spirit that dwells within you to keep you tranquil while you listen. When your spouse has finished and gives you an opportunity to speak, first try to name the emotion he or she is feeling. For example, "You sound really upset" or "You seem really frustrated." If you misinterpreted the emotion, allow your spouse to name the emotion he or she feels. Then, try to repeat what your partner said using your own words. Check with your partner if your interpretation of what was communicated was correct. Ask "Do you want my opinion or advice?" It might not be wanted. If that is the case, don't give it. After your spouse feels understood, you can switch roles and express your view. The goal is to clarify both viewpoints of a situation, not to resolve it. After you both feel understood, you are more likely to resolve a situation amicably. Are you a good listener?

Dear Lord, Form my words in my heart kindly, gently, and serenely so that they can enter [*name*]'s heart. Teach me how to embrace his or her thoughts and feelings and tell me, Lord, what to do with them. Teach us how to enjoy the peace, love, and joy that you bring into our marriage. Thank you, Lord. Amen.

September 19

To one he gave five talents; to another, two; to a third, one—to each according
to his ability. Then he went away. Immediately the one who received five
talents went and traded with them, and made another five. Likewise,
the one who received two made another two. But the man who received one
went off and dug a hole in the ground and buried his master's money.

MATTHEW 25:15–18

When I was in grade school, I participated in a savings program where
I brought a few coins in an envelope to class each week. I learned to
save money, invest in my future, and watch the interest grow. Holy Scripture
indicates that investing money to increase its value is wiser than burying it.
Ponder your current financial situation. Are you in credit card debt, or do you
have healthy portfolio of investments? How did you decide what is "yours,"
"mine," and "ours" and is that plan working? You might have to try several
different methods before you find the one that works best for your marriage.

Some couples pool their money, pay their bills, stash some in a savings
account, and split the leftover cash between them. Resentment could build
over individual purchases made. This method divides the spending power,
eradicating some of the financial value of marriage. What sum of money have
you established that you may spend without consulting your partner? Always
consult with your mate before purchasing a big-ticket item. Having some of
your own money enables you to feel like you haven't lost yourself in order
to be married. Establish a policy and stick to it. Don't spend money secretly.
Set boundaries and live within those parameters. Never justify purchasing
something you cannot afford. Instead, save for it.

Consider the type of debt you brought into your marriage or now have:
school or car loans, credit cards, mortgage, or gambling debt. What is your
plan to become debt-free? Consider past discussions about income and
spending. Your personality plays a part in your spending, saving, and how
you discuss it with your spouse. Consider the type of money issues you dealt
with as a child growing up; that plays a role too. Examine what is behind your
spending habits; emotional problems cannot be solved by spending money.

Do you and your spouse have dual incomes or is one partner a stay-at-
home parent? Perhaps one spouse is unemployed. Whatever your financial
situation, it is important for both of you to cooperate as a team in decisions
regarding spending and saving. Create a realistic budget; hire a financial
planner if necessary. What role do you play in your finances?

Dear Lord, bless me with the knowledge to make wise financial
exchanges. Bring the right people into my life to help me. Amen.

September 20

Therefore, neither the one who plants nor the one who waters is anything,
but only God, who causes the growth. The one who plants and the one
who waters are equal, and each will receive wages in proportion to his
labor. For we are God's co-workers; you are God's field, God's building.

1 Corinthians 3:7–9

A scorekeeper is typically an official who records team and player earnings in sports. Music librarians are "scorekeepers" also. They catalog musical scores and recordings. Anyone can be their own scorekeeper using a phone app. Consider if you are a scorekeeper in your marriage, calculating "who has done what chore."

Scorekeeping is an indicator of marital distress. Should you dispute "who did what chore," you create an atmosphere of separation instead of teamwork. Try to avoid scrutinizing everything your spouse does in your marriage. If you don't like the way a chore was done, look the other way. If your spouse is doing the job, he or she gets to decide how to do it. By expressing disappointment, you end up hurting your marriage. If you don't like the way your spouse does a chore, leave the room. Don't discredit your spouse's contribution. Recognize it and compliment it because then your partner feels appreciated, valued, and loved.

Critical scorekeeping makes each partner a marital "accountant" of chores. Eventually, it will make you and your spouse feel resentful and prove problematic to resolve this growing tension between you both. Telling your partner to do a better job is condescending and a disrespectful thing to do. Ask yourself if you keep score because you are angry with your partner because he or she is neglecting the marriage or has there been a recent change in your life: perhaps a new job, new baby, or relocation? Change that rearranges plans can lead to score keeping. Consider if you could be fighting over time and energy.

Ask your partner if you both can do better as a team, to solve problems together and stop keeping score, blaming, being critical, and being sarcastic. Discuss complaints amicably and lovingly, not by making your spouse the problem. Can you set reasonable expectations by prioritizing chores and working as a team?

Dear Lord, remove all critical thoughts from my mind. Replace them with loving thoughts so that only kind words flow from my heart and out of my mouth. Remind me to appreciate the contributions [*name*] makes for our marriage. Help me to be a better spouse, Lord. Amen.

September 21

You made the moon to mark the seasons,
the sun that knows the hour of its setting.
You bring darkness and night falls,
then all the animals of the forest wander about.

PSALM 104:19–20

In the northern hemisphere, the first day of autumn occurs when the sun crosses the celestial equator, known as the Autumnal Equinox. The climate cools because the earth turns to face a colder part of the solar system, away from the sun. Consider what actions cool off your marriage. Perhaps you are considering a separation from your spouse. A separation can offer a "cooling-off period," allowing you to accurately assess the strengths and weakness of your marriage. The time apart might enable you recall your spouse's better qualities, those that made you fall in love. It can provide a vivid viewpoint on unhealthy features of your relationship.

If you are contemplating a separation, speak with your parish priest to solicit advice and direction. Perhaps you might schedule time with a marriage counselor. Consider the possible consequences of a separation. How will your spouse handle it: as rejection or time apart to discover amicable solutions to problems? You and your spouse will have to work out the logistics of it: determine how your separation will be designed, what it means to you, legal issues, co-parenting, how long should it last, and how will you both work on your relationship? A separation can be a time for healing and personal growth in your relationship. You and your spouse could emerge with a stronger marriage. If you work earnestly to restore your marriage by building healthy patterns and working together as a team, you might find the greatest improvement in revitalizing your marriage.

Make time to talk to the Lord. Find a church that offers eucharistic adoration, where you can be still and mull over your problems with your Lord and Savior. You will receive an abundant amount of grace when sit before the Lord, filling Jesus with jubilation. Adoration will strengthen your relationship with Jesus, allowing you to express your love, gratitude, and respect. It can be more consoling than anything the world can offer you. It will not only strengthen you, but your family and marriage as well. You can adore Jesus reserved in the tabernacle while your church is open; call for times and go today.

Dear Lord, let me reach out to you in my time of need. Touch my heart with your healing grace and transform my soul to be the loving creature you meant for me to be. Heal my marriage, Lord. Help me be kind, considerate, and compassionate. Bless my every thought, my words, my touch, and my work. I do it all for you. Amen.

September 22

When Joseph's brothers came, they bowed down to him with their faces to the ground. He recognized them as soon as he saw them. But he concealed his own identity from them and spoke harshly to them. "Where do you come from?" he asked them. They answered, "From the land of Canaan, to buy food." When Joseph recognized his brothers, although they did not recognize him, he was reminded of the dreams he had about them. He said to them: "You are spies. You have come to see the weak points of the land."

GENESIS 42:6–9

Identity theft happens when a thief steals another person's personal information: Social Security number, driver's license number, or credit card number, to pretend to be that person and commit crimes. Unfortunately, stealing an identity from an unsuspecting person is easy to do. Ponder if you lost some of your identity when you married due to compromises, making joint decisions, or even accepting a new title or role as husband or wife. Marriage is the joining of two individuals sharing a home, money, time, meals, and so much more, which is all fantastic. However, it's good to maintain your own identity while being married through preserving a balance of self by focusing on what makes you happy.

It's easy to get absorbed in your title as "husband" or "wife." Instead, decide what you want to become and identify what is missing from your life that you want to reclaim. Perhaps it's time with friends or time and space to reenergize, relax, and pray. Maybe you miss your physical activities or hobbies. You can maintain your sense of self by continuing your education, pursuing your career, or following your dreams. Reconnect with yourself and do the things that bring you joy. Don't depend on your spouse to make you happy. Happiness comes from within.

Your marriage should add to your personality, not take away from it. The key is finding a harmonious balance between your private moments and sharing time with your loved one as you journey through life. Your partner was attracted to who you were before he or she found you. Strive to be the best version of yourself.

Dear Lord, thank you for making me truly unique. Help me to appreciate my differences as well as our similarities. Teach me to be a good spouse while maintaining my individuality. I ask this in your loving name, Lord. Amen.

September 23

I will bless the LORD at all times; his praise shall be always in my mouth.
My soul will glory in the LORD; let the poor hear and be glad. Magnify
the LORD with me; and let us exalt his name together. I sought the LORD,
and he answered me, delivered me from all my fears. Look to him and
be radiant, and your faces may not blush for shame. This poor one cried
out and the LORD heard, and from all his distress he saved him.

PSALM 34:2–7

The sunflower is an annual plant that possesses a large flowering head. Its name is derived from the sun, the flower's shape. The flower's head consists of many individual flowers that mature into seeds that are an excellent source of calories, essential fatty acids, vitamins, and minerals. No matter where they are planted, the face of the flower always turns toward the sun. In life, no matter where you might be planted, you will thrive by focusing on God the father, God the Son, and God the Holy Spirit. Ponder if God is the center of your life and your marriage.

Apply biblical principles to your marriage because that will give you a stronger foundation compared to your friends and neighbors who don't believe. Use the challenges, joys, struggles, and celebrations of marriage to draw you closer to God. There is a purpose for it all or else God wouldn't give it to you. God designed marriage to make you happy and holy. Appreciate what God designed marriage to provide: partnership, spiritual intimacy, and the ability to pursue God together. It isn't always easy to find your fulfillment and purpose in God, especially when you are having a bad day. Despite your inadequacies, God created you to guide your partner in his direction.

Loving your spouse through difficult moments can be challenging. However, the issues you struggle with are what you probably value the most in your relationship. Don't make achieving happiness or receiving love your goal. Instead, strive to model God's love and commitment to your family. Do this by emphasizing your spouse's strengths, gifts, and talents, not his or her weaknesses. Do not criticize your partner. Instead, inspire, encourage, and love unconditionally. Embrace your spouse's differences because God created him or her that way, especially for you. Offer your spouse support, respect, and prayers.

Dear Lord, teach me how to be a better partner and have a successful and holy marriage centered on you. Enable me to have an unwavering commitment to make it flourish as you designed it to be. Thank you for bringing [*name*] into my life. Amen.

September 24

Then his wife said to him, "Are you still holding to your innocence?
Curse God and die!" But he said to her, "You speak as foolish women do.
We accept good things from God; should we not accept evil?"
Through all this, Job did not sin in what he said.

JOB 2:9–10

In a darkened movie theater without windows it's hard to tell what the weather is like outside. The sun could be shining brilliantly, or it could be raining cats and dogs. Absorbed in the movie, it's nearly impossible to know what's happening outside the theater. Ponder if you ever feel like you're in the dark with your spouse. Perhaps you are clueless to what he or she is feeling or thinking. Do you feel lonely in your marriage even when your partner is with you? Perhaps you could examine your role in the marriage problems. Don't just blame your spouse; if you are hurting emotionally, that pain skews your insight, immobilizing you from fixing your problems, making them drag on or worsen. The best way to tackle the problem is through open and honest communication.

Begin by acting with integrity and be compassionate, loving, and loyal, because so much rides on how you make your spouse feel through this vulnerability by relaying that you really care. Perhaps you misread your spouse's body language and there isn't a marriage problem at all. Maybe your spouse is dwelling on a work-related problem. Your spouse could be worrying about the economy and together you could revise your financial situation, which could bring him or her peace. Keep an open mind throughout it all, not taking anything personally by only attacking the problem, not your spouse. The only way to know for sure what is wrong is to ask and reassure your partner that whatever is troubling him or her, you will both get through it together.

The best way to start is through prayer. Ask God to bless you as you listen with your heart. Remember that the Holy Spirit dwells within, and he can empower you to gain bigger and better insight than you could on your own accord. Try to define what the problem is without being defensive. After you understand the issue, list as many solutions as possible even if some sound absurd. Sometimes, a crazy idea could work! When you think you have all imaginable options, list the pros and cons to each. Spend time together discussing them at length. Often, you only need to talk aloud to notice the obvious results. So much can be accomplished by "talking it out."

Dear Lord, thank you for giving me a compassionate spouse who cares enough to want to work out problems so they don't fester into huge fights. Thank you for keeping me composed and giving me insight to work through our issues. I love you, Lord. Amen.

September 25

Now Abraham and Sarah were old, advanced in years, and Sarah had stopped having her menstrual periods. So Sarah laughed to herself and said, "Now that I am worn out and my husband is old, am I still to have sexual pleasure?" But the LORD said to Abraham: "Why did Sarah laugh and say, 'Will I really bear a child, old as I am?' Is anything too marvelous for the LORD to do? At the appointed time, about this time next year, I will return to you, and Sarah will have a son."

GENESIS 18:10–15

I ndian summer is a period of unseasonably warm temperatures after the end of the summer, typically after there has been a frost. The nice weather is welcome before the winter winds blow in. It's hard to take winter seriously when high temperatures tease everyone with a few more days of sunshine. Consider how easy (or difficult) it is to take your spouse seriously.

Is your spouse a jokester? Laughter with a sense of humor can buoy your relationship if it is done in good jest. For some, teasing can be a frisky way of showing love and affection. For others, teasing could be a way of interacting with people, a power play, or a way of trying to be the center of attention or liven up a dull conversation. Some forms of teasing are not funny; these areas of your lives should be off-limits. Maybe your spouse has a demanding personality or embarrasses you with what he or she considers "playful teasing." The key is not to ignore it because that only makes the problem worse. You cannot change your spouse, but you can change your attitude, your reactions, and your responses.

Reinforce positive behavior each time you see it. When your spouse demonstrates good behavior, let him or her know how happy it makes you. Try to model good behavior for your spouse to emulate by being honest about yourself. If you make a mistake, admit it. Listen with both your heart and your mind. Ask the Lord to keep you strong.

Are there times throughout your relationship that you do not take your spouse seriously? Whatever is important to him or her, it also needs to be important to you. If it is important for your spouse to return to school to get a degree, let that goal be important to you too. By providing this emotional support, you are telling your spouse that you genuinely care about what motivates them to succeed. Spouses are not mind readers, so it's essential to verbally communicate exactly what you need from your spouse. If you are seeking encouragement, appreciation, and praise, ask for that.

Dear Lord, let my words be light as air, to tickle and delight in, and also warm and loving. Amen.

September 26

During those days Mary set out and traveled to the hill country
in haste to a town of Judah, where she entered the house of
Zechariah and greeted Elizabeth....Mary remained with her
about three months and then returned to her home.

LUKE 1:39–40, 56

The Virgin Mary visited relatives as her body was making room to carry the infant Jesus. She found camaraderie with Zechariah and Elizabeth. Consider if you have sought the comfort and love that visiting relatives can offer? Do your parents, in-laws, or other family members live nearby? Are family members a source of love and support or a foundation for conflict and stress? Many couples have in-law troubles or issues with extended family members. Sometimes it's nice to see family members come to visit, but it can be nicer to see them go.

Your loyalties need to be to your spouse and children. Establish boundaries so there is a clear understanding when in-laws are invited to your home. Discuss the boundaries with your parents. You and your spouse only have so much time and energy that you can divvy up between family members. If your extended families are stressing you out, discuss reformulating the boundaries with your spouse. Reassure in-laws that you are not shutting them out; you are redirecting back onto yourselves. Negotiate with your partner the role that you want your in-laws to have. Don't criticize your partner for the kind of relationship he or she has with his or her parents because it could snowball into bigger problems. Instead, try to find something positive with it. Maybe no one else can make a raspberry pie like your mother-in-law and she always brings you one—celebrate that!

If you are having a particular problem with your in-laws, your spouse needs to be the one to step up and address it. If your spouse is having a problem with your family, you need to be the one to address it. It's important to have a loving relationship with your parents and in-laws. Do not bring your marriage problem to them. You must work on your marital issues with your spouse, a priest, or marriage counselor.

Remember that your in-laws are connected to your spouse through genetics, history, and complicated psychological dynamics. Try to honor your parents and in-laws by demonstrating love and showing them patience, kindness, gentleness, and respect. Treat them the way you would treat Jesus.

Dear Lord, help me to embrace my nutty family and in-laws. Bless me with the resilience I need to bend without breaking each time they visit. Let me remember how wonderful it was for Mary to visit her relatives in her time of need. Amen.

September 27

For in hope we were saved. Now hope that sees for itself is not hope.
For who hopes for what one sees? But if we hope for what we do not see,
we wait with endurance.

ROMANS 8:24–25

Watching kids run to the bus stop with backpacks filled with a few dollars, laptops, smartphones, and mp3 players is so completely different than when my mom went to school: walking a mile with a chalkboard and a sandwich wrapped in wax paper, plus a few cents to buy milk. Reflect on how times have changed since you walked down the aisle to exchange vows. Perhaps you have changed too. Consider what areas in your marriage might need to be improved upon. How quickly do you jump to conclusions when something seems off?

Do you give your spouse the benefit of the doubt when you are in a quandary? Do you think he or she is out to get you? Do you choose to believe the good about your spouse quicker than something bad? Without full evidence or a clear picture, can you choose to find something positive and give a favorable judgment to your partner? Giving your spouse the benefit of the doubt can reduce your stress because instead of getting aggravated over an issue, consider it an oversight, a distraction, or he or she simply didn't intentionally mean to upset you. Ask God to give you the courage to do this.

Giving your spouse the benefit of the doubt can improve your marriage. Essentially you and your partner both want the same basic things. By accepting that your partner makes mistakes or acts without thinking of the consequences, the more accepting you can be. And the more tolerant you are, the more you'll succeed. Accepting yourself this way means rebounding from blunders sooner and living with your own weaknesses; this bridges you to live peacefully with your spouse including his or her weaknesses.

Perhaps you can offer the benefit of the doubt to a stranger in the grocery store, but not your spouse. The next time you encounter someone who annoys you, think about God dwelling within that person, running late to help someone somewhere. If you can offer Jesus the benefit of the doubt, offer it to your spouse too.

Dear Lord, thank you for giving me the benefit of the doubt when you see my heart and true intentions. You see my sinful nature and still extend grace and forgive me each time I ask. Teach me how to be more forgiving, to cut [*name*] some slack the next time he or she goofs up. Amen.

September 28

And we have this confidence in him, that if we ask anything according to his will, he hears us. And if we know that he hears us in regard to whatever we ask, we know that what we have asked him for is ours.

1 JOHN 5:14–15

There are commercials on TV where one spouse surprises the other with a Mercedes in the driveway with a huge red bow on the roof or plane tickets to New Zealand. While some spouses might like that kind of a surprise, I would prefer to be a part of the decision-making process. I like having the right to be consulted. A decision that affects both you and your spouse should be made jointly. When it comes to making large purchases, such as a new car or big vacation, vow to make those decisions together. Major expenditures affect both of you with a mutual budget, and to an extent, a joint credit rating. Consult with your spouse if you want to take out a loan or acquire a major credit card. If you are unable to make the payments, the responsibility would fall on your spouse's shoulders.

When one spouse applies for a job halfway around the country, he or she should consult with his or her spouse because it impacts both of you. Before accepting a higher-paying job that involves relocation, consult with your spouse or you may be moving alone. When it comes to choosing a home to live in, you and your spouse should decide together. Promise to include your spouse if you spend more than a particular dollar amount. Agree ahead of time what that amount is; whether it is $100 or $1,000, because with that pledge there won't be any unpleasant surprises.

Your spouse has a right to be consulted about when to include children in your family. If you cannot reach an agreement, hold off until you are both ready. Nothing will impact you both as much as much as having a child or having another child. Always make this decision as a couple. Consult with your spouse before you enroll in college classes, travel with a friend, or invite someone home for dinner. It is wise to check with your spouse before signing up for a couples' seminar at church or purchasing season tickets to basketball or football games. Ask your partner first before accepting an invitation from friends, family, or neighbors. Making decisions together on things that impact you both is the respectful thing to do.

Dear Lord, help me to be more thoughtful and respectful to check with [*name*] before I agree to something. Amen.

September 29

The earth brought forth vegetation: every kind of plant that bears seed
and every kind of fruit tree that bears fruit with its seed in it.
God saw that it was good.

GENESIS 1:12

What can you do with an apple? Make apple pie, applesauce, apple fritters, apple muffins, apple turnovers, apple dumplings, and apple butter. All of those different foods have one thing in common: they are made with apples and the skin is peeled off and thrown away. Did you know the skin has the most nutrients? Sometimes, we overlook the obvious to get to what we think is the "good part." Perhaps there are many differences between you and your partner. Don't automatically cling to the similarities; celebrate your differences as well.

What can you learn from your spouse's differences? God gave us many gifts and talents, why not share them with each other? Reflect on one of your spouse's talents that you would like to learn. You both might enjoy the experience of either teaching or learning. If your spouse can play a musical instrument, maybe he or she could teach you that. Perhaps your spouse has extensive knowledge on computers; you could learn those skills from him or her. If your spouse is a different nationality, learn how to cook traditional meals from that culture, or learn a game from that race. If you have an inter-racial relationship, consider the excitement of being exposed to new ways of thinking and incorporating aspects of the culture, race, or religion into your daily life.

You have the right to be different. If you like to keep methodical paper-work because that quirkiness is a part of your personality, that is acceptable as long as it doesn't overflow out of control and into your spouse's territory. If you can make decisions quickly without a lot of excessive information, that is okay as long as you don't buy two identical cars on the same day, because that would definitely affect your spouse. You have the right to your individualism, to be uniquely yourself, exactly the way God intended.

Consider what aspects of your spouse you have overlooked, similar to the nutritional elements of the apple skin that was discarded. How will you include those new ideas, attitudes, and elements into your everyday life?

Dear Lord, give me the patience to appreciate the aspects my spouse holds near to his or her heart. Let me embrace our differences to learn from them and to grow in your eternal love. Thank you for bringing us together and for enabling us to our love to flourish. Amen.

September 30

Is there anyone who has planted a vineyard and not yet plucked its fruit?
Let him return home, lest he die in battle and another pluck its fruit.
Is there anyone who has betrothed a woman and not yet married her?

DEUTERONOMY 20:6–7

When record high temperatures scorched the Finger Lakes region of New York State, grapes thrived and wine producers rejoiced because it created better-tasting wine. Warm temperatures impacted an entire wine industry with a favorable economy. Ponder how much warmth is in your marriage. Consider if you offer a genuine love to your spouse where you care about his or her happiness without thought for what you get out of it for yourself. Real love is when your partner makes mistakes or inconveniences you, but you're not angry.

How frequent are your expressions of love? Saying "I love you" is important, but showing love is vital. Consider how you pay attention to your spouse and demonstrate your love. Try to compliment your spouse each day and affirm your appreciation for what he or she does for you. Reflect on when you last spent quality time together. Hopefully, you find a way to connect each day. However, it's also good to step away and do something fun together, even if it's meeting each other for lunch once a week. Wrap a blanket around yourselves and watch the sunrise or a sunset. It's a simple thing to do and gives you quiet time to reflect on the day you have in front of you as well as end your day on a loving note. Go outside at night and look at the stars together, marvel over them, and perhaps make a wish on a falling star. What would that wish be? Share it with your partner; maybe he or she can help make your dreams come true.

How can you foster a more loving atmosphere? Ask yourself if what you are doing in your marriage is pleasing to God. If it is, keep it up. If you are not promoting an amicable environment, pray for God's intervention. Ponder ways to nurture your marriage, not destroy it.

Dear Lord, fill my mind, heart, and soul with loving solutions to my marriage difficulties. Enable me to be more caring to my partner even when I do not feel like it. You didn't want a crown of thorns, but you wore it for me. Amen.

October 1

Woe to those who sew amulets for the wrists of every arm
and make veils for every head size to snare lives!

EZEKIEL 13:18

Yarn is a series of twisted fibers that can be woven into just about anything: sweaters, hats, or scarves. Knitting is an easy concept if you understand it; however, the skill requires a lot of practice and patience. It's amazing to watch a tiny piece of yarn be transformed into a wearable object. What conflict-resolution skill could you weave into your marriage? Perhaps establishing a policy that you both agree upon would work best in your household.

When one person's need trumps the other spouse's desire, the policy gives into the spouse with a need. An example of this could be if one spouse is sick on the sofa watching a movie, while the other spouse sits nearby watching it too. When the phone rings, the spouse who is well answers the phone.

If one spouse's likings are not as strong, he or she will yield to the spouse who feels strongly. An example of this policy is planning dinner. If the wife doesn't care what she eats, but the husband really wants spaghetti, then they both will eat spaghetti.

When a job needs to be done, the spouse who can do it more capably or efficiently will be the one to do the task. An example of this rule can be established over emptying the dishwasher. If you have more time and you know where everything goes, just do it automatically. There will be other jobs your spouse can do.

The spouse who is doing a chore, or making some sacrifice, gets to do it the way he or she chooses. While some of these policies might work in your relationship, discuss them before you implement them. Initially, mistakes might be made if one person forgets, but use loving reminders that build up your partner while you are both learning to embrace establishing policies in your home. After practicing positive methods, they will become second nature, and you will wonder how you ever lived without them. They save a lot of aggravation! Soon you will become masterful and your relationship will be strengthened as a result. Invoke the Holy Spirit to help you remember the techniques. Can you intertwine more constructive elements into your marriage today?

Dear Lord, fill my mind and heart with all that is wise, loving, and honest so that I can effectively communicate and implement policies to my spouse. Thank you for helping me raise my relationship to a higher level of mature respect and love. I love you, Lord. Amen.

October 2

As the people grumbled against Moses, saying, "What are we to drink?"
he cried out to the LORD, who pointed out to him a certain piece of wood.
When he threw it into the water, the water became fresh.

EXODUS 15:24–25

After water, tea is the most widely consumed beverage in the world. It's made by pouring hot water over leaves. The two simple ingredients have numerous health benefits containing antioxidants, flavonols, and polyphenols. Some say it suppresses pain and nausea and provides calming effects. Your marriage also has health benefits. Your partner has a vested interest in your well-being. Married people have a tendency to take better care of themselves and avoid risky behaviors. Consider if this holds true in your marriage.

The routine of marriage reminds you to eat and sleep well with an increased likelihood of being physically and mentally healthier. The protective effect of marriage applies to minor illnesses such as colds and flu, but also to serious health problems such as cancer, heart disease, and heart attacks. Emotional support from a spouse shortens the recuperation rate from minor or major illnesses. Marriage enables spouses to manage chronic diseases better and can actually boost the immune system warding off some sicknesses altogether. Within your marriage you have social support and are more tolerant of pain with the ability to be happier with increased longevity.

Reflect on other advantages of your union and the goodness that God blessed your relationship with. Like tea that is infused with fruits, contemplate what you can enhance your marriage with. Consider prayer as an option. While it is important to spend time alone with Jesus, it is also good to pray with your spouse. Try praying for a stronger marriage. Reach out to God in your time of need and see what he can do. Just as you might add sugar, milk, or lemon to enhance your tea, consider a few easy steps to improve your marriage. Don't take each other for granted. Make an effort to be respectful, thoughtful, appreciative, supportive, and affirming toward your spouse. Say, "I love you" and "thank you" frequently. Don't put off an opportunity to be affectionate or romantic. Make your sex life a priority. What can you do today to make your marriage richer and more robust?

Dear Lord, allow me to infuse my marriage with more love and devotion. I thirst for your glory and the blessings of my relationship with [*name*]. Thank you, dear Lord, for countless gifts you provide in the sanctity of my marriage. Amen.

October 3

I will give you a new heart, and a new spirit I will put within you.
I will remove the heart of stone from your flesh and give you a heart of flesh.
EZEKIEL 36:26

During the summer, there are slight variations in the green leaves on the trees, but they mostly blend together in the same hue. In the autumn, the same trees have spectacular colors; some are bold yellows, others are brilliant oranges, and there are even deep reds and purples. The change from ordinary green to the motley assortment altogether is breathtakingly beautiful. In relationships, we often show our true colors to our mate, which sometimes is boring, mediocre at best, or downright unappealing. Consider what aspects of your marriage need improving. Perhaps there are a lot of little things that are adding up to one massive weight on your shoulders.

Try breaking them apart and resolving one at a time by asking yourself "what did I expect?" Did you just want your own way, or were your rights violated? Perhaps you assumed the way something "should have" been done, based on the way your parents raised you. Perhaps you formed an opinion based on books you have read or movies you watched. Ask yourself if they were realistic expectations and did you tell your spouse or did you assume he or she could mind read your desires? If you were wrong, apologize. Maybe you asked your spouse in a way that sounded like a demand. Instead, you could turn your requests into hopes. For instance, you could say, "I love it when we do a project together. Do you think we could paint the bedroom over the winter?" If you are unhappy with your spouse's response, negotiate it. For example, "Would you mind if I painted the bedroom?" If your spouse likes the color of the bedroom, and you really want to paint, ask to paint the garage or find another project you can both do together. Try to be open-minded and flexible. Most importantly, reflect on what it is you really want.

With God's grace and glory, it's possible to transform ourselves into a better person, rich with vibrant color. What insincerities do you show your spouse? Are you dishonest or vindictive? Reflect on occasions where you could be more truthful and loving. Use prayer to help you achieve the warmth your marriage craves.

Dear Lord, give me the strength and courage to transform into a more beautiful person. You gave me the capabilities and the desire. Soften my heart, buff out my rough edges, and let me grow in your infinite love and wisdom. Amen.

October 4

*In their actions even children can playact
though their deeds be blameless and right.*

PROVERBS 20:11

Eating chocolate is good for you. It contains antioxidants that enable cells to resist damage from environmental contaminants. Flavonoids found in cocoa lower blood pressure and improve blood flow to the brain and heart. There are myriad health benefits to being married; some aspects you may not realize. The conditions surrounding your childhood impact your married life today. Reflect on emotional baggage that you dragged into your relationship.

Are there any negative feelings from your youth that cause resentment in your relationship today? Are there unmet childhood needs that you expect your spouse to fulfill? Perhaps you did not receive much affection from your parents because they worked many long hours and had other children that you might have felt slighted. Question if you are now seeking the physical contact from your spouse that you did not get as a child. If you were not heard in your childhood, perhaps you are trying to get that from your spouse.

Unfinished business in your childhood can come in many different forms, not just the need to be heard or touched. Everyone has a need to feel accepted and loved unconditionally. If you were a foster child, bounced from one home to another, perhaps you didn't feel accepted and now are seeking to obtain a sense of belonging from your spouse. Reflect on possible risk factors that you were exposed to in your childhood: abuse, abandonment, addictions, or mental illness. If there was divorce in your youth, you might have felt a sense of abandonment, even though you weren't technically "abandoned."

The key is to be aware of the elements that formed your characteristics. Do you have excessive anxiety or guilt, which could be from a controlling, overprotective, or critical parent? Do you have anger from an authoritarian parent who ridiculed or showed favoritism? Do you harbor resentment from unfair dealings in your childhood, possibly in the form of rejection? Is hurt or pain your trigger, possibly caused by trauma? Question what causes any depression you experience. You can decide what aspects of your emotional baggage you want to keep and what you can get rid of. God walks with you as you uncover and resolve past issues. By addressing them, you pave the way for greater stability within your marriage. Which issue will you work through today?

Dear Lord, break the shackles that repressed me from my childhood. Propel me forward in my relationship so that my marriage is stronger and more resilient. Amen.

October 5

The patient are better than warriors,
and those who rule their temper,
better than the conqueror of a city.

PROVERBS 16:32

Water in its natural state is a liquid, but it can also be a gas in the form of steam or a solid in the form of ice. Temperature changes water from one state to another. Fluctuations in the temperature of a relationship can affect it greatly. Have you given your spouse the "cold shoulder?" Have you had a "hot" temper recently? It takes a great deal of control to keep your marriage in the natural state, flowing along nicely. What aspect of your life seems out of control that could be impacting your marriage? Is it your finances, job, children, activities, or in-laws? It could be a combination of all of these.

Don't allow any one of these things to overpower your life. Assert yourself and take the control back. Begin by saying, "no" when you are asked to work overtime. Say no to your children when they ask to take on another sport or activity. If you want them to have one activity, then involve them in the decision-making process. Have them find two other parents to carpool with. Assign chores to your children. Cut back on spending to gain better control of your finances. Hire a financial planner to help find areas where you could do a better job saving money. The key is not to let your life control you; you need to control it.

Is your spouse being too controlling? There are obvious signs of control issues, but did you know there are subtle ways your spouse can exert control? Contemplate if she or he is overly helpful by doing everything him or herself. Does your spouse surprise you with things to get it his or her way? For example, your partner could buy a vacation package for the family at Disneyland, when you had your heart set on going to Hawaii to celebrate your anniversary. Your spouse got his or her way through a surprise when you would like to have helped make the decision. Another way your spouse can be subtly controlling is by being overly sensitive, sickly, or worried.

Perhaps you are attempting to control your partner. God only wants you to control yourself. Focus internally on your spirituality, and once you have tapped into that energy, use it to transform the other areas of your life that need improving.

Dear Lord, Quiet my heart and mind. Let me rest in your love. Feed me strength and courage to regain my composure to forge onward. Lead me back to be in control my life and marriage. Amen.

October 6

One can put on gold and abundant jewels,
but wise lips are the most precious ornament.

PROVERBS 20:15

Certain rocks or minerals found in their natural state are not that pretty. However, once they are cut and polished, they become gemstones and are used in jewelry and admired by many. Does your marriage need polishing or reconfiguration? Do you have unspoken expectations in your marriage? When it comes to birthday celebrations, do you drop hints or suggest how you would like your spouse to honor your special day? Are you disappointed when you had higher expectations? When it comes to birthdays, they seem to conjure disappointment and unfinished childhood issues. Consider if you ever missed out on feeling special on your birthday or if you overindulged. At some point, everyone endures a birthday disappointment. Even your spouse has a particular history and preferences on how to celebrate his or her birthday.

Consider how you act when you are disappointed. Do you sulk or justify it by rationalizing that as an adult you are cherished by your spouse regardless of a cake with candles. Reflect on past birthdays where you were elated with the celebrations or were you sorely disappointed by your spouse? Don't allow birthday malaise to creep in and spoil your day or snowball into an argument with your spouse. Instead of allowing your birthday to pass by unnoticed, have the courage to tell your spouse in a loving manner what you would like to receive for your birthday or how you would like to celebrate. Focus on celebrating another year with your spouse. Become a part of planning the birthday festivity together. It might not be a surprise, but you can negotiate what you really want from the person who means the most to you.

Unsaid expectancy leads your spouse to be a mind reader. And yet, expectations can feel like demands to your loved one. The message delivery is critical. Invoke the Holy Spirit to enable you to find the right words to convey your feelings and desires. How can you turn your yearnings into a hope? Stories of hopefulness are thread throughout the Bible. Hold onto hope the way you grasp God. He is the answer to everything.

Dear Lord, sooth my aching heart and calm my restlessness. Let patience and hopefulness spread over me and seep deeply into my soul. Let me shower my spouse with the richness of unconditional love and fill the spaces were disappointments once resided. You keep me strong despite my fragilities. I love you, sweet and loving Lord. Amen.

October 7

Should not many words be answered,
or must the garrulous man necessarily be right?

JOB 11:2

Each autumn, the wind strips the colorful leaves from the trees' spindly branches and sends them soaring through the air. A few leaves sail down the street into neighbors' yards, miles away, settling in storm drains and clogging them. It would be inconceivable to retrieve any of them. Like the leaves, unkind words can fly out quickly, disperse to places you never intend them to go and cause severe damage. How do you prevent yourself from being provoked to say bad words, gossip, or speak poorly of your spouse?

How do you channel your anger so that you don't explode, attacking your spouse with unhealthy or abusive words? Jesus used a soft and gentle tone when he spoke. Think of Jesus when he delivered messages calmly. Try to recognize early warning signs when you feel anger building within: muscles tense, face reddens, flushed feelings, fidgeting, or voice changes.

Consider healthy ways to use up the energy that you have been suppressing. You could cry; shedding tears could actually flush toxic chemicals from your body and liberate you from tension and stress. Researchers discovered emotional tears are produced when somebody is stressed, containing more protein-based hormones, some of which are natural painkillers; crying can actually reduce pain. Crying indicates to your spouse that you might need help from him or her. Tears can signal a need for a hug. A reassuring touch has been associated with facilitating stress reduction. Frequent episodes of crying are not always good and can signal depression or post-traumatic stress disorder. The healing effect of crying doesn't work for everyone, especially people with mood disorders.

Another healthy outlet to burn pent-up energy is through exercise, even if it is a ten-minute walk. Exercise and the mood-enhancing endorphins it produces will not only improve your health, but it can also reduce emotional stress and anger. A recent study suggests that men may excrete more emotional stress type toxins in their sweat because they sweat more than women.

The best solution for handling anger is to turn to God and ask for his help in your time of need. While some people opt to count to ten, consider saying ten Hail Mary's while focusing on the difficulties Mary endured watching Jesus suffer through his crucifixion.

Dear Lord, bless my mind to conjure sweet words and heartfelt ways to say them. Let each tender word be a useful instrument to unite us. Thank you for the ability to speak wisely and lovingly. Amen.

October 8

For he says: "In an acceptable time I heard you,
and on the day of salvation I helped you."
Behold, now is a very acceptable time;
behold, now is the day of salvation.

2 CORINTHIANS 6:2

Squirrels scamper through my yard, busily collecting and hiding items to retrieve later. They playfully chase each other, scooting up and down trees, jumping from one branch to another. It's enjoyable to watch them frolicking outside; I certainly wouldn't want one inside my house. What are a few unwelcome intruders in your home and marriage?

Reflect on occasions where the time you spent on the computer was more than the actual time you spent with your spouse. Consider using a timer so that you designate a set amount of time to surf the Internet or use social networking sites. Then, spend twice that time with your spouse. Do you spend much time watching TV? Maybe you could designate one or two days a week as TV nights, and spend the remainder of the week doing something else: watching a sunset, counting the stars, volunteering at a food pantry, or painting the family room. Establish one night a week as a "date" night where you go somewhere special.

Reflect on the time you spend with friends, coworkers, or neighbors. Perhaps there are game nights, time allocated to sports, or time to socialize at bars and restaurants. The key is balancing your outside friendships with your spouse and family. While it is important to maintain a life with others, it is essential to spend quality time alone with your spouse. Have a frank discussion with your spouse about time allotted for socializing with friends and with each other. Negotiate and compromise until you reach a schedule with rules about entertaining friends and activities that are acceptable to both of you.

How much time do you spend drawing the Lord into your life and marriage? Don't procrastinate praying. Welcome Jesus into your marriage today. Consider spending an hour each week in adoration with your Lord and Savior.

Dear Lord, extinguish the distractions that compete for my time and keep me from prayer and focusing on my marriage. Bring me into your alliance and become my number one priority. With you, I can do anything. Guide me down the right path, Lord. Don't let me comfort strangers into my home. Let me focus on [*name*] and make our marriage as strong as my bond with you. I love you, Lord. Amen.

October 9

So for one who knows the right thing to do and does not do it, it is a sin.

JAMES 4:17

Raking leaves is an exhausting task. Have you ever wished that your leaves would blow into your neighbor's yard so you didn't have to rake them? Is there a topic in your marriage that you hope you could avoid because it would be too difficult to handle? Perhaps it's a "touchy" topic involving in-laws, money, or sex. Whatever the topic is, it's important not to sweep problems under the rug or hope they will go away, because problems never resolve on their own.

Do you take responsibility for your own feelings, choices, and behaviors? If you find yourself in a negative mood, the easiest way to change your situation is to examine your actions and determine what role they played in bringing about your problem. Your life is your responsibility. You can't control every aspect of your life, what happens, or what others do to you. However, you can control the way you respond. Don't get bogged down in blame and bitterness. Instead, scrutinize your own inadequacies and mistakes you made.

After you reflect on your actions, initiate a conversation by using "I" statements. If you are overly responsible in your marriage, question if have become an enabler. Do you try to do everything so that your spouse doesn't need to help out? Contemplate if you prefer doing things your own way. After honestly evaluating why you try to do it all, consider rendering something to your spouse. If it was a problem of his or her that you were trying to fix, give it back. If you are overly responsible, you need to focus on doing less to stop being an enabler. However, if you are irresponsible, you need to step up to the plate and do more. Instead of avoiding responsibility, you need to accept more and stop allowing your spouse to compensate for your inadequacies. Get yourself out of your predicament by being responsible for yourself.

You can always ask to start over and try to do it again the right way. Ask God for guidance as you accept more accountability in your life and marriage.

Dear Lord, empower me with the capabilities to do more in my marriage. I am sorry I have neglected my spouse and my responsibilities. I will take the problems back, fix them, and try again until I get it right. I want to please you, Lord, and do what is honorable. Thank you for being such a powerful presence in my life. I love you. Amen.

October 10

"Rise, then, for this is your duty! We are with you, so have courage and act!"

EZRA 10:4

When making soup, it's good to have a balanced mixture of vegetables, pasta, and meat. If a soup is loaded with carrots, it might not be as appetizing. In marriage, it's important to offer a mixture of gifts to your partner. If you constantly tell your spouse how much you love him or her, but you are never around to share in chores or activities, how good are those words alone? Words of affection in combination with quality time make your relationship that much better. Therefore, offer your time and talents as well to make a heartier and richer relationship. Ponder what you might be giving too little of to your spouse.

Consider meeting for lunch. It doesn't have to be extravagant, just a place where you both can share a meal and talk in the middle of the day. Maybe you could meet at a park and share a picnic lunch. It's enough to break up the routine and stir the desire for future opportunities to spend time together. Maybe you could plan a mini-vacation, a getaway someplace nearby, but still far enough away to make it exciting and fun. Maybe visit an apple orchard or a pumpkin patch. When is the last time you carved a pumpkin? Trace exotic cutouts to make your jack-o-lantern extra special. Try horseback riding with your spouse or rent bicycles. Take a nature walk; they are splendid with the leaves changing colors and the air crisp and clean. Whatever activity you decide on, remember that you are building memories with your spouse and expressing love by being together.

Have your spouse draft a list of activities he or she would enjoy and make plans to actually do them. Make your own list and incorporate them to balance out your events. Devise a joint bucket list of things you both dream of doing eventually, someday, and start doing them! Don't wait. Reflect on the depth of Jesus love for you and ask him to enable you to find healthy ways to show your love to your mate.

Dear Lord, allow me to see where I am not giving enough support, love, blessings, and gifts to my spouse. I long for a well-balanced relationship and I will strive to achieve it with your guiding hand. I trust in your ways, dear Lord. Thank you for loving me so completely. Amen.

October 11

King Belshazzar gave a great banquet for a thousand of his nobles,
with whom he drank.

DANIEL 5:1

Every year in Munich, Bavaria, Germany, is a sixteen-day festival celebrating beer. The famous celebration, known as Oktoberfest, attracts nearly six million people from around the world. Reflect on the celebrations you and your spouse share each year: your anniversary, birthdays, milestones, work promotions, or personal accomplishments. Perhaps you are not in a festive mood or you haven't celebrated it in the past; however, a wedding anniversary commemorates an important event in your life and should be recognized. Celebrating your anniversary allows you to relive your wedding in the present and recall that special emotion created by your commitment to each other.

Your anniversary celebration should commemorate the continuation of your love for one another throughout the years, even if your life has not unfolded the way you expected it to. God has a plan for you and while it might be different from what you imagined, trust in God that it will be good. How have you celebrated your wedding anniversary in the past and how do you plan to honor it in a memorable way in the future?

Making the effort to acknowledge your anniversary in a special way can be beneficial to your marriage because you remember falling in love and can actually bring some of those feelings back. Look at your wedding photographs, or play "your song." Consider making the same meal that was served at your reception or splurge on a really nice bottle of champagne. Perhaps you could plan a mini-honeymoon or attend a marriage-enrichment workshop or a marriage-encounter weekend. Maybe you could host a small party. You could make a scrapbook of the major milestones since your wedding date or have a portrait taken. If you want to exchange gifts with your spouse, discuss it in advance so that you can agree on the amount spent. You might even consider renewing your vows. Maybe you could have a discussion with your partner a few months before your anniversary to decide how you both want to celebrate it.

Think back to the planning, the money, and work that went into your wedding. Think about the vows you made and the commitment you have agreed to uphold for the rest of your life. Recall the sacrament of marriage that you received. How can you let that anniversary date pass without recognizing it in a jubilant way?

Dear Lord, thank you for bringing [*name*] into my life. Thank you for the love we share and the vow we made to each other. Amen.

October 12

Why would you yet be struck, that you continue to rebel?
The whole head is sick, the whole heart faint. From the sole of the
foot to the head there is no sound spot in it; Just bruise and welt
and oozing wound, not drained, or bandaged, or eased with salve.

ISAIAH 1:5–6

A placebo is a medically useless treatment for a condition that is meant
to deceive the patient. A phenomenon called the placebo effect is when
patients who take a placebo without knowing it is fake show signs of improvement. A placebo can be a substance or procedure including pills, creams,
inhalants, injections, sham surgery, and sham acupuncture. Consider if your
marriage is not quite right and might need some special managing. What
kind of treatment could be helpful to get your marriage back on track?

The best thing you can do is pray. The spiritual connection with the Lord
will provide strength, endurance, and enlightenment. Even though you cannot
see this, you must believe that you have a host of angels encircling you and
the Holy Spirit dwelling within you. Schedule time with God to pray and be
still with him. Ask God to bring the right person or the right treatment to
you. Although placebos don't work all of the time, you can always count on
God. Ask and you shall receive.

Invite your spouse to pray with you. Start off with basic prayer, then
advance into a deeper connection by revealing your intimate secret desires
to God. Hold hands while you pray, light a candle, and pray for each other.
Allow this prayer time together to bond you closer to each other and the
Lord. Convey to your partner the desire to improve your relationship and
work harder to overcome any obstacles that might be in your path through
prayer. God loves your mate even more than you do. God could be taking
your partner on a spiritual journey that might deepen his or her faith. God
may choose to reach your spouse through you.

Your mate will benefit from your companionship when you're serious
about your devotion to Christ and realistic about your struggles. You should
not only share your faith with your spouse, but your concerns as well. Seek
guidance from your parish priest if things do not improve. He might be able
to refer you to a nearby marriage support group, such as Third Option, group
or a marriage counselor.

Dear Lord, let me bask in your glory and depend on you to guide each
step I take. Light my path with your brilliance and keep me safe from
the evils of the world. Amen.

October 13

When the evil spirit from God comes upon you,
he will play and you will feel better."
Saul then told his servants,
"Find me a good harpist and bring him to me."
1 Samuel 16:16–17

Music therapy uses all of music's facets: physical, emotional, mental, and spiritual, in order to improve their clients' health. Music therapists help patients' cognitive functioning, motor skills, emotional, social skills, and quality of life through singing, listening to and discussing music, and moving to music to achieve goals. Music therapy is utilized in hospitals, cancer centers, schools, alcohol and drug recovery programs, psychiatric hospitals, and correctional facilities. With so many different groups of people benefitting from music therapy, what could music do for you and your spouse? Reflect on times when music affected your attitude.

Scientists have proven that music relaxes people, inspires, and motivates them. Music can alter your mood positively or negatively, depending on the type of music you listen to. It can raise your serotonin and dopamine levels. It can change your heart rate, respiration, and body temperature. Music equalizes brain waves, fortifies memory and learning, regulates stress-related hormones, stimulates digestion, and boosts immunity. Music is great medicine for both the mind and the soul, but did you know that it can also play a major role in your marriage?

Whatever your marriage difficulty is, you could find help and learn new communication skills by consulting with a music therapist. A music therapist can assess emotional well-being, physical health, social functioning, communication abilities, and cognitive skills through musical responses. Stress reduction can be achieved through drumming, and passive listening improves relaxation. Music is important for physical exercise. It can enhance romance and sexuality.

Consider playing soft music when you pray or try singing your prayers to the Lord. Music in the church is imperative because it becomes a voice to your beliefs. Also, you might be able to remember what you sung in church longer than what was preached: a true picture of God.

Dear Lord, let me lift my voice up to you in song today, rejoicing over the spirit within me. Thank you for my voice, Lord, to call out to you and know that you will hear and answer me. Thank you for giving me the ability to put my words to a melody; a gift I can give to you, recognizing all that you have given to me. Amen.

October 14

Paul warned them, "Men, I can see that this voyage will result in severe
damage and heavy loss not only to the cargo and the ship, but also to
our lives." For last night an angel of the God to whom [I] belong and
whom I serve stood by me and said, 'Do not be afraid, Paul. You are
destined to stand before Caesar; and behold, for your sake, God has
granted safety to all who are sailing with you.' Therefore, keep up your
courage, men; I trust in God that it will turn out as I have been told.
ACTS 27:9–10, 23–25

Columbus Day celebrates Christopher Columbus' arrival in America, which occurred in October 1492. Imagine his spirit and excitement as he embarked on a significant and historic expedition: a voyage across the ocean to an unknown destination he could only dream of. Think back to the excitement you felt as you walked down the aisle after exchanging wedding vows. You were embarking on an incredible journey through life with your spouse as co-captain. Did you expect to live happily ever after, or did you have more realistic expectations of how your married life would unfold? How long did your honeymoon stage last?

Once the honeymoon is over, disillusionment can settle in. Maybe you didn't know your partner as well as you imagined. Even though you might have discussed everything before the wedding, you might be seeing your spouse now in a totally different light. Keep your faith strong through prayer and reading Holy Scripture to continue building a loving relationship with your spouse as you discover who he or she really is.

Think of Christopher Columbus sailing over the vast ocean searching for land. He might have felt discouraged or scared when storms blew in, or maybe he worried about sickness or disease aboard the ship. When he landed on America's shores, imagine how elated he must have been. Marriage has euphoric beauties and unsuspected dangers. Despite diligent efforts to prepare for marriage, you can't possibly know how you're going to adjust until after you have married. When your love is tested by the ordinary familiarity of living together every day, the uniqueness wears off, taking you by surprise.

However, it's important to know that this is a normal stage of marriage. You both need to work together as captains, navigating your ship where you want it to go, taking each other's differences in stride to find peaceable solutions. When times become difficult in your marriage, remember that God sends angels to protect and guide you as you sail.

Dear Lord, take the anxiety from me and stand beside me as I sail along with [*name*]. Calm the rough waters, stabilize our marriage, Lord, so that I can enjoy the journey you meant for us. Amen.

October 15

Two are better than one: They get a good wage for their toil.
If the one falls, the other will help the fallen one. But woe to the
solitary person! If that one should fall, there is no other to help.

ECCLESIASTES 4:9–10

Everyone has a first-aid kit in their homes. Some people have one at their workplace or maybe in their cars, boats, or trailers. People want to be prepared in the event of an emergency. If you experience a crisis in your marriage, consider what is in your marital first-aid kit. If an argument erupts, the first item in your "kit" is the bandage of resuming courteous and honorable treatment. The basics are essential if you want to get your relationship back on track. It's easy to fall off course from time to time. The important thing is to get back up, dust yourself off, assess the situation, and stay committed to your marriage.

Not only is it important to respect yourself, but it is also critical that you show respect to your spouse, especially during times of conflict. Treat your spouse with civility by being genuine. Say what you mean and mean what you say. Listen to your spouse's needs and desires, while keeping an open mind. Be respectful of his or her space, and treat your partner the way you would like to be treated. Although you may desire your mate earning your respect, it's essential to give it to your partner because it is the right thing to do, even if you think he or she doesn't deserve it. Remember that the Lord dwells within your mate and, in effect, you are showing respect to God each time you show respect to your spouse.

Be kind and loving to your partner in both words and actions. While you might be angry at your spouse, upholding your marriage far outweighs whatever happened to fan the flames of your anger. Honor your commitment by standing beside your spouse and working out your problems, whatever they are. There will be ups and downs in your relationship, but get on the same team because together you can get through any challenge.

You also have the right to disagree. Instead of blowing an argument out of proportion, simply agree to disagree. It's much easier and quicker to maintain your own beliefs without damaging your relationship. Express your love for your partner, emotionally and physically. Your marital first-aid kit might also prompt you to say, "I love you," "I'm sorry," and "Let's start over."

Dear Lord, when my marriage gets wounded, help me to reach for the first-aid kit to make it better. I don't want tiny scratches to fester. Teach me how to be healing and soothing. Restore my relationship back to the healthy union you created it to be. Amen.

October 16

For we are God's co-workers; you are God's field, God's building.
According to the grace of God given to me, like a wise master builder
I laid a foundation, and another is building upon it.
But each one must be careful how he builds upon it, for no one can lay
a foundation other than the one that is there, namely, Jesus Christ.

1 CORINTHIANS 3:9–11

A beautifully wrapped package was mailed to me—a gift from a friend. The gift wrap was gorgeous: a shiny metallic paper with sparkles dotted randomly on it. It was tied with a satin ribbon beckoning me to open it. The inside was damaged in the shipping process. I couldn't tell from the outer wrapping of the gift that the inside was a total wreck.

Have you ever compared your marriage to your neighbors or coworkers, thinking their relationship is stronger? You will never know what really goes on in their marriage; it could be discombobulated, like the present that was mailed to me. You just can't tell from the outer appearance. The best thing you can do is stop comparing. Instead, focus on the good aspect of your marriage and build upon the strengths to fortify them. Begin by reaffirming your strong faith in God. Depend on the Lord to give you greater insight, immeasurable courage, and unconditional love.

A healthy marriage has open and honest communication, companionship, and trust. Mixed messages or misunderstandings can be the cause of many marriage problems. A spouse doesn't always know what their partner is thinking, feeling, or trying to say. That's why it's vital to practice reflective listening techniques and to speak lovingly without interruptions.

For a marriage to truly thrive, you must be able to trust your spouse. With faith in one another, you will rise above any anger flare-ups, or other difficulties. Healthy marriages are also built on trust and respect. With trust, you can spend time apart from each other pursuing your own interests, hobbies, or sports. When you reconnect, you will have interesting stories to share that will contribute to your relationship.

A fulfilling marriage requires two people who are willing to invest totally and completely into building themselves and each other into the very best that they can possibly be. Marriage is a powerful connection between two people who genuinely trust one another and want to help their partner achieve their dreams. When you give of yourself to your partner, it is like getting that pretty package in the mail with a glorious gift inside.

Dear Lord, thank you aligning me with [*name*] and enabling me to fortify my marriage through open and honest communication. Thank you for keeping me on track. Amen.

October 17

The LORD said to him: Who gives one person speech?
Who makes another mute or deaf, seeing or blind? Is it not I, the LORD?
Now, go, I will assist you in speaking and teach you what you are to say."
EXODUS 4:11–12

I use a crystal paperweight as a tool to promote taking turns speaking with my spouse. Whoever has the paperweight may speak. Using a tangible tool enables couples the opportunity to listen without worrying about interruptions from their partner. You can use any object: a paperweight, a wooden block, a spoon, a stone, or a cross. The way you talk to your partner says a lot about how you want your relationship to unfold.

Holding an object reminds you to speak gently, using positive language, both honest and respectful. When your spouse sees that you are trying to be courteous, he or she will put forth an effort to be kind to you too. Even if your partner is brutally honest and your feelings are hurt, stay focused on maintaining self-control so that you don't clam up, shout, or swear. You are only responsible for your half of the dialog. How you act might influence how your spouse acts and speaks. If your spouse calls you a "jerk," as tempting as it may be to return the insult, it will unravel your best efforts that you put into the conversation.

Remember to always use an "I statement," which isn't "I think you're a jerk." However, you can say, "I felt sad when I was called a jerk." Before you delve into a heated conversation with your spouse, invoke the Holy Spirit that dwells within you to form the words you speak. God will assist you in speaking and teach you what to say. Could you hold a cross as a speaking tool? That way you know God is there helping you to form your words. Can you imagine having an argument with your spouse in front of God? Remember that God is always with you, even when you are in the midst of a disagreement.

Dear Lord, fill my heart with an abundance of love so that my words are formed there first before I say them. Enable me to speak kindly and lovingly to [name] so that we can resolve our conflict peacefully. Surround us with your serenity so that we can embrace your essence and live the lives you meant for us. Amen.

October 18

*Similarly, an athlete cannot receive the winner's crown
except by competing according to the rules.*

2 TIMOTHY 2:5

When the dishwasher needs to be emptied but no one wants to do it, there is a good chance that someone will put a dirty dish in thinking the dishwasher needs to be run. It's so exasperating when that happens. I implemented a rule to prevent that from reoccurring in my house. When the dishes are clean, a dishtowel is placed on top of the dishes. Rules or policies are good to have to keep order in the home. Do you have any established strategies in your relationship that work?

When faced with divvying the household chores, if you and your spouse are unable to agree on who does what, have the wife make the final decisions about the inside of the home and the husband have the final say about the outside of the home. How do you and your spouse split the chores?

When it comes to in-laws, try having each spouse be responsible for his or her own parents or family. When my family visits, I do all of the work. When my husband's family visits, he does all of the work. If we decide we want to help each other out, it is purely optional. When it comes to disagreements with family, the same rule applies: if my family is involved, I defend; if his family is involved, he defends. And what happens within the marriage stays within the marriage. Dragging family into marriage problems is never a good thing to do.

How do you decide how much time is allocated to spend with your friends alone without your spouse? One policy option could be to mutually decide how much time each month can be spent alone, with friends, or with each other. It might be wise to have a rule against going out with friends of the opposite sex unless your spouse is included in the plans.

If you advocate establishing ground rules, you might consider one that states you must work out disagreements so that you don't go to bed angry. You may have to iron out any details in the morning, but at least having the rule allows you to practice being forgiving to allow you both a good night's rest. Setting ground rules is a shared agreement to behave in a certain way for the good of the marriage. If you don't have any policies in your marriage, what one policy would you consider implementing?

Dear Lord, thank you for giving me the wisdom I need to decide between what rules I should or should not have. Thank you for letting [*name*] be creative with how we should manage our marriage in your constant stream of never-ending love. Amen.

October 19

He said: "O LORD, my rock, my fortress, my deliverer,
my God, my rock of refuge! My shield, my saving horn,
my stronghold, my refuge, my savior, from violence you keep me safe.
Praised be the LORD, I exclaim! I have been delivered from my enemies.

2 SAMUEL 22:2–4

In ancient Egypt, the parasol was fashioned in a variety of shapes. Some were merely a fan of palm leaves or colored feathers secured on a handle meant to offer shade. A parasol refers to protection from the sun while an umbrella is a waterproof shield from the rain. Protection from the blistering hot sun or drenching rain is paramount.

God is a protector far greater than a parasol or umbrella. God's protection is like a spiritual covering, providing you abide by his ways. Imagine standing under an umbrella in a downpour, symbolizing God's loving shield over you, keeping you dry. The Lord's protection is a place of safety and blessings. When you step away from the umbrella, it emphasizes that you can remove yourself from God's protective covering whenever you step outside of his will. Don't turn your back on God and his guidelines for living. Don't place yourself in harm's way, allowing the devil to cause destruction.

Never utter the word "divorce," because it is not an option. Don't tempt yourself by walking away from God or your spouse. God brought your spouse into your life for a reason, even if you don't know what it is. Even if you cannot understand it, trust that God has a wonderful plan for you, but you must follow his ways, not your own. If you follow your own agenda, you are in effect stepping away from the Lord's loving shield over you. It is as if you are walking in a rainstorm without an umbrella, wondering why you are soaked to the bone, freezing cold, and unable to find your way.

While it might be tempting to give up on your marriage, remember your vow to your spouse that you made in the presence of the Lord. Honor your promise. Use your commitment as momentum to keep going, keep searching, continue loving unconditionally, the way God meant for you. You can do anything with God. Align yourself with him by praying constantly. Even if all you can utter is, "God, help me!" Say it, because God hears your cries. He knows your pain and he will shelter you. He will guide you and tell you what to do. Listen for his voice in the quiet of your heart.

Dear Lord, Lift me up to a place of tranquility because I need to rest in your loving care. Brush the sadness away from me. Keep me out of harm's way. Tell me what to do. I trust you, Lord, with every breath I take. Amen.

October 20

It is this disciple who testifies to these things and has written them, and we know that his testimony is true. There are also many other things that Jesus did, but if these were to be described individually, I do not think the whole world would contain the books that would be written.

JOHN 21:24–25

The first libraries contained clay tablets in cuneiform script dating back to 2600 BC. Today, the library has an organized assortment of information, resources, and books available for communities to borrow. Most people use their local library to borrow books and then return them in good condition. Our time on earth is borrowed and everyone is responsible to return it in good condition back to God. Consider the care you give to your married life knowing that you need to be accountable for it.

You could practice accountability in your marriage through your spirituality. Make prayer time a part of your daily routine, just as brushing your teeth is part of your dental hygiene habit. Having a devoted spouse who cares about you going to heaven, who encourages your devotion to God, and wants to connect with you spiritually, is a gift. Initiate thought-provoking dialog with your mate by opening with remarks such as "What has God been teaching you lately?" or "What is weighing heavy on your heart that you pray about?" Couples who pray together routinely have an accountability mechanism in place.

In addition to your faithfulness to God and to each other, your loyalty to your spouse regarding sexual devotion to him or her is critical. Do not risk inappropriate intimacy with someone of the opposite sex, especially on business trips. Temptations and moral struggles should be dealt with utmost concern to keep your marriage on course. Secrets divide couples; accountability keeps them from ruining your marriage.

Consider how you accept accountability to your partner for your parenting skills. Most people rely on the techniques modeled for them by their parents. Discuss the parenting styles you think are best for your family, including ways you can sharpen your particular parenting styles. If you notice any good tendencies you can encourage those and help each other improve any poor trends. Don't undermine your partner. Instead, be his or her ally, back each other up. Parenting is a hard job, one God didn't intend for you to do alone. Now, consider how accountable of a spouse are you?

Dear Lord, it isn't easy being accountable, especially at times when I feel like hiding. Build me up, Lord, and help me in my desperation. I want to be a responsible spouse. I ask this in your name. Amen.

October 21

They promise them freedom, though they themselves are slaves of corruption,
for a person is a slave of whatever overcomes him. For if they, having
escaped the defilements of the world through the knowledge of [our] Lord
and savior Jesus Christ, again become entangled and overcome by them,
their last condition is worse than their first. For it would have been better
for them not to have known the way of righteousness than after knowing
it to turn back from the holy commandment handed down to them.

2 PETER 2:19–21

X-rays are special invisible waves that are used to allow doctors to see the bones inside their patients' body for diagnostic purposes. While x-rays are a magnificent tool for identifying illness or fractures, too much radiation can actually be harmful. Consider what element in your marriage requires a gentle balance, because too much of something could be detrimental to your union.

Consider if control is equally distributed between you and your spouse. Do you ever feel as if your spouse is too controlling? There is no room for a controlling spouse in your marriage. Assert yourself to take control back. Be in charge of your life. Consider what is out of control in your world. Is spending money out of control? If money is causing marriage difficulties, hire a financial planner to make a budget; then stick to it!

Is your job controlling you? Talk to your manager to take on fewer assignments or reduce your time at the office so that you are home more. Are your children running your life? If so, outline all of the activities that are too time-consuming and consider eliminating some. Is time a factor in your feelings of loss of control? Many people wish for more time in each day, but the fact remains that there is only so much that you can do in twenty-four hours. Pick and choose wisely the activities that stay and the ones that must go. Life can be defined by the decisions that you make.

Reflect on other factors that may be controlling you. Is your spouse obviously too controlling by stepping over your choices and decisions to get his or her way? If so, assert yourself to take control back. However, your spouse could also be controlling you subtly by being overly helpful. For instance, if you are driving to a new location, your spouse may decide to drive you instead of allowing you to figure it out on your own accord. Have an open and honest discussion with your spouse to discover what is really going on in your relationship so that you can fix it, nurture it, and watch it flourish again.

Dear Lord, scoop me up into your loving embrace and fill me with the courage I need to assert myself in my relationship with [*name*]. Caress me with your healing touch so that I can take control back and live my life the way you intended. Amen.

October 22

When Haman entered, the king said to him, "What should be done
for the man whom the king wishes to reward?" Now Haman thought
to himself, "Whom would the king wish to honor more than me?"
So he replied to the king: "For the man whom the king wishes to honor
there should be brought the royal robe the king wore and the horse
the king rode with the royal crest placed on its head. The robe and
the horse should be given to one of the noblest of the king's officials,
who must clothe the man the king wishes to reward, have him ride
on the horse in the public square of the city, and cry out before him,
"This is what is done for the man whom the king wishes to honor!"'

ESTHER 6:6–9

Have you ever yelled across a crowd of people, waving your hand, to
someone you thought you knew, only you discover he wasn't who you
thought he was? It's embarrassing to speak to someone you think you know
but discover it was a case of mistaken identity. Mistaken identity is used as
a defense in criminal law claiming the innocence of a criminal defendant by
undermining evidence by proclaiming that an eyewitness erroneously thought
that they saw the defendant, when the eyewitness actually saw someone else.

Have you ever looked at your spouse and wondered, "Who are you?"
When couples exchange wedding vows, they believe they really know the
person they are marrying, when in reality there is so much they don't know.
Committed love requires work believing that there is no such thing as a
"right person." The presence of sin in the world guarantees there are no 100
percent "right people." When you married your spouse, you hoped he or she
was somewhat compatible.

What is more beautifully accurate is the biblical image of marriage because it portrays two imperfect people committing themselves to each other
until death. They commit to do the sanctifying work of expressing Jesus's
self-sacrificial love so that they might witness their spouse transforming into
the person God has always intended them to be. When you and your spouse
make this commitment, you will experience unbelievably divine marital
intimacy. In addition, you both will become more forgiving, more sensitive,
more loving, and more truthful.

Dear Lord, teach me how to be relentlessly committed to this task with
[name]. Help me to grow into a better person, a better partner. I'm
truly excited, Lord, to see the person you are transforming me into. I'm
truly thankful that I have the honor of sharing it with [name]. Amen.

October 23

Then the eyes of both of them were opened, and they knew that they were naked; so they sewed fig leaves together and made loincloths for themselves.

GENESIS 3:7

Have you ever examined a shirt to see how it was made? Fabric is cut to the dimensions of a shirt pattern. The pattern is pinned to the material and then cut out. One seem is sewn together at a time. Within a few hours, a simple piece of material can be marvelously fashioned into wearable clothing by a seamstress. Non-sewers can still make a shirt, but it will take considerably more time, and there could be flaws in the finished product. Practice makes perfect when it comes to sewing.

Consider what aspects of your marriage might need to be transformed or sewn together with a stronger thread. Married couples are more likely to be happy with their relationship if they both continue educating themselves about marriage, learning new skills, and enriching and nurturing their relationship. It is vital couples learn how to reach decisions harmoniously and communicate effectively with one another and other family members. It is also imperative that their positive actions speak louder than their words.

Many couples settle for mediocrity in their marriage when they would never settle for second best in other areas of their lives. Contemplate if you want a marriage that is a true union of souls with a connection of love, respect, romance, and spiritual oneness. It's possible to build such a relationship. You can create an intimate marriage by fostering affection, warmth, and encouragement. It sounds easy, but with many demands on your time and energy, couples often neglect their relationship first.

This can be accomplished by implementing rules that cater to your specific needs: a date night each week, being away from home two nights a week, and prayer time together even if it's over the phone. Other couples may require a different plan, with five or ten different principles. Just like sewing a shirt, some people might pick fabric with a print or solid color with varying trim; the point is to be intentional about your marriage to make it a priority.

While you are working to build a stronger marriage, you might need to adjust your attitude. You cannot change your spouse, only yourself. Therefore, make a concentrated effort to show affection and warmth. A simple gesture, such as a loving smile, can change your spouse's mood and the atmosphere in your home. When your spouse walks in the door, stop what you are doing, and shower him or her with affection. Can you make changes like these?

Dear Lord, teach me ways to draw [*name*] closer to me through prayer and affectionate words and touch. Let me lose my bad attitude and replace it with affection, warmth, encouragement, and respect. Amen.

October 24

There is a correlation between owning a dog and reducing the risk of cardiovascular problems, including high blood pressure and elevated cholesterol levels. Having a dog may be an important coping mechanism for people suffering with anxiety. Therapy dogs can expedite a patients' healing process from a severe illness or prolonged hospitalization. Service dogs assist people with various disabilities accomplish everyday tasks and reduce dependence on others. If you are a dog lover, consider emulating some of their traits and dispositions.

Do you greet your spouse with excitement, overlook his or her flaws, and easily forgive bad behavior? Everyone has much to learn about how people love their pets. People describe pets as undemanding while providing unconditional love. The reality is that pets require much time, attention, special foods, and care. Dogs ruin furniture, leave "messes" in the house, and steal food from countertops. Yet dog owners accept their pets' flaws because we love them like a member of the family.

Even on bad days, people greet their pets with a happy greeting, and usually a pat on the head or a hug. Do you greet your spouse that way? Reflect on the way you say "good morning" or "hello." Can you put more enthusiasm into your spouse's greetings this week? Consider if you hold grudges against your partner. Would you hold a grudge against your pet for wrecking the furniture or soiling the floor? Why then would you ever think of holding a grudge against your spouse? Do you assuming the best with your mate? If your pet made a mistake, you wouldn't take it personally, and chances are good that you would forgive the dog. People tend to give pets the benefit of the doubt. Yet if your spouse does something wrong, do you react with anger and blame? Perhaps people give rather positively to their pet, summoning unconditional love and a connection that makes people feel good. I think everyone can learn something from this: we all have the potential to improve our relationship. What will you do today to enhance your marriage to make it more desirable? Barking is not allowed!

Dear Lord, thank you for providing us with pets. I have learned so much from them. And now I will think of an excited dog greeting his master at the end of a long day, which is how I plan to welcome my spouse home. I will recall a dog when offering unconditional love and forgiveness. Thank you, dear Lord, for the dogs that roam the earth. Amen.

October 25

The young men who had grown up with him replied, "This is what you must say to this people who have told you, 'Your father made our yoke heavy; you lighten it for us.' You must say, 'My little finger is thicker than my father's loins. My father put a heavy yoke on you, but I will make it heavier. My father beat you with whips, but I will beat you with scorpions.'"
1 KINGS 12:10–11

In ancient times, the wind was harnessed to provide power to grind grain between stones to create flour. The windmill converted the energy of wind into rotational energy through sails and can be adapted for other uses, such as mining groundwater. The idea of harnessing the wind presented people the ability to diversify and develop the technology. Consider where the power in your marriage comes from. Think back to recent arguments to clarify which one of you wins them. Is your spouse more powerful and you feel powerless or vice versa? How do you try to get power back? If only there could be a windmill in your relationship that you both could regulate!

Consider this: when one of you wins an argument, you both lose. The only way for you and your spouse to win together is for you to both get on the same team. Your success depends on cooperation. When you argue with your spouse, a common reaction is to blame him or her. You could be overlooking your role in the situation, hindering any possibility for growth and chance for lasting happiness in your relationship. Therefore, look within first. Remember that you can't change or fix your partner; you can only change and fix yourself. Start with introspection.

Do you go along with what your mate says or does just to "get along?" Think clearly and rationally by compromising or taking turns instead of giving in to your spouse. Do not set ultimatums on your marriage unless it is the only option left to you and it is something you absolutely mean. This would be important if your rights were being violated. For example, if your spouse forbid you attending Mass. With an ultimatum you need to follow through with it, so be absolutely certain it is what you want to do.

Don't blow a riff out of proportion or allow it to escalate. If this happens, take a step back. If you can't control outside matters, can you take control of yourself? Be determined to gain insights on how to avoid situations and make improvements so that it doesn't reoccur. Think about how you can redirect your energies in better ways to attain the life you want and deserve to have.

Dear Lord, encourage and remind me that everything happens for a reason. Help me to consciously find that reason or to accept that you meant for it and I need to trust in you more. Amen.

October 26

Then he had another dream, and told to his brothers.
"Look, I had another dream," he said; "this time, the sun
and the moon and eleven stars were bowing down to me."

GENESIS 37:9

Daydreaming provides your working memory with a workout. Working memory is the place in your brain that allows it to juggle multiple thoughts simultaneously. If you have a large working memory, you can daydream more without forgetting the task you were doing. For example, the plans you make while taking a walk or while showering are aided by working memory. Off-topic thoughts can become the main topic if your mind runs out of working memory without a conscious effort. An example of this is realizing that you didn't comprehend several pages you just read in a book because you were more absorbed in daydreaming. Consider if stress could be impairing your working memory.

Do you think you work better under pressure? You might work better under the pressure of a deadline, but with severe stress in times of a marriage crisis, cognitive performance crumbles. When you become stressed, your body releases cortisol, a stress hormone, which causes changes in the brain. Excessive amounts of cortisol can prevent you from forming new memories in addition to increasing your inability to retrieve existing memories. When couples are in the midst of marital distress, they might not be able to resolve their problems as well as they think they can. The next time you run into conflict with your spouse, remember to pray first. God can release you from the agony you feel when your mind races. Prayer and meditation can help you to refocus. Remove yourself from a stressful situation so you can sit alone in peace and quiet to listen to God. He will tell you what to say and do.

Do not worry if you daydream periodically. It has been associated with creativity; your most inventive moments come through daydreaming and the most intelligent people have high levels of working memory.

Dear Lord, don't let bad thoughts creep into my mind and pollute all the goodness in it. Take away the evil thoughts if they are not from you and clear a path for your words and wisdom, which is exactly what I need. Lift the stress from my shoulders, and let me find refuge in your kindness and mercy. Flush the cortisol out of my brain and replace it with an unending stream of your love. Amen.

October 27

Do not worry about tomorrow; tomorrow will take care of itself.
Sufficient for a day is its own evil.
MATTHEW 6:34

In the late autumn, my pear tree was laden with crimson foliage that flew off with a vengeance, dancing across the lawn in the crisp breeze. By nightfall the bereft tree was barren, standing like a tall skeleton in the moon glow. The next morning snow blanketed the tree, giving it a totally new appearance. What a difference a day makes. Today your marriage might feel like it is heaven blessed, but tomorrow you could feel like you are living in a war zone. Most brides and grooms that walk down the aisle hope love will make their marriage last forever, but most realize they need something more.

How can you concentrate on your marriage one day at a time instead of worrying about what tomorrow will bring? While it's good to be hopeful that love will make your marriage last, it's wise to cultivate a friendship with your partner to sustain your marriage. When bad habits surface, it might be shocking. Deal with them the way you would with any friend, remembering that no one is perfect, no marriage is perfect. Sort it out through negotiations and compromises.

Once you bring children into your family, attitudes tend to change. Sometimes one spouse might lose interest in their mate, putting the child's needs as a top priority. Distance gets created between couples when they lose sight of who they are. You can be a wife or husband first, parent second. If this happens, take control back and nurture your marriage. Have a discussion with your spouse about how you want to raise your family. Keep the lines of communication open so that resentments won't have room to grow or escalate. Check in with each other from time to time to keep ahead of problems that sneak in when bringing up children. It might not be a bad idea to lower the bar, because you might be less disappointed if you can roll with the changes that marriage brings, and manage your expectations.

What troublesome worries are preventing you from living fully with your partner? Each day you have with your spouse is a gift from God. What will you do today to make it wonderful?

Dear Lord, ease my worrisome heart and carry my burdens so that I don't have to. Teach me to focus on the goodness in my midst, my holy union with you and my spouse. Help me to make the best of each day and to find the goodness that is tucked so sweetly inside. Enable me to find it, cherish it, and uphold it in your glory. Amen.

October 28

Again, [amen], I say to you, if two of you agree on earth about anything for which they are to pray, it shall be granted to them by my heavenly Father. For where two or three are gathered together in my name, there am I in the midst of them.

MATTHEW 18:19–20

Influenza can cause death. Every flu season healthy people become ill and spread it to others. People need to get vaccinated against it. Wouldn't it be nice to get a vaccination against marriage difficulties? There is something you can do to give your relationship a shot in the arm: pray together. Couples who pray together, stay together.

Praying with your spouse creates a dramatic effect in building oneness and intimacy in your marriage. God desires couples to pray together because it unites them spiritually. Prayer bonds a couple together in agreement as they make petitions to the Lord. Their hearts align as they focus on a common goal when making requests of God. If you and your spouse long to be of one heart, start praying together. To have a profound relationship that is truly substantial and spiritually cohesive, you and your mate need to pray together.

Unity of heart requires humility, a willingness to bear your soul before your mate and before God by being open, vulnerable, and sincere. Don't be afraid to acknowledge any weakness or need to one another. When your spouse knows your heart and the problems that weigh it down, it draws you both together as one. Good communication is essential for a healthy marriage. When you pray you might reveal intimate secrets to God that you might not reveal to your spouse casually. Prayer together reveals the deepest inner workings of your heart, giving your partner greater insight into who you both really are. This type of pure, open, and honest communication is a gift from God. When you pray together, communicating your common needs before God, you will experience a closer camaraderie and confidence than ever before. The closer you get to God, the closer you'll be to each other.

Reflect on the last problem you solved through prayer. If you haven't tried it before, do it now because it's not too late. The moment you recognize a difficulty, pray together. Even if you don't feel like it, prayer can energize your spirit and fortify your soul. People remember to take care of their bodies by eating and sleeping right, exercising, and getting a flu shot, but neglect their soul. How can you and your spouse nurture your souls?

Dear Lord, keep me well and mindful to pray constantly. With you in my life, everything will be right. I love you. Amen.

October 29

Ah! Those who call evil good, and good evil, who change darkness into light, and light into darkness, who change bitter to sweet, and sweet into bitter!

ISAIAH 5:20

Have you ever played with shadows by making hand puppets? It's entertaining to look for something that isn't really there. Are there other optical illusions in your life? Perhaps you have used some form of trickery in your marriage: dishonesty, delusions, or cheating. Were you deceitful about a friendship that is more than a friend? Do you visit questionable websites that are out of your character? Reflect on past hurts you might have caused through sneaky, deceptive behaviors and plausible reparations you could make. Ask God to empower you to be able to convert dishonest behaviors into honorable ones.

Reflect on the day you made your marriage vows; remember how strongly you felt about them. Try to recapture some of those feelings in an effort to fill your mind and heart with all that is good, honest, and just. Don't even think "divorce," because it is not an option. Why tease yourself with something that can only bring pain and heartbreak when you have within your reach all that you need to mend your relationship? With God, anything is possible.

Perhaps your children are more independent, and you have more free time. This phase of your life can provide an opportunity for an affair. Many people cultivate a physical affair or an "affair of the mind" at some point in their marriage. Nonetheless, don't be one of them. An affair of the mind can occur anywhere, but more so in the workplace where coworkers become confidantes, cultivate crushes on each other, and share secrets. Have you lied to yourself about a colleague recently?

If you are inclined to do this, or if you have contemplated an affair, stop and pray the temptations away. Instead, invite your spouse to dinner via text or e-mail. Send a card reminding him or her how much you appreciate the small things he or she does. Even if you cannot think of one good thing to say, remember that you thought of him or her. That alone might make your partner happy. If you miss the closeness you once had, improve things by spending time with each other. Tell your spouse you miss the closeness and ask what you can do to rekindle the flames that once fanned your love. Make the first step toward your spouse. It might be the best thing you do today.

Dear Lord, shine your light into my life, removing any possibilities of illusions. Flood my soul with your spirit. Help me to make amends and build my marriage into a better, stronger union, the one you meant for it to be. Allow my life to be a radiance of yours. With you, I can do anything. Amen.

October 30

If the one falls, the other will help the fallen one. But woe to the
solitary person! If that one should fall, there is no other to help.
So also, if two sleep together, they keep each other warm.
How can one alone keep warm? Where one alone may be overcome,
two together can resist. A three-ply cord is not easily broken.
ECCLESIASTES 4:10–12).

Pumpkins can be made into pies, cookies, pancakes, ice cream, and even beer! But this delicious vegetable is also carved and illuminated each Halloween, delighting both young and old. Pumpkins adorn fall festivals, are used as table decorations, and filled with flowers. Pumpkins are versatile. Think about all of the wonderful and versatile aspects of marriage: a friend and companion, sounding board, someone to care for, share meals with, cry with, pray with, and volunteer with.

While you and your partner are on a life-long journey together, when was the last time you traveled to an exciting destination together? Consider planning now for a vacation you might take next spring to celebrate your anniversary. Stepping away from a boring routine can kick-start your relationship. Perhaps an off-season vacation can be a meaningful adventure that brings you closer together through shared experiences: navigating through a different city or state, deciphering maps or road signs.

Agree with your partner ahead of time on what kind of travel accommodations you are both comfortable with. It will establish the budget of the trip. Be prepared to compromise or take turns deciding on activities. You could establish policies in advance before taking a trip. For instance, whoever is driving gets to choose the music you listen to or whoever copilots selects the snacks. Decide ahead of time who is packing and loading the car. Establish guidelines regarding calling the office and staying connected to work before you leave.

Prioritize together the attractions that you absolutely want to see and what you can afford. Try to be flexible. Rushing from one place to another can be stressful. God gave you an amazing gift in your spouse. Whatever your reason is for being married, think about how much you value your spouse as a traveling companion through life.

Dear Lord, guide our journey. Take us down the right roads, the ones you want us to travel. Bless us, Lord as we take the bumps and sharp turns of the busy highways of life. Thank you for allowing me to share my life with [*name*] because it is more rewarding, enjoyable, and complete. You know what's best for me, and I trust in you completely. Amen.

October 31

His confidence is but a gossamer thread, his trust is a spider's house
JOB 8:14

S piders are drained of enormous energy when building a web. They use vast amounts of protein to form silk. Because the strength of spider silk is greater than the same weight of steel with greater elasticity, researchers scrutinize it for possible uses, including bulletproof vests and artificial tendons.

Have you felt exhausted repairing one aspect of your relationship, but discovered another benefit of it? Perhaps in developing conflict resolution skills, you discovered better ways to convey your thoughts and feeling by using a rating scale or analogies. Teachers use analogies as a powerful technique in the classroom and surveyors use rating scales to judge customer priorities because they are quick and easy to understand. These two simple methodologies might make conflict resolution doable. It's understandable to avoid conflict in your marriage, but if you continue to circumvent a confrontation, your chances are good that you may not develop effective strategies to resolve your differences.

If you encounter a disagreement with your spouse, do not give in to his or her ways because it's easier to give up than fight. You don't have to fight; you can work through steps to manage your differences. The next time an argument ensues, don't sweep it under the rug or run away, hoping it will resolve itself, or act like a dictator to get your way. Remember the ground rules to conflict resolution: stick to one issue, don't dredge up the past, don't blame each other, set down your swords, and attack the problem, not your spouse. The process begins with honest and open communication and reflective listening skills. Define the problem; write it down if necessary. Be creative, listing possible solutions regardless of whether you like them. Turn it into a game by seeing who can draft a bigger list of options to consider. Then, together list pros and cons to each solution before choosing one.

In working through the steps to resolve your conflict, maybe you discovered you are a great listener. Perhaps you have appreciated the quality time you reserve to reflect, regroup, and rebuild each day. God has woven many gifts, talents, and miniature miracles throughout your life. What are yours?

Dear Lord, thank you for your generous, loving touch. Thank you for showing me the silver lining in each dark cloud that looms overhead. I once felt only heavy, cold raindrops, but now I see the rainbow and a hint of sunshine peeking through. Thank you for transforming my heart with your warmth. Amen.

November 1

In my thoughts during visions of the night, when deep sleep falls on mortals,
Fear came upon me, and shuddering, that terrified me to the bone.
JOB 4:13–14

The right mattress can determine if you have a good night's sleep and wake up refreshed and feeling rested, or if you endure sleeplessness, back pain, and body aches. It's critical for some people with back problems to have a good-fitting mattress so that their pain doesn't worsen. What can you do preventively in your marriage to ensure it remains healthy? Make every minute count. If you learned that you only had one more day left to live, how would you treat your spouse? Consider how often you might say, "I love you." Consider other compliments you would give. You never know for certain what day will be your last; treat each new day that you have with your partner as if it's the last. Be more affectionate, loving, and nurturing. As your body needs nutritious meals to survive, your marriage needs frequent doses of affection to grow. Question if your spouse could be starving for affection.

Affection is an essential way to connect with your spouse involving expressions that result in feelings of closeness, passion, and security. God created you with a need to belong and to give and receive love. However, there is a difference between healthy and unhealthy needs. Healthy needs include the desire to be understood and accepted for who you are without criticism. It implies a responsibility to be loved for affection and intimacy, with a yearning to feel safe from emotional or physical harm. Unhealthy needs involve controlling your spouse in order to get your own way. You can't change your spouse; however, you can change yourself by augmenting your expectations.

Tell your spouse each day what you're thankful for in your marriage. Also, tell God what you're thankful for. God can meet all of your needs. Pray about improvements you'd like to see in your marriage and trust God to help you. Can you spend more quality time together with your spouse in prayer? How can you enhance your devotion, loyalty, and dependability to your spouse?

If something is keeping you up at night, talk to God about it. As important as a good mattress is, it's wiser to have a clear conscious. Whatever is weighing heavy on your heart, give those qualms to God and trust that he will resolve everything; he is more knowledgeable than you.

Dear Lord, take my problems and tell me what to do. I long for a peaceful relationship with you and my partner. Allow tranquil sleep to come easily each night wrapped in your endless love. Amen.

November 2

He also said to the crowds, "When you see [a] cloud rising in the west you say immediately that it is going to rain—and so it does; and when you notice that the wind is blowing from the south you say that it is going to be hot—and so it is. You hypocrites! You know how to interpret the appearance of the earth and the sky; why do you not know how to interpret the present time? Why do you not judge for yourselves what is right?"

LUKE 12:54–57

The weatherman is wrong nearly 50 percent of the time, and yet people depend of their knowledge of weather patterns and expertise in the field of meteorology. What other occupation could you work in with such poor results and still be well-thought of? What would your marriage be like if you were not committed 100 percent of the time? Are you giving your marriage 100 percent loyalty and devotion? Consider if you show selfless affection for your mate. Do you have qualities of loyalty, kindness, and faithfulness to your partner?

Because of many different obligations, you might pour yourself into them and leave your marriage last to receive whatever energy is leftover. If your marriage is last on the list, what state is it in? Ponder if you make your children's activities a priority over your marriage. You might have school functions, sports, or parties to tend to. When making your weekly plans, schedule quality time to tend to your marriage first by scheduling dates to go out or stay home and spend time together doing something you both enjoy. Make your marriage a priority by nurturing each other now similarly to the way you acted when you started dating each other. God created marriage so try to hold it up to an esteemed place in your life.

If you feel pulled by your children's commitments because you want to give them the best, consider how important it is for you and your spouse to model a loving couple and congenial family. What distinguishes one student from another is their ability to relate amiably to others. Your well-balanced marriage centered on God will influence children who are able to make the world a better place to live and thrive. God provided a wonderful system to produce and raise children to love, honor, and serve him. Imagine your marriage and home as an evangelism tool. Devote yourself to your marriage and reap the fruits of your labors.

Change isn't easy; therefore, give yourself time to adjust slowly to making your marriage a top priority by giving it 100 percent. Include more prayer through your transition by asking God to help you.

Dear Lord, sometimes I feel a storm brewing and I fear its fury. Flood my relationship with your glorious brightness and warmth. Elevate my spirits, and shine your face on my life for now and always. Amen.

November 3

Let them be yours alone, not shared with outsiders;
Let your fountain be blessed and have joy of the wife of your youth,
your lovely hind, your graceful doe. Of whose love you will ever
have your fill, and by her ardor always be intoxicated.

PROVERBS 5:17–19

The white-tailed deer has protective coloring to enable it to hide in brush and undergrowth. The color of its fur is gray in the winter, and more red emerges during the summer. The ability to blend into its surroundings is a gift God gave these creatures to survive. Have you and your spouse blended talents, traditions, or ethnic cultures to adapt into your communities and how well has that worked? While this could present difficulties to accommodate you and your spouse's desires, anticipate it with excitement, for you will be creating something unique to your own family. Even if your family unit consists of just you and your spouse, the size doesn't matter. If your spouse's family always served a chestnut stuffing on Thanksgiving, and your family always served an apple stuffing, create your own stuffing recipe, or don't make any at all. Make your own traditions.

Ponder if you appreciate, celebrate, and learn from your differences. Perhaps your partner is a socialite and you are an introvert; you can rely on each other for balance in both areas to keep your relationship harmonious. God gave you the ability to learn from each other to grow and adapt in different circumstances. Reflect on other areas where you can blend talents to maintain equilibrium in your marriage.

Compatibility is not measured by how many things you have in common, but is measured by how you resolve the things that you don't have in common. Consider how willing you and your mate are to resolving your differences. This enthusiasm is what will make you compatible with your spouse. You can choose to work as a unit to blend your differences, create something new, or alternate. Sometimes, the most important things in life come down to a series of choices. Choices are good. Imagine going to a restaurant where there is only one item on the menu with no choices.

You also must decide whether or not you are willing to choose what pleases God as it connects to the struggles you might be experiencing with your spouse. Are you willing to do what God wants of you?

Dear Lord, thank you for my spouse's differences. I can learn from them and grow into a well-rounded individual. You blessed us both with countless talents and gifts; for them I am eternally grateful. Amen.

November 4

The crucible for silver, and the furnace for gold,
but the tester of hearts is the LORD.

PROVERBS 17:3

Gold is highly valued in society. It's symbolic of power, strength, wealth, happiness, love, justice, intelligence, and perfection. Great human achievements are often rewarded with gold in the form of medals, trophies, and other decorations. When you initially married, was your union as precious as gold, but now it's not so much? Ponder what has changed in your relationship or what has changed in your life. Consider whether marital hardships have fallen on you and you are struggling with them. How do you cope with your difficulties?

When gold is tested in the fire, it changes by melting. Silver and gold are made pure by melting them down with intense heat. When the precious metals are melted, impurities float to the surface and can be skimmed off the top. You might be experiencing a fiery trial in your marriage, but this hardship could transform your heart into something more pure. God burns all of the impurities out of you and makes you clean and wholesome before him.

You don't really know your heart thoroughly nor can you search your spouse's heart; only God knows them, tries them, and purifies them. Gold also must be purified by the action of the fire. God tries hearts. He sends afflictions that can penetrate your soul, and convince you to see his way. God destroys what cannot withstand the fire, as a means to separate the good from the bad and incinerate the trash, leaving all that is good, true, and pure.

Consider if you or your spouse has become more powerful. Who seems to be always winning arguments in your marriage? When one of you wins, you both lose. How can you work toward a win-win situation each time there is a disagreement? Try cooperating with each other. Be supportive of each other the way you used to be before you got married. Don't sabotage your relationship by getting even with your spouse because that just digs you deeper into a hole that you may not be able to climb out of. Jesus didn't teach to seek revenge; he taught love and forgiveness.

What can you do to ensure you both make it into your golden years together? Perhaps you could spend more time in prayer, reading the Bible, and revisit the Ten Commandments.

Dear Lord, sometimes I see my partner as an enemy; therefore, I will love [name] as I love myself. Whenever I struggle to forgive, I will remember what Jesus said as he hung on the cross, "Forgive them." I will look at my problems the way Christ looked at his: through love. Amen.

November 5

When a man makes a vow to the LORD or binds himself
under oath to a pledge, he shall not violate his word,
but must fulfill exactly the promise he has uttered.

NUMBERS 30:3

Cardboard signs litter lawns, boasting the best candidate for Republicans and Democrats. TV reports and commercials are swamped with smear campaign tactics that worsen as election day arrives. Most people vote for their candidate knowing that they probably won't keep their promises. Imagine making your marriage vow knowing your spouse might not keep their promise to you. Promises mean a great deal, but if they are broken, it is not the end of the world, even if it feels that way. Have you broken a promise to your mate? Humans are bound to make mistakes.

Perhaps your spouse didn't follow through with an intention, or said one thing and did another. Breaking promises shatters emotional and physical intimacy in your relationship. Do you or your spouse have a negative attitude, struggle to keep a job, become verbally abusive, or drink or spend excessively? Such behaviors could devastate your marriage. Coping in these situations can be difficult if only one of you wants change.

Ask God to help you with endurance to tolerate. You cannot change your spouse, but you can change yourself, your thoughts, and reactions. It's possible that your spouse will make changes once he or she notices your modifications. Examine your attitudes and behaviors and evaluate your expectations, hopes, concerns, and fears. Contemplate what you will do if your marriage doesn't improve. Consult with your parish priest and seek counseling to understand your role in the marital discord. Assess which of your spouse's undesirable actions you can accept and which are intolerable.

Remember what you love about your partner and convey that as you express your concerns and fears about the future of your marriage. Invite your spouse to begin an open conversation to confront the issues that are bothersome, mindful of your role in it. Do you need to seek or offer forgiveness? Do you hold a grudge or forgive too easily? Forgiveness is a process; therefore, resume respectful treatment and initiate honest communication focusing on reconciliation. Consider heartfelt contemplations and receiving the sacrament of reconciliation as you attempt to heal your relationship.

Dear Lord, take my pain, and rectify the wrongs. Fill me with your love and mercy. Teach me how to be more loving and accepting of my spouse's shortcomings, and enable him or her to take mine. You brought us together for a reason, sweet Lord. Don't let us drift apart. I ask this in your holiness. Amen.

November 6

"Bad, bad!" says the buyer, then goes away only to boast.
One can put on gold and abundant jewels, but wise lips are the
most precious ornament. Take the garment of the one who became
surety for a stranger; if for foreigners, exact the pledge!
PROVERBS 20:14–16

With the impending holiday season, it's tempting to get caught up in the Christmas shopping frenzy. There are sale fliers stuffed in your mailbox, newspapers are filled with sale ads, and TV commercials boast one commercial after another prodding you off the sofa and into their store. Christmas is not an excuse to shop till you drop. Consider if you are a compulsive spender, addicted to shopping. Do you shop online as well as in stores, buying items you don't really need or want? Are these items affordable, or do you buy them on credit hoping to pay it off, but then don't? Do you shop because you have been disappointed or angry, or because it creates a euphoric rush with anxiety simultaneously?

Reckless shopping not only causes emotional chaos in your life, it will also wreak havoc with your marriage. Arguments could spiral out of control as your spouse realizes your spending habits are slowly deteriorating your relationship. You might hide items or lie about the money you spent and juggle accounts to justify your spending spree. Afterward, you might feel guilty or confused. There are steps you can take to get your spending under control. First, invoke the Holy Spirit to keep you strong as you fight the urge to shop. Don't allow yourself to browse either online or in stores. If you don't know what to do with that time, volunteer at a food pantry or soup kitchen. Your gift of time and talent can make a difference in someone else's life.

Discuss this problem with your spouse so it's not a secret between you. Ask for his or her support and explain why you need to destroy your credit cards and limit the amount of cash you have access to. Be accountable for every cent you spend. Maybe shopping with your spouse will help keep your spending in control. With God, all things are possible, even overcoming excessive spending. What steps will you take today so that you don't overspend during this Christmas season?

Dear Lord, keep me strong so that I am in control of my spending. Teach me how to walk away from a sale sign and give to the poor instead. Help me to invest in building memories with my spouse and family instead of buying useless things. Help me, Lord. I cannot do this without you! Amen.

November 7

Trust in the LORD and do good that you may dwell in the land and live secure.
Find your delight in the LORD who will give you your heart's desire.
Commit your way to the LORD; trust in him and he will act And make
your righteousness shine like the dawn, your justice like noonday.

PSALM 37:3–6

In some places, November is part of the rainy season. Where I live it's typically gloomy, dark, and depressing in November, resulting in many people experiencing seasonal depression. However, the promise of white, fluffy snow, and the upcoming holidays give enough hope to those overcome by the miserable weather. Consider if your mood could use a lift.

Start the day off right by opening your eyes and thanking God that he gave you a gift: another day to live. Begin your day on a positive note with a prayer as you make your bed. Some experts believe that a neat bed reflects the state of your head. The act of straightening your sheets and blankets gives you time to talk to Jesus about what you hope to accomplish.

Establish a good routine for your day. Routines can declutter your mind. Hug your spouse several times throughout the morning. Some experts believe you need eight prolonged hugs each day. Try to hug your spouse at least four times before you leave your house each day.

Listen to music while you eat breakfast. Perhaps you can sing in the shower or sing in the car as you drive to work. Music can lift your spirits. Doctors listen to music to help them operate on patients. Mornings can be difficult for many families as they make breakfast and lunches, hustle their children to the bus stop, and get themselves to work. It might be more relaxing to get ready for the day to music.

Wear a smile; it is the best thing you can put on when you are getting dressed for the day. Even if you must "fake it," the act of smiling will make those around you smile too. After a while, your smile will come naturally. If you have to force it, some believe that biting a pencil will manipulate your facial muscles into those used to smile. When you smile, your heart rate drops and things appear funnier.

During your lunch break if the sun is shining, go for a walk. Sunlight can make you happier and the exercise will relieve stress. When you return to work, look at family photographs, buy flowers for your desk, and send a bouquet of flowers to your spouse just because. Practice gratitude and expressions of optimism. Perhaps you could spend one hour a week volunteering with your spouse and children. How will you celebrate the joy of today?

Dear Lord, thank you for giving me another day to live on earth; sharing the joys and sorrows of my spouse and children. Amen.

November 8

"Look, all these years I served you and not once did I disobey your orders;
yet you never gave me even a young goat to feast on with my friends.
But when your son returns who swallowed up your property
with prostitutes, for him you slaughter the fattened calf."
LUKE 15:28–30

Do you feel like you are doing everything around the house yourself with little help from your spouse? Do you make the meals, do the dishes, the laundry, the kid's assignments and activities, carpooling, grocery shopping, and anything else that falls on the chore list? Is your spouse's idea of helping staying out of your way? The unbalance can create resentment. Don't mandate ultimatums, because that will only make matters worse. Keeping score may make you feel better, even more powerful that you can juggle so much. However, if you lived alone, you would still be doing everything alone.

Keeping score in your marriage will unravel it with arguments and hostility. Some couples keep score as a way to teach their partner a lesson. Sometimes the pain within your marriage morphs into wanting to hurt your partner so that he or she will suffer and understand the discomfort you feel. The problem with that is that everyone is sensitive to different things, and what hurts one person looks childish or punitive to another.

The one doing all of the chores might also feel powerful, getting a thrill from being indispensable. Ponder if you are the family manager, schedule keeper, event organizer, and decision-maker. This fosters a lack of respect by your partner. Your spouse might feel your behavior weakens marital trust and intimacy.

If you are feeling resentful that you must do everything or it won't get done, remind yourself that when you resent someone you give them control of your emotions. Keep your emotions in check by praying. Ask God to strengthen you. When you respond with hatred, anger, and bitterness, you become part of the problem. Convince your brain to think more loving thoughts because your positive energy will attract affirmative results.

If you are tired of carrying the burden alone, spend time with your spouse divvying up the chores in a more equitable style that you both agree to. Offer assistance to your spouse when you see him or her overwhelmed. Living peacefully makes you more attractive, like a love magnet. Living a happy, successful, and peace-filled life is the best revenge!

Dear Lord, grant me the wisdom to stop trying to do everything myself. Help me to stop keeping score. Teach me how to surrender to your love and let you fill my days with endless wonder. You, who give me everything, are my light and salvation. I love you, Lord. Amen.

November 9

Hallelujah! Give thanks to the LORD, who is good, whose mercy endures forever.
Who can recount the mighty deeds of the LORD, proclaim in full God's praise?
Blessed those who do what is right, whose deeds are always just.

PSALM 106:1–3

It is necessary to thank someone when they have done something nice for you: perhaps when someone changed your flat tire, carried your groceries to your car, or held the door open for you. When you receive a gift, send a thank you note to show your gratitude, because it's important to let people know that they're appreciated. The notes don't have to be long or elaborate, but they require genuine appreciation and letting them know that the small things they do make a difference. It's important to send a handwritten note of thanks because you're taking the time to recognize someone who has done something nice for you. A thank you note can make someone's day, because that person could read it once or a dozen times. It shows that you thought of them after the initial gift-giving and receiving moment, and that you are genuinely appreciative. And it's good manners.

After a job interview, most people send a note of appreciation for the time that was spent. Proper business etiquette calls for sending a thank you note to your potential future employer to reiterate your appreciation for their consideration. Consider how many people pray to God asking for favors. When God grants their requests, I wonder if they ever send prayers of thanksgiving to God for the blessing they received. It is much more than simply good manners to thank God for all he gives you. Everyone likes to be acknowledged for the good that they do—even God! A more complicated question is: have you ever thanked God for the bad things that have happened in your life too? If you haven't, then you need to start.

Hidden inside each and every bad circumstance is something good. It's important to thank God for all that is good and bad. There is a reason for everything God does, even if you don't understand it. You are not expected to understand everything God does, because after all, he is God! Eventually, you may begin to see the reason, but even if you never comprehend it, you still need to thank God. Trust in him and his ways.

Dear Lord, I place all of my worries and cares in your hands. You know how to sort it all out, you know what to do with it; I do not. I trust you, Lord that you will take me down the path that you planned for me to take. Guide me, Lord, and keep me safe in your love. Amen.

November 10

The righteous cry out, the LORD hears and he rescues them from all their afflictions. The LORD is close to the brokenhearted, saves those whose spirit is crushed. Many are the troubles of the righteous, but the LORD delivers him from them all. He watches over all his bones; not one of them shall be broken.

PSALM 34:18–21

The English language has numerous words that sound alike but are spelled differently and have diverse meanings. An example of this is son and sun. Words are important and it's critical to use them correctly. Consider the last time you used the words, "I'm sorry" or "I was wrong" or "I made a mistake." Not only are these words tough to say, but it's even harder when you don't think you've done anything wrong. Ponder if pride prevents you from apologizing. Denying an apology could hurt you and possibly harm your relationship.

Apologizing releases you from carrying an unnecessary burden that could be remedied by saying two simple words: I'm sorry. When you apologize to your spouse, it signifies that you respect him or her. By accepting responsibility for an unfortunate situation, regardless if it was intentional or not, demonstrates that you value your spouse and want to restore your marriage. Chances are good that your partner wouldn't intentionally hurt you, so after he or she is made aware of the offense, your spouse has the opportunity to rectify it. An effortless way to bring a situation like this to light is to say, "Ouch!" It's plausible that your spouse was oblivious to what was said or done to insult you.

Expressing regret is liberating to your conscience. An apology enables you to move past the offense and prevent bitterness from festering. Deal with the problem right away to avoid unnecessary turmoil and guilt. If the tables were turned, wouldn't you want the same consideration extended to you? If your spouse is unwilling to accept your apology, rest assured that you tried to make things right. You cannot force anyone into forgiveness.

An apology is only half of the equation; a plan not to repeat the action is required too. It's also nice to follow up with a nice gesture to show your partner that you mean what you say. Maybe you could buy your spouses' favorite coffee, CD, or a plant. If you were the injured person, grieve and let it go, working to reconcile with your spouse. If your spouse is unable to apologize, you might have to accept inner peace until he or she is ready to do so. You cannot force someone to apologize.

Dear Lord, make me strong, Lord, so that I can withstand the blows of life. Let me bend without breaking; love without forsaking. Thank you for the gift of forgiveness. Amen.

November 11

"What is your name?" the man asked. He answered, "Jacob."...
Jacob then asked him, "Please tell me your name." He answered,
"Why do you ask for my name?" With that, he blessed him
GENESIS 32:28, 30

The US Marines use tactical call signs for company-sized units. Fighter pilots use funny nicknames: Boo-Boo, Grumpy, and Burning Bush. It's part of a long-standing military tradition leftover from the old days that is still done today for fun.

Do you have a special "pet name" for your partner: sweetheart, honey, or babe? Perhaps you could resurrect an old one from the past or generate a new one for fun. Researchers say it's a sign that couples who use pet names have a healthy and strong relationship. Pet names identify the relationship as exclusive because when people around you overhear your cutesy conversation, they know you're committed to each other.

A "coded language" demonstrates how well you know each other. For instance, if you and your spouse are at a party and one of you says, "mistletoe," the other understands that it's a secret code for "It's time to leave." Ponder if you and your spouse are deeply bonded so that you have constructed your own "mini-world" with its own language.

If your spouse stops calling you by your pet name, it's a warning to pay attention to. Experts feel it's similar to calling a disobedient child by his full name. This tells your partner that you are no longer being intimate with him or her. If this happens, figure out what is happening in your relationship that needs attention. It could be a misunderstanding; but you should check it out. Maybe your spouse is derailed by work and needs to be reminded not to take life so seriously.

In the day-to-day grind of work, chores, and obligations, how much fun do you have each day with your spouse? Perhaps it's time to create more smiles and laughter. When is the last time you called your spouse an endearing name? Using an affectionate pet name might set a completely different tone today. Try it, you may possibly like it, or better yet, your spouse might like it.

Dear Lord, let me find loving ways to connect with my spouse. Let me call [name] a pet name that will be adored and cherished between us the way a key fits perfectly into a lock. Teach me to be more open to trying new things to brighten my partner's life. Amen.

November 12

I will pray with the spirit, but I will also pray with the mind.
I will sing praise with the spirit, but I will also sing praise with the mind.
1 CORINTHIANS 14:15

When you sing, you produce endorphins that produce a feeling of well-being. Singing in a group is even more beneficial because you actually produce oxytocin, the chemical you produce when you're making love. It boosts the immune system, lowers blood pressure, and blocks pain receptors. You don't have to be "good at it" to reap the effects; you just have to do it. Try singing while you are sorting the laundry, doing the dishes, or singing in the shower to get the endorphins flowing and make chores more fun. Turn on the radio and sing in the car with your spouse or join your church choir. St. Augustine said he who sings prays twice.

Have you considered participating in a flash mob? A flash mob is comprised of a group of people who congregate in a public setting to partake in a coordinated performance that usually involves singing. Flash mobs are intended to look accidental. The flash mob phenomenon has evolved over time to incorporate a wide range of people and causes used to generate buzz. They draw attention to important issues: homelessness, abuse, poverty, love, and compassion. Could you organize a flash mob in your local parish or community to raise awareness to a cause that is near to your heart?

Having the ability to sing is a gift from God. Imagine what you can do with your voice to serve God's people. You can use it to reveal loving messages in simple words, rhyming words, or words with melodies. Could you sing to entertain residents of a nursing home, a soup kitchen, or nearby hospital? Contemplate different ways that you can use your voice to serve God's people. Maybe you could teach children to read music, sing, or play an instrument. Maybe you could organize a chorus of new refugees in your area. God wants you to reach out to his people in loving ways using the gifts he gave you. What can you do to raise your voice to the Lord today?

Dear Lord, let me sing praises to you, Almighty God in heaven. Look down upon me and lift me up throughout the bleakness of November. Remind me to sing my heart out and to offer my songs to you. Thank you for hearing my voice. Amen.

November 13

Rejoice in hope, endure in affliction, persevere in prayer.
Contribute to the needs of the holy ones, exercise hospitality.
ROMANS 12:12–13

As trees lose their leaves, they resemble lifeless skeletons; yet evergreen trees remain the same throughout the entire year. Is your marriage consistent like the evergreen? What do you do to build up your marriage and keep it reliable and healthy? Reflect on what you did last week to create an amicable environment. How did your spouse react to that?

A good marriage is as good as its foundation. How sturdy is your foundation? A solid marriage is built on the secure foundation of Christ, which requires daily care and attention. You wouldn't dream of building a house on a crumbled foundation, so ensure your footing is solid by reading and living the Holy word of God. You can strengthen your marriage by building on your friendship with your spouse and Savior. While it's good to have many friends, make your spouse your exclusive confidant, be his or her biggest and best supporter, and form an intimacy that is holy and decent. Live in the spirit of love by remembering and keeping your partner's heart sacred.

It takes discipline, effort, and drive to foster consistent quality moments with your spouse. You cannot wait for good times to happen; you have to make plans in advance because it signifies to your spouse that you care about your marriage. Hire a babysitter, make reservations, and step away from the humdrum routine to safeguard your marriage by creating memories to reflect on years from now.

Perhaps your mate could use your help with a project at home. You just might enjoy spending time with him or her while being supportive. Your home needs maintenance, just as your marriage does. Consider how spending time together creating a loving and stable family life is good for your relationship too. Maybe you could treat your spouse with a special meal or suggest eating dinner out at a favorite restaurant. If your spouse doesn't accept your help or support, could you pray together for resolution? Prayer is the best medicine.

Dear Lord, shower me with your infinite stream of love so that it permeates my soul and transforms me into a more loving and supportive spouse. Teach me to be more giving of myself, my time, and my talents. Teach me how to create a solid foundation for my marriage. I trust you. You are my saving Lord. Amen.

November 14

To you our vows must be fulfilled, you who hear our prayers.

PSALM 65:2–3

Doctors recommend washing your hands for as long as it takes to sing "Happy Birthday." Instead of singing a song, why not say a Hail Mary? Fervent prayer to Jesus's mother can only be helpful. Or maybe you could sing the Hail Mary to your own tune. Think of how many times you wash your hands each day. If you said a Hail Mary each time you washed your hands, you might be able to say the rosary throughout the day. Imagine how happy that would make Mary!

In your marriage, do you do rote behaviors without much thought to them? Perhaps it would be better to do something with a purposeful intention to try to improve and strengthen your marriage bonds. Could you send your spouse a lighthearted e-mail at work to say you prayed for him or her today? What would it hurt to tell your spouse "You look great" or "I love you"? Maybe you could give your spouse a card with the words, "I'm sorry, I was wrong," or "You're the greatest!" Whatever special words your spouse needs to hear, say them today. Make your words count. You have the power to say something trite or something tremendous. You decide.

How can you take something you already have and transform it into something quite special for your spouse? For example, you have an ordinary voice; however, you can use it to lift up your partner by giving compliments, words of affection, or singing a love song. Take what you have been given and use it is a marvelous way. Maybe you are a wonderful cook. Could you bake a special treat for your mate? What are your talents? Are you an artist? Try painting a picture for your spouse or photograph something you think he or she would appreciate. Frame it with a handwritten note about why you chose that gift. Having a special meaning behind a gift makes it that much more special.

Would you consider taking an exercise class, a cooking class, or painting class with your spouse? You might not know your special talent and need to tap into your interests by having a venue to your creativity. Maybe you could take piano lessons or learn a foreign language and then visit that country. The sky is the limit to what you can do. Live life to its fullest by sharing it with the one you love.

Dear Lord, inspire me to be uplifting to my spouse. Whisper the words he or she needs to hear from me. Give me the courage to say them and mean them. Let me grow in your love to share it with [*name*]. Amen.

November 15

The covetous are never satisfied with money, nor lovers of wealth
with their gain; so this too is vanity. Where there are great riches,
there are also many to devour them. Of what use are they
to the owner except to feast for the eyes alone?

ECCLESIASTES 5:9–10

If your house was on fire and you had one minute to get your valuables, what would you take? Some materially minded people would take their wallets, laptops, photographs, phone, or jewelry. We live in a consumer-driven economy, so it's not surprising that people would automatically think of possessions to save from a fire. Is there an underlying opinion that money and what it provides are vital for your life, happiness, and success? Do the house you live in and the car you drive reflect your financial status and marital joy?

Consider the type of conflicts you grapple with in your marriage. Are there disagreements between you and your mate on the basics of money: saving and spending? Ponder the elements that are a source of contention when formulating a household budget. Experts say couples are better off when both spouses ranked low on the materialism scale. Consider where you and your spouse would rate your materialism levels. Couples at greatest risk of marital woes are those who place a high priority on earning and spending money.

The reason materialism causes so much strife is because it provokes spouses to spend money imprudently. People who rate money with great significance can be less responsive to their partner and unclear on their marriage probably because they find happiness in possessions instead of each other. Ponder if you put a greater emphasis on money and less time and energy into making your marriage successful. Instead of focusing on money, shift the center of your life on God and giving your time, talents, and financial resources to the less fortunate in your community. When you are giving of yourself in this manner, it is pleasing to God. Make your time and love for one another more valuable than money and possessions. You cannot take things to heaven. Look around your home now and identify what you would save if there was a fire.

Dear Lord, help me to discern between what [name] and I need in our relationship, instead of what we want. Help me to stay focused on all that is good, true, pure, and wise in our marriage. Don't let me get distracted by "things" that could clutter our marriage. Amen.

November 16

Let love be sincere; hate what is evil, hold on to what is good;
love one another with mutual affection;
anticipate one another in showing honor.
Do not grow slack in zeal, be fervent in spirit, serve the Lord.

ROMANS 12:9–11

Bowling is a leisure activity where the players roll a heavy ball down a lane with the goal of knocking over pins. Whoever knocks down the most pins wins the game. Opponents practice one-upmanship to successively outdo their competitors. Ponder if you try to outdo your spouse as if he or she is a competitor. Do you feel competitive with your spouse when enjoying friendly challenges with word games, board games, or sports? Is there a "poor sport" between you? It's okay to have a competitive edge during play time, but don't allow it to infiltrate your relationship.

In your marriage you both need to be on the same team building each other up. If you want your union to be successful, you need total cooperation from each other. Hold onto what is good in your marriage and let go of what is a hindrance. Try to stop doing one annoying habit that bugs your spouse and strengthen a different habit that is pleasing. If you are constantly keeping score of how much work you are doing compared to your partner, that negative behavior will erode the bonds that hold you together. Cut them off by giving 100 percent to your marriage.

Listen to how you speak to one another, especially in front of your children or friends. Do you act dismissively, roll your eyes disrespectfully, or yell needlessly? Stop the rude behavior today and begin acting polite to your mate. Start by noticing the small things he or she does. Then acknowledge it with gratitude. Saying "Thank you" is a good first step in the right direction. Even if you are busy, stop what you are doing to recognize your spouse's kindnesses.

Everyone gets tired sometimes. You might even get tired of each other. Don't stay in that corrosive rut. If you want to criticize or be argumentative, suppress the urge. If your spouse says something that wounds your pride, don't respond. Instead, ask yourself if he or she could be right. Always focus on self-improvement. Revive your passion by listening to the same music you enjoyed when you first dated. Remind your spouse of the traits you admired then and what you value today. Look at your wedding album or old photographs taken of you both in the early years together.

Dear Lord, transform me into the perfect version of what a good spouse should be. Teach me how to stop being disrespectful to [*name*]. Let me build him or her up so that we walk united into your kingdom together. Amen.

November 17

*Would he contend against me with his great power? No, he himself
would heed me! There an upright man might argue with him, and
I would once and for all be delivered from my judge. But if I go east,
he is not there; or west, I cannot perceive him; The north enfolds him,
and I cannot catch sight of him; The south hides him, and I cannot see him.
Yet he knows my way; if he tested me, I should come forth like gold.*

JOB 23:6–10

A diamond is a girls' best friend. Do you know how a diamond is created? A diamond is a mere lump of coal. The difference between a diamond and coal is that the diamond underwent a long, hard, hot, and intense pressure. Scientists believe that it takes 1,000 or more years for a diamond to actually form. Consider if your marriage has endured intense heat, pressures, or difficulties. What test has your marriage recently survived?

No one likes trials, but in the Bible, Job overcame his test with God's help. Job proved his faithfulness and was rewarded. Similarly, you can grow stronger and receive God's rewards if you stay true to him and are thankful for the hard times. Try to be identified with Jesus Christ so that when you suffer, while being thankful, you are embracing Christ's attitude. Later, you will be capable of helping others because of the strength that God gave you during your difficult moments. The hard times you went through make you stronger.

Have you heard the expression, "What doesn't kill you makes you stronger?" The reason you need to be appreciative of difficulties is because strength comes from the hard times. Think about how your body hurts during a new exercise routine. The muscles of the human body grow stronger when they are broken down. The "breaking down" comes through the hard, tough training. It's the same for most sports, or for any study, for that matter. Hard work, hard training, and hard study produce great results later. While your marriage might appear broken, thank God for it; during the brokenness it can be rebuilt stronger and lovelier than ever.

Dear Lord, thank you for the difficulties that surround my marriage. Please don't let me give up and walk away from it because I feel so week and alone. Scoop me up into your loving embrace and guide me down the path of recovery. Unite us again, like when we were first married. And let our love carry us throughout the rest of our lives in your gentle mercies. I love you, Lord. Amen.

November 18

Do not return evil for evil, or insult for insult; but, on the contrary, a
blessing, because to this you were called, that you might inherit a blessing.
For: "Whoever would love life and see good days must keep the tongue from
evil and the lips from speaking deceit, must turn from evil and do good, seek
peace and follow after it. For the eyes of the Lord are on the righteous and
his ears turned to their prayer, but the face of the Lord is against evildoers."
Now who is going to harm you if you are enthusiastic for what is good?

1 PETER 3:9–13

A hiccup is a spontaneous contraction of the diaphragm that could happen several times a minute. Hiccups may occur alone or in sessions. The rhythm of the hiccups, or the time between them, is fairly constant. Hiccups usually resolve on their own or with home remedies used to shorten the duration. Medical treatment is usually sought with prolonged hiccups. Reflect on your relationship with your spouse to determine if your marriage has several minor bouts of hiccups or a chronic case that requires intervention.

Regardless of what led to the hiccup, it's possible that the way you view your marriage is keeping you stuck. The minute you feel down, you begin to notice problems with your marriage that you overlooked before because you were happy. Your frame of mind and thoughts play a big role impacting the way you feel and act. Your actions have consequences and can self-perpetuate your situation. Therefore, change the way you are thinking. If your partner leaves for work leaving a trail of clutter behind, consider how distracted work has made him or her feel. Instead of taking the mess personally, look underneath it to learn what is weighing heavy on your mate's mind. If your partner makes a negative comment, give him or her the benefit of the doubt that he or she didn't mean to be hurtful. You can prevent it from festering and overreacting.

If the situation intensifies, talk to your partner openly, honestly, and with love in your heart. It isn't easy to do without it escalating. Begin the conversation with the mindset of fixing the problem, not highlighting your partner's faults. Try using a tangible reminder to focus on throughout your discussion so that you speak wisely, not harshly. Try holding a crucifix as a symbolic reminder that Jesus suffered for your sins to grant you a wonderful afterlife in heaven. Perhaps that will enable you to stay focused on achieving a resolution and not verbally attack your partner.

Dear Lord, enable me to keep the hiccups of life in proper perspective so that they don't ruin my marriage. I want to be more Christ-like. I will try harder. I will do better. I will pray longer. I will endure. Amen.

November 19

On the way of wisdom I direct you, I lead you on straight paths.
When you walk, your step will not be impeded, and should you run,
you will not stumble. Hold fast to instruction, never let her go; keep it,
for it is your life....Survey the path for your feet, and all your ways will
be sure. Turn neither to right nor to left, keep your foot far from evil.
PROVERBS 4:11–13, 26–27

I walked to solve my marital conflict. The physical aspect of marching up and down hills consumed the restless energy that grew from anger, negativity, and frustration. The longer and harder I strolled, the more I prayed to God for enlightenment. After a while, I relaxed and could think clearly and intelligently to resolve my dilemma. Soon, walking became my coping strategy and I felt healthier and more physically fit. What I once loathed became a dearly loved passion. Now my husband and I walk together, hiking up mountains, down wild nature trails, and over winding country roads. I transformed a method to solve conflict into a much-loved activity. What can you do to expunge negativity created from marital squabbles?

Through daily exercise you can promote an overall sense of wellbeing. Instead of viewing exercise as a self-centered activity to simply look good or feel good about yourself, consider it a service to your spouse. Exercise improves your self-confidence, moods, health, enthusiasm, and energy levels. Couples who exercise are less likely to get sick. Being physically fit teaches you to stay true to your goals and see them through to completion; this is especially helpful when striving to reach marriage goals while maintaining a positive outlook. Couples who work out are less stressed. When you encourage your spouse to stay fit with you, it demonstrates a concern for his or her well-being.

Before you were married you might have enjoyed tennis matches with each other, shooting baskets, taking long walks, or riding bikes. Don't allow the business of life to get in the way of this form of physical connectedness. If you can't exercise together, then allow each other some time to work out individually, and hopefully you'll be able to exercise together from time to time.

Housework can be a form of exercise. How many calories do you burn when scrubbing the kitchen floor, vacuuming the carpet, or washing windows? Divvy up the chores as a way to get your house clean while getting physically fit. Clean to your favorite tunes and it's twice as good. Or better yet, whistle while you work.

Dear Lord, I love the body you designed for me. Thank you for allowing me to use it constructively. Help me to take good care of my health and well-being so that I can honor you all of the days of my life. I truly love you, Lord, God Almighty. Amen.

November 20

With all vigilance guard your heart, for in it are the sources of life.
Dishonest mouth put away from you, deceitful lips put far from you.
Let your eyes look straight ahead and your gaze be focused forward.

PROVERBS 4:23–25

This is the time of year when people start dressing in layers depending on where they live. Temperatures dip down at night making a chilly morning commute to work. You might need a hat, gloves, scarf, sweater, and jacket; all of which take effort to find and put on. When the sun pops out in the later afternoon, temperatures rise and one by one a layer get peeled off to provide ample comfort. Ponder what aspect of your marriage requires layers.

Often in relationships, when there is heat from anger or hurt, you might need to peel back emotional layers to determine what is driving your pain. If you have been hurt, tell your spouse immediately, even though it might feel unnatural, because it verbalizes that you were harmed by words or actions. Open amicable dialog with your spouse. Don't start a war; simply have a conversation with your spouse about what just happened. Your mate is not a mind reader and could be oblivious to your feelings. It's up to you to tell him or her in a loving manner.

Begin by questioning yourself: "I feel angry because…" or "I feel hurt because…". Then ask yourself, "I am afraid that…" and "I regret that…" and "I wish that…". By peeling back these emotional layers, you will uncover what is driving your true feelings. This introspection work is like peeling layers of an onion because it can make you cry. Don't let your ego try to reassert power in the form of irrational outbursts, judging others or yourself, dwelling on painful emotions of the past, worrying about the future, or trying to control your spouse. Instead, lean into God, your divine savior. Ask God to bless your self-examination process and step you through it in his loving mercy.

Don't allow the hurt cycle to spiral down out of control by using hurtful zingers or retaliations. Keep your emotions in check. Take baby steps if you need to. Just keep moving in the right direction.

Dear Lord, strengthen me with your divine power to work through this introspection process to better understand myself and all that is painful to me. Help me to get to the bottom of it, Lord, so that I can fix it and repair my brokenness. Help me to be a good spouse. Don't let me hide behind emotional layers. Raise me up, Lord, to where I need to be. I ask this in your holy name. Amen.

November 21

But now they hold me in derision who are younger than I;
Whose fathers I should have disdained to rank with the dogs of my flock.
Such strength as they had meant nothing to me; their vigor had perished.

JOB 30:1–2

Years of research has proven that living with pets provides health benefits. Having a dog can lower your blood pressure, lessen anxiety, and boost your immunity. Dog owners are less likely to suffer from depression, and because dogs need to be walked, most dog owners get daily exercise that keeps them in better overall shape. I am not advocating couples buy dogs to make their marriages better, although I do see the benefit of it. I am suggesting that you consider dogs, taking daily walks with your partner, playing with your spouse more frequently, even "roughhouse" by tickling each other. Acting "dog-like" might put more happiness in your heart. If that works—great! If it doesn't work for you, try getting a dog and share the responsibility of caring for it together. Maybe you could start out small by buying a goldfish; if that goes well, then get a dog.

A dog can be a great friend. After a long and difficult workday, dog owners feel loved by their pets. Consider what you do to help your spouse feel rejuvenated after a long day of work. The dog's enthusiastic reactions to his master when arriving home teaches couples how to greet their spouses after being away. Stop what you are doing even if you don't feel like it, smile, greet, and embrace your partner, welcoming him or her back fervently. It's such a simple gesture that goes a long way to lifting your partner's mood. It doesn't cost anything and is minimal effort to reap such a wonderful reward: pleasing your mate.

People trust dog owners more than random people walking on the street. Dog owners are more likely to approach and interact with "friendly" strangers. Consider just how much we can learn from a dog: how to forgive and forget and how to stay close when our loved ones are sad or sick. It seems that canine pals have the ability to smell cancer in the human body. Stories have recently surfaced about owners whose dogs sniffed or licked a particular body part that was later determined to be cancerous.

Consider the tricks dogs do to please their master. What would you do to please your spouse? Think about being "dog-like" just for today. Maybe showing your playful and loyal side to your spouse will do the trick.

Dear Lord, thank you for blessing mankind with dogs. Remind me to be more spirited with [name]. Fill me with the enthusiasm I need to make my marriage more exciting. Amen.

November 22

"For this reason a man shall leave [his] father and [his] mother and be joined to his wife, and the two shall become one flesh."...In any case, each one of you should love his wife as himself, and the wife should respect her husband.

EPHESIANS 5:31, 33

Love is a choice. When you exchanged your marriage vows at your wedding, you chose love. And the love you create can build up your relationship, leading to a stream of intimate moments. Intimacy is a need and a prerequisite for happiness. You can live without it, but you will thrive with it. Until you experience true unadulterated intimacy, your heart will be restless and discontented. Intimacy shares secrets of your heart, mind, and soul. It moves, inspires, and motivates. The greatest gift you can give your spouse is to remove your mask and reveal your personal strengths, weaknesses, faults, defects, talents, achievements, and potential. Consider how you create intimacy in your marriage.

Couples need to constantly work at keeping their marriage healthy. It doesn't come easy for most people; it takes thought-provoked effort. Consider whether you might have been neglecting your spouse's needs for affection, comfort, and camaraderie. Reflect on times you have felt closest to your mate. What made the difference? What are your expectations concerning your spouse's friendship today?

You set the mood, tone, and atmosphere in your marriage. It's too easy to blame your partner for not setting the necessary atmosphere to create an intimate marriage. You can change the mood of your marriage immediately with affection, warmth, and encouragement. Don't allow the tone to fluctuate according to what your spouse does or forgets to do. Decide not to react to the stresses of life, because that allows negativity to settle in. Focus on intimacy with your partner.

Create an attitude of intimacy and closeness through affection: hold hands, kiss, and bring gifts such as flowers and chocolates. Back rubs or neck massages work, say "I love you" in different ways, and display tenderness. Sometimes marriages slip into bad habits such as indifference or aloofness. Why live with a negative atmosphere when you could enjoy warmth, intimacy, and abundant love? Use the power from encouragement and affirmation by being present in your marriage. Consider if your spouse enjoys receiving encouragement through words, through your presence, through gifts, or through kind actions. How will you create an atmosphere of intimacy in your marriage today?

Dear Lord, enlighten me to be more warm and loving to my spouse.
Help me create intimacy between us. Amen.

November 23

*Immorality or any impurity or greed must not even be mentioned among you,
as is fitting among holy ones, no obscenity or silly or suggestive talk,
which is out of place, but instead, thanksgiving. Be sure of this, that
no immoral or impure or greedy person, that is, an idolater, has any
inheritance in the kingdom of Christ and of God. Let no one deceive
you with empty arguments, for because of these things the wrath of God
is coming upon the disobedient. So do not be associated with them.*

EPHESIANS 5:3–7

D oes your spouse have rude or annoying habits? Ponder if you complain,
criticize, or act disrespectfully when the unappealing habits surface.
If the rudeness slips outside your home exposing friends and family to it,
have a conversation about it with your partner. Let him or her know how
you feel about the offensive behavior using honesty and discretion while
staying calm. Question what made your spouse act rude to begin with.
Once you realize what caused this issue to surface, you might have more
luck resolving it. Remember not to use "you statements" or be a critical nag.
Instead of saying, "You have been extremely rude, belching so loud," say, "I
am concerned about your belching. Maybe we should see a doctor. What if
you have food allergies?"

Step away from the mundaneness of life and enjoy an evening alone with
your spouse; like the dates you once went on when you started dating each
other. Back then you were on your best behavior and wouldn't dream of
belching at a restaurant. Did you open the car door and wait in a long line
for popcorn and candy at the movie your partner chose? Treat your spouse
with that same respect and consideration.

Reflect on the positive characteristics that you love about your spouse.
Remind him or her about them, focusing on them, and be thankful for the
positive qualities. Show your thankfulness to your spouse frequently. If
your partner fills up your car with gas, express your gratitude. Bake his or
her favorite dessert or buy his or her favorite doughnut. If vulgarity sneaks
into a conversation, change the tone by reminiscing about the good times
instead of dwelling on the bad. Who brings rudeness into your relationship,
and what do you plan to do about it?

Dear Lord, keep me strong as I face the impoliteness's that surface in
my marriage. Replace every foul thought that enters my mind with
those that are lovely, pure, and genuine. If the thoughts and actions
are from you, then those I gratefully embrace. If they are not from
you, remove them from me. Let every word that leaves my mouth be
from you. I truly love you. Amen.

November 24

When you build a new house, put a parapet around the roof,
so that you do not bring bloodguilt upon your house if someone falls off.

Deuteronomy 22:8

When a daredevil walked a tightrope over Niagara Falls, people gasped when they realized he didn't use a safety strap. Don't most people want a safety net underneath them as they journey through life? Cars have seatbelts, computers have antivirus software, and highways have guardrails. Consider if your marriage has a safety net, and if it does, what is it?

Think of relationship traits that your marriage absolutely must have: trust, loyalty, good communication, abundant love. These qualities woven together make your marriage safety net. When you stumble in your marriage and seek forgiveness, that safety net will be there to spare you from a hard, possibly irrecoverable relationship crash.

If your spouse makes a mistake or is offensive to you, the opportunity exists for you to be either self-righteous or a safety net. Because you are both human frail and faulty, you both will make mistakes: that is a given. Hurt exists at some point in every marriage. When you are on the receiving end of your spouse's blunder, it's understandable to be indignant. That position however, puts you at odds with your spouse. Instead, get on the same team, moving forward in the same direction.

If your spouse owns up to his or her mistakes, it signifies their desire to be closer and to make a repair. If your spouse tells you to sit down because he or she has something to say, take a seat, say a quiet prayer, and open your heart as well as your ears. Your partner's willingness to keep you informed and to work it out is a good sign. While you are listening, refrain from holding your spouse to unrealistic standards; choose to be his or her safety net.

The best thing you can do to be a safety net for your spouse, is to forgive little things quickly, completely, and let them go. Don't bring them up again. Create an atmosphere of warmth, acceptance, and unconditional love, like that of Jesus Christ. If your goal is striving for perfection, no one can live up to that which makes you unapproachable. How can you love your spouse during and after confessions?

Dear Lord, thank you for making me human; capable of bending and not breaking. Strengthen me to accept confessions when they come without being judgmental. Reinforce my safety net with unconditional love and plenty of forgiveness to carry us through the rest of our lives together. Amen.

November 25

One who slanders reveals secrets, but a trustworthy person keeps a confidence.
PROVERBS 11:13

S ome people think recipes are meant to be shared, while others believe their formulas, instructions, and ingredients should be kept a secret. Most food companies go to great lengths to keep their product manufacturing techniques a highly prized secret. What is the secret ingredient to making your marriage successful? Reflect on your communication skills, your empathy toward one another, or your selflessness. What areas can you improve upon?

Do you have secrets in your relationship that you don't want to share with your partner? Does your spouse keep secrets from you? You have the right to space in your marriage. You also need to respect your partner's boundaries. Contemplate what emotional space you provide to each other. The key in any relationship is the ability to honor each other's request to keep your spouse's confidences safe in your heart. Safeguard your heart by keeping the Lord in it. Make God the secret to keeping your marriage alive and well.

All married couples want to be happy, yet happiness will come and go. Truly successful couples learn to intentionally do things that will bring happiness back when life pulls it away. Consider what deliberate action you could count on to keep waves of happiness floating through your relationship. A routine of date nights, prayer time, and service to each other could help some couples. What's your solution?

When you hit a rough patch and don't know what to do, simply hang in there and be supportive for your spouse by remembering your marriage vows: honoring each other in good times and in bad. Time has a way of allowing couples to work things out. Remember also to pray your way through your difficulties. God will present opportunities to reduce stress and help you to overcome challenges if you continue to trust and hope in the Lord. If you do what you always do, you will get same result. That is great if everything is going well. However, when things go awry, try a different approach to your problems and you might get better results. Even minor changes in your attitude can make the biggest difference in marriage. Changing behavior is important, but it can be critical if you have a bad attitude that needs adjusting. A bad attitude can drive negative feelings, actions, and emotions. How you think, feel, and believe about your spouse greatly impacts how you perceive each other.

Dear Lord, thank you for providing the security for my secrets, and building me up to provide a safe dwelling place for me and [*name*]. Thank you for allowing our love to flourish. You are my salvation, Lord. Amen.

November 26

Jacob then gave him some bread and the lentil stew;
and Esau ate, drank, got up, and went his way.

GENESIS 25:34

Instead of letting leftover meats, vegetables, and pastas spoil, make soup with them. The only constant ingredient in each different batch is broth. The one constant ingredient in each marriage is love. However, other things inadvertently get mixed in sometimes, such as hurt, resentment, or discontentment. If there is a solid foundation of love, the overall stew is still nourishing and worth saving. What unpleasant element came into your marriage and how can you repair it? In stews you could add more spices; in a marriage you can add more prayers. If something is missing, always add God.

The first step to fixing marital discord is to maintain respectful treatment. Open honest dialog with your spouse, being direct and using reflective listening techniques to understand the message your spouse might be trying to convey to you. Don't interrupt with responses or rebuttals. Allow your spouse to speak without noises of your house or children interrupting. Find a quiet place where you can give your full attention to discuss your situation privately and with love for each other. Speak using "I statements." Ask your spouse for what you want in a cordial fashion, not complaining or being rude. Make sure you choose a topic your spouse can relate to. For instance, if your mate is a gardener, use a plant metaphor. One of the most important things you can do during your conversation is to make sure your partner understands your message.

It is essential not to be brutally honest with your spouse, but use tact instead when you are striving to make your point. Also, it is important not to clam up and keep your thoughts and feelings to yourself, because remaining silent is a form of dishonesty. The purpose of dialog is to understand each other and strive to make your marriage better, not worse. Work together in a congenial manner to figure out what is causing conflict in your union. Brainstorm different solutions. Propose taking turns or each giving a little to get to the bottom of your difficulty. If you are unable to rectify it, take a break and go for a walk. Listen to lively music and dance in the kitchen. Eat something, say a prayer, and then go back to trying to fix your problem with a fresh start; you just might be more successful.

Dear Lord, help me to identify what is causing discontentment in my relationship. Teach me how to repair and rebuild my marriage. I don't want it to be merely palatable; I want it to be delicious, like it once was. Help me to stop, think, and pray more to keep my life on track. Amen.

November 27

If your offering is a grain offering that is fried on a griddle, it must be of bran flour mixed with oil and unleavened....If you offer a grain offering of first ripe fruits to the LORD, you shall offer it in the form of fresh early grain, roasted by fire and crushed as a grain offering of your first ripe fruits.

LEVITICUS 2:5, 14

If a baker mixes together all of the ingredients to make chocolate chip cookies at once, the cookies will turn out basically okay. If the entire ingredients for an apple pie are all mixed together, the outcome will be disastrous. There are specific steps to make an apple pie: dough must be made, rolled thin, and lined in a dish, and then filled with sliced apples. It takes more thought, time, and work. Similar elements are essential when working through the forgiveness process in a marriage.

Have you offered an apology and wondered why it didn't yield better results? Was your apology sincere? Perhaps you forgot to provide a plan to ensure the offense doesn't reoccur. A plan tells your spouse that you want to make a conscious effort to improve. It's also a good idea to provide your mate with a gesture that signifies just how sorry you are. You could buy flowers or your spouse's favorite candy bar with a card informing your spouse just how much you value your marriage. You cannot demand forgiveness. It is a gift only your spouse can grant you. Remember that forgiveness is a long process that takes time, energy, and love. The goal is reconciliation or to start over.

Sometimes people want the process to be over quickly, but forgiveness cannot be rushed. It's similar to a broken bone healing. The leg's strength will eventually be restored, but only after rest, medication, therapy. Your marriage needs something similar to that too. After a serious offence in your marriage, your spouse may need time before he or she accepts or digests what has happened. Give your mate time to grieve and think. Your spouse might be holding a grudge and it might take a lot of convincing that you are truly sorry. You must be patient. Your actions will speak volumes to how quickly your spouse will let his or her guard down and trust you once again. So make sure your actions are just, loyal, and loving. What are the steps that you require in your forgiveness strategy? Think of God's tender mercies when you ask for forgiveness.

Dear Lord, with your divine intervention, touch my heart, lighten, and melt the pain that has been festering there from past hurts. Teach me how to be merciful and a thoughtful partner. Amen.

November 28

"And brought us to this place, and gave us this land, a land flowing with milk and honey. Now, therefore, I have brought the first fruits of the products of the soil which you, LORD, have given me." You shall set them before the LORD, your God, and you shall bow down before the LORD, your God. Then you and your household, together with the Levite and the resident aliens who live among you, shall celebrate with all these good things which the LORD, your God, has given you.

DEUTERONOMY 26:9–11

Early Thanksgiving celebrations were centered on prayer and fasting. It was not until much later that it evolved into the holiday we currently celebrate. Often, it takes time for things to work out the way you intended, which happens in relationships too. You might have married your partner believing it would be one way, and then it morphed into something completely different. Maybe you were blessed with children earlier than you anticipated or perhaps your careers changed. Whatever transformations occurred, remember that life is a journey, unfolding as you go. You write the story. If you are unhappy with one chapter, change it, and help it to progress. With God, you can do anything.

When you got married, did you think it would take champagne, chocolate, and roses to keep your marriage going, or would it take work? Most people think love just happens. But the reality of it is your marriage takes time, commitment, thought, and work. Every day when you wake up, thank God that he gave you another day to spend with your spouse. It's a gift. What you do with your day is a gift that you can give to your spouse and to God. Begin by committing yourself to your spouse the way you did when you exchanged your marriage vows. You promised to love, honor, and cherish your spouse. You pledged to remain faithful to him or her, and do it in good times and bad, in sickness and in health forever. What if you held your spouse in your arms and recited your vows each day? Imagine how that would shape your attitude.

Dear Lord, thank you for my past mistakes because they molded me into the person I am today. Thank you for the ability to move past them and make tomorrow better. Help me to cultivate my marriage into a beautiful union, the one you wanted it to be. I am truly thankful, Lord, for all you have blessed me with this year. Amen.

November 29

The LORD *is my strength and my shield, in whom my heart trusts....*
Save your people, bless your inheritance; pasture and carry them forever!
PSALM 28:7, 9

Turkey contains L-Tryptophan, an amino acid that induces sleepiness. However, L-Tryptophan must be taken on an empty stomach and without any other amino acids or protein in order to be most effective. Turkey has copious amounts of protein. Even if you passed on the meat, you would likely feel tired from everything else you ate at your Thanksgiving feast. The culprit: rapid blood sugar swings and general fullness.

There might be scientific explanations for the state your marriage is in, with statistics backing them up, but put your faith in God; let him guide you. God has a magnificent plan for you. Perhaps your spouse is on a military deployment or struggling with a medical issue. Reflect on a past problem that God carried you through, and believe he will do it again.

You have to believe in things you cannot see, such as the Holy Spirit. Embrace God's love and passion for your life. Ask God to lead you down the right path, the one with opportunities to improve your marriage. Reflect on ways you can do that. Maybe you could prepare a special meal using some of the leftovers from Thanksgiving dinner and do all of the dishes to allow your spouse a rest. Consider what your spouse would enjoy having as a special treat: a long back rub, someone to clean the bathroom, or an hour of peace and quiet. Give your partner the gifts from your heart to bring him or her to a new level of love.

With the holiday season right around the corner, how will you begin Advent with your spouse? Are there special programs at your church or a nearby parish that you could attend? Maybe you could incorporate Advent prayers and time for spiritual reflection with your partner. Mull over the options available to you both to volunteer together as a couple. Inquire with your parish priest opportunities to provide a blessed Christmas to the less fortunate. By shifting the focus away from yourself and onto those needy individuals, you will find God's love—the best gift you could possibly receive.

Dear Lord, remove the distractions and explanations why my marriage is wavering. Keep me resilient, working persistently to keep it together in your love. All of my trust is in you, kind and merciful Lord, as I give it to you. Amen.

November 30

In the same way, the Lord ordered that those who preach the gospel should live by the gospel....If I preach the gospel, this is no reason for me to boast, for an obligation has been imposed on me, and woe to me if I do not preach it! If I do so willingly, I have a recompense, but if unwillingly, then I have been entrusted with a stewardship.

1 CORINTHIANS 9:14, 16–17

The biggest shopping weekend of the year is upon you, beckoning you to spend crazily. It marks the beginning of the Christmas shopping time where retailers open doors earlier than ever, offering irresistible deals. Don't succumb to societal pressures. Instead, think of ways you can bond with your spouse during the holiday season. Consider lingering after Mass to say the rosary with your spouse. On the way home from Mass, consider enjoying a cup of coffee and a doughnut in the quiet of your car while you make plans for your day. Find a cozy spot that you would not normally go to just to share a few quiet moments together. Stand in your bedroom closet embracing each other while you ask God to bless your day. Those quirky moments will be remembered and even possibly repeated. Think outside the box.

Try lateral thinking just for today. If one method doesn't work, test another one. The long lines at Disney World appeared shorter when engineers used convoluted patterns leading anxious guests into unique areas with an enjoyable atmosphere. The line was just as long but it was more enjoyable because the surroundings were enhanced. Consider how you can augment your home to make it more conducive to warmth and happiness. Could you do less for yourselves and more for others?

What worthy organizations would you and your spouse volunteer together for or contribute to? Stepping outside of your comfort zone to volunteer might bring you more rewards than challenges. Could you be a bell ringer for the Salvation Army or collect items for the Toys for Tots program sponsored by the Marines? Could you work in a soup kitchen or food bank? Whatever contribution you make together, God will bless you for it; for it is in giving that we receive.

Dear Lord, make me resistant to the myriad sale fliers that bombard me this time of year. If I give into the shopping, then let me buy for indigent families, the giving tree program at church, or food for the destitute. Amen.

December 1

We know that all things work for good for those who love God,
who are called according to his purpose.

ROMANS 8:28

To make a chocolate cake, the individual ingredients do not taste good alone; cocoa powder is bitter and unpalatable. However, when all of the ingredients are mixed together and baked, the result is a delicious dessert. The same can be said for marriages; there are some components that could be unpleasant, like adjusting to your partner's bathroom etiquette or juggling holidays between families and in-laws. When all of the different aspects of your marriage come together as a whole, it is basically good and can be endearing. Are you focusing on a solitary aspect of your relationship that you are not fond of? Contemplate what you can do to get past your mate's trivial nuances. Start with the foundation of your marriage, building on your faithfulness to God and to each other.

One irritating note about annoying habits is that they are usually trivial yet they can drive you crazy! While you should be able to shrug it off, no matter how hard you try, sometimes you can't let it go. It's like the constant drip of water in the sink. You try to turn the nozzle as tightly as possible, but it still drips. And the drip left alone will add up to gallons lost down the drain; which in reality is throwing money down the drain. It all adds up. Annoying habits will erode your patience away.

When you explain to your spouse how their behavior is bothersome and your request to stop gets ignored, you might consider him or her inconsiderate. Maybe your spouse cracks his or her knuckles, or forgets to close the door, or talks with a mouthful of food; the actual behavior is not a deal breaker. It's the thought that your spouse doesn't appear to care. Ponder if you have any annoying habits that you downplay, and consider why you don't stop your own insensitive behavior.

Combining your habits and activities defines your lifestyle, which can be gratifying for you together or alone. When you both enjoy your habits and activities, you build a strong foundation for your marriage. Replace the weak footing by making an effort to eliminate insensitive behavior. The moment you realize you are bothering your spouse, stop that behavior. Can you devise a plan to eliminate weakness in your relationship?

Dear Lord, thank you for bringing my partner into my life with all of [name]'s quirkiness. Thank you for allowing us to live amicably, in our sacred union as husband and wife. Allow me to embrace the constructive criticism to build a stronger, lasting relationship so that our time together will be enjoyable. Amen.

December 2

"The holy Spirit will come upon you, and the power of the Most High will overshadow you. Therefore the child to be born will be called holy, the Son of God. And behold, Elizabeth, your relative, has also conceived a son in her old age, and this is the sixth month for her who was called barren; for nothing will be impossible for God."

LUKE 1:35–37

The thought of whether or not to have children is a topic most couples discuss at some point in their marriage. Has God blessed you with children already, or do you long for them someday? Do you have children from a blended family or are you considering adoption? God has a special purpose for you regarding children and the number of them he wants you to embrace: it could be one, several, or none at all. Children can complicate a marriage while making it richer, fuller, and more satisfying. Trust in God's plan for the size of your family and how it is created because nothing is impossible with God.

Maybe the thought of parenting is frightening; being responsible for the welfare of other human beings. Perhaps you don't want to pass on an illness genetically or maybe it's an exciting notion to peer into the eyes of a child seeing a semblance of yourself. Maybe you want to build up a nest egg first, or experiment parenting skills on a pet before a child. Contemplate if you fear losing a part of yourself or if children will strain your marriage. The stuff kids can throw at you and demand from you and need from you is challenging. With children, you will have more to juggle, no matter how old or young the children are. Always focus on God and remain on the same team.

Each time you fly on a plane the crew reminds adults in the event of an emergency to put oxygen masks on themselves first. In everyday life put your symbolic oxygen mask on: take care of yourself, your spouse, and then your children—all encircling God's love. And don't take life too seriously. Try to find humor in everyday experiences because they will uplift your spirit and keep your family happier. Always search for little ways to make your family members happy; even if it's just a quick hug. Sometimes the littlest things mean the most. Be kind to your spouse and children, even if they are driving you crazy. It's during those frenzied moments that kindness is needed the most. Remember that the best gift you can give your children is a good marriage. How will you model a stable marriage for your children?

Dear Lord, strengthen my conviction that children will come to me according to your divine plan. Though I may not understand it today, I appreciate how someday I will. You are my saving Lord, and I love you. Amen.

December 3

During those days Mary set out and traveled to the hill country
in haste to a town of Judah, where she entered
the house of Zechariah and greeted Elizabeth.
LUKE 1:39–40).

Mary sought comfort in her visit with Elizabeth. Do you have plans for impending holiday travels? Perhaps you are planning to reconnect with distant family members or spend time with close friends. Do you anticipate it with a mixture of excitement and anxiety? Vacations can bring stress to the calmest family, especially during the Christmas season, which can become hectic when travel plans are involved. There are traffic jams, winter weather, delayed or cancelled flights, and crowds everywhere you turn. The trick to smooth sailing is to nix "winging it" and opt for careful planning while being flexible.

Ponder coping strategies that can alleviate apprehension; incorporate quiet time to regroup, reconnect, and reenergize. First, remember that the holidays are a time of spirituality recognizing the birth of Jesus. It's the perfect time to renew your spirituality by spending more time in contemplation and prayer. Consider attending Mass more frequently, joining your church choir, attending Advent events at your church or nearby parish, or spending time in adoration. By doing this, it could enable you to comprehend your motivations and your relationships with your spouse or others who are near and dear to you.

Consider the activities and hobbies that have helped you in the past. Perhaps you can exercise, read, meditate, and pray with your spouse. Keep busy by doing things that bring you pleasure. Is it plausible for you and your spouse to volunteer some free time at a hospital or nursing home?

You may have more visitors in your home during the holidays, or you may travel for family get-togethers. The disruption of your day-to-day routine can be stressful or throw you off balance by interfering with your eating, sleeping, and exercise schedules. Be mindful that it can increase your emotional vulnerability leaving you feeling irritable or moody. Try curbing your alcohol or caffeine consumption. Take a long, hot shower or bath, listen to soothing music, watch a funny movie, or take a brisk walk. Be kind to yourself. Don't try to do everything yourself; ask your spouse, your children, or family for help. How can you make your holiday travels a productive and loving experience for yourself, your spouse, family, and friends the way Mary and Elizabeth did?

Dear Lord, bless my holiday travels. Keep me safe and healthy while I am away. Enliven my heart to be more tolerant, loving, and forgiving. Revitalize my spirit to be more caring. Amen.

December 4

Who provides nourishment for the raven when its young cry out to God,
wandering about without food?

Job 38:41

The male cardinal is a vibrant red color and is breathtakingly beautiful in winter's snowy backyards. It has a distinctive plume on the head and a black face mask on the male and gray in the female. The male behaves territorially, marking his area with song. During courtship, the male feeds the female beak to beak.

During Advent, what can you do differently to show your spouse you care? Perhaps you could invite your mate into your special space at home and spend more quality time with each other. Maybe you could prepare your spouse's favorite meal or bake his or her preferred Christmas cookie. Could you formulate new Advent traditions around special prayers? If you don't have an Advent wreath, contemplate buying or making one.

During Advent it's important to balance the sacredness of the season with the other Christmas preparations you are making. Set aside time for quiet reflection and prayer to stay spiritually connected to the Lord. The pink and purple colors used throughout the Advent season reflect a spirit of penitence and the need to prepare your heart. Pink is a secondary Advent color that symbolizes the joy of the season. The evergreens in the Advent wreath signify eternal life that comes through Jesus.

How will you and your partner prepare yourselves spiritually during Advent? Consider what voluntary acts of fasting, penance, and almsgiving you can do together. If your partner is tired and snaps at you, can you offer it up as penance? Chances are your spouse was overtired and it might be worth letting the little things go instead of blowing them out of proportion. The next time a small annoyance pops up, try not reacting.

The Christmas season is the perfect time to feed the hungry, clothe the poor, and be satisfied with what you have. After you find a way to accomplish this, consider not stopping once the Christmas season is over. Why not keep the spirit of the Christmas season going all year long? How can you reaffirm your love of God and your devotion to each other during this blessed season?

Dear Lord, allow me and [*name*] spiritual fulfillment during Advent. Let us nourish each other with food, prayer, and love as we revisit old traditions and create new ones centered on you. Enable us to focus on enriching our lives in your indelible love. Amen.

December 5

Therefore I praised joy, because there is nothing better for mortals under the sun than to eat and to drink and to be joyful: this will accompany them in their toil through the limited days of life God gives them under the sun.

ECCLESIASTES 8:15

Can you justify a slice of apple crumb pie à la mode as a nutritious lunch? The crust and topping contains wheat, oats, and nuts; all healthy. The apple, a fruit, is also wholesome. A scoop of ice cream is dairy, essential to fortify bones. While you might not indulge in lunches like that often, it's an enjoyable treat to indulge in every now and then. What do you and your spouse splurge on occasionally? Perhaps you score tickets to a show or sporting event. Or do you pamper yourselves with an extravagant weekend away or a romantic dinner at a favorite restaurant? God wants you and your partner to enjoy the pleasures of life. It isn't easy to step away from your obligations and responsibilities, but it is healthy and good for your marriage to step away from chores to have fun.

A great way to rekindle romance in your relationship is not to take it for granted. It takes work to strengthen your bond. Therefore, find fun ways to enjoy spending time together. If you like to go see plays, buy tickets and turn it into a special date by getting dressed up and going out for coffee afterward. Maybe you and your partner could start Christmas shopping and find a quiet place to have lunch together. Find ways to reconnect no matter how simple or elaborate.

Be good role models for your children. When your children witness your affection and love for each other, it teaches them the value of a committed marriage that it is more important than work. Even if you haven't done this in the past, begin to do it now. Be thankful for the baby steps you can take, like bringing your mate a cup of coffee, or giving a long passionate kiss with a warm embrace. Don't put it off. If your relationship has gone awry, make a conscious choice and commitment to get your marriage back on track. Turn to God for help; he will never lead you astray.

Dear Lord, tell me what to do to get my marriage back on track. Fill my head with noble ideas and direction. I trust in you, Lord. Let me see the goodness in my partner and build our relationship into the perfect union you wanted it to be. Teach me how to look at everything you have given to me and help me to find the joy in it. Amen.

December 6

For I decided not to come to you again in painful circumstances. For if I inflict pain upon you, then who is there to cheer me except the one pained by me?

2 CORINTHIANS 2:1–2

When do you and your spouse put up your Christmas tree? What kind of tree do you select: artificial, freshly chopped from a farm, or one purchased from a lot? There are many varieties: Douglas Firs, Fraser Firs, Blue Spruces, Scotch Pines, Red Cedars. Despite the myriad choices, you both ultimately must reach an agreement. Is the selection based on family traditions, compromises, or taking turns? Can you implement similar decision making methodologies in other areas of your life? What painful circumstances can you work through using similar decision strategies such as: agreeing to disagree, establishing a policy, or trade-offs? During this process, suppress the urge to inflict pain on each other. The purpose is to unite harmoniously and decide amicably in God's graces.

Throughout each day you will make countless decisions, such as what to make for dinner, who will cook, when to do the laundry, and how to fold the clothes. When decisions are forced on you in difficult and stressed times, it's vital to talk about how the decisions will be made because they can have a lasting impact on your relationship. Decisions such as how many children you will have and what kind of parenting styles you will use, or how you will spend and save money will greatly impact your life. Making decisions needs to be a shared responsibility. In shared decision-making, neither you nor your spouse can be blamed for making a bad decision. You're in it together.

The topics you discuss may change, but the process of healthy decision-making never does. The goal of the decision making process is to have a conversation of thoughts and sharing of opinions, not an argument over who is right or wrong. If you stray from the topic, refocus or take a break. Don't allow strong emotional responses to derail your discussion. Write the problem on a piece of paper and remind each other that two intelligent brains work better than one; tell your partner that together you can do it. Sometimes decisions made in the present could dredge up memories of the past. Consider if there are inherent views in what is being advocated that extend back to childhood. Beliefs that were formulated during childhood are deeply imbedded in them; therefore, each perception of what is right or wrong will vary. Ask God to enable you to understand each other's frame of reference.

Dear Lord, bless me as I work through issues with my partner. Enable me to be open minded to reach feasible solutions regardless of their desirability. Make my heart malleable to accepting circumstances that I might not be able to change. Amen.

December 7

Pursue love, but strive eagerly for the spiritual gifts,
above all that you may prophesy.

1 Corinthians 14:1

As you resurrect Christmas decorations from storage places in the attic or basement, it can be a delightful experience sifting through everything and deciding how to adorn your home for the holidays. Ponder the skills you once used when you courted your partner. Maybe you looked or acted differently. Did you buy flowers or write letters, poems, or songs? Try pursuing your partner again, the way you once did, because it worked in the past and it might work again. Try calling your partner at work to make a date. Send an e-mail to say how much you appreciate and adore them. Send an arrangement of flowers to your spouse's office and simply write "I love you" on the card.

Perhaps you could use this time to reflect on the talents and attributes you may have forgotten you possess. If you are a musician, write your spouse a love song, then, play it for him or her. If you are a painter, paint a lovely scene for your partner. Make a meatloaf in the shape of a heart. Write a sweet note and leave it on your partner's computer, or leave a small gift on his or her chair. Write a message on a steamy shower door or leave a card under his or her bed pillow. In the spirit of Christmas giving, consider giving physical gifts to your spouse. Is your partner starved for affection or hungry for attention? Give frequent hugs, back rubs, or foot massages.

During this time of giving, it's easy to provide for everyone else and ignore your own needs. Set aside time to replenish your own energy through a brisk walk or long bubble bath. Remember to eat well-balanced meals and take much-needed rests. You need to take care of yourself and be in the right frame of mind before you can do any good to your spouse or family. Spend time in prayer with the Lord asking him to strengthen you and keep you well.

Dear Lord, Awaken my senses to the needs of my partner and the desires of my soul. Imbed in me the strength to replenish the vanished love I long for. Fill me up with your love so that I recognize it when my spouse gives it to me. Let me be appreciative of whatever forms it comes to in and allow me to be loving in return. I ask this in your sweet and holy name. Amen.

December 8

Face to face I speak to him, plainly and not in riddles.

NUMBERS 12:8

Before you drape Christmas lights in or around your home, it's important to check them out first to ensure they are working properly. It can be frustrating to hang lights only to discover later that they don't work. When you listen to your spouse, how do you know that you fully understand the message? Try naming the emotion you detect when listening: frustration, sadness, anger, hurt. Attempt to reflect the message back in your own words so that your partner realizes that you truly understand the intended message.

For example, you might ask your partner, "Are you saying the reason you are late is because you were in an unscheduled meeting with your boss?" Your job as a listener is to understand, not to fix the problem or cast judgment. It's a bonus when understanding the problem can be easily resolved, but that is not always the case. Consider if you provide your undivided attention. Reflective listening is one of the best ways you can concentrate hearing and appreciating what is driving your spouse's thoughts and words. Invite God through prayer to enable you to become a better listener.

While listening, it's important to pay attention to your spouse's body language. This nonverbal type of communication discloses hints as to some unspoken intention or feeling through physical behavior. For instance, crossing your arms in front of your chest might indicate that your spouse is putting up a barrier between you both. In a confrontational situation, it could mean that your mate is expressing opposition. A blank facial expression often shows hostility. Eye contact can indicate that your spouse is thinking positively on what you said, while the lack of eye contact can indicate negativity. Because body language provides clues of your spouse's attitude, it's wise to pay attention to it.

In marriage, listening can be one of the most important challenging things you do. It's not easy listening to your spouse point out your mistakes or acknowledging and admitting your failures. If God was your marriage counselor, what would he say to you? If you are struggling in your marriage, petition God for guidance and inspiration. When you ask, he listens and responds. In the silence of your heart, wait patiently for his reply.

Dear Lord, open my ears to your word and to the voice of my partner. Allow me to understand and appreciate his or her messages. Give me the patience to hear with my heart and to act upon those words. Teach me to be a better listener. Amen.

December 9

This is now, beloved, the second letter I am writing to you;
through them by way of reminder I am trying to stir up your
sincere disposition, to recall the words previously spoken.

2 PETER 3:1–2

Do you send salutations to friends and relatives in Christmas cards? Sending holiday greetings is a nice way to keep in touch with the friends you rarely see. It's also delightful to receive cards from friends you see every day. How do you convey warm feelings of affection to your partner, someone you see every day?

Consider writing a special card and tucking it under your spouse's bed covers or placing it on his or her pillow. Draft a love poem or a simple note of thanks for something he or she did that you appreciated. Sometimes, reflecting on the gentle side of your partner, and conveying it in a letter, gives him or her something positive to think about throughout the day. Even if writing is not your forte, it could be worth the effort to your mate. Invoke the Holy Spirit that dwells within to bless you with the perfect words to convey your heartfelt message. It could be the best gift your spouse receives.

Jot down your ideas as they pop into your head. Don't worry if they initially appear wild. The letter is coming from your heart therefore whatever you write cannot be wrong. Consider focusing on one aspect of your spouse that you are particularly fond of and write four descriptive words that feature that area. For instance, if you choose your spouse's eyes to write about, you might describe them as twinkling, loving, truthful windows of his or her soul, and joyous. Writing a love letter is an opportunity to reveal your truest and deepest love for your spouse. Allow your emotions to flow freely onto the paper. The words are an extension of you and your deep feelings for your mate.

You could write something such as: Each morning when you open your eyes, I thank God that he gave me another day to spend with you. Your twinkling eyes sparkle like the sunshine on crisp white snow. When I gaze into your loving eyes, I am instantly warm and feel safe with you beside me. Your eyes are reflective pools of my love allowing me submerge myself entirely, knowing how deeply you care. Your eyes are truthful windows of your soul, which elevates my spirit as I start a new day with you beside me.

Dear Lord, thank you for the gift of words and the ability to use them in charitable and compassionate ways. Amen.

December 10

Whoever cares for the poor lends to the LORD,
who will pay back the sum in full.

PROVERBS 19:17

Take a look around and admire all that you have: a roof over your head, food in your cupboards, and love in your heart. During the second week of Advent, you might be searching for a charity you can be generous with. Maybe you could volunteer in a soup kitchen or food pantry, or make a donation to another worthy organization. This time of year our heartstrings are tugged in many different directions. What tugs on your heartstrings? Have you and your partner worked together on missions in the past? Could you and your spouse volunteer together on a church-related project or a local charitable organization within your community? Sometimes stepping away from your own problems and spending quality time with others less fortunate enables you to appreciate all you have. For the duration of the week, stop focusing on yourself and open your heart to a worthy cause.

The individuals who are on the receiving end of love reap many benefits of generosity and compassion, in addition to experiencing a positive effect on their overall health and well-being. Recently, researchers have evaluated a "helper's high," which has widespread positive effects on the body, health, and longevity. In the story of Ebenezer Scrooge, who was the epitome of selfishness, he discovered the joy of good deeds and totally transformed with a "helper's high" as his spirit of giving was revitalized.

Cornell University studied a group of older adults who routinely volunteered and determined they reaped overall health benefits and well-being. Those who volunteered were living longer than non-volunteers. Another study found a 44 percent reduction in early death among those who volunteered a great deal. Volunteering has a greater effect on the human body compared to exercising four times a week. Engaging in good deeds reduces your stress, including the physiological changes that ensue when you're strained. Stress hormones, such as cortisol, are released during anxious moments, causing an increase in respiratory and heart rate. If the stress response stays on too long, it adversely affects the immune and cardiovascular systems by weakening the body's defenses, making it more vulnerable to abnormal cellular changes that cause premature aging. The "helper's high" gains power over the stress response. When someone feels loved, they have lower stress responses and improved immunity.

Dear Lord, I pray to you for peace in my heart, home, and neighborhood. Bring the needy into my life and teach me how to be caring and compassionate to them. Amen.

December 11

If I speak in human and angelic tongues but do not have love,
I am a resounding gong or a clashing cymbal....
Love is patient, love is kind....It bears all things, believes all things,
hopes all things, endures all things. Love never fails.

1 CORINTHIANS 13:1, 4, 7–8

Does your relationship ever suffer because of uncontrollable outbursts? Excessive anger is a major source of marital stress. Recognizing and understanding it will help you to resolve it, which is important for the health and happiness of your marriage. Do you explode over things that don't go your way, or do you suppress your feelings, sweeping them under the rug and not addressing them? Neither are good ways to handle your anger. If you stuff your anger, you are being dishonest to yourself and your mate. Stuffing it doesn't solve anything and can cause depression and your physical health to suffer.

Ask yourself if your anger is really sadness over a loss, or if it is fear. Contemplate if it is hurt, frustration, or fatigue that could be causing you to overreact. Consider if it has resulted from an unmet expectation or if it is from your childhood. Could it be misdirected anger? Once you have identified where it originated from, you are better equipped to address it with your spouse in a calm and honest manner. Consider if the anger signals that you want your own way, or if one of your rights is being violated. Maybe the stresses of the holidays are taking a toll on your relationship with houseguests to prepare for, gifts to buy and wrap, and meals to prepare. Consider if you might be teetering on the border of verbal abusiveness. Cruel words can crush your spouse's spirit, cripple his or her confidence, or cause a physical illness. Consider how often you lash out to your spouse. If you are irritated several times a week, you might have a hormone imbalance or other medical problem that requires help from your family doctor. Be cognizant to recognize early warning signs of anger building: muscles tighten, face flushes, or voice escalates. The moment you identify any signs, try to channel it in a positive way.

Explain calmly to your spouse that you need to regulate your anger by taking a walk and thinking things through before you can discuss it. You could take a shower, listen to music, or pray if that works better for you. Find what works best to allow you to think about what caused your anger to escalate. It would be lovely to quell the intrusive racket with something sweet. Instead of reaching for candy, perhaps you could use kindness, with respectful words, gratifying thoughts, and endearing prayers. Love conquers all.

Dear Lord, Quiet the noise that is blaring through my life. Let your compassionate love erase all of my pains and problems. Let me make you the center of Christmas. Amen.

December 12

"We saw his star at its rising and have come to do him homage."
MATTHEW 2:2

I s there a star at the top of your Christmas tree? The tree is not complete without it because it represents the star of Bethlehem that led the wise men on the long journey to find the Christ child. Can you imagine following a sign as simple as a shining star in the evening sky? What unassuming signs do you notice in your relationship that you can act on? Does your spouse seem happy to be near you? Perhaps the smile shining brightly on his or her face is a sign that you could act on. Maybe you both could spend more quality time together in pleasant conversation and prayer. Go for a walk in the evening for the chance to gaze at the stars that dot the sky. How can you be a shining example of Christ's infinite love to your partner this Christmas?

Listen to the way you talk to each other. Do you blame your spouse for things that don't go as planned, or do you share equal responsibility for the way things enfold in your relationship? Talk nicely to your partner, the way you might with your best friend. Better yet, make friends with your spouse because some of the basic principles of friendship apply to marriage. Friends have more patience, kindness, and forgiveness with each other. Be your spouse's best friend and start having more fun in your marriage. Give your spouse your own special version of the "Twelve Days of Christmas." Instead of having twelve drummers, create something else he or she will enjoy, such as a back rub with you drumming in between the massage. Make a list of twelve good reasons why you are grateful for your spouse and present it as a gift.

Nurture your spiritual growth during the Advent season. Start your day by saying daily prayers for your spouse and your relationship. Consider attending worship services together, developing a regular time to pray together, read Holy Scripture, or meditate together. Reflect, review, and renew your marriage vows privately or in a small ceremony. Vow renewal ceremonies are often more meaningful than the wedding because you know how much effort is expended into preserving your relationship. Reviewing and renewing your vows will move you toward spiritual intimacy. If you have too many activities scheduled before Christmas, try planning something for the first of the new year.

Dear Lord, thank you for the humble gifts, signs of your love and generosity. Enable me to act on the signs in my marriage to create a sacred dwelling place of love. Amen.

December 13

Then the angel said to her, "Do not be afraid,
Mary, for you have found favor with God."

LUKE 1:30

There are many magnificent angelic aspects of the Christmas story; none more significant than the Christmas angel, which represents the angel Gabriel who first appeared to Mary. Another angel visited Joseph in a dream. Myriad angels appeared in the sky over Bethlehem to announce and celebrate Jesus's birth as the world's savior. How can you be more angelic to your spouse during the holiday season? Is it possible to give your mate gifts of service? Perhaps you could fill up his or her car with gas, run errands, or do a chore. How would your spouse feel if you made a favorite meal and cleaned the kitchen afterward? Small acts of kindness, done with great love, will make a huge impact. Possibly the best thing you could do for your partner is pray for him or her.

Discover what you can do for your spouse; it might require time and ingenuity. However, the acts of service should be done with great love and pleasure in order for them to be professed as a gift of love. In other words, you cannot be grumbling while you are vacuuming or complain while you are taking care of the children.

Consider what type of gift you would like to receive from your partner. Instead of feeling resentment over your spouse not knowing intuitively, try asking him or her for it in a loving manner. For instance, "I would be so grateful if you could rub my back this afternoon." If your spouse is unable to deliver, refrain from sulking over it. Keep asking without nagging. After a while, your spouse will realize what gift will make you happy.

Think about the last time you thanked your partner for something he or she did for you. When did you thank your spouse for working hard, being a good parent, or just being fun to go through life with? Your marriage takes effort so remember that it is important to acknowledge a good deed instead of making excuses or blaming. Start showing appreciation for all he or she does, especially in front of your children.

Dear Lord, whisper in my ear the kind gestures I can do for [*name*]. Give me the stamina to accomplish all that is set before me. I offer this work, sacrifices, and prayers to you, loving Father. Let me also recognize and be appreciative of the gifts offered to me. Teach me to be the very best version of myself that I can possibly be. Amen.

December 14

Is anyone among you suffering? He should pray.
Is anyone in good spirits? He should sing praise.

JAMES 5:13

Christmas carols can be sung by a church choir or sung in the street by amateurs. Carolers can be found in shopping malls, schools, hospitals, and other public places throughout the holiday season. The amalgamation of voices makes people pause to listen and enjoy the lift in spirit they feel. It might bring to the surface delightful childhood memories of school plays or concerts.

What are your fond childhood memories? Do any of those remembrances impact your marriage as you celebrate Christmas with your partner? Perhaps you and your spouse have incorporated special traditions from your childhoods. Consider building off them as your family grows or shrinks. Could you create a new unique Christmas custom as husband and wife? What if you organized an afternoon of caroling in a nearby nursing home? Whatever you decide, keep Christ as the focal point of your Christmas experiences because Jesus is the reason for the season.

Consider setting time aside to pray with light music playing softly in the background. Perhaps you could buy a CD of chanting monks, singing nuns, or classical Christmas hymns. Contemplate singing your prayers to God. Perhaps you could begin singing the "Our Father," a prayer that is often sung in Mass. You don't have to sing well, just open your mouth and let it flow. Even if you are afraid that you don't sound angelic when you sing, do it anyway. In the Bible it says to make a joyful "noise" to the Lord. It doesn't say, "Sing perfectly in range, harmony, or melody." It doesn't matter to the Lord if you are singing the wrong notes; sing anyway. It will make his heart rejoice.

When babies cry, parents often sing lullabies to quell them back to sleep. The soothing cadence of music relaxes most people. It's played in most doctor's and dentist's offices for a reason: to keep patients calm. Remember to incorporate more music in your heart and homes during this Christmas season.

Dear Lord, open my heart to the opportunities that await me during this glorious season. Awaken my senses to those around me who need their spirits lifted. If it is my voice they need to hear, then, speak through me. I ask this in your sweet and holy name. Amen.

December 15

The people who walked in darkness have seen a great light;
Upon those who lived in a land of gloom a light has shone.

ISAIAH 9:1

Advent wreaths originated during December's darkness in Europe, where evergreen wreaths were set ablaze as a sign of hope. By the sixteenth century, Catholics used the symbol to celebrate their hope in Christ, the everlasting light. It represents eternal life brought through Jesus; the circular shape represents God with no beginning or end. Turn to God for hope in the darkness of your marriage difficulties. Ponder the problems that weigh heavy on your heart. Are you being truthful with yourself or your spouse?

Consider if you have lost your way by overspending. It is easy to do during the holidays, trying to make everything perfect and then realizing that you bought too much. Parties, gifts for your kids' teachers, and shopping for gifts to put under your tree can result in huge bills. A common mistake of shoppers is waiting for the last minute. When you procrastinate, panic sets in and you could spend twice as much. The good news is that some stores slash prices at the last minute, so try to get only what is on sale. Make a list and stick to it. Next year, try to rake in the good deals that spring up early in the season.

Another lethal mistake is buying on credit. It's too easy to swipe the plastic card. It's best to make a budget and withdraw only the amount you think you will need. Once it's gone, you stop shopping. Use coupons and search for savings before you make purchases. Handmade treats usually costs less than something purchased from a store. Consider giving a plate of homemade cookies or pumpkin bread. Get your family involved in the kitchen to make it a fun activity you can all do together.

One of the best gifts you can give is prayers. It doesn't cost anything but your time, which is the most valuable gift. Open your Bible and read passages that will inspire and guide you. God gives you the tools; ask him for the wisdom to implement them. God can light your path.

Dear Lord, take my hand and lead me down the right path. Show me the way for I feel lost and forgotten. I know you are always with me; where I go, you go too. Allow me to extinguish this misery and bask in your love and graces. Amen.

December 16

Come to me, all you who labor and are burdened, and I will give you rest.

MATTHEW 11:28

There are many choices to make when stringing lights around your Christmas tree. There are: all white, multicolored, only red and green, all blue, blinkers, icicles, old-fashioned big bulbs, or new age high-tech bulbs. How do you select one?

You also have many decisions to make in your marriage. Some are easy, but others require much deliberation. Do you take responsibility for the decisions you make? Reflect on past occurrences where you were irresponsible. What can you do to accept accountability in the future? Remember that your choices define you and you are never alone in the decision-making process; the Lord is always with you and you can trust in his help and guidance.

If you are overly responsible, you need to do less and give the problems back to your spouse to handle. You are only held accountable for yourself, your choices, and your feelings. If you are feeling resentment, that is a sign that your relationship is off-kilter. While it's okay to care about your partner, you need to focus on taking care of yourself and doing less. If you are irresponsible, you need to pick up the slack and do more.

When faced with self-responsibility, use "I" statements and avoid the accusing "you" statements. For example, don't say, "You never clear the table." Instead say, "I would be so happy if you could clear the table for me." If you make a mistake with the wording, ask for a "do-over." While you are perfecting this skill, it takes practice, so keep trying until you get it right. Depending on your circumstances—whether you need to do more or do less—continue to pray while you implement the changes. In stillness, reflect and listen for God's message. In the silence of your heart, God will tell you what to do. Especially during the holiday season, when there is so much commotion and noise, tune out the clamor and search for God's love within you.

Dear Lord, take my weary body and provide nourishment through your merciful and abundant love. Revive my soul and teach me to search for you in the quiet of my heart. Fill my mind with wisdom, so that I can hold my marriage together, keeping it strong, despite the distractions of this world. Rejuvenate me, Lord, and build me up to be a wise and wonderful partner to [name]. Amen.

December 17

*David and all the house of Israel danced before the L*ORD *with all their might,
with singing, and with lyres, harps, tambourines, sistrums, and cymbals.*

2 SAMUEL 6:5

Do you have Christmas parties to attend this year? Maybe you have a celebration with coworkers, neighbors, friends, or relatives. Do you look forward to them or anticipate them with dread? Are you a social butterfly or an introvert who abhors social interactions? How does this socialization, or lack of it, impact your marriage?

During the holidays it can be a wonderful opportunity to socialize, reconnect with friends, and be grateful for the people in your life. But if you're shy or have trouble with social interactions, holiday get-togethers can be difficult. Ponder how holiday celebrations wreak havoc with your relationship and cognitively plan how to avoid mayhem this year. Discuss your feelings with your spouse about what you can and cannot handle. Make a list of events that you will be expected to attend. Maybe you could compromise and attend one party or downsize the event you plan to host.

Contemplate eliminating socially awkward events that you are not obligated to attend. If you absolutely must attend, establish ground rules that you and your partner can live with. For example, agree in advance what time you will leave the party. Sometimes, knowing that you only have to socialize for two hours will help you actually enjoy yourself more. If you become overwrought with anxiety, have an agreed-upon signal with your partner so you can leave the event without embarrassment. For example, if you use the word "mistletoe," your spouse will know that you need his or her help. Whether you have a social anxiety or are just shy, remember to stay calm when you are in public. Ask your angels and the Holy Spirit that dwell within you to be reinforced with positive energy and love to be your very best.

Schedule private moments for you to talk to your spouse before, during, and after the party. Reconnect on an emotional level and keep praying. Bring God into the equation when making your holiday plans. The Lord, God, Almighty can help you through anything if you just let him.

Dear Lord, with so many obligations pulling me in many different directions, keep me grounded, Lord. Be the stabilizer in my life and my marriage. You are the reason for the season. Thank you for opening my heart to your gracious love, my Lord and savior. Amen.

December 18

Then Jacob kissed Rachel.

GENESIS 29:11

Mistletoe is commonly used as a Christmas decoration. An ancient custom of hanging mistletoe from the ceiling, enticing couples to kisses under it, is still prevalent today. It's amusing that a tiny piece of greenery serves as a reminder to kiss throughout the Christmas season. A kiss conveys affection and value. It signifies exclusiveness and expresses fondness with each other.

Some couples have lost the desire to kiss. Has this happened to you? Perhaps you could try a few small kisses, because that might lead to more meaningful ones. Kisses release pheromones, dopamine, oxytocin, and adrenaline. The release of oxytocin induces feelings of satisfaction, reduces anxiety, and promotes tranquility and security with your mate. How many times a day do you kiss your spouse? What is preventing you from expressing affection? Reflect on the underlying reasons, pray about them, and consider hanging a sprig of mistletoe where you can kiss your spouse more often.

Kissing builds connectedness between partners. It can be more intimate than having sex, and is often the first thing to go in a waning marriage. If you have noticed a decrease in kissing in your relationship, hang some mistletoe and pucker up. Kissing relaxes couples. It is an important expression of desire, intimacy, adoration, and passion for your partner. Contemplate if you are more comfortable with physical affection than your spouse.

It's common for women to want kissing more than men. Research indicates that kissing is more important to women than men. Women use kissing in the dating ritual to assess the suitability of their partner as a mate. One kiss allows a woman to determine if she wants to a relationship to last. Both sexes agree that kissing symbolizes a promising romantic intensity and intimacy.

In your marriage, you might compromise and do things more often than you would like in order to maintain a happy and stable relationship. Remember how important kissing is to your partner and how much pleasure he or she derives from it. In return, remind your mate what's important to you physically. Allow for your differences, respecting them, and share in what makes each of you happy. If kissing is not your thing, find other ways to make him or her feel loved, cherished, and desired.

Dear Lord, thank you for making my lips sensual. You designed my body perfectly, making it respond beautifully to the chemistry between [*name*] and me. Give me gentle reminders to stay physically connected to my partner for life. I am richly blessed. Amen.

December 19

*The wilderness and the parched land will exult;
the Arabah will rejoice and bloom....
The glory of Lebanon will be given to it,
the splendor of Carmel and Sharon;
They will see the glory of the Lord,
the splendor of our God.*

Isaiah 35:1–2*

The Christmas poinsettia plant decorates many homes throughout America. The legend began in Mexico that an impoverished girl was unable to provide a gift for Jesus's celebration. She gathered a clump of weeds and placed them on the church altar. Poinsettias miraculously blossomed from the weeds. During the Christmas season, tiny miracles can blossom from seemingly insignificant but thoughtful gifts. Perhaps a compliment would be considered a "small" gift, but it goes a long way to making your spouse feel cherished and loved.

Perhaps you could grant a small wish to your spouse; even though it may seem small to you, it might mean a great deal to him or her. Perhaps your spouse wants you to accompany him or her to a concert, to donate blood, or to visit an elderly relative. A kind gesture, no matter how inconsequential it might seem to you, if done with good intentions, could mean the world to your partner. It has been said that great things come in small packages. What small package will you present to your partner during this Christmas season? Perhaps a poinsettia plant with a promise of prayers will be an eloquent present, or long sought after words.

Consider giving your spouse a vow to do better. A promise to try harder to improve is a gift in itself when it is carried through. Could you give your spouse a small gift each morning leading up to Christmas? Maybe it would be bringing your mate a cup of coffee served in a special mug or making a special breakfast. Maybe it could be a small love poem, a holy card, or note tucked sweetly beside a cereal bowl. Small surprises can turn an ordinary day into a spectacular one with just a little ingenuity and thoughtfulness. How will you put a smile on your partner's face today?

Dear Lord, let me sit patiently in silence with you and wait for your precious words to enlighten me. Words are simple, like roadside weeds, blossoming into something meaningful and quite extraordinary. I truly love you, sweet miraculous, Lord. Thank you for building me up into the person you always meant for me to be. Keep me on the right path, following you the rest of days. Amen.

December 20

Behold, magi from the east arrived in Jerusalem,
saying, "Where is the newborn king of the Jews?
We saw his star at its rising and have come to do him homage."
MATTHEW 2:1–2

The three wise men—Melchior, Caspar, and Balthazar—traveled a great distance hoping to find the Christ child. They made the long, arduous journey based on their beliefs and hopes. They lacked any tangible proof, yet followed their heart. You had no proof that your marriage journey would be successful, you had to trust in God that it would be good.

Reflect on the journey through marriage that you are taking with your spouse. You gave each other three noble gifts: your honor, love, and respect. For the magi, it was all about the destination: finding and worshiping Jesus. For your marriage, it's about the day-to-day happenings: remembering and living by your vows. Each new day is an enchanted gift that you give to your spouse. Make the day overflow with happiness and goodness, unfolding with love and endearments. Smile; offer compliments; and be thankful, welcoming, and warm in God's radiant love. How can you make the journey with your spouse better?

Try putting your best foot forward by beginning the day joyfully. You can choose to be happy. Smile, because they are contagious and they cultivate an atmosphere of happiness. Be respectful of your partner's wishes. If something is important to your mate, make it paramount to you too. Overlook his or her flaws and weaknesses by instead focusing on the attributes you admire the most. When your spouse speaks to you, stop what you are doing, look him or her in the eye and give your undivided attention without interruptions. Resist the temptation to nag; instead, build up your spouse and cultivate an attitude of gratitude. Don't take your partner for granted; always say thank you. Honor your partner in the manner you speak of him or her to family and friends. Safeguard his or her reputation by always speaking positively about him or her. Then, it will become obvious to others why your marriage is solid. Are you enjoying your marriage journey? What actions will you take today to improve your relationship?

Dear Lord, as I journey through Advent with [name], I joyfully embrace your wisdom to experience the challenges and rewards that come with married life. I am thankful for the many gifts you continue to give me, sweet and generous, Lord. Bless the path we take in your trust and hopefulness. Amen.

December 21

They prostrated themselves and did him homage. Then they opened their treasures and offered him gifts of gold, frankincense, and myrrh.

MATTHEW 2:11

The wise men offered gifts fit for a king, with gold being valuable. It's easy to get drawn into the commercialism of Christmas with tempting sale fliers and TV commercials. It's understandable how the holiday hype drives people crazy in stores, baiting with price wars, longer shopping hours, and online specials. How do you stay true to yourself and your budget? Do you reflect on the wise men's gifts when shopping for a Christmas present for your spouse? Is it possible to give your spouse one gift of symbolic significance representing something to make him or her "feel" like royalty? What one gift would make your spouse feel loved totally and completely? Consider giving that gift this year.

You don't have to spend royally to make your spouse feel like a king. Consider the many things that you could do that cost very little, but would mean so much to your partner. Maybe you could bake your spouse's favorite Christmas cookie. Perhaps you could make a holiday ornament together. Visit your library and check out different Christmas CDs to listen to or play the music your spouse enjoys the most. Consider listening to nuns sing this year. Go outside and play in the snow: build a snowman, make snow angels, go sledding, and have a snowball fight where you let your spouse win. Shovel the driveway together. Warm up with a mugful of hot cocoa. Adorn your house with twinkling lights this year. Walk through your neighborhood at night admiring everyone else's decorations while holding your spouse's hand. Give your spouse a foot massage or back rub. Give your spouse a compliment. Read a book of poems to him or her. Tell your spouse what saint reminds you of him or her. Pray for your partner. These frugal suggestions might win over your spouse's affections.

The number one topic that couples argue over the most is money. Consider shifting your focus off money and center more onto Christ this Christmas through the spirit of giving to others. Instead of thinking about what you want this year, think about what others would want to receive from you. If you have been holding back, now is the time to open up and give freely.

Dear Lord, thank you for the endless stream of gifts that you shower me with every day. I am especially grateful for your mercy and unconditional love. Let me share the blessings of your good favor with everyone around me. Amen.

December 22

Joseph her husband, since he was a righteous man,
yet unwilling to expose her to shame, decided to divorce her quietly.
MATTHEW 1:19

Think about the confusion and tumultuousness Joseph felt when he realized Mary was pregnant. His solution was to divorce her quietly until an angel appeared to him in a dream. If you are contemplating divorce, don't act on it right now. Instead, give it to God and pray on it.

Ponder why God brought you both together in the first place and what purpose do you have as a couple? God had a blessed reason for Mary and Joseph's union. You might not initially see it in your relationship right now, but trust in God's plan for your marriage. Even if you feel as if your marriage is in shambles, give it to God. If your relationship feels like a library with every book off the shelf, stop what you are doing, pick one book up, and place it on the shelf. Slowly, with God's help, put your marriage back together.

If you will be traveling, entertaining, or staying home alone to celebrate Christmas, set aside time to reflect on your marriage goals. Contemplate ways you can achieve them throughout the holiday season. Envision the questions Joseph and Mary must have had and by trusting in the Lord, they overcame every obstacle that they encountered.

This Christmas, the best gift you can give to your partner is the commitment to build your marriage back up stronger than before. Start by being each other's best friend; be there when things go wrong, or go right. Accept your partner's shortcomings and be willing to forgive transgressions, both large and small. Start out by taking small, simple steps because they can bring big results. Thank your spouse for taking out the trash, for emptying the dishwasher, or paying the bills. "I truly appreciate you preparing dinner tonight." Praising your partner is reminiscent that you love him or her, and knowing that you are loved makes you more willing to work out any differences.

Consider doing random acts of kindness. When you're thoughtful to your partner, he or she is more inclined to be thoughtful too. Take on your spouse's chore or watch his or her favorite TV show without complaining. Do service projects together all year long, not just during the holidays. Giving to others less fortunate removes you from your own problems and supports a more spiritual view of life. Choose an organization that appeal to you both, whether it's working at a food pantry or in the local soup kitchen. Shifting the focus away from yourself will bring you closer to each other and to God.

Dear Lord, wipe away my confusion and help me to be more trusting of your plan for my life with [*name*]. Let my marriage be as blessed as Joseph and Mary's union. Amen.

December 23

She wrapped him in swaddling clothes and laid him in a manger,
because there was no room for them in the inn.

LUKE 2:7

If Joseph and Mary knocked on your door, would you make room for them? With so many charities vying for financial support or volunteer hours during the holidays, it's understandable to get overwhelmed with requests. How do you make room for all of them? It isn't easy juggling family life, obligations, and caring for the less fortunate during the Christmas season. With many organizations and duties pulling you in different directions, it's essential to make room in your heart for your spouse. Money might be tight, free time could be almost nonexistent, and opportunities for "alone time" with your partner might be hard to finagle. Remember how Mary and Joseph made the best of what they had in the humblest of ways. How can you make the best of your situation?

Seek opportunities within your day to reach out to your spouse and create a slice of heaven in your world together. Perhaps you could set your alarm to wake up fifteen minutes earlier each day and use that time to snuggle in bed and chat about your hopes and dreams for the day. Include prayer in this time asking God to bless your chores and all that you say, think, and do. Use your lunch break to reconnect again. Maybe you could send an e-mail to your spouse; it doesn't have to be long or witty. For example you might say, "I have been thinking about you. I hope your day is going well." Maybe you could meet for lunch one day a month.

Evenings can be hectic depending on your circumstances. If you have children, they have specific needs that you must tend to as parents. However, that doesn't mean that you can't set aside time to reconnect, even if it's only fifteen minutes. Instead of watching the news or reading the paper, use that time to talk about your day over a cup of decaf. Or go to bed an hour early to massage each other. You only have so many hours each day to work with. Sift through the redundancy and monotony to eliminate some of those tasks and add time alone with your spouse. Life is what you make it; take what you have and really make it something wonderful.

Dear Lord, help me to be more like the holy family: offering a smile amidst chaos, a warm caress, a loving touch, a lasting prayer. Enable me to make room in my heart and in my life for my spouse. Amen.

December 24

So they went in haste and found Mary and Joseph,
and the infant lying in the manger.

LUKE 2:16

Have you wondered why Jesus arrived into the world so humbly, with only a manger for his bed? Maybe it happened that way in order for you to be able to relate to him. If he were born in a gold palace with extravagant silks wrapped around him, would he be as relatable? Jesus was born homeless among dirty and smelly animals.

Was Jesus's humble birth a sign meant for us to believe that he would be the food that nourishes our soul? How does Jesus nourish your soul? How can you provide sustenance to your spouse in a spiritual sense? When you drive to Christmas Mass, instead of turning on the radio, talk to each other about the readings and what you have taken from them and how you plan to incorporate them into your daily life. Time spent traveling in a car could be the perfect forum for prayer as a couple. What creative measures can you take to provide or lift up your spouse during this sacred season?

It is so easy to get caught up in the rigmarole of Santa Claus because of the consumerism that bombards you on TV, radio, and stores. Don't allow society to commercialize your Christmas season. Go to Mass early and meditate on the many gifts that Jesus provided. Keep Christ in your Christmas by focusing on Jesus, not Santa Claus. If you struggle to do this, imagine Joseph as he helped his new wife Mary to deliver their baby in such rough conditions.

There were no nurses, doctors, family, or friends to help them. They relied on each other. They were beckons of hope and strength for each other. Even if your spouse has been irritating to you, set those feelings of disdain and discontentment aside as a gift. Act like Joseph and Mary instead. When you bring such reverence into your marriage, it will be pleasing to you, your spouse, your children, and to God. Strive to achieve this behavior as long as you possibly can. Use the Holy Family as your role models.

Dear Lord, thank you for nourishing my soul and blessing me with someone to share my life with. Teach me how to provide a welcoming place in my heart for him or her. Enable us to grow closer in your constant love and protection. I want to be as selfless as you are. Amen.

December 25

Behold, the virgin shall be with child and bear a son, and they
shall name him Emmanuel, which means "God is with us."
MATTHEW 1:23

God is with you wherever you go, whatever you do. There will be diffi-culties throughout your life, but trust that the Lord is with you and he
can help you through anything. If you are struggling to hold your marriage
together, ask God to help you with that. If your job is unstable, or your health
is questionable, ask God for help. Whatever your troubles are, call out to the
Lord because he wants to hear your voice. Think of the many problems Mary
and Joseph encountered on their arduous journey to Bethlehem. Whenever
they called out for God's help, he was there to see them through it.

What are you struggling with? Perhaps you must face a family crisis or
socialize with extended family members who bring you tumultuousness
and grief. Maybe you must interact with siblings knowing a rivalry exists
between you. Sometimes the preparations of Christmas become overwhelm-ing because of what society deems important. Discuss with your spouse what
family traditions are essential for your family to keep and which ones you
can stop doing. How can you work together with your partner to make your
Christmas celebration truly meaningful? Perhaps after Mass you can linger
by the manger scene and ask a favor of the Christ child.

Try to capture some of the Christmas spirit and bring it into your mar-riage to build off it. Let go of problems that have weighted you down. Let
past hurts go, and replace them with an abundance of love that Christmas
spirit can bring. Consider giving gifts to someone who would never expect
them. Put a small box of homemade fudge in the mailbox for the postman,
or leave a gift-wrapped package for the trash man. Giving this way can fill
your heart with much love. Consider leaving a small package on your spouse's
nightstand so it can be opened right away. It could be something simple such
as wrapping up the baby Jesus and asking to fill your hearts with the Lord
on this special day, hoping that your relationship will always have Jesus in
it. Start today.

Dear Lord, thank you for sending your only begotten son. As I pause
to remember the difficulties surrounding Jesus's birth, let me embrace
my troubles and find purpose and meaning in them. Thank you for
the good and the bad. I love you, Lord. Amen.

December 26

On entering the house they saw the child with Mary his mother.
MATTHEW 2:11

St. Francis of Assisi created the first nativity scene in 1223. Over time, distinctive nativity scenes have been designed around the world and are exhibited throughout the Christmas season in churches, homes, and other public venues. What are your family's nativity scene traditions? If you don't have any, start now to create meaningful customs that your family will enjoy participating in for years to come.

Did you and your spouse buy a nativity set together the first year you were married, or was one handed down or bought for you? Is there a special significance to it? Can you compliment it with your own special touch? Some families arrange their nativity set in a place of prominence or display it before anything else. What could you do to enhance your nativity scene traditions?

What aspect of your marriage has a similar sacredness or significance to you? What facet of your relationship is set apart or holy? Like the nativity sets, there are many different kinds of marriages; some are esteemed, others are not. Hone in on the aspects that revolve around God and cherish them. Perhaps your vows are sanctified. Consider repeating them to each other as a new tradition, a reaffirmation of your love and commitment to each other each year on Boxing Day, a traditional holiday celebrated the day after Christmas when servants would receive gifts from their employers. The tradition would symbolize that you are each a servant of Christ in your marriage and to each other.

Dear Lord, keep my eyes open to the abiding love I have witnessed in my marriage. Let me hold it in high regard, revering it, as the prized gift you meant it to be. Amen.

December 27

And Mary kept all these things, reflecting on them in her heart
LUKE 2:19

After Jesus was born, Mary had to be thinking, "What now?" She was young and without her mother or relatives for help; she had to rely solely on Joseph. She needed to be patient and contemplate her thoughts quietly in her restless heart. How can you be more like Mary: reflecting on your thoughts? After Christmas there can be periods of sleep deprivation, depression, disappointment, or disparity. Can you contemplate your thoughts before acting on them? Mary only had Joseph to comfort her; can you depend on your spouse with the same confidence? Mary also trusted in the Almighty to help her through her difficulties. Remember her throughout this blessed season.

Dear Lord, give me the strength to ponder all that is weighing heavy on my heart. Let me give it all to you and trust that you know what is best for me. Teach me patience and the ability to accept the outcome you want for me. You have showered me with many marvelous gift and favors; thank you for them all, kind and generous Lord. Amen.

December 28

When Jesus was born in Bethlehem of Judea, in the days of King Herod,
behold, magi from the east arrived in Jerusalem, saying,
"Where is the newborn king of the Jews? We saw his star
at its rising and have come to do him homage."
MATTHEW 2:1–2

The three wise men were on a long and difficult journey toward Christ.
Stop and think about the type of journey your marriage is on. All marriages—all relationships—have ups and downs. Has the path been bumpy or
smooth lately? Along the way, were you complaining or competing, holding
back or hurrying? Think of the times when you were wooing, cheering, and
supporting, and try to reconnect with your spouse in these ways. Whatever
steps it takes are well worth it, and they will lead you to a better place.

Now reflect on your own life. Is it orientated around your career, focused
on creating a lovely home, traveling to exotic vacation spots, or are you
simply providing food, clothing, and shelter for your family? Is what you're
doing good, honest, and pleasing to God? Redirect your life toward God and
journey toward him. In all that you do, regardless of how arduous or agonizing, make sure that it is leading you toward the Almighty. Questions about
your life—or your marriage—can be can be answered by reading the Bible.

Dear Lord, I feel lost. Bring me back into your graces and tender
mercies. Let me live a humble life; caring for others more and my
own self less. Let my hands be your hands. Amen.

December 29

And having been warned in a dream not to return to Herod,
they departed for their country by another way.

MATTHEW 2:12

When you encounter road construction on your travels, do you automatically consider another route to reach your destination? Like the Magi, it's good to have alternative directions. If one way of handling your marriage difficulties isn't yielding favorable results, try another means to solve them. Draft a list of possible solutions incorporating your spouse's ideas, regardless of their feasibility. How many options can you conjure together? Are there resources from social, professional, and religious groups you can tap? Rule out less favorable choices and consider more realistic possibilities after prayerful reflection. Bringing God into your decision-making process can make a world of difference in the outcome of your dilemmas.

Dear Lord, enable me to isolate my emotions from my marriage problems. Allow me to attack it constructively while building up my spouse, keeping our marriage sacred. Open my heart to seek and consider all possible solutions. Help me to embrace and carry through the one you deem essential for me. I want to do what is good, honest, and just. Empower me to sort through my quandaries and decide what to keep and what to get rid of. Amen.

December 30

Then the shepherds returned, glorifying and praising God for all they had heard and seen, just as it had been told to them.

LUKE 2:20

The Christ child attracted impoverished shepherds and wealthy kings despite the variances between them. They united in glorifying God at the manger. Couples with varying affluence and circumstances are drawn together in the lifelong banns of marriage. Love unites them despite their dissimilarities. However, eventually those differences can become irritating and complicate a marriage. What annoyances are bothersome in your relationship? Perhaps you clean as you cook while your mate leaves the kitchen a disaster zone. Consider implementing a rule: whoever does the job chooses how to do it. Celebrate your shared traits and interests: love for each other, hobbies, sports, music, and your Divine Savior. Ponder how you can center your life more wholly on God.

Dear Lord, don't let me focus on the differences between my spouse and me. Enable me to build off of our similarities and dwell on all that is good. Let me center my life on you and appreciate all you have provided: food to nourish me physically, mentally, emotionally, and spiritually. I thank you for it all. Amen.

December 31

All bitterness, fury, anger, shouting, and reviling must be removed from you, along with all malice. [And] be kind to one another, compassionate, forgiving one another as God has forgiven you in Christ.

EPHESIANS 4:31–32

A s you approach a new year, you have an opportunity to change or prove and be more Christ-like. God calls you to forgive and uplift your partner. Check your compliancy and modify the relationship you have with others, including your spouse. Make a New Year's resolution to be more amicable and peaceful, and to be an ambassador of Jesus Christ. In reflecting over the hurts and problems of the past year, what mistakes can you learn from? Leave blunders in the past and move forward by beginning over. Wipe the slate clean and hit the "restart" button on your marriage.

Dear Lord, thank you for bestowing countless blessing on me: for keeping me safe and well, and for my food, shelter, and clothing. Thank you for the warmth of your love on chilly evenings and for being a beacon of hopefulness when all seemed lost. Thank you for the peacefulness that filled my heart on chaotic afternoons. I love you, kind and merciful, Lord. Amen.

Prayers

May today there be peace within.
May you trust God that you are exactly where you are meant to be.
May you not forget the infinite possibilities that are born of faith.
May you use those gifts that you have received,
    and pass on the love that has been given to you.
May you be content knowing you are a child of God.
Let this presence settle into your bones,
    and allow your soul the freedom to sing, dance, praise, and love.
It is there for each and every one of us.

ATTRIBUTED TO ST. TERESA OF ÁVILA

The Serenity Prayer

God, give us grace to accept with serenity
the things that cannot be changed,
Courage to change the things that should be changed,
and the Wisdom to distinguish the one from the other.

Living one day at a time,
Enjoying one moment at a time,
Accepting hardship as a pathway to peace,
Taking, as Jesus did, this sinful world as it is,
Not as I would have it,

Trusting that You will make all things right,
If I surrender to Your will,
So that I may be reasonably happy in this life,
And supremely happy with You forever in the next. Amen.

DR. REINHOLD NIEBUHR, 1943

The Peace Prayer of St. Francis of Assisi

Lord, make me an instrument of Thy peace;
Where there is hatred, let me sow charity;
Where there is injury, pardon;

Where there is error, the truth;
Where there is doubt, the faith;
Where there is despair, hope;
Where there is darkness, light; and
Where there is sadness, joy.

O, Divine Master,
Grant that I may not so much seek to be consoled, as to console;
To be understood as to understand;
To be loved as to love.

For it is in giving that we receive;
It is in pardoning that we are pardoned;
And it is in dying to ourselves that we are born to eternal life.

Amen.

Resources

WEBSITES

Christian Family Movement. cfm.org/home.html. © 2013.
This international support network of families offers spiritual
support and social activities for couples. Headquartered in Omaha,
Nebraska, it has a grassroots history dating back to the 1940s.

For Your Marriage. foryourmarriage.org. © 2014.
This initiative of the United States Conference of Catholic Bishops
offers daily tips, articles, and resources for dating couples, parents,
and spouses of every age and stage.

National Marriage Encounter. marriage-encounter.org. © 2013.
Marriage Encounter began with a priest in Spain, then came to
the US in 1966. These weekend retreats strengthen all marriages:
new or old, troubled or thriving. In Catholic circles, it is also
known as World Wide Marriage Encounter (wwme.org/).

The National Registry of Marriage Friendly Therapists.
marriagefriendlytherapists.com/index.php. © 2005-2014. This
registry lists therapists whose goal is to restore the marriage (vs.
taking a neutral stance on marriage vs. divorce). It has no religious or political affiliation.

Pastoral Solutions Institute. exceptionalmarriages.com © 2014.
Dr. Gregory K. Popcak is a nationally known Catholic radio host,
author, and counselor. His institute was founded in 1999 and
offers Catholic psychological help, including call-in radio advice
and personal telephone counseling.

RECLAiM Sexual Health. reclaimsexualhealth.com/. © 2011, 2014.
RECLAiM is a confidential, science-based Catholic program
for healing from pornography, masturbation, and other sexual
addictions. It was born from the founders of Elizabeth Ministry
International (elizabethministry.com, founded in 1991 in Wis-
consin), whose programs help women dealing with childbearing,
sexuality, and relationship issues.

Retrouvaille. retrouvaille.org/. © 2014.
This international resource for hurting marriages was founded in 1977. Catholic in origin, Christian Multi-Denominational weekends are also available in some areas.

The Third Option. thethirdoption.com/index.htm.
This group program was created by Patricia Crane Ennis, MSW, in the 1980s.

BOOKS

Chapman, Gary D. *The 5 Love Languages: The Secret to Love That Lasts.* © 2009, Northfield Publishing.

Coleman, William L. *What Makes a Marriage Last? Secrets for a Lasting Relationship.* © 1990, Here's Life Publishers.

Harley, Jr., Dr. Willard F. *His Needs, Her Needs: Building an Affair-Proof Marriage.* © 2001, 2011, Baker Publishing Group. marriage-builders.com. Dr. Harley is an acclaimed clinical psychologist and marriage counselor and hosts a daily call-in radio show from Minnesota.

More Resources From

9 Ways To Nurture Your Marriage
William E. Rabior and Susan C. Rabior
805851

This collection of lighthearted anecdotes has been compiled from conversations with couples who have found the key to a happy, fulfilling marriage. From these interviews, the Rabiors derived nine ways to energize your marriage, nurture spiritual life, and to cultivate physical intimacy. Spouses will discover how to communicate more clearly, develop trust, enjoy a better sexual relationship, put a stop to pointless power struggles, deal creatively with anger, and more. At the end of each chapter, the authors have provided points for discussion to generate dialogue—helping with new growth and possibilities.

A Daring Promise
A Spirituality of Christian Marriage
Richard R. Gaillardetz
815591

Christian marriage offers the daring proposition that, inspired by faith, two people might unconditionally bind themselves together for life—without destroying each other in the process. This revised and updated edition offers a set of honest and penetrating reflections on the challenges of living faithful Christian marriage today. Gaillardetz creatively draws on the deep wisdom of our Christian tradition while reflecting on the lived experience of marriage. Written with a refreshing sense of candor and humor, this book is informative, lively, and personal, providing wonderful insight into the daring adventure of Christian marriage.

Liguori
ONE LIGUORI DRIVE
LIGUORI MO 63057-9999

Liguori Publications

Stay Mr. and Mrs. After You're Mom and Dad

David and Christine Gibson
821875

Marital satisfaction has a U-shaped curve. Marriage tends to reach its low point during the childbearing years. Divorce is common, as most people think the problem is with their spouse, and Catholic couples are no exception. While you babyproof your house, it's just as important to babyproof your marriage. *Stay Mr. & Mrs. After You're Mom & Dad* will prepare your marriage for the changes that come with parenting. This book guides expectant couples—with research, prayer, and Scripture—through practical day-to-day issues like delegating chores, planning time alone and together, and dealing with fatigue.

Grow Old Along With Me

Marriage in the Later Years
William E. Rabior and Susan C. Rabior
809590

This book looks at the many elements that make a marriage more loving and fulfilling as two people grow older. In a mature relationship, spouses recognize and appreciate the good in their marriage, not only in the past, but right here and now. A mature couple is in a unique position to eliminate frustrations as they are drawn ever closer. Intimacy finds a new dimension—a dimension that moves beyond the physical encounter and joins them in spirit as well as body. Complete with spousal discussion starters.

About the Author

Barbara Canale's writing career began in 1994 with the publication of a nonfiction book titled *Our Labor of Love: A Romanian Adoption Chronicle*, about her experiences adopting two orphans with enormous medical needs. Feeling God calling her to change her life drastically, she decided to write about the sagas of raising post-institutionalized children with unique medical problems. She documented her daughters' growth and development through lighthearted stories that she published in a variety of magazines, including *Seek*, *Exceptional Family*, and *Whispers From Heaven*.

After her daughters' health improved, Barbara returned to her career in healthcare and wrote more spiritual pieces, particularly twelve narrative inspirational stories for the *Chicken Soup for the Soul* series. In 2007, she began writing "The Word of the Lord," a column for the Syracuse diocese's *Catholic Sun*, as well as other journalistic pieces. She also began writing for *55 Plus Magazine*, a retirement publication, and *In Good Health—Central New York's Healthcare Newspaper*. Today, Barbara Canale is a full-time writer. Her previous work with Liguori Publications is titled *Prayers, Papers, and Play: Devotions for Every College Student* (2013).

CPSIA information can be obtained
at www.ICGtesting.com
Printed in the USA
FSOW02n1138300317
32422FS